日本生物武器作战调查资料

〔日〕近藤昭二　王　选／主编

第三册

SSAP 社会科学文献出版社
SOCIAL SCIENCES ACADEMIC PRESS (CHINA)

目 录

6 美国四任调查官赴日调查

6.4.2 Interview of Doctors

6　美国四任调查官赴日调查

6.1 Murray Sanders 调查

6.1.1 14 Aug. 1945: Investigation of BW Targets in Japan Basic Letter from Lt. Col. Cole, CWS, To Chief, Military Intelligence Service, From: FREDERICK D. SHARP, Col. GSC, Deputy Director of Intelligence

资料出处： National Archives of the United States, R112, E295A, B8.

内容点评： 第二次世界大战刚结束，美国为得到日军的细菌战研究资料，接连派遣四任调查官赴日调查。本资料为 1945 年 8 月 14 日情报局副局长 Frederick D. Sharp 上校向军事情报主任提交的特别项目部情报分局主任、化学战部队中校 Howard I. Cole 来信，题目：赴日调查日本细菌战。

SECRET

SPINT 1st Ind FDS/ghm-72622

Army Service Forces, Office of the Commanding General, Washington 25, DC, 14 August 1945

TO: Chief, Military Intelligence Service
Major Osborn.

Information is requested as to the necessity and practicability of such a project in view of the current situation.

FOR THE COMMANDING GENERAL:

FREDERICK D. SHARP
Colonel, GSC
Deputy Director of Intelligence

Officer: Col Sharp/ghm - 72622

SUBJECT: Investigation of BW Targets in Japan

Basic letter frm ~~LT.~~Colonel Cole, CWS

62720

16 AUG 1945
DIRECTOR OF INTELLIGENCE
ARMY SERVICE FORCES

SECURITY CLASSIFICATION NOT REGRADED
REVIEW FOR SEC ARMY BY TAG PER OJ 3

SECRET

14 August 1945

SUBJECT: Investigation of BW Targets in Japan

TO : Commanding General
Army Service Forces
Washington 25, D. C.
ATTN: Director of Intelligence

1. Experience of our BW investigators attached to the Alsos Mission proves that the Japanese BW targets should be investigated and key personnel interrogated at the earliest possible moment.

2. It is recommended that two teams, each consisting of two specially qualified officers and one interpreter be assigned to Headquarters, Invasion Forces for temporary duty of 60 days for the purpose of investigating alleged BW targets now in our possession and interrogation of scientific personnel.

3. In order to be most effective it is felt that these teams should land in Japan with the first troops or as shortly thereafter as possible.

4. This office will furnish the names of officers to comprise these teams upon request but has no information as to qualified Japanese interpreters.

FOR THE CHIEF, CHEMICAL WARFARE SERVICE:

HOWARD I. COLE
Lt Col, CWS
Chief, Intelligence Branch
Special Projects Division

SECRET

SPD
1.942

6.1.2 27 Sep. 1945: Letter from Murray Sanders, Lt. Col. CWS to Col. Worthley, TO: The Surgeon General, FROM: Intelligence Branch Special Projects Division, 12 Oct. 1945

资料出处： National Archives of the United States, R112, E295A, B8.

内容点评： 本资料为 1945 年 10 月 12 日特别项目部情报分局主任、化学战部队中校 Howard I. Cole 提交美军军医总长的 1945 年 9 月 27 日化学战部队中校 Murray Sanders 予特别项目部化学战部队长官部上校 Harlan Worthley 信函：日军细菌战活动调查报告。

SECURITY CLASSIFICATION (If any)

~~SECRET~~

SERVICE FORCES

TRANSMITTAL SHEET

FILE No.	SUBJECT
	Copy of Letter from Lt. Col. Sanders

TO—	FROM—	DATE	COMMENT No. 1
The Surgeon General U. S. Army 1818 H St. Washington, D. C. ATTN: Lt. Col. G. W. Anderson Room 1214	Intelligence Branch Special Projects Division	12 Oct 45	HIC/bjc

The attached letter is for your information and file.

Howard I. Cole
HOWARD I. COLE, Lt Col, CWS
Chief, Intelligence Branch
Special Projects Division

1 Incl.

DECLASSIFIED
Sec. 3.3
785050
NARS, Date 16/4/80

~~SECRET~~
76923

~~SECRET~~

SPD
1986

WD AGO FORM 0105
1 JAN 1945

This Form supersedes WD AGO Form 0105, 10 January 1944, which may be used until existing stocks are exhausted.

16—38245-2 GPO

SECRET

GENERAL HEADQUARTERS
UNITED STATES ARMY FORCES, PACIFIC
Scientific and Technical Advisory Section

APO 500-Advanced Echelon
c/o PM, S. F. Calif
27 September 1945

SUBJECT: Report

TO: Colonel Harlan Worthley, Office of the Chief Chemical Warfare Service, Special Project Division, Gravelly Point, Washington, D.C.

Dear Colonel Worthley,

Sufficient time has elapsed since my arrival in Japan to permit a preliminary analysis of Japanese BW activities. While this is a purely informal statement sent to you with Colonel Copthorne's permission, it will give you an idea of what may generally be expected in the near future. Detailed reports will of course be available soon through channels.

To begin with, I was very fortunate in being assigned to the scientific section under Drs K T Compton and E L Moreland. This was entirely due to the energetic and timely action of Colonel Copthorne. I feel quite strongly that this temporary attachment permitted a type of investigation that would not have been possible under other circumstances. I should also like to emphasize that the chief chemical officer has demonstrated an unusual appreciation of technical problems. As a result of being associated with this committee my work has had an impetus which will, I think, permit evaluation of the problem (for whatever it is worth).

However, as a result of my status with the committee it is also apparent that the present and the immediate future will be the productive periods. Dr. Moreland plans to leave Japan in five or six weeks and it will be necessary for me to carry out my principal investigations during this time. Colonel Copthorne is in agreement with me that my mission will probably be completed shortly after this committee is dissolved. I plan to return to the United States when my work is brought to an end, which should be sometime in November. This may perhaps raise a question in your mind concerning the desirability for an assistant in the short period of time left for our work. I can assure you that even if Lt Youngs arrives approximately the first week in October there will be enough work for him to do to justify his assignment here. Having a vigorous individual with technical training in BW will be of immense help to me during the most critical period.

RHK

SECRET

E.O.
785050
By

SECRET

To date, I have been able to assemble the defensive aspects of BW in great detail. It appears that our G-2 information has been accurate insofar as the general defensive organization is concerned. But of course there are many hiatuses to be filled and detailed data to be obtained. Yesterday I had a 2½ hour conference with Lt General Kubayashi, Surgeon General of the Japanese Army. He has committed himself to providing me all defensive details and protocols. I am to obtain this tomorrow during the visit to the Army Medical College. Checking the details and compiling reports promises to be a good-sized job.

One of my principal problems is to contact Lt General Ishii, supposedly in Harbin, Manchuria. I would venture a rather strong guess that this individual has been concerned with major field activities in BW. I suspect that this may include both offensive and defensive activities. It is likely that General Ishii has a large and independent BW organization. My reason for assuming that his group is of considerable size is based on the statement made by General Kubayashi that, as an incidental activity, General Ishii can produce sufficient vaccine to immunize many people. (He was apparently thinking in terms of one, two, or three million doses.) Furthermore, the scope of the vaccine production is extensive, varying from the ordinary typhoid type of vaccine to typhus fever vaccine. I hope to get the details tomorrow but there is obviously an implication that the Manchurian facilities are extensive, the personnel numerous, and technically trained. This aspect of the problem should certainly be thoroughly examined. I have the backing of both Dr Moreland and Colonel Copthorne in this regard, but since Harbin is in Russian territory there may be some difficulty associated with any attempt to carry on investigations in that area. I am rather optimistic that these difficulties will be overcome and that permission for a temporary assignment to Manchuria will be obtained.

In addition to the formal BW activity, I have been carrying on for the Theater Surgeon an investigation of Japanese research activities in infectious diseases during the war years. This is a major assignment since there has been a surprising amount of excellent work carried out by civilian scientists. Even at this time I can state that the work of the past five years will rate not only with some of our best contributions, but is also superior to much of the Japanese work done previous to 1940, (insofar as infectious diseases are concerned.)

The work carried on in conjunction with the surgeon's office provides a good coordinating force for the BW mission. It has two effects: first, it gains entree for me into all types of scientific circles; second, it permits a broad examination of the infectious disease field which will provide data of interest in BW aside from any formal result in that field.

2

SECRET

SECRET

I am enjoying my work and I am grateful for the technical opportunity provided by the organization here. This is an intensive period of work but is well worth any effort. If you have any suggestion or criticisms please do not hesitate to send them to me since our relations here are quite informal. I hope you are well and that it will not be too long before I can report to you in person.

With best personal regards,

/s/ Murray Sanders
MURRAY SANDERS
Lt Col, CWS

3

SECRET

6.1.3 4 Oct. 1945: Preliminary Report on Japanese BW Investigation, HOWARD I. COLE, Lt. Col. CWS, Chief, Intelligence Branch, Special Projects Division

资料出处： National Archives of the United States, R112, E295A, B8.

内容点评： 本资料为 1945 年 10 月 4 日特别项目部情报分局主任、化学战部队中校 Howard I. Cole 的报告，题目：日本细菌战调查初期报告。

SECRET

WAR DEPARTMENT
OFFICE CHIEF CHEMICAL WARFARE SERVICE
WASHINGTON, D. C.

By authority of the Chief, CWS.
Date 4-10-45 Initials [illegible]

In reply refer to

4 October 1945

MEMORANDUM TO: Distribution List

Subject: Preliminary Report on Japanese BW Investigation

1. Our investigator attached to a scientific group investigating Japanese activities has furnished the following interim report on BW as of 21 September 1945: He states that considering the short time the investigation has been pursued the general pattern is sufficiently apparent to permit an initial expression of opinion. During the war years, Japanese civilian scientists have carried out first class investigations in the field of infectious diseases. These scientists appear to be completely cooperative and have made available all detailed data down to the last protocol. They have even promised to furnish various strains of agents with which they have been working. The investigator states, "These civilians have almost surely not been associated with BW". He goes on to add that the Japanese BW activities appear to have been carried on by Army technical officers and that to date the general defensive pattern for BW is quite in agreement with our G-2 reports. He states that the Japanese Army officials have committed themselves to provide him with defensive records within the next few days and that an appointment has also been secured to examine some of the laboratories where the work has been done.

2. This paragraph from the investigator's report is quoted: "We have uncovered absolutely no evidence of offensive BW activities, but I can assure you that every effort will be made to continue this search. At the moment I am anxious to obtain the records and data for defensive BW before bringing pressure to bear on exposure of offensive BW." One other sentence is significant and is quoted: "It is my impression that Japanese BW was not a major activity and that it will not be necessary to extend this investigation as originally planned."

Comment: It should be noted that this is a preliminary report made after only a very brief period of investigation and inspection.

FOR VICTORY
BUY
UNITED STATES
WAR
BONDS
AND
STAMPS

RHK

SECRET

SECRET

Subsequent developments may not bear out the predictions and thoughts expressed above.

The investigator making the above report is a Medical Corps officer with a background of 2 years research in BW at Camp Detrick.

Howard I. Cole
HOWARD I. COLE
Lt Col, CWS
Chief, Intelligence Branch
Special Projects Division

DISTRIBUTION:
- Gen. Porter
- Gen. Ditto
- Gen. Waitt
- Mr. Merck
- Col. Worthley
- Capt. Fothergill
- MIS - Scientific Branch
- New Developments Division
- Director, ASF Intelligence
- Dr. Maass
- Lt. Col. Talbot (2 copies)
- The Surgeon General's Office

SECRET

6.1.4 5 Oct. 1945: MEMORANDUM TO: Lt. Col. Gaylord W. Anderson, SGO: Extract from Personal Letter from Col. Sanders, from: HOWARD I. COLE, Lt. Col. CWS, Chief, Intelligence Branch, Special Projects Division

资料出处： National Archives of the United States, R112, E295A, B8.

内容点评： 本资料为 1945 年 10 月 5 日特别项目部情报分局主任、化学战部队中校 Howard I. Cole 提交美军医总长办公室 Gaylord W. Anderson 中校的备忘录，题目：Sanders 中校私人来信摘录。

WAR DEPARTMENT
OFFICE CHIEF CHEMICAL WARFARE SERVICE
WASHINGTON, D. C.

5 October 1945

In reply refer MEMORANDUM TO: Lt. Col. Gaylord W. Anderson, SGO

Subject: Extract from Personal Letter from Col. Sanders

The following has been extracted from a personal letter from Lt. Col. Murray Sanders, dated 15 September 1945:

* * * * * *

"Progress is being made at this end and I think the pace will soon be greatly accelerated. So far as my mission is concerned, it has been necessary to follow GHQ policy in dealing with the Japs. However, efforts have been made to place me in an advantageous position. Up to this time, I have been permitted to contact only civilians and have spent a good deal of time at the Ministry of Public Health and the Government Institute for Infectious Diseases. Most fortunatly one of my number one targets in the person of Prof. Miyagawa has been in the latter institution. He is a virus man, is familiar with all my work and is apparently most anxious to stay in my good graces (I trust none of them). I have approached Miyagawa as the Theatre Surgeon's representative. It is fortunate that this is true and that I am investigating recent advances in infectious diseases for the Surgeon. It provides an excellent means of entry and to date I have not mentioned our subject for fear that the target will vanish.

However, I am amassing a prodigious file and will have material for reports soon. I do think it will be desirable to write a very detailed report for Special Projects Division when I return, more detailed than the Chemical Theatre officer or Surgeon would wish.

Thanks to Miyagawa I have had extensive conferences with senior scientists and have several things to report:

1. A great deal of work has been done in infectious diseases. If half of the Jap claims are true -- and I am going to have a chance to check -- then there is a tremendous amount of investigation to do.
2. For the past 2 or 3 years, Miyagawa himself (he seems to be top dog in the field) has worked on a method for large scale preservation of biological materials at room temperature. He claims to have perfected this method and has tested the following substances after one year of preservation (no loss of potency):

FOR VICTORY
BUY
UNITED STATES
WAR
BONDS
AND
STAMPS

(a) Bacillus coli
(b) B. prodigiosus
(c) Rickettsia
(d) Lymphogranuloma
(e) Drugs
(f) Blood constituents
(g) Colloidal suspensions of certain metals which he claims have marvellous therapeutic qualities

The bacteria are mixed with silicates. Next week I am taking a trip with him to investigate the apparatus and to meet his colleague, a physicist. Naturally, as a medical officer representing the Surgeon, I am interested in blood components and in drugs which may be of therapeutic value.

I also have appointments at the Army Medical College and certain other installations. On the whole I am impressed with potentialities here and elsewhere and feel that I can say a definite start has been made.

No mention of several vaccines and certain epidemiological observations have been made because I wish to check protocols and laboratory findings.

* * * * * * * * * * * *

/s/ Murray

HOWARD I. COLE
Lt Col, CWS
Chief, Intelligence Branch
Special Projects Division

6.1.5 5 Oct. 1945: Letter to Col. Harlan Worthley, Office of Chief, Chemical Warfare Service, Special Project Division, from MURRAY SANDERS

资料出处： National Archives of the United States, R112, E295A, B8.

内容点评： 本资料为 1945 年 10 月 5 日 Murray Sanders 予特别项目部化学战部队上校 Harlan Worthley 的信件，提及 Sanders 正在争取前往哈尔滨。

SECRET

GENERAL HEADQUARTERS
UNITED STATES ARMY FORCES, PACIFIC MS/lr
Scientific and Technical Advisory Section

Advanced Echelon
APO 500
5 October 1945

Colonel Harlan Worthley
Office of Chief
Chemical Warfare Service
Special Projects Division
Gravelly Point .
Washington, D.C.

Dear Colonel Worthley:

Colonel Copthorne has recently returned to Manila and Colonel Whiteside, now in charge, has given me permission to write this letter.

Because of a number of important incidents which occurred recently, it would be helpful for you to receive an impression of the current status of my mission. During the past few days the whole problem with which I am concerned has been completely and successfully precipitated beyond reasonable expectations. (That is, expectations which one might have after arriving in Tokyo). There are a good number of details to check but as of this date there is sufficient documentary evidence to permit a coherent analysis of Japanese activities--defensive and offensive. I am pleased to be able to report these facts to you because the situation here has been most delicate and the information has been received under circumstances necessitating the greatest degree of secrecy. I am transmitting this information to you because I think it is within your providence to be acquainted with the progress of my work.

When detailed reports are available (in a few weeks), it will be apparent that: a) the organization of the Special Projects Division was certainly justified; b) the program of the Special Projects Division was sound; c) our intelligence on defense was accurate but this was only partially true of offensive activities; for example, the Mark 7 was not important; you will be much more interested in three other types; d) while this activity on the part of the Japanese was probably never crystallized into action, the scope of the organization and the extent of their effort were such as to make it clear that our phase of work can never be neglected. The scale of activity must, of course, be decided by competent authorities after consideration of the data; e) to give you just a corner of the picture I can tell you that the activities of Watson, Cromartie, and Bloom were justified and that the contract to K F Myer was an excellent idea. However, there is much more to the problem than these two activities.

SECRET

SECRET

As you can easily guess, there is too much information available to do more than give you a glimpse. As a matter of fact, it is going to take some intensive work on my part to record only the general picture.

* * * * * * * * * * * *

Action is being taken this date to attempt to get me over to Harbin in the near future. I hope this attempt is successful because our G-2 was right about that area and about Ishii.

With best personal regards,

MURRAY SANDERS

SECRET

6.1.6　12 Oct. 1945: MEMORANDUM FOR: Lt. Col. G. W. Anderson, MC: Talk by Dr. K. T. Compton on Scientific War Work in Japan, from HARTWIG KUHLENBECK, Captain, Medical Corps

资料出处： National Archives of the United States, R112, E295A, B8.

内容点评： 本资料为 1945 年 10 月 12 日美军卫生部队上尉 Hartwig Kuhlenbeck 提交卫生部队中校 G.W.Anderson 的备忘录，题目：K. T. Compton 博士有关日本战争科学研究的谈话。Compton 博士为麻省理工大学校长、赴日调查的美军太平洋部队科学技术顾问团领队。

S E C R E T

SECRET

12 October 1945

785050 16/4/86

HK/mc

MEMORANDUM FOR: Lt. Col. G. W. Anderson, MC.

SUBJECT : Talk by Dr. K. T. Compton on scientific war work in Japan.

1. Undersigned attended a meeting in the Pentagon Auditorium at 14:30 on 11 October 1945 in which Dr. K. T. Compton, President of MIT, who has just returned from a mission to Japan, reported on his survey of scientific war work carried out by the Japanese.

2. Dr. Compton and his associates investigated the Japanese equivalent of our OSRD, interrogated civilian scientists and military personnel connected with scientific projects, and visited institutes and laboratories.

3. Dr. Compton's report dealt mainly with work in the field of radar, electronics, and similar technical subjects. According to his statement, the Japanese developments were definitely behind our own. Japanese production was on a rather small scale and very slow. In one case it took 18 months to prepare a pilot model of a high priority device for which blueprints and samples had been brought to Japan by a German specialist landed by submarine. There was little coordination, as the military did not trust the universities and did not reveal to civilian scientists the purpose of the research projects which these scientists were ordered to carry out. Thus for a complicated project concerning a homing bomb, various universities were ordered to develop the separate devices without knowledge of their significance. This lack of proper teamwork prevented a successful working of the assembled mechanism and resulted in failure of the project. There also was much friction and ill feeling between army and navy.

Industrial plants were heavily damaged by our bombing and the average loss of productive capacity was estimated at 60% as far as the industries investigated by Dr. Compton were concerned.

4. Dr. Compton stated that while the Japanese were behind our own technical developments they seemed to be more advanced in some aspects of medical science, namely "treatment of some tropical diseases", and some bacteriological techniques, especially "preserving or culturing organisms at room temperature".

SECRET

S E C R E T

S E C R E T SECRET

Memorandum for Lt. Col. G. W. Anderson, 12 October 1945, page 2.

5. Concerning bacteriological warfare, Dr. Compton stated that the Japanese had done a certain amount of defensive or protective work, apparently expecting such warfare from our side, but that they denied having made preparations for offensive bacteriological warfare. Dr. Compton was inclined to doubt this and believed that they might be holding back.

6. Dr. Compton stated that the Japanese were very cooperative and willing to show and explain all their scientific war work. The only exception was offensive bacteriological warfare and he stated that Japanese scientists had been overheard in conversations among themselves to make remarks like "we are not supposed to talk about this".

7. Undersigned talked to Dr. Compton after the meeting and asked further questions about Japanese medical research developments. Dr. Compton replied that he had no detailed knowledge on these matters, but that he had been told about them by Cols. W. M. Moore and M. Saunders working on his team. He thought that the advanced "treatment methods" consisted of new laboratory procedures to obtain colloidal antimony preparations and of new methods of obtaining fine dispersions, including dispersions of microorganisms on sugar (coating ?) but stated that he was not sufficiently familiar with the subject and referred to forthcoming reports by the above mentioned officers.

Hartwig Kuhlenbeck

HARTWIG KUHLENBECK
Captain, Medical Corps

SECRET

S E C R E T

6.1.7 22 Oct. 1945: MEMORANDUM TO: Lt. Col. Anderson: Preliminary Report on Investigation of Japanese BW Activities, from HOWARD I. COLE, Lt. Col. CNS, Chief, Intelligence Branch, Special Projects Division

资料出处： National Archives of the United States, R112, E295A, B8.

内容点评： 本资料为 1945 年 10 月 22 日特别项目部情报分局主任、化学战部队中校 Howard I. Cole 提交中校 Anderson 的备忘录，题目：关于日本细菌战活动初步报告。

SECRET

WAR DEPARTMENT
OFFICE CHIEF CHEMICAL WARFARE SERVICE
WASHINGTON, D. C.

By authority of the Chief, CWS.
Date 22-10-45 Initials [illegible]

22 October 1945

In reply refer to

MEMORANDUM TO: Lt. Col. Anderson

Subject: Preliminary Report on Investigation of Japanese BW Activities

1. Japanese BW activities are being investigated by a Medical Corps officer formerly engaged in BW research at Camp Detrick. This officer was assigned overseas at the suggestion of this office and was attached to the scientific intelligence mission under the leadership of Dr. Compton.

2. We have received to date a number of personal letters outlining his findings. Detailed official reports will follow shortly.

3. The following information, which indicates developments during the early stages of this investigation, has been extracted from these letters:

a. The Japanese have done extensive work on infectious diseases. Much of this work was concentrated on developing methods for large scale preservation of biological materials at room temperature.

b. BW was studied and developed both defensively and offensively.

c. Drawings and production figures on eight BW munitions are in the hands of our investigator in Tokyo, as well as much offensive data concerning tactics, clouds, persistence, method of sampling, etc.

d. There is no evidence to date that the Japanese BW activities ever crystallized into action. However, the scope of their organization and the extent of their effort indicates that our own BW activities were completely justified.

e. Plague, cholera, dysentery, anthrax and salmonellae were the agents most studied. No filterable viruses were studied.

f. Most of the experimental work was done at the Pingfan Institute at Harbin. A small amount however was done in Nanking and at the Army Medical College in Tokyo. We are advised that the Pingfan Institute, including all munitions, probably has been destroyed.

SECRET

SECRET

g. There is some likelihood that the head of the BW organization, Lt. Gen. Ishii Shiro, will be apprehended shortly.

4. It is gratifying to note that our intelligence on Japanese BW activities collected during the war was accurate insofar as the defensive organization was concerned.

HOWARD I. COLE
Lt Col, CWS
Chief, Intelligence Branch
Special Projects Division

DISTRIBUTION:
Director of Intelligence, ASF
MIS, Scientific Branch
Mr. Merck
Lt. Col. Anderson
Technical Director, Camp Detrick

6.1.8 26 Oct. 1945: MEMORANDUM TO: Lt. Col. Anderson: Investigation of Japanese Activities in Biological Warfare, from HOWARD I. COLE, Lt. Col. CNS, Chief, Intelligence Branch, Special Projects Division

资料出处：National Archives of the United States, R112, E295A, B8.

内容点评：本资料为 1945 年 10 月 26 日特别项目部情报分局主任、化学战部队中校 Howard I. Cole 提交中校 Anderson 的备忘录，题目：日本细菌战活动调查。

SECRET

WAR DEPARTMENT
OFFICE CHIEF CHEMICAL WARFARE SERVICE
WASHINGTON, D. C.

By authority of the Chief, CWS.
Date 26-10-45 Initials [illegible]

26 October 1945

In reply refer to

MEMORANDUM TO: Lt. Col. Anderson

Subject: Investigation of Japanese Activities in Biological Warfare

1. The attached report dated 15 October 1945 has just been received from our investigator in Japan. It is actually an outline of a detailed report presently being written and which will be forwarded as part of the Compton-Moreland Committee Report, GHQ, AFPAC. Although the following report contains few details it does indicate:

a. That the Japanese have been studying BW intensively for several years.

b. That at least eleven different types of BW bombs have been made experimentally and tested since 1937.

HOWARD I. COLE
Lt Col, CWS
Chief, Intelligence Branch
Special Projects Division

1 Incl

DISTRIBUTION:
Gen. Porter
Gen. Waitt
Mr. Merck
MIS, Scientific Branch
Director of Intelligence, ASF
Lt. Col. Anderson
Technical Director, Camp Detrick
File

SECRET

SECRET

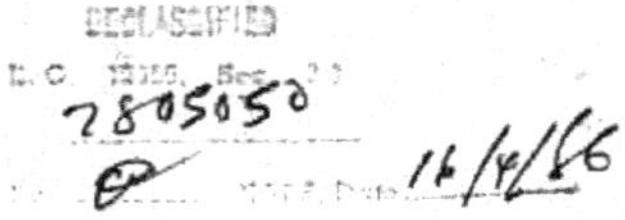

SUMMARY OF INFORMATION EXTRACTED FROM A REPORT BY A MEMBER OF THE STAFF OF THE ARMY MEDICAL COLLEGE, TOKYO

The following information was furnished on 4 October 1945 by Lt. Col. Naito, a Japanese Medical Officer. It was written in very poor English, difficult to understand. An attempt has been made to rewrite the information in proper English and at the same time interpret the meaning intended.

Colonel Naito states that he is divulging this information, which was considered by the Japanese as secret, only because he feels that the information will be developed later and that by an effort on their part to be truthful we will be more lenient with them. The request of our investigator in Tokyo for the military to supply us with information on BW, according to Naito, created consternation among the higher officers of the General Headquarters of the Japanese Army. After much discussion and debate, it was decided by the General Staff to furnish us with the information requested. Naito indicates that the Chief of the Bureau of Medicine of the Japanese Army and the Chief of the Section of Sanitation and other technical personnel were in favor of furnishing us with all details. On the other hand the members of the General Staff, comparable to our OPD, were opposed to giving this information.

Naito states that the Japanese Army had an organization for BW, both defensive and offensive. The offensive operations were under "Second Section of War Operation" under the General Staff. (See attached chart). The research and defensive work was under the Bureau of Medical Affairs and known as "Section of Sanitation". Three organizations figured prominently in the actual work. Foremost of these was the installation at Harbin, Manchuria under the jurisdiction of the Kwantung Army. The other two were under the China Army in Nanking and at the Army Medical College in Tokyo.

The main research work at Harbin was under the direction of Lt. Gen. Shirō Ishii and apparently was conducted between the years 1936 and 1945. The organization at Harbin consisted of eight sections as follows: (The chief of each section was a Colonel or Major General).

General Administration
1 Section (Scientific Research)
2 Section (Preparing Active Offensive)
3 Section (Kwantung Army Water Supply)
4 Section (Manufacturing Preventive Products, Sera, Prophylactics)
Material (Supply and Equipment)
Education (Training)
Clinic (Hospital)

SECRET

Colonel Naito states that the reason for planning offensive research was because the Japanese expected that Soviet Russia might attack Japan with BW, especially in Manchuria. He states that there was some BW sabotage (inoculating horses with anthrax) in the northern part of Manchuria during 1944 or 1945 while the Japanese were building the Peiangcheng-Heiho-Railway. Further he states that Japan should be prepared for revenge in case the enemy uses illegal warfare.

Naito advises that the Emperor did not like the preparation for chemical warfare by the Japanese Army or Navy. Because of this the scale of research for chemical warfare was not permitted to be large. Since the General Staff was cognizant of the Emperor's feeling on chemical warfare they therefore insisted that the work on biological warfare should not refer to offensive preparations. They therefore referred to all work on BW as being purely defensive.

He states that General Headquarters made no attempt to begin active BW and did not plan to unless the enemy initiated this type of warfare. As an after thought he states that the circumstances during the last period of the war became such that the Japanese were unable to start BW.

Research workers were instructed by General Ishii and other high ranking officers on methods of employment of BW, but these instructions were very limited and contained information which was of common knowledge, i.e. means of dissemination:

Airplanes	-	Bombs Direct dispersing
Artillery	-	Shells
Spy	-	Also with parachute

NOTE: Our investigator notes at this point in the report that bombs were the main research work in Harbin, but the details were not known to Colonel Naito.

The following agents are listed by Naito as having been studied: Plague, cholera, dysentery, salmonellas and anthrax. He states that none of the filterable viruses were studied because of, "the difficulty to get them in mass"?

Many research workers were mobilized for this work, each being assigned a specific problem. In order to maintain secrecy the results of the experiments were not published and each worker was uninformed regarding the work of the others.

Colonel Naito fears that all the experimental records at Harbin may have been burned at the beginning of Russia's sudden invasion. However, he states that if we succeed in securing one of the key personnel of the Harbin installation, it should be possible to obtain information concerning the work carried on there.

SECRET

SECRET

The following studies were made at the Army Medical College in Tokyo:

a. Studies on Cheopis-flea, zoological studies for the purpose of defense and tests of insecticides.

b. Studies on mass production of bacteria, in connection with possible sudden large demands for immunizing agents to combat large cholera or plague epidemics.

c. Studies on some poisons which are hard to detect, for instance "Fugu"-toxin.

d. Studies on keeping bacteria in a living state by the lyophile process.

Comment: Our investigator advises that he asked the informant whether prisoners were ever used as experimental "guinea pigs". The informant "vows" that this was never done.

HOWARD I. COLE
Lt. Col., CWS

SECRET

CHART

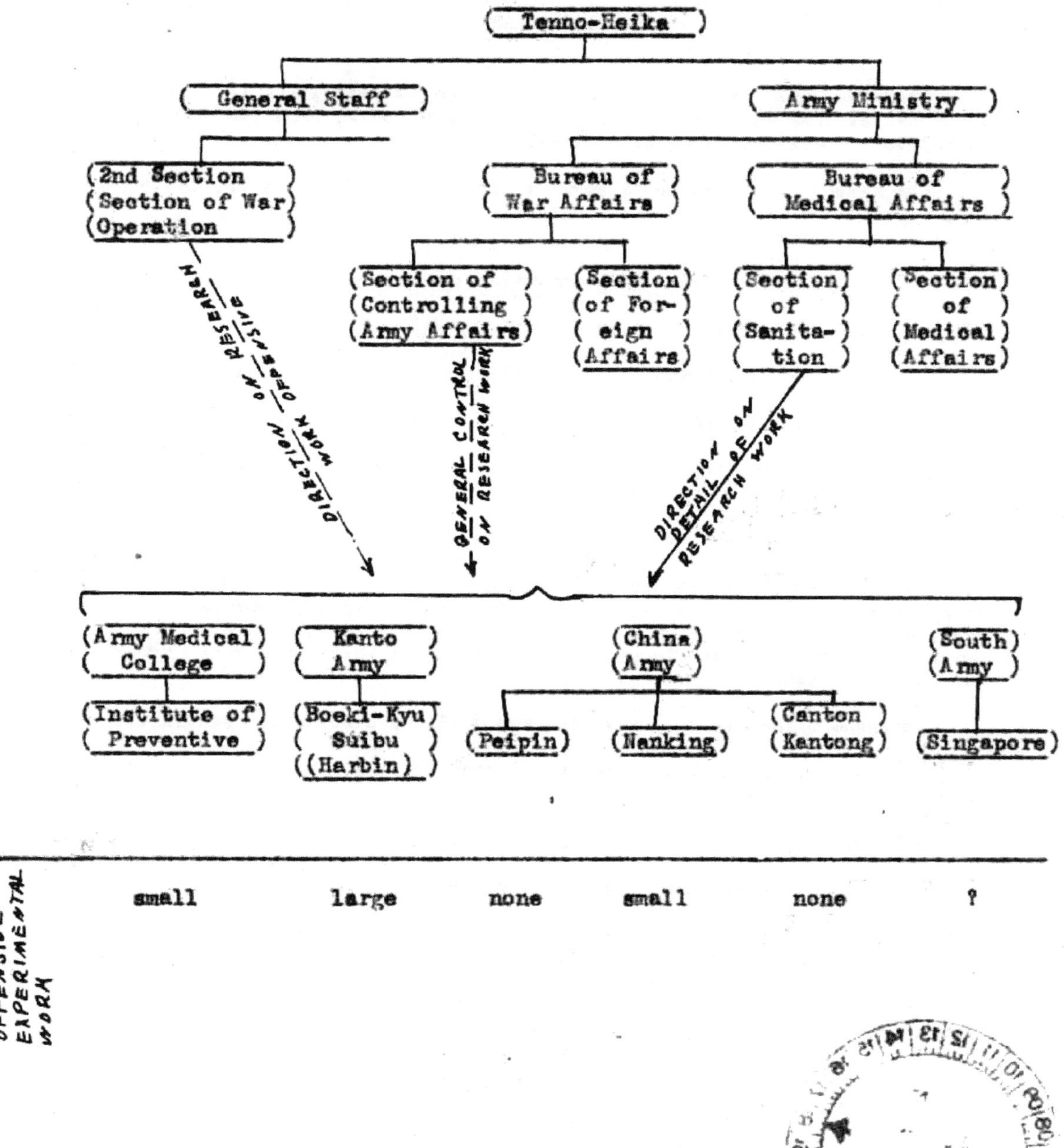
Tenno-Heika
General Staff
Army Ministry
2nd Section
Section of War
Operation
Bureau of
War Affairs
Bureau of
Medical Affairs
Section of
Controlling
Army Affairs
Section
of For-
eign
Affairs
Section
of
Sanita-
tion
Section
of
Medical
Affairs
DIRECTION ON RESEARCH WORK OFFENSIVE
GENERAL CONTROL ON RESEARCH WORK
DIRECTION ON DETAIL OF RESEARCH WORK
Army Medical
College
Institute of
Preventive
Kanto
Army
Boeki-Kyu
Suibu
(Harbin)
China
Army
Peipin
Nanking
Canton
Kantong
South
Army
Singapore
OFFENSIVE EXPERIMENTAL WORK
small
large
none
small
none
?

SECRET

SUMMARY OF A PROVISIONAL REPORT ON INVESTIGATION OF JAPANESE ACTIVITIES IN BIOLOGICAL WARFARE

Lt. Gen. Shiro Ishii was the leader of the BW activities in Japan. Japanese interest in BW was initiated and stimulated by Japanese suspicions of Russian intentions along these lines.

The history of Japanese BW work is divided into two periods, i.e.

A. 1932-1937

1. The period of preparation and organization.

B. 1937-1945

1. The period of construction and preliminary experimentation.

2. Intensive investigation of BW munition models.

3. Testing of BW munitions in the field and attempts at bomb production.

4. Defensive activities.

The report will contain a description of the organization of the Water Purification Department, its position in the Japanese War Department, types of installations, tables of organization, duties; the Kwantung organization in which was incorporated the Pingfan installation at Harbin, Manchuria; munitions.

Japanese offensive BW activities are outlined under seven headings, i.e.

A. Organisms considered and tested in preliminary fashion and the methods of evaluation.

B. Methods of dissemination considered.

1. Artillery shells (discarded)

2. Bombs (only the symbol, the year of their development and the number tested is furnished in the outline as follows):

I (1937) - Approximately 300 made and tested

Ro (1937) - Approximately 300 made and tested

Ha (1938) - Approximately 500 made and tested

U (1938) - Approximately 20 made and tested

SECRET

Uji-old type (1938) - Approximately 300 made and tested

Ni (1939) - Approximately 300 made and tested

Uji-type 50 (Feb 1939) - Approximately 2,000 made and tested. Total production not known

Uji-type 100 (1939) - Approximately 200 made and tested

Ga (1938) - Modification of Uji-type 50 - Approximately 50 made and tested

"Mother and daughter" Radio (1934) - General information only

The Navy Mark VII - No tests

3. Dispersion of BW agents from planes (not in munitions)

4. Sabotage activity

C. Methods of sampling in field trials.

D. Particle size determination.

E. Animal results.

F. Incidental human casualities.

G. Cloud chamber studies (it is claimed that no work was done in this phase)

Japanese defensive BW activities are outlined under five headings, i.e.

A. The development of an organization to meet this problem

B. Preventive medicine procedures

C. The BW defense institute

D. Protective clothing

E. Protection against respiratory assaults (it is claimed that no work was done in this field)

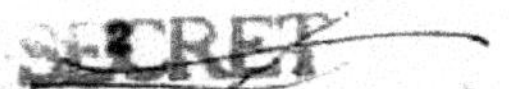

6.1.9 26 Oct. 1945: MEMORANDUM TO: Director of Intelligence, ASF: Investigation of Japanese Activities in Biological Warfare, from HOWARD I. COLE, Lt. Col. CNS, Chief, Intelligence Branch, Special Projects Division

资料出处： National Archives of the United States, R112, E295A, B8.

内容点评： 本资料为 1945 年 10 月 26 日特别项目部情报分局主任、化学战部队中校 Howard I. Cole 提交美军情报长官的备忘录，题目：日本细菌战活动调查。

SECRET

WAR DEPARTMENT
OFFICE CHIEF CHEMICAL WARFARE SERVICE
WASHINGTON, D. C.

By authority of the Chief, CWS.
Date 26-10-45 *Initials* [illegible]

26 October 1945

In reply refer to

MEMORANDUM TO: Director of Intelligence, ASF

Subject: Investigation of Japanese Activities in Biological Warfare

1. The attached report dated 15 October 1945 has just been received from our investigator in Japan. It is actually an outline of a detailed report presently being written and which will be forwarded as part of the Compton-Moreland Committee Report, GHQ, AFPAC. Although the following report contains few details it does indicate:

a. That the Japanese have been studying BW intensively for several years.

b. That at least eleven different types of BW bombs have been made experimentally and tested since 1937.

HOWARD I. COLE
Lt Col, CWS
Chief, Intelligence Branch
Special Projects Division

1 Incl

DISTRIBUTION:
Gen. Porter
Gen. Waitt
Mr. Merck
MIS, Scientific Branch
Director of Intelligence, ASF
Lt. Col. Anderson
Technical Director, Camp Detrick
File

SECRET

SUMMARY OF A PROVISIONAL REPORT ON INVESTIGATION OF JAPANESE ACTIVITIES IN BIOLOGICAL WARFARE

Lt. Gen. Shiro Ishii was the leader of the BW activities in Japan. Japanese interest in BW was initiated and stimulated by Japanese suspicions of Russian intentions along these lines.

The history of Japanese BW work is divided into two periods, i.e.

A. 1932-1937

1. The period of preparation and organization.

B. 1937-1945

1. The period of construction and preliminary experimentation.

2. Intensive investigation of BW munition models.

3. Testing of BW munitions in the field and attempts at bomb production.

4. Defensive activities.

The report will contain a description of the organization of the Water Purification Department, its position in the Japanese War Department, types of installations, tables of organization, duties; the Kwantung organization in which was incorporated the Pingfan installation at Harbin, Manchuria; munitions.

Japanese offensive BW activities are outlined under seven headings, i.e.

A. Organisms considered and tested in preliminary fashion and the methods of evaluation.

B. Methods of dissemination considered.

1. Artillery shells (discarded)

2. Bombs (only the symbol, the year of their development and the number tested is furnished in the outline as follows):

I (1937) - Approximately 300 made and tested

Ro (1937) - Approximately 300 made and tested

Ha (1938) - Approximately 500 made and tested

U (1938) - Approximately 20 made and tested

SECRET

Uji-old type (1938) - Approximately 300 made and tested

Hi (1939) - Approximately 300 made and tested

Uji-type 50 (Feb 1939) - Approximately 2,000 made and tested. Total production not known

Uji-type 100 (1939) - Approximately 200 made and tested

Ga (1938) - Modification of Uji-type 50 - Approximately 50 made and tested

"Mother and daughter" Radio (1934) - General information only

The Navy Mark VII - No tests

3. Dispersion of BW agents from planes (not in munitions)

4. Sabotage activity

C. Methods of sampling in field trials.

D. Particle size detemination.

E. Animal results.

F. Incidental human casualities.

G. Cloud chamber studies (it is claimed that no work was done in this phase)

Japanese defensive BW activities are outlined under five headings, i.e.

A. The development of an organization to meet this problem

B. Preventive medicine procedures

C. The BW defense institute

D. Protective clothing

E. Protection against respiratory assault (it is claimed that no work was done in this field)

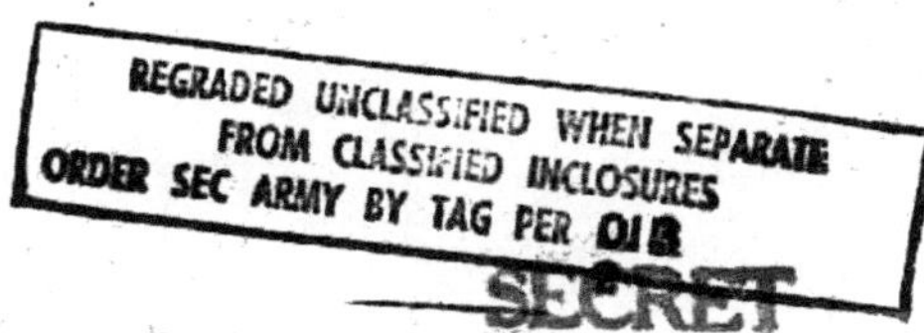

REGRADED UNCLASSIFIED WHEN SEPARATE FROM CLASSIFIED INCLOSURES ORDER SEC ARMY BY TAG PER

SECRET

6.1.10 1 Nov. 1945: Memorandum For: The Deputy Chief of Staff, from Howard C. Peterson, Special Assistant to Secretary of War

资料出处：National Archives of the United States, R112, E295A, B8.

内容点评：本资料为 1945 年 11 月 1 日美国陆军部长特别助理 Howard C. Peterson 提交副总参谋长的备忘录：立即电令麦克阿瑟将军，科学情报调查报告中有关细菌战的部分另行处理，细菌战资料尽快秘密送达陆军部 G-2 科学分局。

SECRET

1 November 1945

MEMORANDUM FOR: The Deputy Chief of Staff

It is urgently required that the following cable be sent at once to General MacArthur signed personal from the Secretary of War.

"That portion of the report of the Scientific Intelligence Mission (Compton-Moreland) dealing with biological warfare must be handled separately from the remainder of the report. The biological warfare material will be transmitted at the earliest opportunity to the Scientific Branch, G-2, War Department. In transmittal, this material will be classified SECRET."

General Surles concurs in the sending of this message.

(Signed) Howard C. Petersen

Howard C. Petersen
Special Assistant to
Secretary of War.

HCP:mec

ORIGINAL carried by HPC
OFFICE SECRETARY OF WAR

NOV 1 1945

SECRET

6.1.11 1 Nov. 1945: Report of Scientific Intelligence Survey in Japan Sep. and Oct. 1945 Vol. V Biological Warfare

资料出处： National Archives of the United States, R112, E295A, B8.

内容点评： 本资料为1945年11月1日的《日本科学情报调查报告（1945年9~10月）》第5卷《细菌战》(《Sanders报告》)。

GENERAL HEADQUARTERS
UNITED STATES ARMY FORCES, PACIFIC
Scientific and Technical Advisory Section

REPORT

OF

SCIENTIFIC INTELLIGENCE SURVEY IN JAPAN

September and October 1945

VOLUME V

BIOLOGICAL WARFARE

MIS 216476
+ Sur. 28
Ports
Lib
CWS-3
Med. 2
OSW-1
NDD-1
WDICC-1
OVI. 3

1 November 1945

COPY 50 OF 52 COPIES

SECRET

BIOLOGICAL WARFARE (BW)

TABLE OF CONTENTS

Classification changed from Restricted to Secret as directed by War Dept. Telegr No: W 80510.

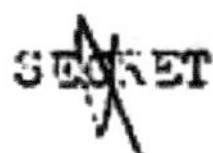

DISTRIBUTION

Report on Scientific Intelligence Survey

Agency	Vol V	Cy No
C/S, GHQ, AFPAC	1	1
Chief Surgeon, GHQ, AFPAC	2	3 & 4
Chief Chemical Officer, GHQ, AFPAC	2	5 & 6
Nav Tech Jap	2	7 & 8
A C of S, G-2 Att: War Department Intelligence Target Section.	3	2, 9 & 10
War Department, G-2 Att: Scientific Branch	39	11 thru 40 43 thru 51
Air Technical Intel Group, FEAF	2	41 & 42
Lt Col M. W. Sanders	1	52

Stencils have been sent to G-2, War Department, where additional copies may be made available upon request.

SUMMARY

BIOLOGICAL WARFARE (BW)

1. Responsible officers of both the Army and Navy have freely admitted to an interest in defensive BW.

2. Naval officers maintained that offensive BW had not been investigated.

3. Information has been obtained that from 1936 to 1945 the Japanese Army fostered offensive BW, probably on a large scale. This was apparently done without the knowledge (and possibly contrary to the wishes) of the Emperor. If this was the case, reluctance to give information relative to offensive BW is partially explained.

4. BW seems to have been largely a military activity, with civilian talent excluded in all but minor roles.

5. The initial stimulus for Japanese participation in BW seems to have been twofold:

a. The influence of Lt Gen Shiro Ishii.

b. The conviction that the Russians had practiced BW in Manchuria in 1935, and that they might use it again. (The Chinese were similarly accused)

6. The principal BW center was situated in Pingfan, near Harbin, Manchuria. This was a large, self-sufficient installation with a garrison of 3,000 in 1939-1940. (Reduced to 1,500 in 1945).

7. Intensive efforts were expended to develop BW into a practical weapon, at least eight types of special bombs being tested for large-scale dissemination of bacteria.

8. The most thoroughly investigated munition was the Uji type 50 bomb. More than 2,000 of these bombs were used in field trials.

9. Employing static explosion techniques and drop tests from planes, approximately 4,000 bombs were used in field trials at Pingfan.

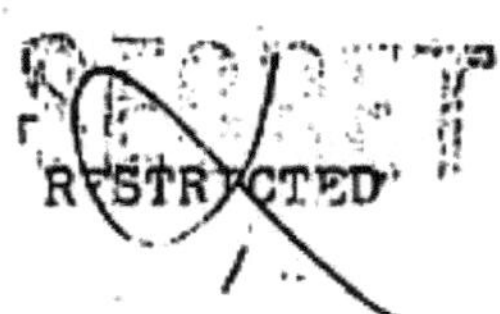

10. By 1939, definite progress had been made, but the Japanese at no time were in a position to use BW as a weapon. However, their advances in certain bomb types was such as to warrant the closest scrutiny of the Japanese work.

11. Japanese offensive BW was characterized by a curious mixture of foresight, energy, ingenuity, and at the same time, lack of imagination with surprisingly amateurish approaches to some aspects of the work.

12. Organisms which were considered as possible candidates for BW, and which were tested in the laboratory or in the field included:

All types of gastro intestinal bacterial pathogens, P. pestis (plague), B. anthracis (anthrax), and M. malleomyces (glanders).

13. Japanese defensive BW stressed:

a. Organization of fixed and mobile preventive medicine units (with emphasis on water purification)

b. An accelerated vaccine production program.

c. A system of BW education of medical officers in all echelons (BW Defensive Intelligence Institute)

14. The principal reasons for the Japanese failure were:

a. Limited or improper selection of BW agents.

b. Denial (even prohibition) of cooperated scientific effort.

c. Lack of cooperation of the various elements of the Army (e.g., ordnance)

d. Exclusion of civilian scientists, thus denying the project the best technical talent in the empire.

e. A policy of retrenchment at a crucial point in the development of the project.

CONCLUSION

It is the opinion of the investigating officers that:

a. If a policy had been followed in 1939 which would have permitted the reasonably generous budget to be strengthened by an organization with some power in the Japanese military system, and which would have stressed integration of services and cooperation amongst the workers, the Japanese BW project might well have produced a practicable weapon.

b. However, since the Japanese dreaded the United States' capacity for retaliating in kind (i.e., BW) or with Chemical Warfare agents, it is most unlikely that they would have used a BW attack against American troops even if the weapon had been at hand.

c. The Japanese are fully aware of the reasons for their failure in the development of BW. It is extremely unlikely that they would repeat their mistakes.

BIOLOGICAL WARFARE (BW)

1. INTRODUCTION. The purpose of this investigation has been twofold: a) to evaluate the intentions and capabilities of the Japanese military in regard to BW; b) to apply these findings in an attempt to estimate the potentialities of BW as a weapon at the present time or in the immediate future.

The basis of the statements in this report stem from numerous interviews and laboratory examinations carried out in Japan during the period immediately following the signing of peace in Tokyo Bay, 2 September 1945. In Appendix 29, an effort has been made to provide a documentary background by recording selected interviews.

It must be remembered that at the time of the investigation, certain unavoidable difficulties inherent to the military situation precluded a searching examination of laboratory records. For one thing, the massive destruction of such key areas as Tokyo, Nagasaki, and Kobe made it impossible to check the claims of those interviewed that records had been burned. Indeed, it was surprising that some records were still extant in such centers as the Tokyo Army Medical College, which was more than 90% destroyed.

It also became apparent early in the investigation that in dealing with the subject of BW, the investigators were faced with obtaining information which the highest authorities in the War Ministry were reluctant to give. This fact, coupled with the lack of recorded data, made it necessary to rely on verbal evidence. In order to reduce the error as much as possible, attempts were made to obtain information from presumably independent sources, using the data from each as confirmation. Although an occasional discrepancy was noted, they were of minor nature, and it is felt that the information obtained from the interviews is reasonably accurate within the limits of error of human memory. Certainly it seems logical to assume that information on offensive BW activities is significant, since the greatest reluctance was encountered in obtaining data relative to this phase. In view of the political situation, the shortcomings of offensive information would be omission rather than commission.

2. INITIAL STIMULUS. There is some conflict in the statements concerning the motives which precipitated the Japanese commitment to BW. According to Naito (App 29-E-a), in 1932 Gen Shiro Ishii (then a Major) returned to Japan after a European tour and attempted to obtain funds for constructing facilities where BW could be developed as a weapon. His hypothesis was based upon the implication of the prohibition by the League of Nations, some years earlier, against the use of bacterial agents in warfare. He reasoned that BW might be effective; otherwise, it would not have been forbidden. Regardless of whether Ishii's efforts were responsible for the birth of the Japanese BW movement, all informants are agreed that this individual was the compelling force behind the scenes throughout the period of Japanese investigations in the field of biological warfare.

Emphasis has also been placed upon the role which Russian BW activities played in stimulating the organization of Japanese BW. According to one informant, Masuda, (App 29-E-d), it was learned in 1935 by the Kwantung Army, that many Russian spies carrying bottles filled with bacteria had crossed into Kwantung territory. It is the claim of this individual that he personally examined containers found on such spies and demonstrated the presence of B. anthracis. A similar contention was made by Dr Naito.

3. HISTORICAL. Regardless of the nature of the initial stimulus, it is apparent that by 1935 Japan was activel engaged in the development of munitions for offensive BW. This work was carried out in the laboratories attached to the Harbin Military Hospital. Nor were their investigations limited to bomb construction. Field trials and preliminary offensive evaluation of organisms, in addition to defensive investigations, were simultaneously in progress. Throughout this period, and indeed at all times during the BW picture, Gen Ishii moved prominently. Although his efforts to obtain support for a BW center were not formally accepted until 1937, he seems to have provided an impetus for the work even before it received quasi-official status.

By 1937, BW investigation apparently showed sufficient promise to warrant support from the Japanese War Ministry. It has been emphasized that the BW project was carried out from beginning to end without the approval or knowledge of the Emperor. This is an important factor in contributing to the weaknesses in the organizational structure, which later proved to be fatal to the success of the mission.

3

With the support of the highest military authorities assured (with the exception of the Emperor), the BW project progressed rapidly. A large institute was constructed in Pingfan, south of Harbin. Buildings were apparently completed with some rapidity, because by 1939 it was possible to house the garrison of 3,000 individuals who were directed by Ishii in all phases of BW investigations. By 1940, the Pingfan Institute reached its present physical strength, although it has been stated that this does not represent the completed plan.

4. ORGANIZATION OF THE BOEKI KYUSUIBU. There is no doubt that the responsibility of BW investigation in all its phases rested in the Boeki Kyusuibu or Water Purification Dept.* To understand the unique opportunity which this group had for pursuing an activity apparently prohibited by the Emperor, the bivalent responsibilities which were lodged in Gen Ishii's hands must be clarified. As head of the Boeki Kyusuibu, he controlled many installations, both within Japan proper and outside the homeland. (Supp 1, a & b). It should be emphasized that the Medical Dept exercised no control over the Boeki Kyusuibu, whatsoever, and functioned in a purely advisory capacity to the military commanders in the various echelons of command. The Water Purification units, on the other hand, were directly responsible to these same military commanders through an independent channel. Furthermore, the Kwantung Armies, perhaps the most powerful military unit in Japan, functioned independently of all authorities, and the commanding general was responsible only to the Emperor. Thus, since Ishii was not only the chief of the Boeki Kyusuibu in general, with headquarters in Harbin, but at the same time was specifically in charge of the Kwantung Boeki Kyusuibu, he was able to carry on in an unhampered fashion so long as he satisfied the commanding general of the Kwantung Armies. For clarification of the channels of command, for appreciation of the magnitude of the organizations involved, with emphasis on the Kwantung group, it is recommended that Supplement 1 be consulted. It is to be further emphasized that the Boeki Kyusuibu Dept, in all its ramifications, was originally organized as the defensive mechanism against BW, and was given the mission of developing this means of warfare as an offensive, retaliatory measure.

a. The Pingfan Institute was the great Japanese BW installation.

---

* The literal translation of Boeki Kyusuibu is "Anti-Epidemic Water Supply Unit."

It can be seen from a plan of the grounds and buildings at Pingfan (Supp 2a, b) that the institute was of considerable size and was self-supporting (even to the extent of raising its own vegetables and livestock).

Unfortunately, no original documents are available because of the stringent command that complete destruction of the installation be carried out at the approach of an enemy. With the entrance of the Russians into Manchuria, this command was supposedly obeyed to the letter. There is no reason to doubt this because the Japanese had ample time to burn records and demolish all buildings and their contents.

Perhaps no better indication of the magnitude of the Pingfan project can be gained than consideration of the fact that in addition to various offensive activities, the vaccine production capacity of the plant was of the order of twenty million doses annually. Furthermore, the spectrum of vaccines ranged from typhoid to typhus.

The Pingfan Institute epitomizes the paradoxical character of the Japanese BW project. On the one hand, modern methods and machinery were utilized in seemingly efficient manner and the experiments which were done revealed ingenuity and imagination. On the other hand, a curiously primitive and limited approach appeared throughout the pattern of the organization. For example, in order to meet typhus vaccine production, the institute maintained its own flock of 50,000 hens and roosters (for obtaining fertilized eggs). These chickens were distributed in lots of 100-200 to farmers. It was the duty of the farmers to tag these chickens and to supply the fertilized eggs to collectors from the institute.

5. JAPANESE OFFENSIVE ACTIVITIES IN BW

a. Organisms. Various sources of information have agreed that the following organisms were considered likely candidates for BW:

(1) B Typhi
(2) Paratyphoid A and B
(3) B dysenteriae
(4) V cholerae
(5) P pestis
(6) B anthracis
(7) M malleomyces (glanders)
(8) Anerobes

RESTRICTED

5

(a) B welchii
(b) B novyii
(c) B hystolyticus
(d) B tetani

However, there is a difference of opinion as to the amount of experimentation carried out with each agent. According to Kaneko (App 29-E-b), organisms which were studied in the BW munitions included B prodigiosus, V cholerae, P pestis, various types of dysentery organisms, B typhosus, and B anthracis. Efforts were principally directed toward the study of pestis and anthracis organisms.

In contrast to this opinion is the statement of Col Masuda (App 29-E-d), that only B prodigiosus and B anthracis were tested in the bombs. Since all records have been presumably destroyed, it was not possible to clarify this point.

b. <u>The Method of Evaluating</u>. BW potentialities of organisms were crude and unsatisfactory. The bacteria under consideration were stored at room temperature and tested at daily intervals. Depending upon viability curves or percentage survival, the decision was made regarding further studies. Since the investigation of preservative materials for extending the life expectancy of the bacteria beyond natural limits was insufficiently studied, the seledtion of BW candidates constitutes one of the basic errors in the Japanese project.

General Ishii and his assistants also exhibited a curiously limited imagination insofar as the virus-rickettsial agents were concerned. Why this group of pathogems was not even considered in the selection of agents is not clear. This is especially puzzling since rickettsia in mass production were available at the typhus vaccine plant. It is, of course, quite possible that fear of retroactivity was the important brake in the policy of agent selection. (See App 29-E-a for details)

c. <u>Methods of Dissemination</u>. The Japanese offensive plans in BW included four general methods of bacterial dispersion: (1) Artillery shells; (2) Bombs; (3) Dispersion from planes (not in munitions); (4) Sabotage activity.

(1) Artillery shells. Two types of shells were investigated and were quickly discarded (1937) because of their impracticality as BW vehicles. The "H" shell was supposedly an ordinary gas shell and the only information available refers to an unsatisfactory trajectory. The "S" shell is supposed to have been a 75 or 90 mm shell with bacterial suspensions replacing the powder charge.

(2) Bombs. The principal offensive effort was expended on attempting to develop a bomb or bombs which could effectively disseminate organisms. Whatever detailed data have been made available on this subject have been incorporated in the drawings and summary chart (Supp 3). For purposes of this report, a brief discussion is given of the two principal munitions, the Uji and Ha bombs, with additional reference to recent trends in bomb research.

The Uji bomb was probably studied at Pingfan since 1936. It represents an ingenious approach to the problem of bacterial dissemination since the friable porcelain casing required little charge for shattering, with subsequently little destruction of the organisms due to explosion heat. That the Japanese investigated this model with vigor may be seen from the fact that at least three types of Uji bombs were exhaustively studied from 1936 to 1943, or even later. Again, the work on this munition emphasized the shortcomings of the Japanese system of investigation. Having made excellent progress in the early phase of their work, the scientific investigators were limited by their inability to obtain adequate equipment to rectify the deficiencies of the munition. One of the sources of information (App 29-E-d) who participated in numerous experiments has emphatically claimed that he would have resolved the munition problem except for the fact that he was only able to procure obsolete fuses. Much effort was wasted because of this fact, since the principle upon which the munition functioned was an accurately timed explosion in the air. (While it is true that he might have improved this weapon, serious doubts may be cast upon the possible solution because of a more basic error; i.e., the poor choice of organisms. (MS and HY)

Another serious error in the Japanese activities was the apparent inability (or the disinclination) of responsible authorities to permit cooperation within their own organization or with other branches of the service. For example, the Uji bombs were produced in the Mukden Army Arsenal by individuals who remained in total ignorance of the purpose for which the bombs were intended. As a result,

7

the deficiencies were not considered by competent bomb experts. Also, workers at Pingfan carried on their work in isolated fashion without intra-departmental discussion.

The nearest approach to mass production was made in the Uji bomb. According to one source of information (App 29-E-b), more than 500 such bombs had been tested in field trials by 1941. According to another informant (App. 29-E-d), more recently concerned with the project, over 2,000 Uji type 50's were tested experimentally. It was also stated that this figure did not represent the total production (figures not available). If one considers the fact that the payload of the Uji bomb varied from 10-100 liters, and that this munition was only one of eight tested in Pingfan, then it becomes apparent that the Japanese offensive BW study was one of no mean magnitude.

Whereas the Uji bomb was an all-purpose munition, the Ha bomb was constructed and produced with only one purpose in mind--the dispersion of anthrax spores. The immediate effect was gained by shrapnel bursts with secondary considerations given to ground contamination. The statement has been made that a scratch wound from a single piece of shrapnel was sufficient to produce illness and death in 50-90% of the horses, and in 90-100% of sheep exposed in experiments. More than 500 sheep were used in such field trials and estimates of horses similarly expended vary from 100 (App 29-E-a) to 200 (App 20-E-b).

Both static explosions and drop-tests were investigated with the Ha bomb. A final opinion of responsible authorities indicates that they considered this munition, or a modification thereof, satisfactory for contamination of pastures. The implication is made that field trials with the Ha bombs filled with anthrax organisms were of a fairly extensive nature, since it was stated that three types of planes were used in such field tests. These planes consisted of:

a. Scout planes, type 94, capacity four Ha bombs.
b. Light bombers, type 88, capacity six Ha bombs.
c. Heavy bombers, type 97, capacity twelve Ha bombs.

The search for a satisfactory BW munition continued until 1944 when a new type of weapon was tested, in an attempt to accurately control the height at which the explosion occurred. This was done by the use of "mother and daughter" radio bombs. The munition consisted of one large "mother" bomb and a cluster of small "daughter" bombs. The large missile contained radio-sending apparatus and was dropped from the plane just before the target was reached. The cluster of bombs, containing radio-receiving apparatus, was loosed within a given period after the "mother" bomb had left the plane. Cessation of the radio impulses, which occurred when the "mother" bomb exploded on contact with the terrain, caused the "daughter" bombs to explode. The only information available concerning this weapon is that the bombs used in clusters were thin-walled and that the trend of research was considered highly promising. Only one set of bombs was made and tested and the investigation ceased because of the high cost of the bombs.

Although details on various other bomb types are available in Supplement 3, it is of interest to summarize information available on types of bombs, the approximate production figures, and the year in which they were made and tested.

BOMB	APPROXIMATE PRODUCTION	YEAR MADE AND TESTED
I	300	1937
RO	300	1937
HA	500	1938
NI	300	1939
U	20	1938
UJI (old type)	300	1938
UJI (type 50)	2,000*	1939
UJI (type 100)	200	1939
GA	20	1938

* This number of bombs was used for field trials. The total production figures are not known, although it has been established that additional UJI type 50 bombs were made.

9 SECRET RESTRICTED

Because the Mark 7 bomb has been frequently mentioned as the Japanese bacillus bomb in Theater G-2 reports, attempts were made to obtain information relative to this munition. In brief, it was found that the Mark 7 was a Navy bomb but its existence had been limited to the drawing board. According to the source of information (App 29-D-b), the Mark 7 bomb was suggested about ten years ago when the Japanese General Staff was considering all possible types of bombs. It has been repeatedly emphasized by responsible officers in the Navy that their interest in BW was not only limited to defensive aspects, but that this interest never exceeded simple theoretical considerations with defensive responsibilities allocated to the Bureau of Medicine. The group at the Naval Medical College maintained that they had carried out no experimentation whatsoever involving BW, and had considered the subject in terms of preventive medicine only.

The naval authorities further maintained that the Mark 7 bomb never advanced beyond a preliminary informal drawing. The photograph of this munition (Supp 3f) is from a copy of the original "informal" drawing. Since the naval developmental group was located adjacent to an air arsenal where naval officers were instructed in ordnance, it is considered likely that a reference to the Mark 7 was seen by one of the instructors who then entered the (theoretical?) bomb in his lecture notes. No evidence refuting these claims was obtained during the course of the investigation. Certainly the Mark 7 based on the drawing is a crude and unsatisfactory BW munition.

(3) Dispersion from Planes (not in munitions). Some consideration by the Japanese has been given regarding the dispersion of bacterial agents from planes, in the form of fluid or dried material. It was the opinion of one of the central figures in the project (Col Masuda), that desiccated material dispersed directly from a plane would undoubtedly be an effective means of waging BW. Because of the hazard to the workers and limited facilities for desiccating biological substances en masse, such considerations have remained hypothetical.

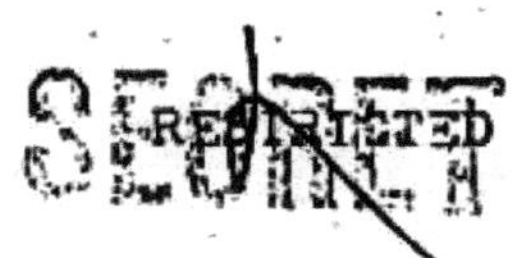

The direct dispersion of fluid material was limited to a few preliminary experiments. Tests with colored material, dispersed at a height of 4,000 meters, revealed that the particles descended to the surface of the earth in one hour. When B prodigiosus was used in such tests, the organisms could not be recovered in viable form. It was further established that the viscosity of the solution and rapidity of dispersion were important factors for successful dissemination of test materials. The best substances for producing the proper degree of viscosity were 50% glycerine and 10% gelatin. In one series of experiments, adequate dispersion was obtained when a dissemination rate of 920 liters per second was maintained over the test area. The number of experiments was small and additional information concerning other substances tested was not forthcoming. However, it was learned that similar tests had been carried out at altitudes of 2,000, 1,000, and 200 meters--with somewhat better results than at 4,000 meters.

Whether this was the complete story of direct dispersion could not be ascertained. However, it was certainly possible for the Japanese to indulge in such activities since the test field at Pingfan is a square, 10 x 10 km, and various planes were at the disposal of the project.

(4) Sabotage Activities. The Japanese have repeatedly emphasized this phase of BW activity, but have invariably placed the responsibility upon China or Russia. Indeed, the only technical reference to saboteurs, so far as the Japanese were concerned, was an explanation as to why the study of contaminated wells came under the defensive program.

Regardless of whether or not the Chinese or Russians indulged in this type of activity, it is suggested that the Japanese statement in respect to their own intentions be considered with some reservation. It is not intended to convey in this report that the Japanese used individuals to disseminate infectious materials, nor that they proposed to do so. However, there are several reasons for accepting, with some question, their purely defensive connotation to BW by sabotage methods. These reasons are as follows:

11 

(a) In the selection of BW agents, the Japanese concentrated to a great extent on organisms spread via the gastro-intestinal tract. In such circumstances, water might be the vehicle of transmission, par excellence.

(b) It is difficult to understand how the Japanese offensive program intended, even theoretically, to disperse such organisms as B typhi, V cholerae, and dysentery by means of the munitions studied at Pingfan. Yet, these bacteria remained on the list of offensive agents.

(c) Not only do G-2 reports emphasize Japanese BW offensive thinking in terms of accentuation of endemic disease, but a similar line of reasoning has been noted in various discussions with Japanese officers. If this reasoning is indicative of Japanese thought on the subject of BW, then the selection of enteric organisms is further explained.

As previously mentioned, there is little concrete evidence, with one exception, of Japanese studies using saboteurs for spreading disease. A large number of experiments were carried out by units under the direction of Col Masuda, which tested the capacity of organisms to survive in water. More than a thousand wells in a given district were tested. Further details on this study can be found in App 29-7-a, and it may suffice to say here that Col Masuda came to the conclusion that contamination of wells in China was not practical.

d. Assessment of Field Trials. The methods used at Pingfan to accumulate and evaluate data from field trials, provide an interesting and significant insight into Japanese BW capabilities. While the methods were essentially of a qualitative character, they were, nevertheless, simple, direct, and undoubtedly provided significant data.

It is important to note that the authorities at Pingfan disregarded any possible need for accumulation of quantitative data in cloud chambers preliminary to setting up field trials. (Indeed, such chamber studies were never attempted). Showing little concern for finesse, they proceeded to test in the field bacterial dissemination from various types of munitions. This activity was initiated as early as 1935 and was energetically maintained for almost ten years.

SECRET
RESTRICTED

SECRET
RESTRICTED

Whatever details are available on such aspects of field trials as persistence of clouds, sampling methods, particle size determination, and pattern of dispersion, can be found in App 29-F-a.

Admittedly crude and possibly unsound as part of a permanent policy, Japanese methods of obtaining data from field trials served an important purpose in demonstrating BW potentialities. It would be a serious error to minimize them.

6. JAPANESE DEFENSIVE BW ACTIVITIES. In spite of the energy which the Japanese expended on offensive BW investigations, the importance which they attached to the BW problem is best appreciated from a consideration of the defensive phase. This is true in spite of two cardinal principles of the Boeki Kyusuibu that: (a) Offensive BW was the best defense; (b) If a large-scale BW attack were to be launched against Japanese forces or civilians (especially in the homeland), defensive measures would be of little avail. Japanese defensive measures may be divided into three phases: (See App 29-F-a) (a) An organization to meet the BW problem; (b) Preventive medicine; (c) The BW Defense Intelligence Institute.

a. <u>Organization to Meet the BW Problem</u>. This was considered the most important defense measure.

During the summer of 1938, Col Masuda recommended that the Boeki Kyusuibu be greatly expanded. His plan was accepted and by October of the same year, 18 water purification centers were established in Chinese territory controlled by Japan. Each of these installations served as a central bureau, assigning their allotment of 300 persons to satellite branches. The 18 larger installations were distributed as follows: 3 in north China, 13 in central China, and 2 in south China.

At the risk of appearing repetitious, it is considered sufficiently important to point out that fear of BW (presumably in China) was the basis of this expansion involving a minimum of 5,000 personnel with varying degrees of technical training. While it is true that the water purification centers of necessity contributed to a health program, it has, nevertheless, been emphasized that only later, when BW attacks did not materialize, was the emphasis permitted to shift.

SECRET
RESTRICTED

13

SECRET

b. Preventive Medicine. This phase of the defense must certainly be considered part of a normal medical program of a nation at war. Nevertheless, the emphasis on BW was a definite and independent part.

To begin with, the vaccine production program was accelerated and expanded. Measures were taken to permit the large, fixed installations to produce all types of vaccines for those individuals in the areas for which the Boeki Kyusuibu was responsible. This, of course, required transfer of personnel and equipment. But the vigor of the program can be noted from the fact that at the Pingfan installation alone, more vaccine was produced annually than in the whole Japanese homeland during a comparable period.

Another, perhaps more specific phase of defensive BW included research in preventive medicine in various localities. Because this type of work was generally acceptable as a medical activity, it was not only carried on at Pingfan but also at the Army Medical College at Tokyo (and possibly at the corresponding institution at Niigata).

It has been difficult to isolate the experiments which were done for the purpose of contributing to BW defense. However, there is no question but that many investigations would have been omitted had it not been for the stimulus of BW

As has been noted in Appendix 29, the records at the Tokyo Medical College were destroyed. Just as the investigation was being concluded, a complete set of records was found at the Niigata branch of the Army Medical College covering all experimental work which was done in Tokyo during the past ten years. An analysis of these records, including detailed findings in defensive BW research, will be presented in a supplementary report.

c. The BW Defense Intelligence Institute. This phase of the defensive activity might well be considered as part of the general organization for combating BW. However, Ishii considered it independently and used this system for teaching purposes. The term, system, has been used advisedly since the Defense Intelligence "Institute" seems to have referred to a function rather than to an organization. The Boeki Kyusuibu had the responsibility of briefing medical officers in all echelons down to battalions, on the subject of BW. It was the duty of these officers to organize epidemiological teams to trace all outbreaks of disease to the source to determine whether or not they were dealing with an artificially initiated epidemic (i.e., BW). While this may

SECRET

SECRET

to be somewhat far-fetched, it may be pointed out that such an attitude was no more incredible than the field testing of some 2,000 Uji type 50 bombs (practically a fait accompli by the time the BW Defense Intelligence Institute began to functio-

Since no BW attacks were experienced, the contribution of the epidemiological teams was limited to control of disease outbreaks occurring in the natural course of events. However, the case may have been, it is the method of thought in the BW Defense Intelligence Institute that is pertinent to this report.

It may be further noted that it had been planned originally to assign specially-trained BW officers in various echelons of the Army, but a dearth of personnel made it necessary for the medical officers to take on the additional duty of BW technical intelligence.

SECRET

SECRET

PREFACE TO APPENDIX 29

Statements in the interviews (Appendix 29) have been largely left in their original form and may therefore appear foreign or unwieldy.

IT IS REQUESTED, IN THE EVENT THAT ANY USE IS MADE OF MATERIAL IN THE INTERVIEWS, THAT JAPANESE NAMES AND SOURCES BE KEPT CONFIDENTIAL BECAUSE INFORMATION WAS OCCASIONALLY GIVEN CONTRARY TO THE WISHES OF SUPERIOR OFFICERS.

SECRET

Appendix 29-A-a-1

ARMY MEDICAL COLLEGE

SUBJECT : Biological Warfare (BW)
DATE : 20 September 1945
INTERVIEWED : Col Saburo Idezuki, Chief, Division Preventive Medicine, Army Medical College, Col Takatomo Inoue, Director Department of Bacteriology, Army Medical College,
INTERVIEWERS: Lt Col M Sanders, Lt Col W Moore, Maj H F Skipper.

1. When these officers were questioned regarding their relationship to BW they answered that the department of Preventive Medicine had been given the responsibility of organizing defense measures in that field.

2. The question was raised regarding the unit of defense and the answer given referred to it as the Water Purification Unit. (WPU)

3. When asked to reproduce a chart showing the organization and details of BW groups in the field the following was given:

Commander of Division

Bacteriological Group (225 men)

(Lt Col or Maj)

4. The duties of the divisional WPU were listed as follows:

a. Prevention of Infectious Disease
b. Water Purification
c. Investigation of Epidemics

5. Fixed units, larger in organization, also prepared vaccines. Futhermore, emphasis was placed upon the fact that the units had no offensive duties but only those considered as preventive medical activities.

6. Equipment for divisional WPU included: 4 water purification units (motorized filters plus trucks); some units contained only 2 filters with 28 trucks for water and material transportation.

7. Army Water Purification Units were twice the size of divisional units and were commanded by colonels.

8. The organization of the permanent fixed stations was somewhat different than that of the army divisional WPU. The permanent fixed stations were situated at:

a. Harbin (Manchuria)
b. Peking (China)
c. Nanking (China)
d. Canton (China)
e. Singapore (Malay States)

RESTRICTED

Appendix 29-A-a-1

29-A-a-2

9. The following questions and answers were recorded:

Q. Where is there water purification equipment which may be examined?
A. In the Army Medical College. Part of the equipment has been moved to Niigata to avoid bombing.

Q. Did you have defensive measures against BW other than "P"?
A. Just cloth masks.

Q. Did you investigate the possibility of the gas masks as a means of defense?
A. No.

Q. Did you produce any protective clothing especially designed for BW defense?
A. Only for people who studied Plague.

Q. Did you expect a BW attack?
A. Yes. (Col Idezuki stated that after the last war they had heard that all countries were studying offensive BW.)

Q. What work has been carried out here on offensive BW?
A. None, The offensive phase of BW was never studied.

Q. Which BW agents did you think would be the most likely candidates in the event of an attack?
A. Typhoid and intestinal type germs.

Q. Did you think ordinary precautions were adequate?
A. We felt that the weakest point of the Japanese soldier was his inadequate knowledge in regard to his hygiene. Because of this weakness, boiling water and proper preparation of foods were stressed.

Q. What vaccines were produced in Japan.
A. a. Typhoid.
   b. Para typhoid A, para typhoid B.
   c. Plague
   d. Meningitis
   e. Typhus
   f. Weil's Disease
   g. Small pox

Q. Am I to understand that you have carried on absolutely no offensive studies on BW?
A. No studies concerned with offensive BW. Only studies to avoid attack of enemy. These studies were carried out at the Army Medical College.

Q. What type of defensive studies have been carried out?
A. Studies of diseases endemic in a given area. For example, in Manchuria—typhus studies; in South China—malaria.

RESTRICTED

29-A-a-2

SECRET RESTRICTED 29-A-c-3

Q. What do you know of a BW bomb?
A. We know nothing.

Q. We have reports from independent sources that you possess a BW munition. All reports agree on the description of this munition.
A. This is a strategic (?) fact. It is not within our responsibility and we would naturally be ignorant of it.

Q. Who would know of this?
A. General Staff.

Q. Who in General Staff?
A. We do not know.

Q. How could you carry on intelligent defensive studies withou offensive knowledge?
A. We believed we could take general measures.

Q. We wish to see your records on the defensive work.
A. Most of the buildings have been burned and with them the medical studies in which BW is described.

10. The interview was terminated and the Japanese officers voluntarily promised to try to find out the individuals on the General Staff who were responsible for policy and who might have had the responsibility for offensive studies.

ESTIMATE: This, the first conference on BW was manifestly unsatisfactory. If the statements of the Japanese officers were to be credited then the defensive aspects of the subject were indeed amateurish and crude. Cols Idezuki and Inoue had been summoned because of the policy current at GHQ of frankly requesting that officers engaged in specific activities be called for interview. Thus, they had come in response to a request for officers concerned with BW.

It is to be noted that the claims made for BW activities were limited to enteric organisms and emphasized the accentuation of endemic disease. Although the paucity of information cannot be denied, it is interesting that these statements were made which were in agreement with our intelligence reports. Also in agreement with such reports was the association of WPU with BW.

Because of the unsatisfactory nature of this interview it was decided that the Surgeon General of the Army be summoned.

29-A-c-3

Appendix 29-A-b-1

ARMY MEDICAL COLLEGE

SUBJECT : Japanese Defensive Activities in Biological Warfare (BW).
DATE : 1 October 1945.
INTERVIEWED : Col Takatomo INOUE, Lt Col Ryoichi NAITO.
INTERVIEWER : Lt Col Murray Sanders.

1. This conference held at the Army Medical College emphasized the reluctance with which Japanese officials discussed BW. Col Inoue who is chief of the Bacteriological Section in the Army Medical College was given the responsibility of defensive BW. He stated that BW was part of the research program in preventive medicine. When asked for the records of this research he said that none were available since all the files had been burned as a result of bombing. This was certainly likely since more than 90% of the Army Medical College has been completely destroyed by air attack.

2. In response to a question concerning the extent of the BW activities in the Army Medical College Col Inoue stated that no type of artificial infection experiment had been carried out and that the approach to the problem of BW was based on general medical concept. Furthermore, 90% of their efforts had been expended toward the improvement of vaccines.

3. In response to orders from Gen Kombayashi, Col Inoue prepared a resume (?) of his departments activities during the war years. Since no detailed records were available the summary was prepared from memory. A translation of this statement is appended. It is apparent that his material deals only with generalities and provides absolutely no information on BW. Col Inoue provided a list of personnel within his department. They are:

Maj Ikebe, Kichitaro	Differentiation of Vibrio cholerae from non-pathogenic
Army expert Miyauchi, Mashiro	Water analysis
Col Inoue, Takatomo	Director 1942-1945
Lt Col Naito, Ryoichi	Water supply, Drying of Sera
Maj Yamada, Masatsugu	Education, Lecturer
" Idei, Katsushige	" "
" Nakano, Minoru	Plague prophylactic vaccine
" Hirooka, Tadashi	Cultivation of Bac tuberculosis
" Miyasaki, Tadaomi	Prophylactic of tetanue and gas gangreno
" Hayashi, Masao	BCG vaccine
" Kondo, Masabumi	Spirochetae icterohaemorrh
" Kaseno, Toshio	B. tuberculosis
" Tsuyama, Yoshibumi	Water supply & Disinfection
Lt. Usiba, Daizoo	Penicillin
Maj Komori	Classification of salmonella

Appendix 29-A-b-1

29-A-b-2

Studies for the Prevention of Epidemics in the Army

I Studies on Malaria

A. On investigations of the mosquitoes which carry malaria.

B. The study for destroying mosquitoes.

1. On insecticides.
2. On a certain insecticide invented by the Chemical Department.

C. Studies with bird-malaria.

1. Precipitin tests between the organs of (liver, spleen) malaria-infected birds and human serum. This was reported to be of no diagnostic value.
2. Sulfachinin (Sulfanilamide + chinine) was found to have no effect on bird malaria.

D. The cultivation of the plasmodium.

1. It was reported that they were able to preserve the bird malaria plasodium in an ice chamber longer than in former times (5 days).
2. Tissue-culture was given up owing to the death of the investigator.
3. The object for cultivation was to discover a good Plasmodium-antigene for diagnosis and prophylaxis.

E. Summary of Japanese references on malaria.

F. On the prophylaxis of malaria.

1. Against the plasmodium in the human blood.
2. The destroying of mosquitoes and larvae.
3. The prevention against mosquito bites.

G. On investigations of the malaria in the occupied areas.

II Studies on immunizing. This was regarded as one of the most important studies.

A. Typhoid Fever
B. Paratyphoid A
C. Paratyphoid B
D. Cholera
E. Plague

29-A-b-2

29-A-b-3

F. Epidemic cerebro-spinal meningitis
G. Typhus
H. Dysentery
I. Tuberculosis
J. Small-pox
K. Tetanua
L. Infectious jaundice

III Studies on tuberculosis.

A. Culture media for the tubercle bacilli. Oka-Kata-kura's media was reported to be the best.

B. On culture medias using eggs.

C. On the resistance of the tubercle bacilli.

D. On the non-pathogenic acid fast bacilli in the sputum.

E. The studies on immunixing solutions, B. C. G.

F. On the manufacturing of "tuberkulin" for diagnostic use.

G. On a simpler method for collecting the sputum.

H. On the effect of the Spirochaeta morsus-muris. The inosoculation of the Spirochaeta to the tuberculosis-infected guinea-pig was reported to show a tendency to the healing of tuberculous ulcers.

IV Studies on Penicillin, especially on the conditions for culture.

V Studies on some pathogenic bacilli.

A. Studies on the Salmonella group.

1. Morphological, biological and serological studies on the bacilli collected from various parts of the continent of Asia.
2. On a simpler way for increasing the bacilli 1% glucose solution, and even sterile water served the purpose.

B. Studies on the dysentery bacilli.

C. Studies on the cholera vibrio.

D. Studies on the Plague bacilli.

29-A-b-3

VI Studies on substitutional culture medias.
Studies on serums for diagnostic use.
Studies on improvement of culture medias for the front.

VII A. On destroying insects which are carriers of infectious diseases: on D.D.T.

B. On the habits of mosquitoes. The colours mosquitoes like are red and yellow.

VIII Studies on the filtering apparatus. The Berkefeld type was adopted by the Army owing to the following reasons:

KIND OF FILTER	METHOD TO DISPOSE OF FILTER CAKE
A soft filter using asbestos.	It needs to be renewed every time.
A hard filter consisting of porcelain.	To be delt with chemicals or flames (fire).
A hard filter made from Diatomaceous earth.	Brushing the surface is sufficient for the purpose.

The types adopted by the Army are:

TYPES	STRUCTURE OF APPARATUS	WATER FILTERED PER HOUR	WEIGHT	ARRANGEMENT
A	Transported by motor truck	36 kl	5 tons	4 to each div.
B	Transported by a cart	1000 l.	100 kg.	1 to each bn.
C	Transported by horse	700 l.	70 kg.	1 to a company
D	Transported by men	100 l.	20 kg.	1 to a section
D	Transported by one man	20 l.	5 kg.	1 to each squad

A. Studies on the raw materials for the filter.

B. Studies on the manufacturing of the filter.

C. On testing the filter.

1. Mean pore diameter.
2. Maximal pore-diameter.
3. The amount of water filtered per hour.
4. The power of checking bacterias.
5. The absorption power.

29-A-b-5

D. On the filtering power and methods for using the apparatus.

E. On the structure of the filter.

F. On the preservation of the filter. For preserving the filter from mold it was soaked in a solution of $Ca\ Cl_2$ and Phenol.

IX <u>Studies on disinfecting trucks</u>. (Trucks for disinfecting) Two motor trucks were used for this purpose.

A. Consisting of:

1. Water tank (containing 1 L. of water).
2. Boiler.
3. Turbine pump for spraying.
4. A shower.

B. Consisting of:

1. A bag to disinfect clothes in.
2. An apparatus for causing hot air.

The trucks A and B combined, the following disinfections are performed:

1. Soldiers - chemical baths.
2. Clothes - steam, then dried with hot air.
3. Horses and carriages - sprayed with disinfectants.

100 (in summer 200) soldiers per hour could be disinfected in this manner.

X <u>Studies on preserving serum</u>.

XI <u>Studies on the typhus vaccine</u>. For producing the vaccine the lungs of rats, or the chicken embryo were used and not the louse nor tissue culture.

A. Vaccine produced from the lung of rats (Rickettsia Mooseri used - R. M. Vaccine)

1. Liquid vaccine.
2. Dry vaccine.

B. Vaccine produced from the chicken embryo using the Rickettsia Provaseki as the virus strain. (R. P. Vaccine).

1. Liquid vaccine.
2. Dry vaccine.

29-A-b-5

SECRET 29-A-b-6

C. The comparison of the two vaccines as antigenes by animal experiments.

Guinea pigs were used for the purpose. The guinea pig was immunized with each vaccine, and after 3 weeks of the injection, 1 cc of brain emulsion from an infected guinea pig was injected. A rise of temperature, decrease of weight, and if considered necessary, monocytosis, Fraenkel's nodules were examined.

1. With the R. M. Vaccine in using 1 cc in the first injection, and 2 cc in the second injection 20% of the guinea pigs were infected, but by using 2 cc in the first, and 4 cc in the second injection, the infection was completely prevented. The only fault was that a large dose was necessary for acquiring complete immunity. The liquid and dry vaccines are almost the same in their antigene powers.

2. With the R. P. Vaccine 0.5 cc in the first, and 1.0 cc in the second injection were enough to prevent the outbreak of the desease. The liquid vaccine, if preserved in a dark cool place, retained its power for about one year, while the dry vaccine can preserve its power for several years even in room temperature.

D. The immunizing of human beings.

In both vaccines the following method was adopted; The liquid vaccine, after preserving for two weeks in an ice chamber, the dry vaccine after dissolving the powder.

1. Local reactions.

Considerable pain is felt in both vaccines when injected, owing to the formalin as a preservative. This, however, disappears in less than a minute.

With the liquid vaccine swelling and reddening of the skin may be seen for a few days, but not with the dry vaccine.

2. The minimal dose:

a. R. M. Vaccine - 1 cc in the first, and 2 cc in the second injection.
b. R. P. Vaccine - 0.5 cc in the first, and 1.0 cc in the second injection.

As there has been no great epidemic, the dose for injection should be further studied. R. M. Vaccine for 6 persons can be gotten from 1 rat. R. P. Vaccine for 30-40 persons can be gotten from 1 egg.

29-A-b-6

29-A-b-7

E. Summary.

The R. P. Vaccine is superior to the R. M. Vaccine because of the following three reasons.

1. The immunizing power being greater.
2. The manufacturing process being simpler.
3. The amount of vaccine available being greater.

XII Studies on the examination of water.

A. An emergency test.

In cases of battle, and marching, examination boxes are used chiefly to remove poisonous substances.

To find poisonous substances in water quickly, and with simplicity, a testing paper for cyanide, sublimate, arsenic were invented.

B. Examinations in camp.

Not only examinations for poisonous substances, but also physico-chemical examinations to prove the contamination of the water by pathogenic bacterias indirectly are adopted. The examinations are made for:

1. Atmospheric temperature.
2. Temperature of the water.
3. Colour.
4. Chlorides.
5. Ammonia.
6. Subnitrates.
7. Nitrates.
8. Hardness.
9. Free chlorine.

C. Thorough examinations for permanent water supplies.

XIII On the water supply in Io Jima (Io Island).

Though the source of water in Io Jima is very scarce, well water is available on the coast, but as it contains much mineral salts, it does not serve as drinking water.

By using it for drinking use many soldiers suffered from diarrhea, the chief cause of which was considered to be the presence of magnesium sulfuricum, and so the following methods were adopted to remove $Mg\ SO_4$:

A. The quantative measuring of $Mg\ SO_4$.

B. The removing of $Mg\ SO_4$.

1. The $Ca\ (OH)_2$ method; $Ca(OH)_2 + Mg\ SO_4 = CaSO_4 + Mg(OH)_2$
2. The $Ba(OH)_2$ method; $Ca(OH)_2 + MgSO_4 = BaSO_4 + Mg(OH)_2$
3. The $Ca(OH)_2$ - $Ba(OH)_2$ method. The two methods above combined.

SECRET RESTRICTED 29-A-b-7

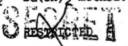

Appendix 29-B-a-1

JAPANESE GENERAL STAFF

SUBJECT : Biological Warfare (BW).
DATE : 1 October 1945.
INTERVIEWED : Lt Col Seiichi Niizuma and Lt Col Ryoichi Naito.

INTERVIEWERS: Lt Col Sanders.

1. Col Niizuma's position was given as "My appointment controls all technical research work for the Japanese Army." Questioning revealed that his position carried extensive responsibilities including: Ordnance (bombs, weapons), Radar, Medicine, Communications, Foods, Clothing (including protective), Fuel, Buildings, Veterinary Medicine.

2. Col Niizuma was frankly questioned on Japanese BW offensive activities and on the official lists which referred to a bomb as the "Mark 7 bacillary bomb".

3. The Japanese officer stated that he had no information concerning Japanese BW since the subject as a whole had been handled in the Medical Bureau.

4. In reference to the Mark 7 bomb Col Niizuma gave the following explanation. It is not the custom of the Japanese Army to place numbers on bombs. The army classification of bombs is based on letters and symbols and so far as he knew the Japanese had never experimented with a bacillus bomb. He suggested that the Mark 7 may have been confused with a 1 kg "Ta" bomb since the symbol for this missile resembles a 7 (タ = "Ta").

5. The statement was made that numbers were placed by the army on rocket bombs and arrangements were made for inspection of the NO. 7 rocket bomb.

6. In answer to the question as to which army bomb was colored green or purple or grey purple Col Niizuma stated that there were no bombs with such colorings.

7. Information was requested concerning protective clothing for BW. Col Niizuma stated that the Japanese Army had no BW protective clothing. Col Naito proferred information that in the Medical Bureau protective clothing was used for special post mortem work (plague) and for plague studies.

8. The following questions and answers were recorded: (NOTE: Since adequate information is available concerning plague protective clothing, this subject was not pursued.)

Appendix 29-B-a-1

Appendix 29-B-a-2

Q. Am I to understand that BW was handled entirely by the Medical Bureau?
A. Yes. General responsibility was lodged in the Chief of the Bureau, (Surgeon General) but specific tactical responsibility may have been placed elsewhere.

Q. Who would have specific tactical responsibility?
A. I do not know.

Q. What was the opinion of the Japanese General Staff in regard to BW?
A. Reports were received based on literature studies that such attacks could be made and would spread misery.

Q. Did the Japanese General Staff expect a BW attack by the U.S.?
A. In view of the Air Force spreading glass and gasoline on rice fields the Japanese General Staff expected BW attacks.

Q. In what form did you expect such an attack?
A. We had no detailed concept. We attempted no protection because it was felt that protective measures were hopeless in view of the number of aircraft available to the U.S. We even felt helpless in view of the threat of rice crop destruction by burning.

Q. Did you take any measures to preserve the rice crop?
A. Only simple ones. (NOTE: Col Niizuma states that the Japanese General Staff planned to vary rice field patterns in order to preserve part of the crop. This was to be done in 1946 in the following manner:

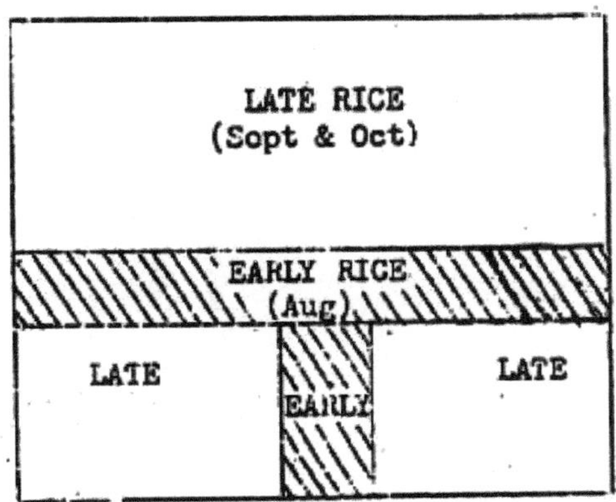

The harvesting of early rice (August) would leave spaces or alleys between sections of late rice (Sept & Oct) so that part of the crop might be protected if incendiaries or gasoline fell on sections of late rice.

Q. What does the Japanese General Staff think of BW as a weapon?
A. We had no idea of its potentialities because we did so little work in that field.

SECRET RESTRICTED

29-B-a-2

29-B-a-3

Q. Would it be possible for independent BW research to be carried out by individual army units e.g. Kwantung authorities?
A. We are responsible for the general directions of research and I made budget estimates for all divisions. BW was not included.

Q. I would like to see these directions and estimates.
A. They were burned previous to the entrance of American forces into Japan. This was reported to General MacArthur.

Q. Did you feel that any BW defensive measures should be directed toward domestic animals?
A. Protective measures did not extend to domestic animals in view of our inability to cope with the human problem.

Q. Who was in charge of the veterinary research?
A. There is no veterinary bureau and I do not know who was responsible for research in this field.

ESTIMATE: It was evident that Col Niizuma either had little or no tactical information on the subject of BW or was under orders to conceal such information. This officer however voluntarily expressed a great desire to assist in the compilation of BW material. Three days later he returned with an explanation for the Mark 7 bomb. (See interview with Cmdr Ishiwata, Oct 3, 1945).

29-B-a-3.

Appendix 29-C-a-1

JAPANESE SURGEON GENERALS

SUBJECT: Biological Warfare (BW)
DATE: 25 September 1945
INTERVIEWED: Lt Gen Hiroshi KAMBAYASH
INTERVIEWERS: Lt Col M Sanders

1. When Gen KUMBAYASHI was asked concerning the Japanese activities in BW, he requested permission to first state his personal opinion on the subject. A free translation of his statement follows: "Should the Japanese Army use BW, I think it would have the same effect on our people as CW. Not only would the Japanese people suffer, but also the Emperor. I am personally opposed to BW, not only on a humane basis but also on a practical basis." The reasons are as follows:

a. New organisms are not easily found. Note: Gen KAMBAYASHI apparently felt that in the absence of new types of organisms unknown to the enemy, BW could not be waged.

b. Many types of organisms are everywhere and disinfection can be practised if they are further disseminated. Organisms cannot be disseminated with much general effect.

c. This work cannot be done with complete secrecy and world opinion would be entirely against such work.

d. If such work is attempted, perfect protection cannot be obtained. Note: The General apparently referred to his fear of retroactivity of organisms.

2. Gen KUMBAYASHI then continued in answer to the question of Japanese activities in BW. He stated that he did not expect any country to wage BW but that "under the press of circumstances" some attempt might be made to carry out BW. As protection against such an attack, methods were perfected in Japan for purification of water. Since this officer had little technical knowledge in the field of bacteriology, he assumed from what he had heard that a BW attack consists largely of gastrointestinal pathogens.

Appendix 29-C-a-1

29-C-a-2

3. The question was asked concerning Japanese efforts to provide protective clothing against BW. The answer stated that no special protective clothing had been devised and that countermeasures were limited to the action of sun and to disinfectants (lysol and mercuric chloride were apparently the favorite disinfectants).

4. The question was asked whether measures had been taken to protect against respiratory assault. The answer was definitely in the negative.

5. When asked what the Japanese offensive activities had been, the Surgeon General stated that no offensive studies had been carried out to his knowledge. However, he said that certain offensive activities might have been carried out in relation to defensive evaluation and that he would attempt to obtain this information. Such work was the responsibility of Col INOUE, Superior Inspector of the Army Medical School. Col INOUE investigated disinfection (boeki-kyoshitsu).

6. He also stated in response to questioning that Lt Gen SHIRO ISHII was chief of the water purification system in Manchuria (Kwantung Army). Gen ISHII was a specialist in disinfection and the inventor of the filters used by the Japanese for the purification of water. It was apparent from information obtained in the interview that Gen ISHII is disliked by medical authorities in the homeland. He is considered an ambitious boaster who has built an organization in Manchuria during the last ten years. Because of the independent organization of the Kwantung Army, Gen ISHII was in a position to organize research along any lines which he desired.

ESTIMATE. In spite of the lack of concrete information received in this interview, a strong impression was gained that Gen KOBAYASHI desired to cooperate fully, that his inability to provide information was probably based on lack of technical knowledge as an administrator of a large bureau and possibly also because of general staff restrictions. The Surgeon General promised to look into the matter of BW and to obtain specific information concerning:

a. Defense activities in BW.

b. The organization of the Japanese Surgeon General's office.

29-C-a-2

29-C-a-3

c. Detailed organization of water purification units in general and also of the Kwantung water purification system under General ISHII.

On the following day, 26 September, another conference was held with Gen KUMBAYASHI and his staff. (See BW report supplement 1-a,b,c,d,e)

29-C-a-3

Appendix 29-C-b-1

JAPANESE SURGEON GENERALS

SUBJECT: Biological Warfare (BW)
DATE: 2 October 1945
INTERVIEWED: Lt Gen Hiroshi KAMBAYASHI, Surgeon Gen, Vice- Admiral Nobuaki HORI, Surgeon Gen,
INTERVIEWERS: Lt Col Murray Sanders

1. This interview was held as a means of summarizing information to date on the subject of BW. On the basis of the material previously provided by officers responsible to the Surgeon Generals of Army and Navy, a tentative conclusion had been drawn that Japanese BW activities in the military program constituted an unimportant minor activity. As a matter of fact, beyond broad generalities limited to defensive experimentation and organizational details, no specific data had been received.

2. Summarizing the information to date and emphasizing its vagueness, it was pointed out by the investigating officer that:

a. There was no reason to doubt the allegations concerning BW as set forth by Japanese officers.

b. Because of a desire to deal frankly with the Surgeon Generals, it was felt that certain information should be given them before a final report on the subject of BW was written. Intelligence reports from the theater based on prisoner of war statements and captured documents had accurately revealed the interest of the Japanese military in defensive BW. The information had also included the role played by the Boeki Kyusuibu (Water Purification Dept); inasmuch as information received from Gen KAMBAYASHI completely confirmed the intelligence reports on the defensive aspect, it was considered desirable that the Surgeon Generals should also become familiar with some of the evidence available on the offensive aspects of BW.

NOTE: At this point several statements were read from an intelligence document* which pointed to Japanese interests in offensive tactics and in bacterial bombs.

---

* Intelligence Research Project, Project No. 2263, 26 Jul 45, "Japanese Biological Warfare", copy No. 23, pg 23

RESTRICTED A.

Appendix 29-C-b-1

29-C-b-2

3. It was further pointed out to the Surgeon Generals that the investigating officer was perfectly willing to accept the Japanese version on BW, but that in view of the complete absence of offensive data, it would be difficult to convince others that the whole story had been told. (This was particularly true because of defensive intelligence confirmation).

4. Thus, the purpose of the interview was emphasized to impress upon the Surgeon Generals that in the event any information relative to offensive BW would be forthcoming in the future, they would have to accept the responsibility for contributing to a poor impression on the General Headquarters in regard to Japanese integrity.

5. General KAMBAYASHI and Admiral Hori gave strong assurance of their desire to cooperate. They promised to look into the matter further and requested that the final report be delayed for two or three days.

29-C-b-2

Appendix 29-D-a-1

MARK 7 BOMB

SUBJECT : Mark 7 Bomb.
DATE : 3 October 1945.
INTERVIEWED : Commander Hiroshi Ishiwata
INTERVIEWERS: Lt Col Murray Sanders.

1. Commander Ishiwata explained the markings on Navy bombs. Each munition was originally labeled with a mark and number in the order of construction. Later, as the variety of special bombs increased this was discarded. Five or six years ago all markings were officially rearranged. Marks 1 to 20 were allotted for special bombs as well as those used in attacks on vessels. Marks 21 to 30 were for antiaircraft or airfield munitions. Marks over 31 were for land targets.

At the time that designations were considered, marks were given to all conceivable types. This is apparent in table #2 where reference is made to the #7 bacillary bomb.

2. The question was raised in regard to the period of construction of of the #7 bomb. Commander Ishiwata was emphatic in stating that the Mark 7 bomb was never constructed or used. The designation was simply an hypothetcal one at a time when all conceivable types were being considered.

3. It was pointed out that frequent reference had been made to Mark 7 bombs in the field. Futhermore specific quotations were read to the commander. He explained that the list was used for education pamphlets for officers and that the bacillary mention was made in air force headquarters and air bureaus.

4. When asked what the Navy had done in BW Commander Ishiwata was of the definite opinion that the Navy had never experimented with BW if only because of tactical and social disadvantages associated from such a weapon. The Navy General Staff had absolutely no interest in BW. And indeed what little defense work was carried out was limited to water purification studies and production of vaccines.

5. Commander Ishiwata volunteered the information that in 1943 when the Japanese Imperial Navy was in difficulties he had personally investigated the possibility of BW to the extent of discussing the subject with responsible Navy officers in the Navy Medical College. He was flatly told that BW was impractical due to the natu e of the organisms.

SECRET RESTRICTED

Appendix 29-D-a-1

Appendix 29-D-b-1

MARK 7 BOMB

NOTE: The interview with Commander Ishiwata was not satisfactory. Emphasis had been placed upon intelligence reports in order that the Japanese officer might realize why the reference to the Mark 7 bomb could not be lightly discarded. Without any warning Commander Ishiwata requested an interview on October 5 and brought with him Commander M. Hayashi. Present also at this conference was Lt Col Murray Sanders. The evidence presented at this time is herewith given. Commander Ishiwata introduced Commander Hayashi as the individual who had made the plans for the original Mark 7 bomb. Both officers re-emphasized the fact that the simple drawing which they presented was the sum total of official Navy action and no formal plans had been drafted.

6. As can be seen from the diagram (See BW Report; Supplement 3-f) the Mark 7 bomb was intended to be a bacterial bomb containing little or no charge and depending on payload distribution by simple scattering after contact.

7. The Mark 7 bomb as presented here is a crude impractical weapon that would certainly be useless for dispersion of bacteria.

8. The drawing was made about 10 years ago unofficially and voluntarily by Commander Hayashi. Its basis was the modification of the 1 kg training bomb.

9. The few officers who saw the plans for the Mark 7 did not approach the Navy Medical Bureau on this subject. However Commander Hayashi worked at the Air Arsenal which is adjacent to the Yokosuka Navy Air Unit specializing in the teaching of Air Armament. It is considered likely that an instructor at Yokosuka saw the rough drawing made some notes and mentioned this munition in his lectures. Subsequent instructors may have followed suit.

10. In regard to coloring no explanation was given for the several references in intelligence reports which stated the Mark 7 bomb was colored "green purple, grey purple" (Intelligence Research Project No. 2263, Date 26 July 1945).

It was stated that all explosive bombs in the Navy had green marks and that purple was placed on depth charges.

ESTIMATE: It was felt that the explanation presented by Commander Ishiwata clarified the references to the Mark 7 bomb. It seems quite possible that the Japanese Imperial Navy was too busy with numerous problems to indulge in activity which at best constituted a direct departure from Navy policy. This was confirmed by a letter from another informant. The informant's letter follows:

"About 10 years ago, Imperial Navy planned to adapt new type of bombs and altogether to systematize various categories of bombs.

SECRET RESTRICTED

Appendix 29-D-b-1

SECRET
RESTRICTED

29-D-b-2

It is acceded that the 7th category should be of bacteriological bombs and Navy has so arranged the colors, so far as I personally am informed. At that time and even thence, no remarkable progress has been attained. But officers cadets, and crews are informed of the enterprise in several Naval instructional institutions the contents given in these lectures have been of imaginary nature. The information concerning the facts might have caused suspicions and caused you to be commissioned on your present investigations. This in return to your confidence placed on me I proceed to tell you. This information gathered by me through reliable and ardently desire that you never disclose the fact that you got this information through me. Otherwise it would become impossible that I be of any assistance in execution of your investigation."

29-D-b-2

29-D-b-3

Table No. 1

Table of Special Bombs used by I.J.N.

Mark	Name	Use	Year of formal adoption as arm
Mark 1	6th No. 1 Land-Bomb	To oppress land area with gas	1936
Mark 6	Style 98, 7th, No. 6 Bomb, Type 1	As land incendiary	1938
Mark 6	Style 98, 7th, No. 6 Bomb, Type 2	As land incendiary	1938
Mark 2	Style 99, 6th, No. 2 Bomb improved type 1	To attack submerged submarines	1940
Mark 3	Style 99, 3d, No. 3 Bomb	An incendiary to attack larger type planes	1939
Mark 2	Style 1, 25th, No. 2 Bomb, Type 1, improved type 1	To attack submerged submarines	1941
Mark 5	Style 99, 80th, No. 5 Bomb	To attack battleships	1941
Mark 5	Style 2, 80th, No. 5 Bomb, Type 1	To attack battleships	1942
Mark 6	Style 1, 7th, No. 6 Bomb, Type 3 improved type 1	Incendiary	1942
Mark 3	Style 2, 25th, No. 3 Bomb, Type 1 improved type 1	An incendiary to attack airfield	1943
Mark 23	Style 3, 6th, No. 23 Bomb, Type 1	Non-penetrating bomb to oppress airfield	1943
Mark 4	Style 3, 25th, No. 4 Bomb, Type 1	Rocket-bomb to attack battle-ship or heavy cruiser	1944
Mark 3	Style 2, 25th, No.3 Bomb, Type 2	Incendiary to attack air-field or formation of larger planes	1944
Mark 8	Style.3, 25th, No.8 Bomb	To attack surface ships by skipping	1944
Mark 8	Style 3, 80th, No. 8 Bomb	"	1944
Mark 31	Style 3, 25th, No. 31 Bomb, Type 1	To attack air-field or landing space (light-electric bulb)	1944
Mark 31	Style 3, 80th, No. 31 Bomb, Type 1	"	1944
Mark 21	Style 2, 6th, No. 21 Bomb, Type 2	To attack airfield (case-shot)	1944
Mark 9	Style 5, 1st, No. 9 Bomb	To attack landing craft (ordinary rocket)	1944
Mark 28	Style 3, 1st, No. 28 Bomb Type 1	To attack larger plane (rocket)	1944
Mark 27	Style 3, 6th, No. 27	To attack larger plane (rocket case-shot)	1944
Mark 1	(Temporary name) Style 4, 6th, No.1 Land-bomb, Type 1	To oppress land (gas)	Under experiments
Mark 1	" Type 2	"	"
Mark 9	(Temporary name) Style 5, 6th, No. 9 Bomb, Type 1	To attack landing craft	"

29-D-b-3

29-D-b-4

Mark	Name	Use	Year of formal adoption as arms
Mark 29	(Temporary name) Style 5, 25th, No. 29 Bomb	To attack formation of larger planes	Under experiments
Mark 32	(Temporary name) Style 3, 6th, No. 32 Bomb, Type 1	To attack airfield (spiral bomb)	"
Mark 33	(Temporary name) Style 5, 25th, No. 33 Bomb	To attack airfield, landing space (with plumb)	"

Table No. 2

Marks and Characteristics of the Special Bombs used in I.J.N.

Mark	Characteristics
Mark 1	Gas
Mark 2	Underwater explosion (anti-submarine bomb)
Mark 3	Anti-aircraft incendiary bomb
Mark 4	Rocket armour-piercing bomb
Mark 5	Armour piercing bomb
Mark 6	Land attack incodiary bomb
Mark 7	Bacillary bomb
Mark 8	Ship bomb
Mark 9	Vessel attack rocket bomb
Mark 21	Anti-aircraft case shot
Mark 23	Aerodrome attack non-penetrating bomb
Mark 27	Anti-aircraft rocket case shot
Mark 28	Anti-aircraft rocket bomb
Mark 29	Case shot to attack formation of planes
Mark 31	Aerial explosive bomb with light electric bulb
Mark 32	Spiral bomb
Mark 33	Aerial explosive bomb with plumb

29-D-b-4

Appendix 29-E-a-1

JAPANESE BW ACTIVITIES
(OFFENSIVE AND DEFENSIVE)

SUBJECT: Japanese Offensive Activities in Biological Warfare
DATE: 6 October 1945
INTERVIEWED: Dr Ryoichi Naito
INTERVIEWERS: Lt Col Murray Sanders

Information was given concerning the history, personnel, and offensive activities in BW by the Japanese Army.

1. HISTORY. The origin of the Japanese movement in this field dates to 1932 when Lt Gen Shiro ISHII, then Maj ISHII, returned to Japan after a tour of Europe. The 1922* Geneva Document outlawing BW apparently constituted the initial stimulus. Maj ISHII felt that the formal prohibition against BW implied its potentiality as a weapon. For several years he attempted, without success, to obtain funds and permission which would allow him to test his hypothesis concerning the practicality of BW. His efforts were of no avail until the year 1937 when the War Ministry agreed to provide the means for establishing an institute where BW activities would be carried out. In that year construction of the Pingfan Institute was initiated with additional personnel, equipment, and construction added each year.

NOTE: It would perhaps be best at this point to clarify the location of the Institute. Commonly designated as the Harbin Institute, the BW installation is actually located one hour by motor, due south of Harbin, in the vicinity of the small village of Pingfan, a few miles east of the South-Manchuria Railroad between Harbin and Hsinkiang.

By 1940, the BW installation reached its present physical extent. However, it is likely that the garrison has been greatly increased in recent years. It is estimated that in 1942 the personnel numbered approximately 1,000 officers, engineers, and skilled technical workers.

---

* Reference is made by informant to a League of Nations Document of 1922. This is confusing since a League of Nations Disarmament Conference barring ".....and bacterial warfare agents" was held in 1925.

Appendix 29-E-a-1

29-E-a-2

The mission of the Pingfan Institute, from its beginning, has been the development of BW as a practical weapon. Extensive defensive activities permitted medical research and at the same time large-scale production of serums and vaccines. The actual vaccine production for one year has been estimated as approximately 21,000,000 doses of various types of vaccines. The offensive activities were apparently on an equal scale, and investigations involving hundreds of bombs (probably thousands) filled with simulants and pathogens were carried out.

At the same time, ISHII developed a BW organization that at its height extended from Harbin to the Dutch East Indies and from the island of Hokkaido to the Celibes. For specific reference to the numerous installations and the functions allotted to each, the data provided by Gen KAMBAYASHI may be consulted. (See report on BW, Supplement 1a, b, c, d, e). It has been emphasized that offensive activities were limited to the Pingfan Institute, even the four satellite branches in Manchuria being concerned only with defensive aspects of BW.

Analysis of the studies which were investigated in the central BW installation during the past three years can only be estimated since the highly secret nature of the research (and other factors) did not permit filtration of information to any great extent to the home office.

2. OFFENSIVE ACTIVITIES. Although it has been stated that the Japanese concept of offensive BW included the use of airplanes (bombs and direct dispersion) artillery and saboteur, information at present is limited to the various types of bombs.

a. Uji bomb (ウジ): This all-purpose bomb was first tested in 1941 with simulants. Colored fluid (eosin or methylene blue) mixed with whole egg emulsion to provide viscosity comparable to payloads made up the simulant. Various technical characteristics of the dispersed load remain to be learned (method of particle size measurement, type of cloud, persistence, etc).

It has been stated that the ballistic quality of the Uji bomb was fairly good but not entirely satisfactory. One of the difficulties was due to the timing of the explosion which was not dependable because of terrain variations, and lack of reliable altimeters gave non-reproducible results. This led to the development of the so-called "mother and daughter" bomb. (See "d").

RESTRICTED SECRET

29-E-a-2

29-E-a-3

This bomb, which was produced in fairly large quantity (by the hundreds"), can be seen to have the following characteristics (See BW report, Supplement 3-a)

(1) Porcelain casing 8 mms* thick.

(2) Celluloid fin.

(3) Four meters of primer cord ("explosive string") attached to porcelain in grooves and kept in place with cement.

(4) A type-1 timer fuse in the nose and a type-5 timer posteriorly at the base of the fin.

(5) Powder charge in nose consisting of the common type of "brown" powder. This charge was fairly satisfactory and no comparable data are available since no other types of powder were tested. The size of the powder charge is to be determined. The dimensions of the Uji bomb are:

(a) Length of shell ca 700 mms.
(b) Total length from nose to end of fin ca 1100 mms.
(c) Porcelain wall thickness 8 mms.
(d) Diameter of shell 130 mms.

(6) The payload consisted of 10 liters of fluid. The bomb was filled with fluid and the charge was then screwed in.

(7) Weight empty was 25 kg, and when filled was 35 kg.

b. Ha bomb (ハ): (See BW report; supplement 3-b) This single purpose munition was developed in 1941 for dispersion of anthrax spores and was produced in relatively large numbers ("by the hundreds"). Explosive mechanism

---

* All measurements are stated as approximations. However, these measurements are probably accurate since they were provided as were the drawings of the bombs by the individual who originally designed them for Gen Ishii. His name will be learned if possible.

SECRET RESTRICTED　　29-E-a-3

29-E-a-4

functioned by a contact fuse in the nose and a shock fuse posteriorly at the base of the fin. The munition was made of steel, the two external and internal surfaces being painted with shellac to prevent corrosion. The Ha bomb was designed for ground contamination and as a shrapnel weapon. In contrast to the Uji bomb the powder charge was large and the payload small. Here, too, the common type of "brown" powder was used for the large central bursting charge. It has been stated that this munition was used on horses in field experiments (possibly sheep), infection and death resulting from superficial wounds caused by single contaminated steel unit.

(1) Steel casing ca 10 mms with serrated wall of ca 10 mms.

(2) Central burster chamber ca 110 mms.

(3) Steel fins.

(4) Payload chamber filled with 1,500 units of steel shrapnel weighing 5 kg. The dimensions are:

(a) Length of chamber ca 600 mms.
(b) Length of payload chamber ca 400 mms.
(c) Total diameter ca 150 mms.
(d) Payload chamber diameter ca 20 mms.

(5) The payload consisted of 500 cc of fluid.

(6) Weight empty was ca 40 kg and when filled was ca 41 kg.

c. Ro bomb (口) (See BW report, supplement 3-b). This steel all-purpose munition was developed in 1941 and because of unsuccessful trials never progressed past the experimental stage. The principal feature of the Ro bomb is the loose connection between the large nose and the remainder of the casing. The nose, which is approximately 1/5 of the bomb, explodes on contact and thus blasts the larger posterior portion containing the payload into the air. Due to a small charge, probably urotropin or picric acid the posterior chamber explodes within 1/10 to 1/5 seconds after the primary explosion. In addition to the "small transmission" charge between the nose and posterior chamber, there is a small amount of powder in the forward section of the posterior chamber. A "black" powder of unknown type is used as the explosive charge. This bomb, unlike the previous types, is filled from the rear, closure being effected by a screw type stopper. The dimensions of the Ro bomb are:

SECRET ~~RESTRICTED~~ 29-E-a-4

29-E-a-5

(1) Total length of bomb ca 500 mms.
(2) Loose nose ca 100 mms.
(3) Total diameter ca 100 mms.
(4) The payload volume is 2 liters.
(5) Weight empty is 20 kg and when filled is 22 kg.

d. In 1944, a so-called "mother and daughter" type bomb was devised to overcome difficulties in timing of the explosion encountered in the Uji bomb. Only one set of bombs was constructed and this type was discarded because of the high cost. While no details are known, the general mechanism was as follows: a large bomb with radio-sending apparatus was released from a plane. This was a high explosive type and did not contain bacteria. It was followed within a given period of time by a cluster of small bombs which had radio-receiving apparatus. When the first bomb exploded on contact and radio contact was broken, the small "daughter" bomb exploded in the air. This type of munition was designed by Lt Gondo (first name unknown), an aviation engineer interested in radio. He attempted to stabilize BW offensive tactics over irregular terrain.

3. ADDITIONAL INFORMATION. Two facts should be noted. In 1943, Gen Ishii recommended the study of large-scale drying of bacterial suspensions to be used in BW munitions. He apparently wished to concentrate the organisms and to obtain more stabilized payloads since the fluid material was active for relatively short periods of time. This plan did not materialize due to the pressure of work at the lyophilization centers which were working full time on plasma and vaccines.

Furthermore, plans were in progress to establish a large BW school but the termination of the war brought this to a premature end.

ESTIMATE. The extent of the Japanese BW program is apparent for the first time. Much thought and effort were expended in this field with results that suggest that the forging of a weapon might have been realized in the not too distant future. It must, of course, be emphasized that this statement is based on generalities and that a final analysis can only be made after careful perusal of experimental data. It remains to be seen whether these data will be available.

29-E-a-6

From a general consideration of diagrammatic construction, the Uji bomb offers some interesting possibilities if the point of explosion over variable terrain can be controlled. The casing is easily disintegrated, the charge is small, and consequently, there is little destruction of the payload. It is apparent also that the designer of this bomb wished to destroy all evidence of BW activity since the fins were made of inflammable material and it would be difficult to obtain the scattered fragments of the porcelain casing.

29-E-a-6

SECRET (RESTRICTED) Appendix 29-E-b-1

JAPANESE BW ACTIVITIES (OFFENSIVE AND DEFENSIVE)

SUBJECT : Biological Warfare (BW)
DATE : 7 October 1945
INTERVIEWED : Major Jun-Ichi-KANEKO
INTERVIEWER : Lt Col M. Sanders

1. Major Kaneko had been a medical officer in the Japanese Army and had been assigned to the Pingfan Institute, in Harbin, for 3½ years. In 1941 his duty at Pingfan was brought to a close by his transfer to the Army Medical College, Tokyo. This move was in the nature of a routine rotation procedure for medical officers. The question was raised concerning the apparent inability of General Ishii to retain his services. The answer emphasized that medical officers were transferred after certain periods, and since the BW activities in the Harbin area were not only secret but were being carried on without the permission of the highest authorities (i.e., the Emperor), no effort could be made to obtain special dispensation for personnel.

2. Although Major Kaneko is a medical officer, his interests were primarily in engineering, and he was given the responsibility of assisting a civilian, Yamaguchi, civil engineer, in the construction of BW bombs.

3. At the time that Major Kaneko began his assignment at Pingfan, sometime in 1937, an old model Uji bomb was being tested. (See previous interview)

4. BOMB DESIGN AND PRODUCTION. On the basis of information received from Major Kaneko, the following facts may be stated:

a. Yamaguchi designed both the Uji and the Ha bombs, the most important models being constructed in 1940. (in 1941 Yamaguchi suffered a stroke. He is paralyzed and ill and is not available for questioning.)

b. The bombs were produced in Mukden, in the Army arsenal. The individuals who manufactured these bombs were not told their purpose; consequently, there were technical difficulities frequently encountered and the production activity was fairly inefficient.

c. By the middle of 1941, at least 500 each of the Ha and Uji bombs had been made and tested.

d. There were certain deficiencies in each type which stimulated the search for more satisfactory bombs.

NOTE: It is to be emphasized that Major Kaneko's information extends only to 1941. He does not know what happened at Pingfan after that year.

Appendix 29-E-b-1

SECRET 29-E-b-2

e. DEFICIENCIES OF THE UJI BOMB.

(1) The porcelain casing varied in the different production lots and only one-third were completely satisfactory from the point of view of size and shape.

(2) The friable porcelain cracked frequently.

(3) This bomb was made to explode in the air and the height of explosion could not be satisfactorily determined when it was released over irregular terrain.

f. DEFICIENCIES OF THE Ha BOMB.

(1) The desired shrapnel effect was not obtained when the bomb fell in holes or into depressions.

(2) The pay load was small and relatively unsatisfactory in covering the iron particles, which were supposed to produce the effect by contact injury.

(3) Too much powder was required. The bomb carried a charge of approximately 3 kg.

NOTE: Major Kaneko stated that no experiments were done on heat generated by the explosion; that originally the iron particles were spheres and later cylinders.

g. The bombs were tested in the field attached to the institute (10x10 km). (Kaneko did not know the method of ground decontamination).

h. There were thirty responsible investigators in the second section (bomb research). The personnel included scientists, engineers, and aviators.

i. Three types of planes were used in the field tests:

(1) Scout type 94, capacity 4 Ha-bombs.

(2) Light bomber, type 88, capacity 6 Ha bombs.

(3) Heavy bomber, type 97, capacity 12 Ha bombs.

Newer types of planes were not available.

j. PAY LOAD.

(1) Organizms in the Uji bomb included B. Prodigiosus, V. cholerae, P. pestis, various types of dysentery organisms,

29-E-b-2

29-E-b-3

B. typhosi, B. anthracis. Efforts were principally directed toward the study of P. pestis and B. anthracis, so far as the Uji bomb was concerned.

(2) Organisms studied in the Ha bomb were limited to B. prodigiosus and (principally) B. anthracis.

K. EXPERIMENTAL ANIMALS. It is know that horses and sheep were used in the field experiments. By the early part of 1941, over 300 horses had been expended in experimental trials.

L. STORAGE. The fluid suspensions of the vegetative bacteria were tested at room temperature and a 90% loss of potency in three days was noted. The anthrax spore suspension was maintained with little loss at room temperature for one week. In the case of B. anthracis only the use of solid media was permitted by General Ishii. Frequent requests to investigate fluid media were refused. Other small experimental animals were also used. Because of the unsatisfactory results on storage, two courses were followed:

(1) All preparations were kept at refrigerator temperature. Bombs were loaded just previous to field trials.

(2) The program for large-scale lyophilization was initiated by General Ishii but, as previously stated, this phase of the program was delayed due to the pressure of plasma and vaccine production. (Kaneko was unable to give even an approximate quantitative estimate of any bacterial suspensions or any of the details of the media used).

m. BACTERIAL CLOUDS. Details concerning the character of the cloud resulting from Uji and Ha explosions were not know. Up to 1941, data for particle size and determination of cloud characteristics were obtained by means of a stationary explosion with the bomb suspended in tripod fashion at a height of ten meters. A base line of wind velocity of five meters per second was used, and it is estimated that under such circumstances a "fairly uniform" cloud extended for a distance of 500 meters. Neither the pattern of the cloud not its persistance was known to Kaneko. Apparently little or no information is available (as of 1941) concerning bacterial clouds resulting from munitions dropped from planes.

Discussions of particle size was somewhat vague. The only information that could be obtained was that the mean diameter was 0.5 mm for particles in a cloud resulting from a stationary Uji explosion. The only method of measurement which could be recalled was the use of colored fluid in the bombs, particle size being determined by contact with paper.

n. OTHER BW MUNITIONS. Apparently several modifications of both the Uji and Ha bombs were investigated. The number of models is not known; changes were minor and were essentially concerned with variations in capacity and shape. One modification of the Ha bomb may be mentioned—the I bomb. In this munition a smaller, central burster charge was used than in the original model. Fulminate of mercury constituted the detonator for the central burster charge of organisms pathogenic via the respiratory tract. This bomb was discarded in 1941.

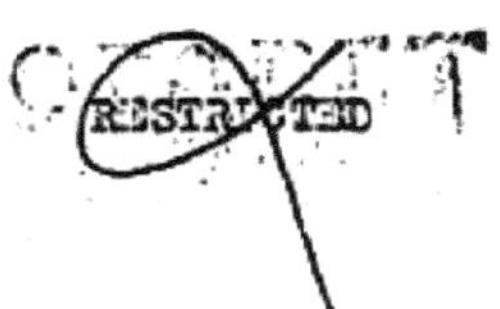

29-E-b-3

SECRET ~~RESTRICTED~~ 29-E-b-4

A so-called "H" shell was tested. It is supposed to have been the ordinary gas shell but the only information available at this interview was the unsatisfactory trajectory and the fact that this shell had been discarded by 1937. Similarly, a so-called "3" shell was tested and discarded before 1937. This is supposed to have been an ordinary 80mm shell with turpentine removed and replaced by bacteria.

29-E-b-4

Appendix 29-E-c

JAPANESE BW ACTIVITIES
(OFFENSIVE AND DEFENSIVE)

SUBJECT: Biological Warfare (BW)
DATE: 8 October 1945
INTERVIEWED: Lt Col Seiichi NIIZUMA
INTERVIEWERS: Lt Col Murray Sanders

Col. Niizuma furnished information this date that he had been successful in making contact with Col. Masuda, Chief of Section 3, at the Pingfan Institute. Col. Masuda has just arrived in Tokyo from Harbin. He is supposed to have been associated with Gen. Isshii during the time that Ishii was in charge of BW. Col. Masuda worked in BW until a month ago and will report for an interview, 9 October.

Appendix 29-E-c

Appendix 29-E-d-1

JAPANESE BW ACTIVITIES
(OFFENSIVE AND DEFENSIVE)

SUBJECT: Biological Warfare (BW)
DATE: 9 October 1945
INTERVIEWED: Lt Col Saichi NIIZUMA (Army); Col. Tomosada MASUD.
INTERVIEWERS: Lt Col Murray Sanders;

1. Col Masuda expressed his desire to cooperate with the investigating officer fully and to provide whatever information he had concerning the subject of BW. He stated that he had been interested in the subject for many years and had either been directly associated with the Japanese work in all its phases or had been kept informed during periodic absences.

In response to the request for his curriculum vitae, Col Masuda provided the following information. The years marked with an asterisk denote the periods during which Col Masuda actually participated in BW activities.

1926 Grad Kyoto Imperial Medical Faculty and thence Army Medical Corps
1926-1929 - Regimental Physician
1929-1931 - Post-Graduate in Bacteriology, Microbiological Institute, Kyoto
1931-1932 - Prof of Bacteriology, Army Medical School
1932-1934 - France & Germany (Berlin) (Prof Erdemann) L'Ecole Militaire Service Sanitaire
1934-1936 - Military Service (Inf Regiment)
1936-1937 - War Ministry - Military Sanitation (Administration)
*1937-1939 - Manchuria - Water Purification Dept, under Gen Ishi:
1939-1941 - To central China
*1941-1943 - Prof of Bacteriology, Military Medical College
March, 1943-December, 1944 - Burma Malaria Control
Jan, 1945 - March, 1945 - Saigon Hq
*April, 1945-August 14, 1945 - Harbin, Manchuria

2. Col Masuda stated that the BW work was carried on by the Boeki Kyusuibu (Anti-epidemic & Water Purification Dept) of the Kwantung Army under Lt Gen Shiro Ishii, and he requested permission to explain the stimulus for the initiation of Japanese BW activities. In 1935, the Kwantung Army was informed that many Russian spies, carrying bacteria in ampules or in glass bottles, had crossed into Kwantung territory. Five spies were apprehended by the Kempei and on these spies were found several glass bottles and ampules.

RESTRICTED Appendix 29-E-d-1

29-E-d-2

Such incidents were not the first nor were they the last, but Col Masuda stated that he can personally vouch for this episode involving five individuals. The examination of the various containers revealed the presence of dysentery organisms (Shiga and Flexner) and bacteria---spore mixtures of B anthracis and V cholerae. He stated that he, personally, saw the anthrax organisms.

Spurred by such incidences, the Kwantung Water Purification Dept investigated the possibilities of artificial epidemics; i.e., a plan was made to investigate BW potentialities. As one method of study of this field, the problem of munitions was investigated and Col Masuda was given the task of obtaining a practical bomb.

While the formal organization of the Kwantung Boeki Kyusuibu was made up of four sections, BW studies were carried out in secret.

To all intents and purposes, the Boeki Kyusuibu had the following sections:

Section I. Fundamental research in Immunology (typhoid, dysentery, anthrax, erysipelas, viruses, and rickettsia)
Section II. Epidemiological research
Section III. Water supply and purification
Section IV. Vaccine production

3. In order that the work might be kept secret, none of the sections which studied various aspects of offensive BW cooperated with each other. Workers were not supposed to discuss their work but carried out problems given them by Ishii.

4. Col Masuda stated that only two individuals have the complete BW story--Ishii and himself. He emphasized that the purpose of the work was to create a weapon so that an adequate defense could be developed.

5. Col Masuda stated that his personal opinion was that no practical bacterial bomb had been developed, but he placed the responsibility for this on organizational difficulties, petty jealousies, and poor equipment. He was bitter regarding the weaknesses of a system which did not recognize a scientific effort and felt that with proper encouragement BW could certainly be made into a practical weapon.

SECRET RESTRICTED 29-E-d-2

29-E-d-3

The fundamental idea of Col Masuda's research was the dispersion of bacterial emulsions at a proper height. He stated that dried organisms would undoubtedly be the ultimate payload of BW weapons, but that they could not be used in preliminary investigations because of danger to the workers. However, with the conclusion of preliminary tests on fluid it would be desirable to substitute dried material. To illustrate the research which had been carried on in his section, he explained a diagram drawn by himself before the interview. A translation of this diagram may be seen in the BW report, Supplement 3-e.

6. Additional statements which were made at the interview are given below because of their general application to the BW problem.

a. Many apologies were presented for the crude nature of the data. Admittedly the work at Harbin was not done scientifically (Masuda's opinion).

b. Destruction of the Harbin installation and its contents including all munitions had been carried out in the early part of August when it was known that the Russian Army had entered the area.

c. It was felt that both the Ha and the Uji bombs could be practical with the improvement of fins to prevent "tumbling" and with the addition of good fuses. NOTE: Masuda was bitter about the obsolete equipment given him for his experiments. Frequent reference was made to poor fuses which were made available. If proximity fuses could have been obtained, both bombs would have been greatly improved. The favored bomb was the Uji No. 50. If a thin iron fin could have been developed to improve the ballistics, this would have made an excellent munition.

d. In 1939, investigation of various types of bombs was stopped and attention was directed on the testing in the field of Uji bomb type No. 50.

7. At this point in the interview, it was suggested by the officer in charge that the discussion be continued on another day. It was obvious that Col Masuda was very ill, and it was learned that he was suffering from acute malaria. The following subjects were given him for which he was to obtain data for the next interview:

29-E-d-3

29-E-d-4

a. Detailed information on bacteria used in BW at Harbin. (Types of organisms, media, methods of mass production, method of field trials, method of assessment, animal experiments, etc)

b. Bacterial clouds (size, shape, persistence, particle size, method of measurement and sampling of cloud)

c. Data on cloud chamber work.

d. Plan of the institute at Harbin.

ESTIMATE: It is to be emphasized that Col Masuda was supposedly unaware of the other sources of information concerning Japanese offensive BW activities (App. 29-E-b). Whether or not this was the fact could not, of course, be established without possible drastic effects upon both sources of information. On the whole, the technical data provided in both this and previous interviews seemed to be consistent. However, in the matter of policy there are two important inconsistencies or omissions. Col Masuda did not explain the cause of secrecy, and when questioned stated that he did not know the answer. It is to be noted it had been disclosed that BW was being carried out without the knowledge of the emperor. Perhaps the most important point is the fact that Col Masuda blames the Russian activities as being the cause for initiation of Japanese BW. According to the previous source of information in this matter, BW originated in Japan because of Gen Ishii's intense interest in the subject.

29-E-d-4

Appendix 29-F-a

BW ACTIVITIES AT PINGFAN

SUBJECT: Biological Warfare (BW)
DATE: 11 October 1945
INTERVIEWED: Col Tomosada MASUDA; Lt Col Seiichi NIIZUMA
INTERVIEWERS: Lt Col Murray Sanders*

1. Col Masuda requested permission to answer questions given to him on his previous conference.

a. Regarding detailed information on bacteria used in BW at Harbin, the following organisms were at one time or another considered potential BW agents and were used in experiments.

(1) B typhi
(2) paratyphoid A and B
(3) B dysenteriae
(4) V cholerae
(5) P pestis
(6) B anthracis
(7) M malleomyces (glanders)
(8) Anerobes

(a) B welchii
(b) B novyii
(c) B hystolyticus
(d) B tetani

No viruses or rickettsia have been used in BW experiments. Generally speaking, S-form for all organisms were used with the exception of the anthrax bacillus, in which instance the R-form was studied.

b. Media. Agar was the common vehicle for cultivation for the bacteria used in all tests. The following formula for the Agar preparation was given:

Peptone - 15 grams
Agar - 30 grams
Sodium chloride - 5 grams
Distilled water - q.s. 1,000 cc

ph 7.45 after sterilization

* Lt Col Babcock, BW officer for FEAF, was invited to attend this conference.

SECRET RESTRICTED Appendix 29-F-a

29-F-a-2

Enteric organisms were harvested after a growth period of 24 hours, at 37° C. In the case of the plague, anthrax and glanders bacteria, a growth period of 48 hours ensued before harvesting. For the anerobes, one week's growth was permitted before collection.

In a few instances, there were some modifications of the basic medium:

For the plague organism, 0.01% saturated solution of gentian violet was used as an anti-contaminant.

For anthrax bacteria, 7.5 grams of peptone were used instead of 15 grams, and 10 grams of sodium chloride instead of 5 grams.

For the glanders bacillus organic iron, 0.01% was added to agar. These modifications resulted in higher bacterial counts than if the basic medium alone was used. Data on bacterial counts are not available.

c. To produce bacteria <u>en masse</u> as required for BW field trials, special small tanks of duralumin have been constructed. The tanks used for mass production are under a military patent and arrangements were made to obtain a sample tank. The surface of this material was oxidized (alemite) for further protection against corrosion.

When Col Masuda was asked concerning the productive capacity of his unit at various times, he replied that he had no figures on this. However, it was possible to obtain some idea of the magnitude of operations by the fact that one duralumin tank yielded 40 grams of B typhi scrapings. In any preparations for bomb experiments, 900 duralumin baths were used.

d. <u>Viability Studies</u>. Before experimenting with the organisms in the munitions, Col Masuda investigated their capacity for remaining alive at room temperature (18-25° C). The technique followed in these determinations consisted of placing bacterial suspensions in large glass containers. (Capacity unknown, but of the order of several liters). The flasks were sealed with rubber, covered with paraffin, and were periodically tested. Following figures for viability of organisms were given by Col Masuda:

SECRET RESTRICTED 29-F-a-2

29-F-a-3

(1) Dysentery organisms died within 5-7 days.

(2) V cholerae died within 3-5 days. (Equal amounts of horse serum and bacterial scrappings were stored in peptone water).

(3) P pestis died within 5-7 days. (dextrose broth).

(4) Spore suspensions of anthrax died within three months. (0.1% phenol was added to the basic medium to prevent fermentation)

(5) M malleomyces died within 3-5 days.

(6) Anerobes were never adequately studied because of lack of apparatus.

As a result of these findings, Col Masuda decided to use only two organisms in bomb field tests: (1) the simulant, B prodigiosus; (2) anthrax spores.

When asked whether any attempts were made to investigate substances which might be added to the organisms for purposes of preservation, he stated that he was unable to apply himself seriously to the problem which he knew was of vital importance. The reasons for this limitation were, as had been previously noted, organizational and financial.

e. Contamination of Well Water. Deliberate contamination of water and testing for viability of organisms might be termed an offensive measure, but the point was made that Col Masuda's interest was limited to possible activities of the Chinese in this respect.

During the course of a year, Col Masuda's units tested more than a thousand wells in Manchuria. It is his opinion that saboteur activity on a large scale is not effective if wells are used as the vehicles for bacteria. He had two reasons for this opinion. In the first place, the enteric organisms which were tested died within a few days (2-4 days) under the best circumstances. Second, he found a tremendous variation in the viability curve of organisms in water samples from different areas. Thus, in one instance, the inoculum might have disappeared from the water within two days, whereas a comparable contamination may have been quite potent, (at least many survivors could be demonstrated) in water from a different area. In an

RESTRICTED 29-F-a-3

SECRET / RESTRICTED 29-F-a-4

attempt to explain this variation, Col Masuda examined factors which might be considered as variables in the problem and made one interesting correlation. In those instances when the death rate of the bacteria in the water was great: that is, when no organisms could be recovered within 24-48 hours, it was found that the water sample came from a district where there had been a recent outbreak of cholera, typhoid, or dysentery. The more recent the outbreak, the greater appeared to be the sterilizating effect of the water. (Col Masuda agreed that this might be a bacteriophage phenomenon.)

f. <u>Experimental Animals</u>. For the most part, the principal small animals used in BW investigations consisted of mice and guinea pigs (marmot?). For field trials, horses and sheep were used. A total of 100 horses and 500 sheep was expended in the course of the investigation of anthrax as a BW weapon. This covered a period of two years.

g. <u>Bacterial Clouds</u>. The nature and characteristics of clouds resulting from bacterial dissemination in munitions were studied in a crude and qualitative fashion. In preliminary tests, clouds were investigated by the use of colored dyes in the material exploded. Based on the principle that <u>dye</u> so used should have a vivid color and should be very <u>soluble</u> in water, rhodamine ($\frac{1}{10,000}$) and fuchsin ($\frac{1}{1,000}$ saturated alcoholic solution) were studied.

A grid on level ground with a radius of 1,000 meters was set up with markers at 10 meter intervals, the munition filled with colored fluid in 2-5% dextrose broth being exploded in the center. For the first 50 meter radii, samples on paper were taken every 10 meters, the evaluation being made visually. Col Masuda claimed that in this fashion he was able to analyze the explosive pattern and particle size down to 50 microns. To determine smaller particle size, the paper was placed in potassium iodide baths after static explosion. Thus, the 2-5% dextrose broth revealed particles as small as 10 microns.

Beyond the 50-meter point on the grid, sampling intervals were not constant, the distances varying with the munition and purpose of individual experiments.

It is interesting to note that the climactic conditions in the vicinity of Pingfan were such that a mild wind could be expected almost year-round. Wind velocities of five meters per second were very common and in winter

SECRET / RESTRICTED 29-F-a-4

the snow-covered ground, instead of paper, was used as a background for the colored particles.* In this season also, it was common for wind velocity to be two meters per second, and a dry, cold winter was the rule.

In the case of munitions dropped from the plane, an instantaneous umbrella-like cloud was discerned. This pattern was quickly dissipated but particles continued to descend for approximately five minutes. In actuality, Masuda was not able to make accurate statements as to particle descent in relation to time since his sampling was made at the end of thirty minutes. However, he stated that quantitative data had been accumulated, based on mathematical formulae.

The size of the field and stable weather conditions permitted both static explosion experiments and drop experiments from planes. When colored fluid was used as an indicator, no bacteria were included in the bomb fluid because of the bacteriostatic effect of the dyes. If bacteria were placed in the munition, dextrose broth (for starch tests) was used as the vehicle.

The question was asked concerning the significance of 10 micron particles; i.e., why was it desireable to obtain smaller particles. Col Masuda answered that he attempted only to produce as small drops as possible in approaching an aerosol.

As was to be expected, the pattern of the explosion was such that large particles were to be found in the immediate vicinity of the point of explosion with a decrease in the size of droplets occurring toward the periphery.

h. A brief discussion was held on the direct dispersion of bacterial agents from planes. While no formal program was planned for this activity, several experiments had been carried out. Again, lack of apparatus and organizational difficulties prevented Col Masuda from obtaining little more than preliminary data. He did feel that dried material would be effective dispersed directly from a plane. However, his own experience was concerned with fluids containing dyes or suspensions of B prodigiosus. The only constructive statement which was mde on this subject was that a great amount of material be dispersed in as short a time as possible. Further details were sparse but it was noted that a tank in the fuselage was used. In one field test 280 liters of simulant were dispersed per second.

---

* Unfortunately, the movies and still-photographs of these winter and summer experiments are not available.

RESTRICTED SECRET

29-F-a-6

Another factor of importance was the viscosity of fluid vehicles for test material. 50% glycerine and 1% gelatine were found to be fairly satisfactory vehicles for direct dispersion. When large amounts of such viscous, colored material was disseminated from a plane at 4,000 meters, one hour elapsed before the colored particles reached the ground. If B prodigiosus was used, no viable organisms were recovered on the ground.

Similar tests were carried out at altitudes of 2,000, 1,000, and 200 meters with somewhat better results.

i. Casualties Amongst the Personnel. In the course of discussion, Masuda incidentally mentioned that two soldiers had died during the course of field trials. Questioning revealed that one of the two individuals had been ordered to cut the grass at the experimental site a day after an anthrax trial. He contacted pneumonic anthrax and passed away after a short course of the disease. The second soldier was the first fatality's roommate and he died of an anthrax septicemia, the result of a contact infection. In addition, five cases of anthrax infection were reported during the course of two years of field trials with this organism. Masuda thinks that other infections may have occurred either during his absences or without his knowledge.

j. Cloud Chambers. No BW investigations were carried on in cloud chambers. Such apparatus was not available and it was Masuda's opinion that chambers were unnecessary since the work could be carried on directly in the field.

2. BUDGET AND PERSONNEL. In the year 1944, six million yen (approximately 2½ million dollars on basis of 1944 rate of exchange) were allotted to Pingfan Institute for research purposes. The impression was gained that this was the result of consecutive budget reductions but no figures were available. It was emphasized that the utilization of the budget was within the jurisdiction of General Ishii.

When asked concerning the size of the technical strength of the Pingfan Institute in recent years, Col Masuda stated that the maximum garrison of 3,000 individuals occurred in 1939-1940. Since that time there was a gradual reduction in strength due to the necessity of meeting Army personnel requisitions and to a policy of retrenchment. By 1945, just previous to the dissolution of the Institute, the garrison strength was 1,500.

SECRET RESTRICTED

29-F-a-6

29-F-a-7

While there was no definite division between defensive and offensive personnel, Ishii and Masuda manipulating their people as desired, the following roster represents a fairly average group concerned with the field-testing of a munition:

Pilot (medical corps officer or flight surgeon)...1*
Ground crew.......................................20
Medical officers for preparatory work............ 2*
Enlisted men (medical corps) as technicians.....50

In addition to the above personnel, Masuda had access to, and could use at will, the hundreds of individuals who made up the staff for vaccine production. These numbers varied from a peak of 400 (1939-1940) to an ebb of 100 in 1945.

3. DEFENSIVE BW IN THE KANTO BOEKI KYUSUIBU. Col Masuda was of the opinion that BW defense would be adequately rebuilt by an alert, comprehensive, medical organization; i.e., unless new pathogens or new methods of dispersion could be found. Basically, an offense was the best defense. (This is a broad interpretation of a dissertation on the subject by Col Masuda). Furthermore, in its present state of technical development, he did not feel that the effects of BW would be realized. Finally, his scientific interest was largely in the offensive phase.

As a result of Masuda's policy, BW defense at the Pingfan Institute emphasized general measures for anti-epidemic control.

a. Organization. This may be divided into three phases. In the summer of 1938, Col Masuda felt that an efficient and large organization was the solution for defensive BW and the Boeki Kyusuibu was expanded and reorganized. (In the meantime, he continued his search for an effective offensive weapon). By October, 1938, 18 large purification units had been set up in China. With these as foci, satellite branches were established covering the whole of Japanese-held China. To each 18 units, approximately 300 individuals were assigned. There were three such units in north China, 13 in central China, and two in south China.

NOTE: For a consideration of Japanese intentions concerning BW, it is important to emphasize at this point that the question was repeatedly and clearly stated concerning the

---

* Were acquainted with the nature of the work.

SECRET RESTRICTED

29-F-a-7

29-F-a-8

basic stimulus for the Boeki Kyusuibu; i.e.: Was the threat of BW so important as to stimulate the Japanese to the creation of an organization covering a huge territory involving hundreds of individuals, many of them technically trained? Or was this organization a manifestation of the desire to improve preventive medical knowledge and procedures in Japanese territories. Certainly the latter reason would have seemed logical. But Col Masuda insisted that in 1938 the Japanese fear of BW was so great that it provided the initial motivation for the Boeki Kyusuibu. Later, when no BW attacks were experienced, the emphasis was shifted.

b. VACCINE program. Another weapon in BW defense was an accelerated and enlarged vaccine program. More vaccines were produced and in larger quantities than heretofore. Furthermore, trained personnel were transferred to four installations in an attempt to make large areas self-sufficient in the manufacture of vaccine. These four centers were Manchuria, north, central, and south China. Such innovations were made as typhoid and cholera "booster" injections for military personnel every three months.

c. BW Defense Intelligence Institute. So important did this subject appear to responsible authorities in the year 1938, that they adopted a system of briefing medical officers in all echelons down to battalions. (In many cases, medical officers were briefed). Originally it had been the intention to place a separate BW-trained officer in various echelons, but because of personnel shortage it was necessary for medical officers to take on the additional duty of BW defensive intelligence.

In the final analysis, the functions of the "BW Defense Intelligence" was simply epidemiological. It was the responsibility of individuals belonging to this group or system to trace all infections to their source.

NOTE: The interesting point of departure from the usual epidemiological investigations was the fact that these teams began their initial investigations with the possibility in mind that the infection they were studying had been disseminated artificially, and that they were dealing with BW.

The military police (Kempei) assisted the medical officers in these BW activities but this help was non-technical and was purely administrative.

RESTRICTED SECRET 29-F-a-8

29-F-a-9

NOTE: Emphasis at this point of the interview was placed on the role of a military police (Kempei) because of G-2 reports which linked them with BW. However, Col Masuda's statements seemed to have solved this puzzle. He did state that during the final phases of organization, medical officers visited military police centers and lectured on BW. Inasmuch as the Kempei were ignorant and untrained individuals, these lectures were maintained on a very elementary basis.

29½F-a-9

Appendix 29-F-b

BW ACTIVITIES AT PINGFAN

SUBJECT: Japanese Activities in Biological Warfare (BW)
DATE: 16 October 1945
INTERVIEWED: Col Tomosada MASUDA, Lt Col Seiichi NIIZUMA
INTERVIEWERS: Lt Col Murray Sanders, Lt Harry Youngs

Q The question of toxin studies in Japanese BW was raised.
A No toxin studies were carried out in the Boeki Kyusuibu.

Q What was the budget of the Institute at Pingfan?
A There was an intensive building program from 1937 to 1940. The operating budget for 1945 was ¥6,000,000; this was the approximate budget for 1944 and did not include expenditures for new buildings. The budget for the years prior to 1945 and 1944 was greater because of building activities at the Institute.

Q What work was done in the "pepiniere" building?
A This building was used for growing all the produce needed for the workers at the Institute. It was also used to supply food for the animals. The garden plot was approximately 5 km square.

Q Give a brief historical background for the Institute.
A The Japanese BW work started in Manchuria when the Japanese gained control of the territory in 1934. In 1934, the Bureau of Laboratories was established at the Harbin Military Hospital. In the same year the Pingfan area was obtained from the Chinese government. There were no buildings in the area at this time. However, in 1937 construction was begun in the area. In the same year, field trials in connection with the BW work were carried out in this area. The actual laboratory work continued to be done at the Harbin Military Hospital where one department was located. In 1940, the building program was completed and three departments were moved to the Pingfan area, the third department remaining at the Harbin Military Hospital.

Q Did BW bomb development stop after 1939?
A All the work and tests were completed by 1939, but work on new bomb developments was continued until 1945. This was on the direct order of Gen. Ishii. Although the developmental work continued after 1939, no new bombs were perfected. All experimental work after 1939 corroborated the previous results.

SECRET RESTRICTED

Appendix 29-F-b.

~~RESTRICTED~~ SECRET 29-F-b-2

Q What protection was offered the field trial workers?
A A completely rubberized, anti-plague suit was worn over street clothing in the field trials. Immediately after the trials, the workers were required to remove all clothing and bathe themselves in 2% cresol or mercuric chloride. The workers were closely observed for any signs of infection after the trials. This routine was followed at each trial. However, as time went on the workers became careless. In 1944, there were two plague deaths as a result of field trials.

Q What protection was offered the laboratory workers?
A Frequent vaccination of all laboratory personnel was required. There were approximately 20 cases of laboratory infection a year. The workers were paid extra for working in the Pingfan Institute; officers were given an extra 60 yen a month; and enlisted men received extra food.

NOTE: According to Col Masuda, there were very few deaths.

Q What therapy for plague was available?
A Surgical treatment was practiced; i.e., exterpation of glands in bubonic cases. The patient also received anti-plague horse serum. Oral administration of sulfonamides was tried.

NOTE: In Masuda's opinion, the effectiveness of sulfanilamide was questionable. The type of sulfanilamide used was called "therapal".

There were no cases of pneumonic plague at the Pingfan Institute; however, there were one or two cases in Manchuria proper.

Q What work was carried out in the drying building?
A This building was used primarily as an experimental unit by the defensive group. It was used by this group for the desiccation of vaccines. Because of excessive cost, no work was done on the desiccation of large amounts of material for offensive BW. Altogether they had 20 drying units but no figures on production were available.

Q What was the glanders program?
A In 1937, undoubtedly due to carelessness on the part of the laboratory workers, two deaths resulted from experimental infection. Because of the severity of the infections, the authorities discontinued the work in this field. There was no therapy for glanders available.

29-F-b-2

29-F-b-3

Q What work on typhus vaccine was done at Pingfan?
A The Institute owned 50,000 chickens. The chickens were loaned out to the local farmers in lots of 100-200 per farmer. All eggs were the property of the Institute, and were given by the farmers to collecting agents from the Institute. In addition to this source, eggs were purchased from local farmers. The total egg supply was approximately 20,000 a week. On the average, 70% of these eggs were fertile.

Q How were fertile eggs supplied?
A Lung and egg vaccines were made.

Only experimental egg work on virus vaccines was carried out at the Institute. No virus vaccines were in production. A good vaccine for the protection of animals against Russian tick-borne encephalitis was developed at the Institute. However, they had not developed any vaccine for human use.

Q What work was done in the machine shop?
A This building was used as a production and repair shop for laboratory supplies; i.e., construction of animal cages, machine shop to repair damaged instruments, etc.

Q If the Japanese had theoretically used BW as an offensive weapon, how did you intend to protect your troops?
A Methods of disinfection:

1. Heat - boil clothing, water, etc.

2. Solutions - use chemical solutions (Hgcl$_2$ or lysol) on skin and material coming in contact with agent.

3. Washing - wash all parts of body (hands, face, body)

B. Serum Therapy - all cases of infection were to be treated with serum.

C. Area decontamination - Col Masuda stated that contaminated territory was denied to troops for three days, since he felt that during this interval, terrain contaminated with B Anthracis would be safe for troops.

29-F-b-3

SECRET

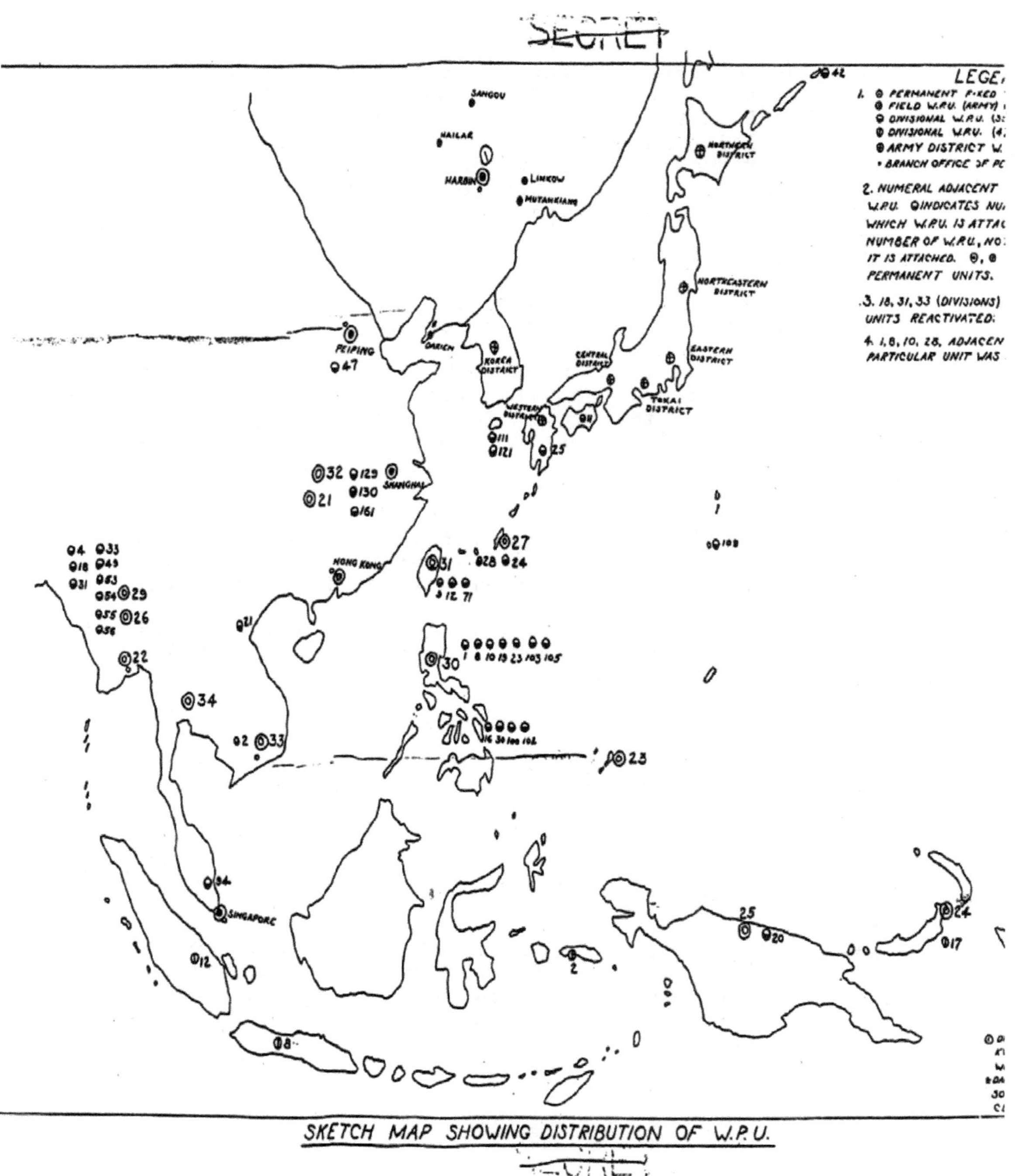

SKETCH MAP SHOWING DISTRIBUTION OF W.P.U.

SECRET

Supplement 1-b

CHART

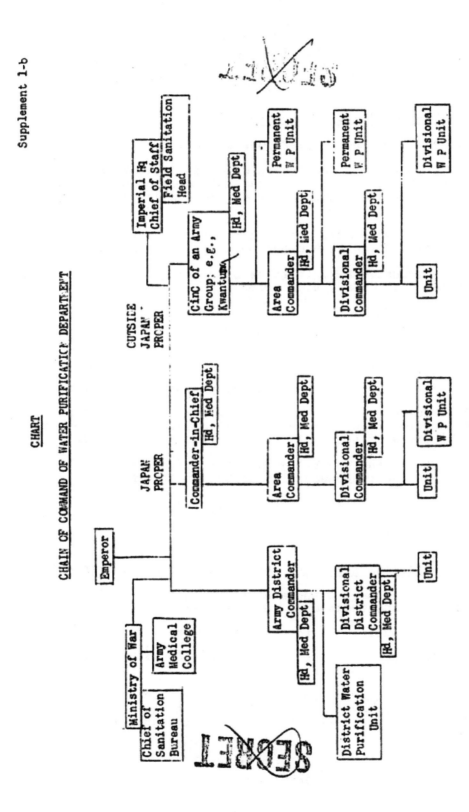

CHAIN OF COMMAND OF WATER PURIFICATION DEPARTMENT

Supplement 1-b

SECRET
RESTRICTED

Supplement 12c

DUTIES OF THE WATER PURIFICATION ~~SECTION~~ DEPARTMENT.

Divisional Water Purification Section

1. Epidemic Prevention (includes malaria prevention).

a. To carry out and direct epidemic prevention work in the div. Mainly analysis of causes and carrying out disinfection. Unit CO is responsible for epidemic prevention work in the unit.

b. When necessary, and upon orders, it takes over part or the entire epidemic prevention work in the area.

c. When necessary, it takes over the quarantine work at an embarkation or debarkation point.

2. Supplying Water.

a. Look for water source.

b. Water analysis (includes analysis for poison).

c. Water purification. Sanitary water filter used.

d. Hauling water. Normally, trucks are used. During combat vehicles, pack horses, or foot soldiers (using water carrier pack) are used to supply water to the front line troops.

e. Direct the supplying of water to the forces. Digging of wells is the responsibility of the engineers.

3. Examination of sanitary conditions in the area.

4. Repair of equipment.

Field Water Purification Section (attached to army or area army).

Duties are the same as those given for division, Differences and additions are indicated below.

1. Supplies water only to rear area forces.

2. Examination and research in connection with epidemic prevention and water supplying.

3. When there is difficulty in supplying vaccines (yoboeki) or when there is a breakout of an epidemic, it will undertake preparation thereof (necessary serums and vaccines).

1

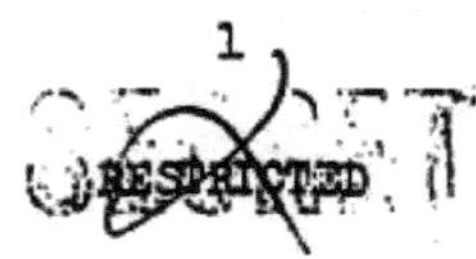

SECRET RESTRICTED Supplement 1-c

4. Quarantine work at a debarkation or embarkation point is mainly done by a Field Water Purification Section or higher. Div water purification section does this work only when necessary.

Fixed Water Purification Section (attached to a general army).

Differences from and additions to those given for Fd Water Purification Sec.

1. Supplying of water limited to line of communication area.

2. Research and examination in connection with epidemic prevention and water supply cover wider scope than that for Fd Water Purification Section.

3. Preparation of standard army vaccines, vaccine lymph (or virus) serums. When necessary, those for civilian use are also prepared.

4. Carry out examination and research on general sanitation.

5. To give training in epidemic prevention and water supply work.

DUTIES OF THE KWANTUNG ARMY WATER PURIFICATION DEPARTMENT (BOEKI KYUSUIBU)

1. Duties.

a. To carry out and direct epidemic prevention and water supplying work in the Kwantung Army.

b. To prepare and supply vaccines and materials for epidemic prevention.

c. Give training in epidemic prevention and water purification and supply work.

d. Examinations and researches in connection with epidemic prevention.

e. Mobilization of the Water Purification Sections of the div and armies of the Kwantung Army.

Supplement 1-c

2. Allocation of Duties within the Department. The duties of the various sections are based on the Kwantung Army service regulations and are determined by the chief of the department, with approval of CG of the Army.

a. General Affairs Section. Plans, control, personnel, routine affairs.

b. Section 1. Prevention and treatment of each type of contagious disease. Research for improvement of vaccines and treatment sera, etc.

c. Section 2. Carrying out and directing epidemic prevention work.

d. Section 3. Carrying out and directing water purification and supply work. Manufacture and repair of equipment used in water purification.

e. Section 4. Preparation of vaccines, serums, and culture media.

f. Supply Section. Purchase, custody, supply of material used in epidemic prevention and research. Breeding of test animals.

3. Duties of the various branches.

a. To carry out and direct water purification and supply and epidemic prevention work in their assigned areas.

b. Dairen (Dalny) Branch. Epidemic prevention work in its area; improvement, research and preparation of vaccines and treatment sera.

4. The Kwantung Army Water Purification Department is responsible for the mobilization of the water purification sections of the divisions and armies in the Kwantung Army. Upon opening of hostilities, it will send out personnel for these sections.

5. In peacetime the various branches are under the department chief and take care of the epidemic prevention and water purification and supply work in their area. Upon opening of hostilities, they are attached to the army, div in their area.

3

SUPPLEMENT 1-d

ORGANIZATION TABLE OF THE KT-
WATER PURIFICATION DEPARTMENT
(Boeki Kyusuibu)

CG, Department	Medical Lt Gen or Maj Gen	1
Chief, Gen Affairs Section	Med Col or Lt Col	1
Chief, No. 1 Section	Med Major Gen	1
Chief, No. 2 Section	Med Col or Lt Col	1
Chief, No. 3 Section	Med Col or Lt Col	1
Chief, No. 4 Section	Med Col or Lt Col	1
Chief, Supply Section	Pharmacy or Med Col or Lt Col	1

Members of Department

Med Officers	35
Pharmacy	18
Sanitation	22
Technical	11
Engineers	29
Professors	3
Interpreter	1
Paymaster	5

Attached to Department

NCO's	98
Assistant Engineers	175
Others - Sanitation corpsmen, hired help	Several

Branches

CO	Medical Lt Colonel (Major)	1
	Med Officer, Company grade	1
	Pharmacy Officer, Co grade	1
	Sanitation Officer, Co grade	1
	Finance Officer, Co grade	1
	NCO's	20
	Assistant Engineers	20
	Privates	400
	Others, hired help	Several

Specific Personnel

CG Dept	Med Lt Gen Shiro ISHII
Chief Gen Affairs Sec	Med Col S OTA
Chief No. 1 Section	Med Maj Gen Hitoshi KIKUCHI
Chief No. 2 Section	Med Col T IKARI
Chief No. 3 Section	Med Col C MASUDA
Chief No. 4 Section	Med Col S OTA
Chief Supply Section	Med Col C MASUDA
CO, Mutankiang Branch	Med Maj M OKAMI
CO, Linkow Branch	Med Maj H SAKAKIHARA
CO, Sungwu Branch	Med Lt Col S NISHI
CO, Hailar Branch	Med Maj T KATO
CO, Dairen (Dalny) Branch	Civilian Engineer K ANDO

SECRET
RESTRICTED

Supplement 1-e

ANNUAL PRODUCTION CAPACITY OF VACCINES AND SERUMS BY THE KWANTUNG ARMY WATER PURIFICATION ~~SECTION~~ DEPARTMENT

The Kwantung Army Water Purification Section on orders from CG, Kwantung Army, prepares and supplies vaccines and serums for the army units, civilian employees of the military and a portion of the general populace in the area under the jurisdiction of the Kwantung Army in Manchuria, No. China, and Korea. Main items and quantities are as given below.

Vaccines

	Item	Approximated Quantity Amt. Handled Annually
1.	Dried vaccine	human doses
2.	Plague vaccine	2,000,000
3.	Typhoid-fever para typhoid vaccine	4,000,000
4.	Gas gangrene vaccine	2,000,000
5.	Tetanus vaccine	2,000,000
6.	Cholera vaccine	500,000
7.	Dysentery vaccine	4,000,000
8.	Scarlet fever vaccine	100,000
9.	Whooping cough vaccine	100,000
10.	Diphtheria vaccine	100,000
11.	Eruptive typhus vaccine	
	a. Chicken egg vaccine	1,000,000
	b. Rat lung vaccine	2,000,000
	c. Field squirrel lung vaccine	1,000,000
12.	Tuberculosis vaccine	500,000
13.	Vaccine lymph	2,000,000

Treatment Anti-Sera

	Item	Liters
1.	Gas gangrene serum	5,000
2.	Tetanus serum	5,000
3.	Diphtheria serum	500
4.	Dysentery treatment serum	1,000
5.	Streptococcal serum	500
6.	Staphylococcal serum	500
7.	Erysipelas treatment serum	500
8.	Pneumonia treatment serum	1,000
9.	Cerebo-spinal meningitis treatment serum	500
10.	Anthrax treatment serum	50
11.	Plague treatment serum	1,000
12.	Plasma for blood transfusion	100,000

Supplement 1-e

Diagnostic Antigens

Item	
1. Typhoid fever, para-typhoid	Each 20 liters
2. Eruptive typhus	5 liters
3. Tuberculin	3,000,000 human doses
4. Dried tuberculin	3,000,000 human doses

Sera for Diagnosis

Item	Liters
1. Typhoid fever, para-typhoid diagnostic serum	5
2. Dysentery (each kind) diagnostic serum	5
3. Cholera (each type) diagnostic serum	5
4. Cerebro-spinal meningitis diagnostic serum	2
5. Pneumonia diagnostic serum	2
6. Salmonella serum	2

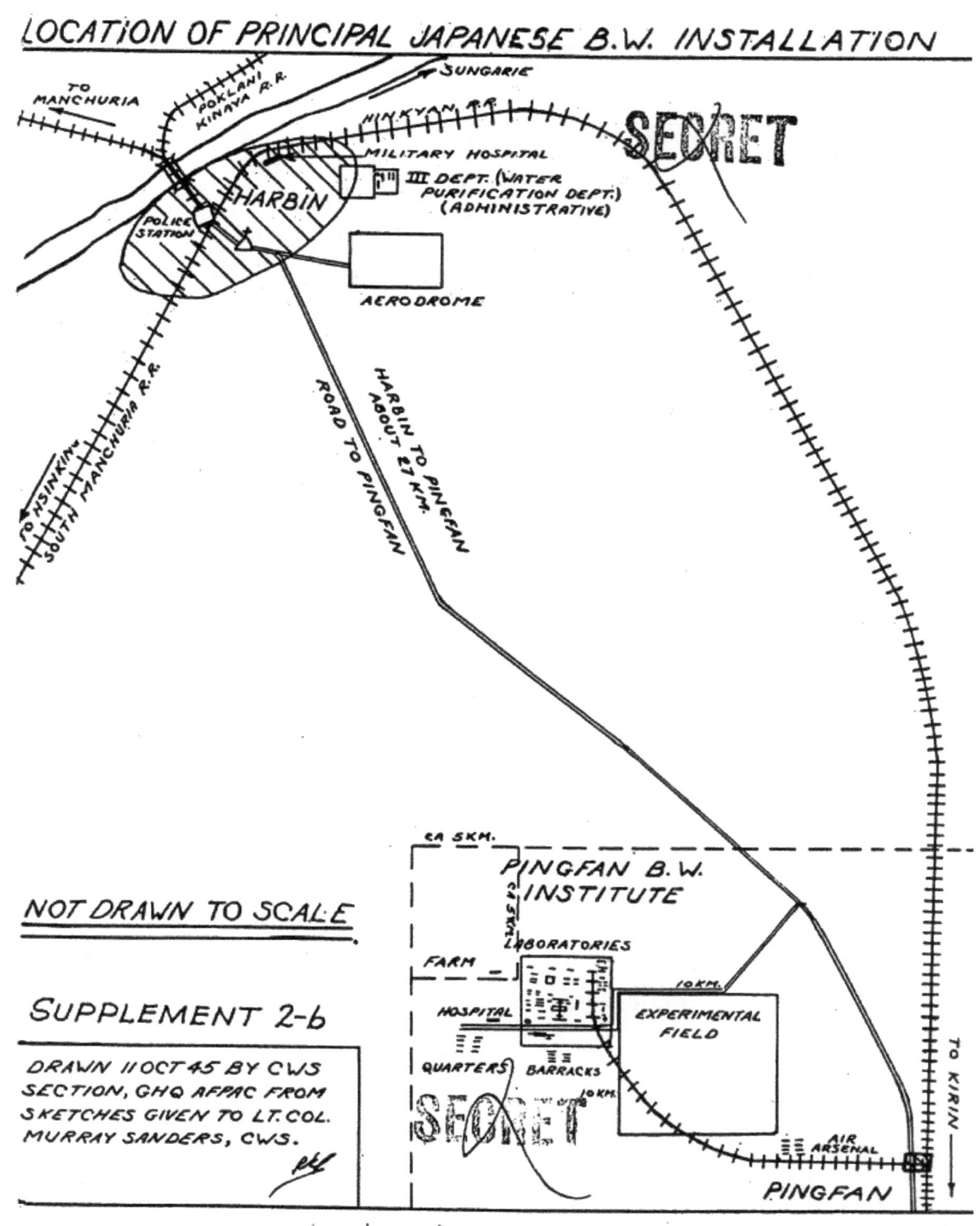

supplement 2-a は?

SUPPLEMENT 3-a

SOURCE OF INFORMATION NO. 1

UJI BOMB

BACTERIAL

ALL PURPOSE TYPE

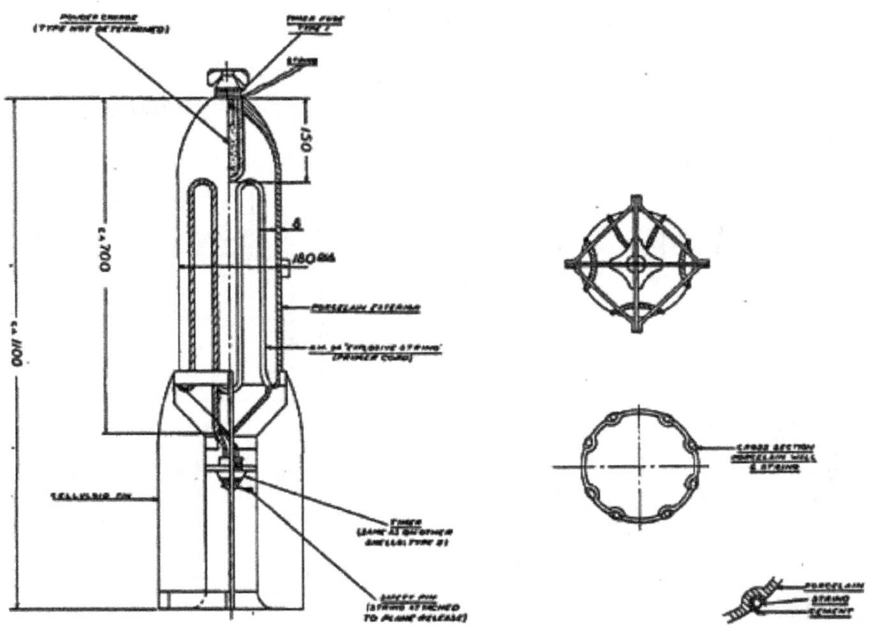

PAY-LOAD 10 L. FLUID
CONTAINING BACTERIA
FLUID IS PLACED IN BOMB
THEN CHARGE IS SCREWED IN

WEIGHT
EMPTY 25 KG.
FILLED 35 KG.

DIMENSIONS IN MILLIMETERS

SUPPLEMENT 3-b

SOURCE OF INFORMATION NO. I

SECRET

HA BOMB BACTERIAL SINGLE PURPOSE TYPE FOR ANTHRAX	RO BOMB BACTERIAL ALL PURPOSE TYPE

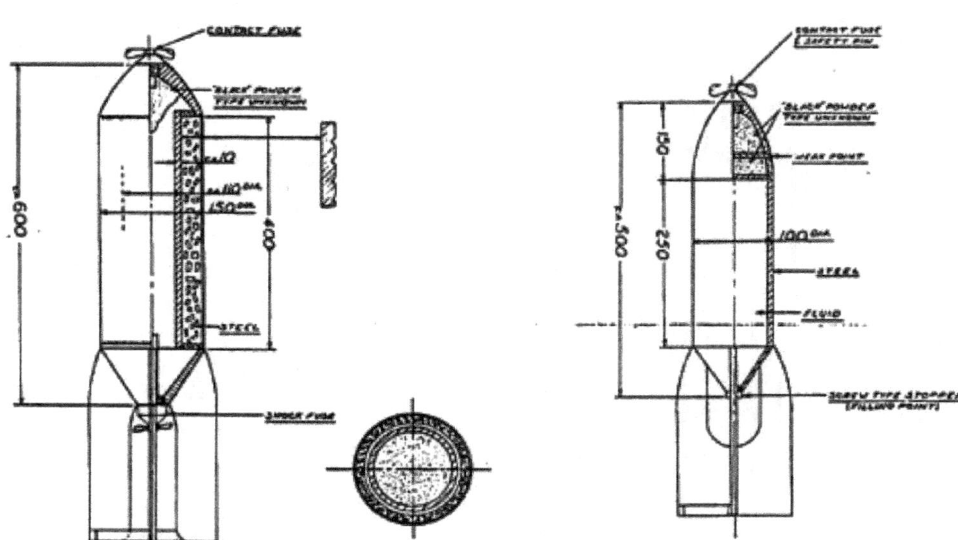

PAY-LOAD 500cc FLUID EMULSION CONTAINING ANTHRAX ORGANISMS

WEIGHT	
EMPTY	40 KG.
FILLED	41 KG.

PAY-LOAD 2 L. FLUID CONTAINING BACTERIA

WEIGHT	
EMPTY	20 KG.
FILLED	22 KG.

STEEL MUNITION WITH INTERNAL AND EXTERNAL SURFACES COATED WITH SHELLAC TO PREVENT CORROSION. CONTAINS 1500 CYLINDRICAL STEEL PARTICLES WHICH WEIGH 8 KG.

DIMENSIONS IN MILLIMETERS

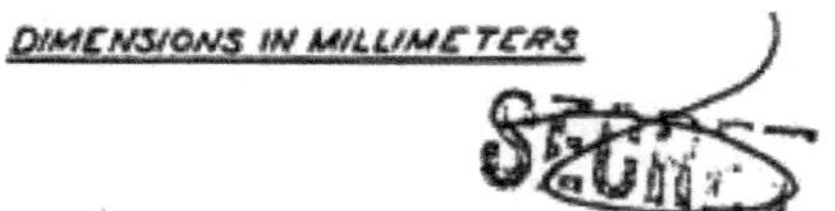

GIVEN TO LT COL. MURRAY SANDERS, CWS.

SUPPLEMENT 3-C

SOURCE OF INFORMATION NO. 2
UJI BOMB
BACTERIAL
ALL PURPOSE TYPE
FORM 50

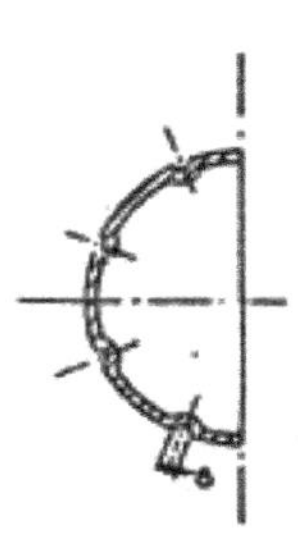

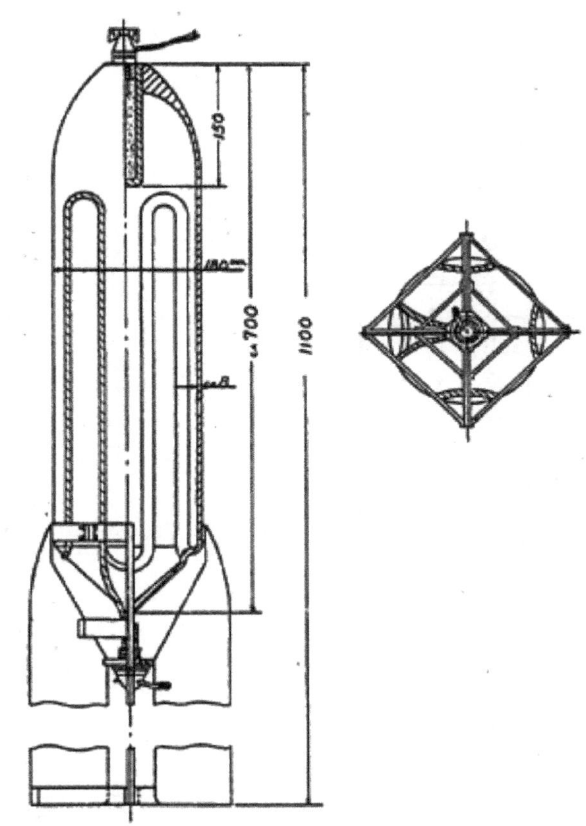

PAY-LOAD 10 L. FLUID
CONTAINING BACTERIA

WEIGHT
EMPTY 25 KG.
FILLED 35 KG.

SCALE IN MILLIMETERS

DRAWN [illegible] BY CWS SECTION GHQ AFPAC FROM SKETCHES GIVEN TO LT. COL. MURRAY SANDERS, CWS.

SUPPLEMENT
3d

SOURCE OF INFORMATION NO. 2

HA BOMB
BACTERIAL
SINGLE PURPOSE TYPE.
FOR ANTHRAX

RO BOMB
BACTERIAL
ALL PURPOSE TYPE

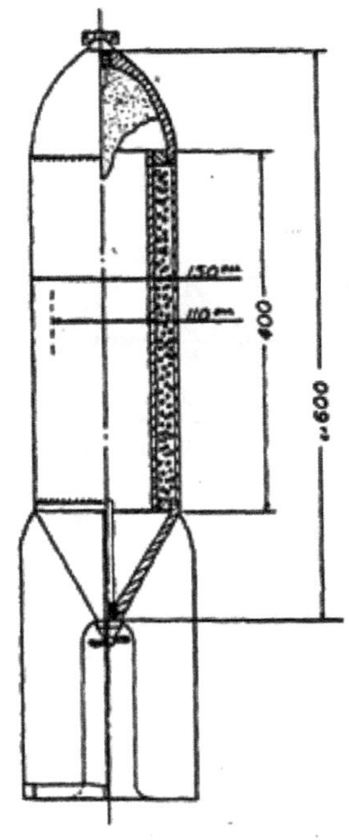

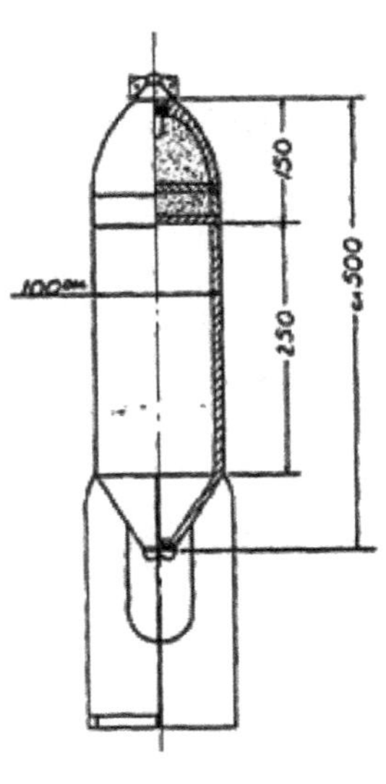

PAY-LOAD 500cc FLUID EMULSION CONTAINING ANTHRAX ORGANISMS	WEIGHT FULL 40 KG. CONTAINS 1500 STEEL BALLS

PAY-LOAD 2 L. FLUID CONTAINING BACTERIA	WEIGHT EMPTY 20 KG. FILLED 22 KG.

SCALE IN MILLIMETERS

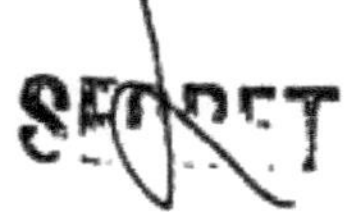

DRAWN [illegible] FROM SKETCHES
GIVEN TO LT. COL. MURRAY
SANDERS, CWS.

TABLE OF EXPERIMENTAL T

BOMB TYPE	MATERIAL	SHAPE AND CONSTRUCTION				
		BOMB PROPER	EXPLOSIVE	FUZE	QUAN. OF BACT. FLUID	TOTAL WGHT.
I CA 300 1937	IRON	500 x 100 MMS. CYLINDRICAL BODY, EGG-SHAPE HEAD. STEEL TAIL FINS. EXPLOSIVE CHAMBER AT HEAD AND CENTER OF BOMB. JUNCTION OF TAIL WEAK. WEAK, BLACK POWDER FINELY GRANULATED, SHORT DELAY POWDER TNT.	FINELY GRANULATED POWDER. (BLACK)	PERCUSSION	2 LITERS	20 KG
RO CA 300 1937	IRON	500 x 100 MMS. CYLINDRICAL BODY, EGG-SHAPE HEAD STEEL TAIL FINS. EXPLOSIVE AT HEAD, BACTERIAL FLUID IN BODY CHAMBER. EXPLOSIVE CHAMBER PARTITIONED INTO FRONT AND REAR SECTIONS. BLACK POWDER IN FRONT SECTION, BROWN POWDER IN REAR SECTION. SECTIONS CONNECTED THRU PARTITIONS BY SHORT DELAY FUZE.	FRONT SECTION FINELY-GRANULATED POWDER. REAR SECTION BROWN POWDER (TNT)	PERCUSSION	2 LITERS	20 KG
* HA CA 500 1938	IRON	600 x 150 MMS. CYLINDRICAL BODY, EGG-SHAPE HEAD STEEL TAIL FINS, DOUBLE CHAMBER. EXPLOSIVE IN INNER CHAMBER AND BOTH ENDS. OUTER CHAMBER FILLED WITH STEEL PELLETS AND BACTERIAL FLUID. THE NUMBER OF PELLETS 1500 (3 GMS. PER PELLET), BACTERIAL FLUID 500 CC.	TNT 3 KGS.	FRONT AND REAR - BOTH PERCUSSION	500 CC	40 KG
NI CA 300 1939	IRON	700 x 150 MMS. SHAPE AND CONSTRUCTION SAME AS HA BOMB EXCEPT THAT CHAMBER RADII ARE TWICE THAT OF HA BOMB.	TNT 1.5 KGS	SAME AS ABOVE	1 LITER	50 KG
U 20 1938	IRON	700 x 180 MMS. JUNCTION BETWEEN HEAD AND BODY WEAK. EXPLOSIVE TUBE IN MIDDLE. SELF-TIMER (SUCH AS USED IN CAMERA) INSERTED IN TAIL AND CONNECTED TO COMPRESSED AIR CHAMBER. WEAK COMPRESSED AIR CHAMBER. SELF-TIMER. PRIMER.	TNT	NONE	CA 10 LITERS	30 KG
UJI OLD TYPE 300 1938	PORCELAIN	750 x 180 MMS. CYLINDRICAL BODY, EGG-SHAPE HEAD, CELLULOID TAIL FINS. GROOVE 8 MMS WIDE AND CIRCLES BOMB 8 TIMES. PRIMER CORD INSERTED IN GROOVES.	PRIMER CORD 2.5 M	TIME FUZE (COMPLEX ACTION FUZE) "5TH YEAR" (OBSOLETE TYPE)	18 LITERS	35 KG
UJI** TYPE 50 1939	PORCELAIN	700 x 180 MMS. GENERAL CONSTRUCTION SAME AS OLD TYPE. SEPERATE EXPLOSIVE CHAMBER OF PORCELAIN ADDED TO HEAD OF BOMB.	PRIMER CORD 4 M. TNT IN HEAD	TIME FUZE IN TAIL (SAME AS ABOVE) PERCUSSION TIME FUZE IN HEAD (TYPE I)	10 LITERS	25 KG
UJI TYPE 100 200 1939	PORCELAIN	900 x 180 MMS. SAME CONSTRUCTION AS TYPE 50.	SAME AS ABOVE	SAME AS ABOVE	25 LITERS	50 KG
GA 20 1938	GLASS	SAME CONSTRUCTION AS OLD TYPE OF UJI BOMB, EXCEPT BOMB PROPER IS MADE OF GLASS.				

* FIRST TO BE TESTED FROM AIR. ** TOTAL PRODUCTION NOT KNOWN. 2000 FOR EXPERIMENTAL PURPOS

SUPPLEMENT 3-e

TYPES OF BACTERIAL BOMBS

ACTION	AREA OF DISPERSION	EFFECTIVENESS	DISADVANTAGE	CONCLUSION
...ad Explodes Upon Percussion, Explosive Pres-...re Transmitted Thru Chamber. After Con-...ents Of Chamber And Rivet At Tail Are ...lown Out, Explosion Is Transferred To ...owder In Center, Breaking And ...cattering Bomb Proper.	Static Explosion 10 to 15 x 200 to 300 m. (Wind Speed 5m/Sec) Drop Test From Plane Embedded 1 to 2 Meters In Ground. No Dispersion.		Drop Test From Plane. Results Very Poor	Unsuitable For Dropping From Plane
Front And Rear Explosive Sections Separate Upon Percussion Throwing Bomb Proper 20 To 30 Meters Into The Air, Together With Rear Explosive Section. Explosion Occurs At This Height And Scatters Contents Of Body Chamber.	Same As Above.		Drop Test From Plane Results Very Poor	Unsuitable For Dropping From Plane
Explodes Upon Percussion Scattering Bomb Fragments And Pellets Together With Bacterial Fluid.	Static Explosion Scatter-Distance Of Pellets 400 to 500 m Radius. Pattern Of Dispersion; About 1 Pellet Per Sq M. Within Radius Of 50 m. From Site Of Explosion.	Path Of Fragments And Pellets Low. Effectiveness Of Wounding And Killing - Great % Adherence Of Bacteria To Pellets: 60 to 70 %	1. Bacterial Fluid Leaks. 2. % Adherence Of Bacteria Low. Explosive Too Strong 3. Unsatisfactory Trajectory 4. Difficult To Make 5. Too Short And Difficult To Handle	Probably Effective In Attacking Pastures
Same As Above	Area Of Dispersion Less Than Ha Bomb.	Increased Percentage Of Adherence Of Bacteria To Pellets.	1. Bacterial Fluid Leaks 2. Explosive Pattern Poor 3. Difficult To Manufacture	Same As Above
...ction Of Self Timer Causes Explosive Tube In Compressed Air Chamber To Advance Separating Bomb Head From Body. Forward Partition Of Compressed Air Chamber Dislodges, Blowing Out Contents Followed By Explosion Of Tube And Scattering Bomb Proper.			1. Basic Construction Poor. (Probably Wrong To Depend On Mechanical Means Of Operation) 2. Too Many Failures, Poor Precision Of Explosion.	Not Usable
Operation Of Complex Action Fuze In Tail Touches Off Primer Cord. Bomb Proper Explodes, Scattering Contents.	Static Expl. At Height 15 m 20 to 30 x 500 to 600 m. (Wind Speed 5 m/Sec) Drop Test From Plane (Height Of Explosion 200 to 300 m) 20 to 30 x 600 to 700 m. (Wind Speed 5m/Sec)(Percussion) Bomb Proper Breaks Before Fuze Operates. Dispersion Poor	Low Internal Explosive Pressure And Lack Of Metallic Effect Are Advantageous For Preserving Bacterial Viability	Trajectory Unsatisfactory	Effectiveness Poor
Operation Of Complex Action Fuze In Tail Touches Off Primer Cord, Causing Bomb To Explode And Scatter Contents	Static Expl. At Height 15 m 20 to 30 x 400 to 500 m. (Wind Speed 5 m/Sec) Drop Test From Plane	Live Stock Eating Grass In Breeze Within Range Of	1. Trajectory Unsatisfactory (Effectiveness 10%) 2. Error Of Fuse	Best Among Uji Bombs

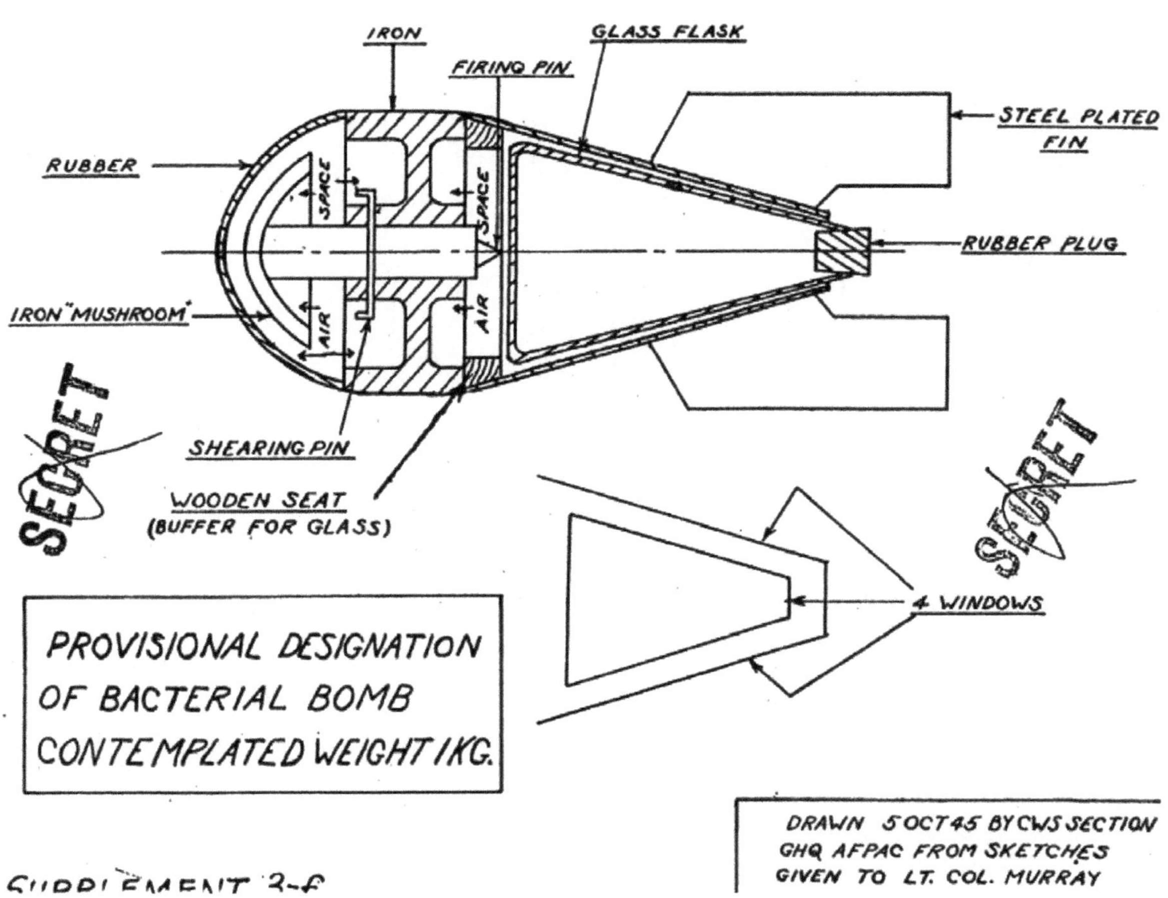
NAVAL MARK 7
MODIFICATION OF TRAINING BOMB
IRON
GLASS FLASK
FIRING PIN
STEEL PLATED FIN
RUBBER
SPACE
SPACE
RUBBER PLUG
IRON "MUSHROOM"
AIR
AIR
SECRET
SHEARING PIN
WOODEN SEAT
(BUFFER FOR GLASS)
SECRET
4 WINDOWS
PROVISIONAL DESIGNATION
OF BACTERIAL BOMB
CONTEMPLATED WEIGHT 1KG.
DRAWN 5 OCT 45 BY CWS SECTION
GHQ AFPAC FROM SKETCHES
GIVEN TO LT. COL. MURRAY

6.1.12　9 Nov. 1945: MEMORAMDUM: Supplementary Biological Warfare Information, TO: Commander-in-Chief, AFPAC, THROUGH: Chief Chemical Officer

资料出处： National Archives of the United States, R407, E261A, B12.

内容点评： 本资料为1945年11月9日美军化学战部队中校Murray Sanders提交美军太平洋部队总司令部司令官备忘录：细菌战情报补充报告（《Sanders报告·补遗》）。为Sanders应美国陆军部要求，对日军将领及内阁成员有关细菌战的讯问记录。

TOP SECRET

WAR DEPARTMENT

TOP SECRET

THE ADJUTANT GENERAL'S OFFICE

WASHINGTON

AG 729.2 9 Nov. 45 (1)

Subject: Supplementary Biological Warfare information in Japan.

OPERATIONS BRANCH A.G.O.

CLASSIFIED FILES

WAR DEPARTMENT

CLASSIFIED DOCUMENT DOWNGRADING COMMITTEE

File No AG 729.2 Date 2 Feb 48

An overall classification of (TOP SECRET)(~~CONFIDENTIAL~~)(~~RESTRICTED~~) is retained for the following reasons:

(1)_____ Inclusion of documents classified by authority outside War Department requires minimum classification of (SECRET)(CONFIDENTIAL)(RESTRICTED).

(2)_____ Good faith toward originator of included matter requires minimum classification of (SECRET)(CONFIDENTIAL)(RESTRICTED).

(3)_____ Included allegations of misconduct or incompetence require for preservation of discipline or harmony a minimum classification of (CONFIDENTIAL)(RESTRICTED).

(4) V Included revelations concerning policies, operations, materiel, or techniques currently classified requires minimum classification of (TOP SECRET)(~~CONFIDENTIAL~~)(~~RESTRICTED~~).

(5)_____ Included literal text of protected cryptograms requires, per par 16c, AR 380-5, Aug 1946, minimum classification of (SECRET)(CONFIDENTIAL)(RESTRICTED).

(6)_____ ____________________

Initials of Reviewing Officer 7W

Form: Classification Retained No. 3 (Copy to be attached to document or file).

AG 729.2 9 Nov. 45

Secret sheet
729.2 USAF in Pacific
do Japan
319.1
333.5
461 SCientific Intelligence
Survey in Japan
370.24
385
ham

TOP SECRET

GENERAL HEADQUARTERS MS/roe
UNITED STATES ARMY FORCES, PACIFIC
Scientific and Technical Advisory Section

Advanced Echelon
APO 500
9 November 1945

MEMORANDUM: Supplementary Biological Warfare Information.

TO : Commander-in-Chief, AFPAC

THROUGH : Chief Chemical Officer

1. Transmitted herewith are four interviews with Japanese General Staff and Cabinet officers on the subject of Biological Warfare. These interviews were held in response to a War Department request, radio No. 80140.

2. Since the formal report on this subject has been included as Volume V in the "Scientific Intelligence Survey in Japan" report, 1 November 1945, the interviews are submitted as supplementary information.

3. The interviews have been reported in the first and second persons for purposes of simplification. However, it should be emphasized, while the context has been accurately transmitted this is not a verbatim, literal record. Interpreters acted as channels in the interviews and questions were frequently stated in the third person. An attempt has been made to record the answers as they were given. Therefore Japanese phraseology is common.

4. An additional statement is also appended concerning information in Army Medical College records which were found in Niigata in the closing days of the Biological Warfare investigation.

Murray Sanders
MURRAY SANDERS
Lt. Col., CWS

370.24

OH 729.2

9 Nov 45

24 Jan 46

TOP SECRET

TOP SECRET

GENERAL HEADQUARTERS
UNITED STATES ARMY FORCES, PACIFIC
Scientific and Technical Advisory Section
Dai-Ichi Bldg - Room 233

Advanced Echelon
APO 500
9 November 1945

SUBJECT: Biological Warfare, (BW).
DATE: 6 November 1945.
INTERVIEWED: Lt. Gen. Tadakasu WAKAMATSU.
INTERVIEWERS: Lt. Col. Murray Sanders.

1. General Wakamatsu stated that he had been the Vice War Minister of Japan for three months from the 12th of July to the 1st of November, 1945.

Q. What was the position of the War Ministry in regard to BW as a weapon either used by hostile powers or one which Japan might employ?

A. I must explain that I held my office for a brief period and was unaware of any official opinion in this matter. However, during my brief tenure the BW investigation was initiated from the U.S. General Headquarters and I received reports concerning its progress.

I had a special interest in the prevention of disease in the event of a Japanese invasion and therefore stimulated the Bureau of Medicine and the Ministry of Welfare to work as hard as possible in that field. Since last year the number of cases due to infectious diseases has greatly increased. I should like to explain that this actual increase did not appear in statistics because for the past three years the Ministry of Welfare had been handling it and did not do a good job. To elucidate this point there is the example of a division transferred from Manchuria to Japan in the last months of the war. Many cases of dysentery occurred and I did not pay much attention to BW but stressed prevention of disease. Until the last moment of capitulation my sole concern was to keep the war going and in the two-fold medical problem of prevention of disease and solution of nutritional difficulties.

Now I would like to give you my personal opinion about BW. I think it is impossible on a large scale. It may be feasible on a small scale and for purposes of deception.

Q. Is this your opinion in regard to Japanese position in BW or in regard to other nations?

A. From what I have heard, no nation is in a position to use BW. After the first world war the opinion was prevalent that BW could be used on a large scale in the future. In line with this thought

- 1 -

TOP SECRET

TOP SECRET

we were suspicious when dysentery outbreaks occurred in large troop centers (permanent garrisons). Investigations were carried out to see whether such outbreaks were tactical infections. However, they proved to be natural infections. Then I heard of the tactical and strategic impossibility of BW from the Chief of the Medical Bureau. However, this was only after the BW investigation from U.S. General Headquarters had been started.

Q. In your position as Vice War Minister did you know that the Japanese were investigating BW?

A. Only after the initiation of the investigation did I hear of it. Previous to that I was fully occupied with preparations for the battle of Japan, and I did not think that BW would be used in this instance.

Q. When you did learn of the Japanese work in BW did you feel that the information should be given to the American investigators of the subject?

A. Yes.

Q. Is it your impression that the Japanese study was a major one?

A. I know very little about it. It would only be in the event that we (i.e., Japan) contemplated the use of BW that I would become familiar with the details.

Q. What position did you hold previous to the Vice War Ministry?

A. (a) I was Chief of Staff of the Second General Army (stationed in the Japanese homeland) for three months.

(b) I was Vice Chief of Staff of the Southern General Army in Saigon for four and one-half months.

(c) I was Commander of the 46th Division, Dutch East Indies, for one year and one month.

Q. In these positions were you given any information about BW?

A. Absolutely none.

Q. You received no order from higher authorities in regard to either offensive or defensive work?

A. I had no warning but I did have an experience in Manchuria in 1933 when many horses died at the same time. This I think was due to the work of Russian spies.

Q. How reliable is your information on this point?

A. I had no direct information, just discussion with brother officers.

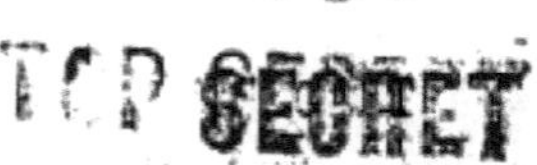

TOP SECRET

GENERAL HEADQUARTERS
UNITED STATES ARMY FORCES, PACIFIC
Scientific and Technical Advisory Section
Dai-Ichi Bldg - Room 233

Advanced Echelon
APO 500
7 November 1945

SUBJECT: Biological Warfare, (BW).
DATE: November 7, 1945.
INTERVIEWED: Lt. Gen. Torashiro KAWABE, Assistant Chief, Japanese General Staff.
INTERVIEWERS: Lt. Col. Murray Sanders.

1. Gen. Kawabe stated that he had held the position of Assistant Chief of the Japanese General Staff from April 1945 to October 15, 1945. Previous to that time he had been Assistant Chief of the Japanese Army Air Corp General Staff. At present he is in charge of Japanese Army demobilization.

2. Q. What is your personal opinion of BW as a weapon?
A. For a long time--at least 25 years--I felt that it could be used effectively as an offensive weapon. Recently I have had doubts concerning the practicality of using this weapon on a grand scale. For one thing, the technical difficulties are great. For another, there are both humane and practical considerations which make it an unlikely weapon. However, I feel that the practical considerations outweigh anything else. From a layman's point of view, the greatest difficulty appears to be the inability of our technical people to maintain bacteria in a viable state and to give them an environment where they may propagate.

Furthermore, there is great danger, once the bacteria are let loose, that one's own soldiers might be adversely affected. It would take much time, energy, and money to overcome the technical difficulties.

Where one is dealing with an enemy with a high degree of civilization the defense against BW is almost automatic because of excellent modern sanitary facilities. In the future, however, the picture may become different and social defenses may be overcome by efficient BW methods.

Q. You have stated that it would be necessary to expend time, energy, and money to overcome technical difficulties. If this were done, do you think BW would be a practical weapon?
A. Yes, provided that there is sufficient preparation, and proper use of technical personnel.

- 1 -

TOP SECRET

TOP SECRET

Q. In your official position did you know of the activities of the Japanese Army in the BW field?

A. Yes, but only the defensive aspects.

Q. Did you learn of offensive studies in BW when you became Assistant Chief of General Staff in April?

A. My previous impression was entirely confirmed. So far as I am concerned the Japanese Army has never studied offensive aspects.

Q. Would it come as a complete surprise if I were to suggest that the Army has attempted to investigate the offensive potentialities of BW?

A. Frankly speaking, I was entirely in ignorance of this until after the cessation of hostilities. Then I was informed that such studies had been carried on only for the purpose of evaluating defense against BW.

Q. When did you learn about the offensive studies?

A. I do not recall the actual date. When the investigation of BW was initiated from American General Headquarters I took a positive attitude and stated that I wished to know the actual picture. With this in mind I ordered Lt. Col. Niizuma to make a thorough investigation and get to the bottom of the matter. I also ordered the medical officers to give me all information.

Q. Did you feel that the U.S. forces (i.e., General Headquarters) should have this information?

A. That is not my interest. It was my desire to obtain a full picture on what had happened.

Q. But having this knowledge, did you have any objections to our having the information?

A. I am a strong advocate of cooperation with the American Forces and in this instance of making the information available to the General Headquarters.

Q. Since you now have this information you know that BW offensive studies were carried on on a fairly large scale. This being the case, how does it happen that such a project could be carried out without the knowledge of the Assistant Chief of the Japanese General Staff?

A. In answer to the first part; I do not know exactly on what scale the work was carried out but I did learn that several hundred bombs were produced and tested in the offensive study.

This needs explanation (i.e., question of General Staff ignorance). The fact is, I took my position in April. Please understand the situation at that time. The only question which concerned me and consumed all my energies was the problem of resistance against United States Ground Forces in Japan.

Q. On the basis of what you have said am I to assume that BW did not enter into the consideration of strategy in the battle of Japan?

TOP SECRET

A. Exactly.

Q. Who was your predecessor as the Assistant Chief of the General Staff?

A. Lt Gen H. Haka. He was transferred to the position of Chief of Staff for the Kwantung Army and is now missing.

Q. You have stated that for many years you believed BW a possible weapon. During this early period did you think it would be used against the Japanese Army?

A. Yes, by the Soviet. According to traditional Japanese military thinking the Soviet was our principal enemy. Approximately ten years ago I heard rumors that Russia was making extensive BW preparations and was experimenting against livestock in Manchuria.

Q. What was the source of your information and how reliable was it?

A. So far as I know this was never proven. It was just a rumor.

Q. You have said that in previous positions, you were officially given defensive but not offensive information. What was the character of this information?

A. As commander of an Air Division, I experienced a severe outbreak of cholera in the Hong Kong and Canton districts. This was effectively handled by the Boeki Kyusuibu and I consequently became interested in this organization. I encouraged the Boeki Kyusuibu and obtained defensive information from that source.

When I took my position in April the most acute problem which faced me was the unsanitary condition under which our people were living. This was due to the effects of air attack and also to the presence of large concentrations of troops assembled for the battle of Japan. Consequently, I attempted to better general conditions to ameliorate the situation. This is not to be construed as defensive BW but emphasizes the anti-epidemic problem which faced us.

GENERAL HEADQUARTERS
UNITED STATES ARMY FORCES, PACIFIC
Scientific and Technical Advisory Section
Dai-Ichi Bldg - Room 233

Advanced Echelon
APO 500
9 November 1945

SUBJECT: Biological Warfare, (BW).
DATE: 8 November 1945.
INTERVIEWED: Yoshijiro UMEZU.
INTERVIEWERS: Lt. Col. Murray Sanders and Lt. H. Youngs.

1. General Umezu stated that at present he is a member of the Military Council which acts as Imperial Advisory Board of Military Affairs. From July 1944 to the de-activation of the Japanese General Staff he held the position of Chief of Staff.

Q. What information have you received in your official capacity on the subject of BW?
A. I have received only a small amount of information as to the BW itself. However, under the supposition that BW could be employed in modern warfare, the Japanese military made a considerable study and research in BW in order that it might be able to cope with it in the event that it were used.

I may say that in this connection, I have received no report on the use of BW by the U.S., Britain, or China. But neither did I receive reports that this weapon would not be used. Therefore the Japanese Army had to extend itself to study BW and to obtain knowledge in this field.

As to the Soviet with which we had been neutral until recently, reports were received concerning their intentions to use BW in the eventuality of war. These reports came from Japanese authorities in Manchuria. Therefore this was considered one of the principal motives of the Japanese study in BW.

I should like to add, that the reason for our major study was defensive. This was due to the state of contamination present in the area of battle. We felt very strongly that we must learn to combat infections. (INTERRUPTION)

(Q. Natural infections?
A. Yes.)

I mentioned Japanese activities during war time, but even in peace time every effort was made to combat cholera, pest, etc. This was done not only for the military but also for civilian population.

TOP SECRET

Such activities were greatly encouraged by the Imperial Japanese Government.

So, for the reasons I have just mentioned the BW study was primarily defensive. Its chief activity was the prevention of epidemics.

Q. Would you say it is fair in summarising that Japanese BW activities emphasised two things; offensive activities because of potential danger from the Soviet, and defensive activities for prevention of epidemics?

A. I can safely say that the Japanese Army never intended to make an offensive study. The only purpose of such a study was to learn the proper counter-measures. Naturally, the researcher must know enough of BW offensive potentialities in order that he may prepare proper defenses. In this connection offensive aspects might have been studied, but the main purpose was defensive.

Furthermore the Soviet was not the only reason for our research in BW. We felt we must expect BW attacks by any nation in any battle in modern warfare.

Q. Would you list the nations in the order of likelihood which you might expect them to employ BW?

A. Judging from the study carried out by the Japanese Army I understand there is little possibility of any nation indulging in offensive BW. But I also know that you cannot state definitely that it might not be waged. Even if chance is one out of a hundred we cannot neglect counter-measures.

Q. What is your impression of the extent of the Japanese offensive studies in BW?

A. The ways and means of research were left in the hands of responsible persons. The central authorities never instructed the technical people how to do their work but the purpose was given them, i.e. the purpose of defense. However, it is understandable that the research workers studied offensive measures for purposes of defense, therefore the offensiveactivities were not a major part of the program. But I have a report that a considerable number of bombs were used, therefore it must have been of some extent. However, I do not have the details.

I also have no details on information concerning the budget. No additional money was given for purposes of offense. Money was just given for defense. On that basis I would think the offensive activities would not be of tremendous scale.

Q. Was the budget assigned to the BW organization for the specific purpose of studying defensive measures or was it given simply for the study of BW?

-2-

TOP SECRET

TOP SECRET

A. I do not recall definitely but there was no specific organization for BW. As you have already heard the study was carried out by the Boeki Kyusuibu. This organization was established for control of epidemics. The budget was assigned to various units and I do not know the details.

Q. The prime purpose of the Boeki Kyusuibu was not to combat BW? It was not organized for purposes of offensive or defensive BW?

A. The prime purpose was the control of epidemics, for purification of water and for the transportation of water to the battle front. As to the appropriations I shall have a subordinate sent to your office. As I recall, the budget was not itemized and specific instructions were not given but I am not certain of this.

Q. If this impression is true, then would you say it was within the jurisdiction of the Boeki Kyusuibu to use as much or as little of their budget for BW purposes as they say fit? In fact, could they not use as much as they wished for offensive purposes?

A. I am not sure but that seems to be the case.

Q. As you know, by this time we have received certain impressions in regard to Japanese BW activities. For one thing, the Boeki Kyusuibu seems to have been quite independent of the Medical Bureau. Was that the case?

A. I think I can safely say that BW research was independent of the Medical Bureau but there was an advisory connection. The Boeki Kyusuibu did not come under command control of the Medical Bureau but received technical advice in medical matters.

Q. How important did you consider BW?

A. Personally, I think BW constitutes an unimportant means of carrying on war. It is not an easy weapon to use in actual operations because of many technical difficulties. Therefore I do not think the Japanese should use BW. From the beginning to the end of the war, I entertained no thought of using it offensively. The reason for this impression was that unless it is waged on a large scale it cannot be significant. In order to use it one must make considerable preparations. To do this one must have tremendous national resources. Therefore it is not a weapon for Japan.

Second, I should like to mention that offensive BW may decrease the fighting strength of the enemy but also affect non-combattants, i.e. civilians. It might also affect our own troops. Even if a specific battle turned in favor of Japan as a result of BW, it might affect our own population. Of course, you might consider a specific battle situation but even if BW were successful it would not turn the tide of war in favor of Japan.

Third, there is a humane consideration. The use of bacterial agents is forbidden by international law. Therefore it is my firm belief that this form of war should not be resorted to in any case.

TOP SECRET

TOP SECRET

Q. Can you tell me whether the Emperor knew of BW i.e., defensive activities?

A. I do not know exactly. While I was Chief of the General Staff I had no chance to explain this problem to the Emperor nor was I ever asked concerning it. Perhaps My predecessor discussed this but I am not certain.

I had the impression that offensive BW might be used against Japan, but we never had such a case. Therefore there was no opportunity for discussion with the Emperor. Only if this situation arose would we take up the matter with the Emperor, again.

Q. What is your general impression of the progress made by the Japanese Army in demonstrating the potentialities of BW as a weapon?

A. So far as Japan is concerned my previous statements were based on the knowledge which I had of our work. However, if the Soviet or the U.S. carried out BW it could be used on a large scale. For a small nation like Japan it is impossible. However, I think it is possible for such a nation as yours or the Soviet to use it in future wars. So far as Japan is concerned there can be no future wars.

Q. You have mentioned that you have received reports concerning Soviet attempts to use BW. How reliable do you consider these sources? Can you enlarge on this? (NOTE: The answer which was given in response to this question was considered so important that General Umezu was requested to submit a written statement of his answer. Aside from information on the reliability of source material it is to be noted that there is a statement in conflict with the early one concerning the purposes of the Boeki Kyusuibu work. The answer herewith given is a true copy of the statement submitted by General Umezu's interpreter.

A. "As to the reports concerning the Soviet possibility of using the bacteorogical warfare offensive, I think they are fairly reliable.* During the China Incident, around 1937, I received and also heard of reports from the Japanese authorities in Manchuria stating that they had captured at several different places on several occasions Soviet spies carrying bacteria in bottles for the purpose of dissemination. Judging from these reports, we concluded that the Soviet Union attached importance to the bacteorogical warfare offensive. As I recall, it was for this reason of coping with the Soviet possibility that Boekikyusuibu was organized and began its study on the bacteorogical warfare deffensive around 1937. Originally we had no intention of waging war against the United States. Soviet Union has always been our future possible enemy and from that point of view, we regarded these reports with great concern and were obliged to lay stress on the study and research of the bacteorogical warfare defensive.

* As originally made by General Umezu this statement was "I considered the reports very reliable." (MS & HY).

- 4 -

TOP SECRET

TOP SECRET
SECRET

"The above is the best of my recollection and knowledge at present, and if it is your wish, I shall look into the matter further to ascertain the exact dates and the original of reports received.

/s/ Interpreter
H. Takeuchi"

Q. Why was so much secrecy maintained for the BW project?

A. To keep the information from our enemies. I might mention another reason. It might create a misunderstanding both here and abroad that we were studying BW offensive whereas we were only studying the defensive.

Q. How would you recommend that the subject be treated in the future?

A. It should not be openly discussed among nations.

Q. Why?

A. BW is clearly against humanity. It is the reason why international law forbids its use. Therefore you might say it is not appropriate to discuss the subject and therefore to stir up feeling against it. On the other hand if discussions are for purposes of reassuring and reaffirming the prohibition against its use then it is well to look into the matter. But it is not good for the scientists to say whether it is possible or not.

TOP SECRET

UNITED STATES ARMY FORCES, PACIFIC
Scientific and Technical Advisory Section
Dai-Ichi Bldg - Room 319

Advanced Echelon
APO 500
10 November 1945

SUBJECT: Biological Warfare, (BW).
DATE: 10 November 1945.
INTERVIEWED: General S. SHIMOMURA, War Minister.
INTERVIEWERS: Lt. Col. Murray Sanders; Lt. Harry Youngs.

1. General Shimomura stated that he has held the position of War Minister since August 23, 1945. Previous to that time he was President of the Staff College at the outbreak of war in December 1941. From October 1942 to March 1944 he held the position of Commanding General of the Japanese Army in the Shanghai area. From March 1944 to November 1944 he held the position of Commanding General of Kyushyu district army. From November 1944 until he received the appointment of War Minister he was Commanding General of the Japanese Army in Northern China.

2. General Shimomura expressed the willingness to answer any and all questions asked of him.

3. Q. Who was your predecessor?
A. Prince Higashi Kuni. At that time Prince Kuni held the positions jointly of Premier and War Minister.

Q. How long did Prince Kuni hold the position of War Minister?
A. One week.

Q. Who held the position of War Minister before Prince Kuni?
A. General K. Anami.

Q. How long did General Anami hold the position?
A. From March 1945 to August 1945.

Q. What is the responsibility of the War Minister in development of new weapons?
A. The War Ministry received requests or demands from the General Staff. If the War Ministry accepted the request for new weapons then the War Minister had the responsibility of supplying them.

- 1 -

TOP SECRET

TOP SECRET

Q. Is the War Ministry responsible for the development of new weapons?

A. As a general rule its not the responsibility of the War Ministry to take up the development of new weapons. It is the responsibility of the Chief of General Staff. After the request is made to the War Ministry the War Minister and the Chief of the General Staff have a consultation in regard to the request. Both the War Minister and the Chief of General Staff exchange conferences in relation to new weapons.

Q. In other words the Chief of the General Staff suggests a new weapon, the War Minister is called, and they have a conference. How does the War Minister help the General Staff in the development of the new weapon?

A. The sole responsibility of the War Ministry once it has agreed to the request is to prepare and supply the required amount at the required time. The initiative of thinking out new weapons is not the responsibility of the War Ministry. The War Minister's responsibility is to prepare the production and produce the required amounts of the weapon. However, the War Ministry has the authority to improve the weapon. For example, if the General Staff requires the War Ministry to provide them with a certain number of airplanes capable of the speed of 400 kilometers per hour, then this request is granted. Should the plane be found lacking and the General Staff requests the War Ministry to increase the speed to 500 kilometers per hour, it is their responsibility to provide such planes. However, the initial suggestions for types of new weapons must come from the General Staff.

Q. Does the War Ministry have a research and development function?

A. Yes, it has.

Q. What relationship has the War Ministry had with BW research?

A. I was not aware of what transpired before I took office. So far as I know the General Staff did not make any requests to the War Ministry regarding that problem. And the War Ministry has never issued any instructions on that question.

When I was Chief of Staff College in 1941 just prior to the outbreak of war I discussed the question of new weapons with the Assistant Chief of the General Staff. The discussion was very extensive but no mention of BW was made by the Assistant Chief of General Staff. My reason for asking about new weapons was based on the fact that I

TOP SECRET

TOP SECRET
SECRET

was expected to instruct the students of the college in this subject. Furthermore, I was also interested in the question of BW because I had previously been one of the Japanese delegates to the Geneva Disarmament Conference. The reply which I received was that the Japanese Army was not thinking of using BW as a weapon.

Q. Does this mean that they did not even study the problem from a defensive point of view?

A. I did not consider the question further. Because of my position (I was Lt. Col. at that time).

Q. When you became War Minister did you learn anything about Japanese activities in BW?

A. When I took office I heard nothing of the subject. Later, the director of the Medical Bureau told me that he had been asked by American General Headquarters concerning BW. He said he would answer that the War Minister and General Staff had never instructed the investigation of that question.

Q. Have you acquired any additional knowledge concerning BW since that time?

A. Yes, not through the Chief of the Medical Bureau but from other officers. I was informed that the Ishii Corps in Manchuria had undertaken the question of defensive BW independently without the knowledge of the War Ministry.

Q. From what sources did you obtain the information?

A. This information was given to me by General Yoshizumi, the director of military affairs. I do not know who informed the General in this matter.

I was further interested in this problem because it will be remembered that I was told there had been no activity in BW when I was Chief at the Staff College. In view of this circumstance I wished to know why the work was done by local authorities rather than from the central agencies. General Yoshizumi was unable to answer me satisfactorily and I inquired further. I learned from several officers (I do not remember their names) that the Ishii Corps had studied the problem for the past 10 years. Presumably the initial motive came from a suspicion that the Russians had practiced BW. I thought this was quite possible since in 1935 I was a Staff Officer in the Kwantung Army and the report concerning Soviet intentions was made directly to me.

-3-

SECRET

TOP SECRET
SECRET

Q. In what form did you receive that information?
A. I am not certain. As I recall, information was received that there was an acute outbreak of anthrax in horses. I myself visited the spot where this attack was supposedly perpetrated. I was unable to ascertain whether this incident was due to Soviet Union intrigue. The next year I left Manchuria and was unable to continue the investigation.

Q. Why do you think the Soviet Union was responsible for the outbreak when it is a natural disease in that area?
A. Of course I am not an expert. However, it is my impression that the outbreak was not normal. The area involved was unusually large and the outbreak was unusually acute.

Q. Were Russian spies captured and were they carrying such material?
A. At that time I received no information that such was the case.

Q. Have you ascertained to what extent the Ishii Corps investigated the question of BW?
A. I ascertained that the Boeki Kyusuibu investigated this question from the defense point of view on a broad basis. This, in spite of the fact that the Boeki Kyusuibu's primary function was antiepidemic and the supplying of pure water. Since becoming War Minister I have learned definitely that the Boeki Kyusuibu did carry on defensive BW.

Q. We have been told by General Umezu and others that the Boeki Kyusuibu was organized for the purpose of studying BW and that this followed Soviet activities. Do you know anything about this?
A. I have not met General Umezu in a long time and cannot answer that question. As War Minister I did not think that was within my jurisdiction but belonged to the General Staff.

Q. I must confess that I am surprised that an organization as large as the Boeki Kyusuibu was able to work for 10 years on this problem without the knowledge of the War Ministry. I
A. I quite agree with you. I myself was quite surprised. That is why I wished to investigate the Boeki Kyusuibu.

TOP SECRET

TOP SECRET

Q. As the Commanding General of two Japanese Armies in China did you ever hear of BW?

A. Not when I was Commanding General of the Northern Army. When I commanded the Shanghai area I inspected the central Boeki Kyusuibu installations at Nanking. This inspection lasted about two hours. At that time the Question of BW was entirely out of my mind.

Q. Who was the Chief of the Nanking installation during the inspection?

A. I do not remember.

Q. Was the Commanding Officer a general?

A. No, he was a medical colonel.

Q. Did this medical officer discuss the subject of BW with you?

A. He made a detailed report on every aspect of the Boeki Kyusuibu but did not mention BW. As a matter of fact the only reason that I inspected the Boeki Kyusuibu was because the usual yearly outbreak of cholera which occurred in that area failed to appear in that year (Oct 1943).

Q. Would you care to express an opinion on the problem of BW?

A. I am quite without knowledge on this sort of thing. I am just an administartive officer therefore my opinion is not based on any specific knowledge of the problem. However, I would like to say that; (1) sentimentally I feel it is against humanity, (2) unless this weapon is used ona grand scale at the right time and place its effect will not be important. On the other hand, one must produce great quantities of bacteria, transport them and store them. These technical difficulties cannot be easily overcome particularly in Japan. Thus BW as a weapon would not be feasibleg i.e. in the case of Japan.

4. In conclusion the General wished to state that he had instructed all officers under him to give all information relative to any invetsigation or questions American General Headquarters might ask of them and to cooperate as fully as possible.

-5-

TOP SECRET

**RECORDS OF EXPERIMENTAL WORK
CARRIED OUT AT THE ARMY MEDICAL COLLEGE**

1. During the early days of the BW investigation, it was learned that all experimental records of the Army Medical College in Tokyo had been burned. Further search revealed that a duplicate set of records had been sent to the subsidiary unit at Niigata.

2. The duplicate records were found during the closing days of the BW investigation, after the formal report was concludéd. The records will be sent to the Committee for Surveying Medical Activities in Japan and thence through channels to the War Department, Washington.

3. It is known which papers represent BW research carried out at the Army Medical College in Tokyo. These papers will be translated and should supply the final data for the investigation of Japanese activities in BW.

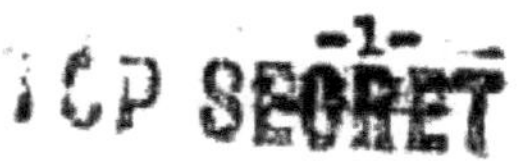

SECRET

DISCUSSION: It is apparent from the interviews which have been recorded that high Japanese Staff and War Ministry officers were either acquainted with only vague generalities in the BW work, or that they were evasive. Clearly, they were well aware of the BW investigation by GHQ, AFPAC and were concerned with the effects which the revelations might have upon their future. However, it is very likely that all the sources of information contributing to this report were not known to the Japanese officials. This assumption is based on the statements occasionally made in the interviews directly contradicting confirmed evidence.

Since no previous attempt has been made to analyse the role of the Soviet in relation to Japanese BW, it might be well to summarize at least a part of the evidence in regard to this question.

While political analysis is not within the province of the present mission, the investigating officers would be negligent of their duty if they did not point out that diatribes against Russian intrigue stem from poorly informed as well as from thoughtful and responsible sources. The colossal effrontery against common sense is thoroughly demonstrated by such a statement as "Originally we had no intention of waging war against the United States. Soviet Union has always been our future possible enemy"* which emanates from no less a person than the recent Chief of Staff. Confused thought and conflicting statements permeate the discussions of the highest Japanese officers and the desire on the part of the investigators to remain objective is strained by frequent and obvious prevarication.

On the other hand, the claim of Russian BW activities is made by almost all informants and can hardly be discounted, without careful evaluation. The contention that anthrax, cholera, and dysentery were deliberately spread in northern Manchuria by Soviet agents is made by two of the best technical sources, Lt. Col. Naito and Col. Masuda. The latter individual went so far as to maintain that he had personally examined specimens taken from spies and that he had demonstrated B. anthracis. While there is no documentary supporting evidence, neither is there available confirmation of some of Masuda's technical data. If details on field tests which were provided by Masuda are to be considered credible, then there is no reason for refusing to accept his information relative to Russian activities.

Another point important to the final evaluation of Japanese BW intentions, is the reason behind the organization of the Boeki Kyusuibu. Here, too, is seen the confusion which

* In his first, unprepared statement, General Umezu said that Japan had never entertained the thought of war except with Russia.

-1-

TOP SECRET
SECRET

disturbs Japanese officialdom. Whereas the assurance has been frequently and blandly made, in the early part of interviews that the Boeki Kyusuibu was formed only for control of epidemics and for supplying the military with pure drinking water, the statement was usually elicited by the end of the conference that its actual *raison d'etre* was to provide an independent organization capable of dealing with BW. Great care has been taken to remove equivocation on this point. Leading questions have not been asked and as much use as possible has been made of information given voluntarily.

Certainly, it was to be expected that a modern nation at war would stress preventive medicine and take strong steps to assure control of epidemics. But it appears equally certain that this is not the whole story of the Boeki Kyusuibu. The impression of the investigating officers in regard to this matter may be summed up as follows; The Boeki Kyusuibu was the BW organization of Japan. The BW activity was a very important responsibility and accounted, at least in some measure, for the powerful and unique position of the Boeki Kyusuibu in the military hierarchy. While the Boeki Kyusuibu served a real purpose in contributing to the general health of Japan's fighting forces, this activity served (in part) as a cloak for the BW investigation. The basis for this impression is not only the recent interviews of General Staff and War Ministry but also the rather numerous interviews and investigations which have been part of the complete BW report. If General Shiro Ishii had succeeded in forging an efficient weapon, there would probably have been nothing to prevent him from using it. It would have only been necessary for him to convince the Japanese General Staff that it could be employed to good purpose, that he could control it, and (possibly) that there would be no repercussions.

-2-

TOP SECRET

BASIC: Memo, GHQ AFPAC, ADV, Scientific and Technical Advisory Section, APO 500, dtd 9 Nov 45, subj: "Supplementary Biological Warfare Information".

AG 385 (9 Nov 45) SIS 1st Ind.

GENERAL HEADQUARTERS, UNITED STATES ARMY FORCES, PACIFIC, APO 500, 2 January 1946.

TO: The Adjutant General, Washington, D. C.

Transmitted in accordance with request contained in radio WX 80140 of 1 November 1945.

FOR THE COMMANDER-IN-CHIEF:

H. W. ALLEN,
Colonel, A.G.D.,
Asst Adjutant General.

RECEIPT ACKNOWLEDGED:
In AGO: 7 Jan 45.
EM/lq 2B-939 Pentagon

TOP SECRET

ARMY SERVICE FORCES

TRANSMITTAL SHEET

EM/lq 2B-939 Pentagon/72401

FILE No.	SUBJECT		
AG 729.2 TS (9 Nov 45)OB-S	Supplementary Biological Warfare Information		
TO	FROM	DATE	COMMENT No. 1
Assistant Chief of Staff, G-2, WDGS	AGO, Operations Br. S & C Section	8 Jan 46	

1 Incl.
Memo fm General Hqs, USAF, Pacific, Scientific and Technical Advisory Section, Advance Echelon, APO 500, 9 Nov 45, to Commander-in-Chief, AFPAC, w/1st Ind. and 4 Incls.
Incl. 1 - Interview of Lt. Gen. Tadakazu WAKAMATSU, 6 Nov. 45
Incl. 2 - Interview of Lt. Gen. Torashiro KAWABE, Asst. Chief, Japanese General Staff, 7 Nov 45
Incl. 3 - Interview of Yoshijiro UMEZU, 8 Nov 45
Incl. 4 - Interview of General S. SHIMOMURA, War Minister, 10 Nov 45

D. E. Boukuight

8 JAN 46 AM

FILE 8 JAN 1946

TOP SECRET

AGASF FORM 897
1 OCT 1943

U. S. GOVERNMENT PRINTING OFFICE

6.1.13　23 Nov. 1945: Report on Japanese Biological Warfare, from Wm. A. Borden, Brigadier General, GSC, Director, New Developments Division

资料出处： National Archives of the United States, R407, B12.

内容点评： 本资料为 1945 年 11 月 23 日新发展部主任、参谋团准将 Wm. A. Borden 提交的《日本科学情报调查报告（1945 年 9~10 月）》第 5 卷《细菌战》摘要。

SECRET

CLASSIFICATION AUTHORIZED BY
Director, NDD
11/23/45
Date Initials

WAR DEPARTMENT
SUMMARY SHEET

FOLD OVER PAPERS AND CLIP

TO			G-4	FOR	1	APPROVAL	FROM	OFFICE OF PREPARATION
	G-1		OPD			SIGNATURE		NDD, WDSS
	G-2	1	CHIEF OF STAFF		2	INFORMATION		GRADE—SURNAME—PHONE
	G-3	2	SECRETARY OF WAR					Col Mills/wgu/73484

FILE NO.	SUBJECT	DATE
	Report on Japanese Biological Warfare	23 Nov 45

Noted H.C.P.
Date 12-5-45 File
(Signed) Howard C. Petersen

SUMMARY

1. Attached for your information is a brief of the "Report on Scientific Intelligence Survey in Japan", (September and October 1945), Volume V, Biological Warfare. This report is based on information obtained from interrogation of responsible Japanese Army and Navy officers now in Japan and is considered "reasonably accurate." Some documentary evidence may be available later.

COORDINATION

2. None required.

Noted H.C.P.
Date 12-5-45
File

John S. Mills
for Col G.S.C.

1 Incl
Rept on Japanese BW

Wm. A. BORDEN
Brigadier General, GSC
Director, New Developments Division

NOTED-DEPUTY CHIEF OF STAFF
U. S. ARMY
27 Nov 45

NOTED BY
SECRETARY OF WAR

WDCSA 385 (23 Nov 45) Secret
(SW 385 (11-23-45) Secret

69.11/26

SECRET

W.D., A.G.O. Form No. 520
26 August 1944

16—41232-1

This form supersedes W. D., A. G. O. Form No. 520, 1 April 1944, which may be used until existing stocks are exhausted.

INSTRUCTIONS

PURPOSE.—Summary Sheet is used to summarize for quick reading in Office, Chief of Staff, papers prepared by War Department General Staff or by major commands for signature or other action in Office, Chief of Staff or Office, Secretary of War. Papers prepared for signature or other action in Office, Secretary of War, but not channeled through Office, Chief of Staff, do not require Summary Sheet. In general, use of Summary Sheet is limited to following:

1. In place of short memorandum for Chief of Staff recommending action or transmitting letter or other paper to be signed or otherwise acted upon in Office, Chief of Staff or Office, Secretary of War. Tissue copy of sheet is prepared for Office, Chief of Staff, as well as comeback and stayback if necessary.

2. As brief of long memorandum for Chief of Staff (three pages or more). Tissue copy of sheet is not necessary.

ROUTING.—Routing information and action requested are indicated by "x," check (√), or number in appropriate box. As Summary Sheet clears each office, abbreviation of that office in routing box is lined out and papers are forwarded to next office indicated on sheet.

IDENTIFICATION.—Office symbol or abbreviation of office of preparation, grade, surname, and telephone number of dictator, file reference, subject, and date are placed in boxes indicated. File number and subject should be as brief as possible consistent with clarity.

COMPOSITION.—Information presented on Summary Sheet should be sufficiently condensed to be contained on face of sheet, although second page on plain bond may be prepared if necessary. Headings used on Summary Sheet are: SUMMARY and COORDINATION.

Under SUMMARY is stated as concisely as possible essential background information on recommended action or on letter or other paper (if any) transmitted for action.

Under COORDINATION are stated organizations and individuals from whom concurrence or nonconcurrence has been obtained and explanation of unresolved concurrences (if any).

INCLOSURES.—Inclosures are listed according to military practice and begin even with left margin on same line as typed signature.

SIGNATURE.—When papers are prepared in major command, signature on Summary Sheet is that of officer authorized by commanding general to sign; when prepared in War Department General Staff, that of head of division or his authorized representative.

APPROVAL.—Approval of commanding general of major command or of head of division of War Department General Staff, or their authorized representatives, is indicated on Summary S[illegible] [illegible]itials or name of approving officer above approval stamp or above typed or stamp[illegible]ature.

U. S. GOVERNMENT PRINTING OFFICE 16—41232-1

SECRET

BRIEF OF REPORT ON JAPANESE BIOLOGICAL WARFARE

1. From 1936 to the end of the war the Japanese Army was actively engaged in both defensive and offensive Biological Warfare research and development (an activity which was apparently carried on without the knowledge of, and possibly even contrary to the wishes of, the Emperor). The Navy interest was only in defensive BW. Two factors apparently stimulated this type of activity, namely: (a) the driving influence of Lt. Gen. Shiro ISHII and (b) the firm belief that the Russians and Chinese had engaged in BW against the Japanese. The principal BW center was located at Pingfan (near Harbin, Manchuria). This installation was self-sufficient with a garrison of 3000 at its peak (1939-40), being reduced to 1500 in 1945.

2. The defensive activity consisted largely in: (a) organization of fixed and mobile preventive medicine units, (b) accelerated vaccine production program and (c) BW education of medical officers.

3. Offensively, the principal objective appears to have been the development of a suitable BW munition, and at least eight types of bacterial disseminating bombs were tested with approximately four thousand (4000) being used in field trials at Pingfan.

4. Of the pathogenic organisms under investigation, those of the gastro-intestinal diseases (cholera, dysentery, typhoid and para-typhoid A and B) and those causing plague, anthrax and glanders were studied most intensely as possible BW agents. The virus-rickettsial group was not considered.

5. It is believed that the Japanese were at no time in a position to wage BW successfully on a large scale in spite of nearly ten years research. This failure apparently is due in part to: (a) limited or improper selection of BW agents, (b) denial or even prohibition of cooperated scientific effort, (c) lack of cooperation of various Army components, (d) lack of use of civilian scientists and (e) policy of retrenchment at a critical period in the development of the project.

SECRET

Incl.

6.1.14　21 Dec. 1945: Japanese Biological Warfare Intelligence, from J. M. BARNES, Lt. Col., R.A.M.C.

资料出处：National Archives of the United States, R407, B12.

内容点评：本资料为 1945 年 12 月 21 日英国皇家陆军军医队中校 J. M. Barnes 提交的日本细菌战情报报告，附《日本科学情报调查报告（1945 年 9~10 月）》第 5 卷《细菌战》综述。

BIO/7453

233036

JAPANESE BIOLOGICAL WARFARE INTELLIGENCE

A report from U.S.A. of approximately 60 pages, together with a ground plan and several drawings of BW munitions, has been received and a summary is attached.

The report consists of a general summary of Japanese BW activities together with some information on the policy of the Japanese military authorities. This information was collected in a series of interviews and interrogations of Japanese officers in Tokyo. Summaries of these interrogations are given as appendices.

No documents or experimental protocols were available to the interrogators, and the drawings included in the report were based on sketches supplied by the Japanese to Colonel Sanders.

The Japanese had a large installation situated near Harbin, Manchuria, which had been investigating the offensive aspects of BW for at least 8 years, and the work had continued until the surrender. At least 2,000 BW bombs were exploded in field trials. Despite all this work, the report has practically no technical information of value, and what little there is suggests the work was carried out in a strangely crude and amateurish manner. The Japanese claim that the whole institute and its contents were destroyed in August 1945 before the place was occupied by the Russians.

The greater part of the information on the work of this institute was obtained from two officers who had worked there for a period of years. It should, therefore, be possible by more detailed interrogation to get more technical details from them.

On the whole the intelligence already received before the fall of Japan and summarized in B.W.I.C. Periodical Summary No.3 (M.I.10/4388 dated 27/6/45) seems to have been fairly good. Major-General Ishii was in charge of the BW program and the laboratory at Pingfan, near Harbin, was part of the Water Purification Department. Directives found on Japanese prisoners were the result of the policy of briefing medical and police officers on the possibilities of BW. This briefing was carried into the lowest echelons.

The Mark 7 'Bacillus bomb' was a naval weapon. It does not appear to have at any time developed beyond the stage of a crude drawing. It did however appear on official naval munition lists. The Navy claim that they never took any part in the work on BW.

This report throws little light on the policy of the Japanese Supreme Command with regard to BW. The General Staff in Tokyo seem to have denied having done any active work on the subject, though admitting they did expect the U.S.A. to use the weapon as they had already used petrol on the rice fields. No active precautionary measures were taken. General Ishii was the head of the Water Purification Department of the Kwantung armies. These are generally considered to have been the extremists of the Japanese and to have done many things independently of the Tokyo authorities. They might almost be considered to be in a similar position to the SS in Germany. In addition they provide useful scapegoats for the other official bodies.

J. M. BARNES

21.12.45

Lt.-Col., R.A.M.C.

INCLOSURE 1 TO REPORT NO. R179-46
MILITARY ATTACHE, LONDON

SECRET

233031-1

SUMMARY OF "REPORT ON SCIENTIFIC INTELLIGENCE SURVEY IN JAPAN - SEPTEMBER AND OCTOBER 1945, VOLUME V, BIOLOGICAL WARFARE"

issued by GHQ; U.S. Army Forces, Pacific. Scientific and Technical Section, 1st November 1945.

Sources of Information

The following officers were interrogated on one or more occasions in Tokyo:-

Lt.Gen. KAMBAYASHI Surgeon General to the Army
Vice-Adm. HORI *Chief Naval Surgeon*
Colonel INOUE Director, Dept. of Bacteriology, Army Medical College
Lt.Col. NAITO Director, Water Supply and Sera Drying, Ditto.
Lt.Col. NIIZUMA Controller of Technical Research (inc. medicine and veterinary medicine) for the Army.
Major KANEKO, Medical Corps. Worked at Pingfan 1937-41
Colonel MASUDA, Medical Corps. Worked at Pingfan 1937-9, 1941-3 and April-August 1945

Policy

The Surgeon General for the Army stated that he personally was opposed to the use of BW on humanitarian and practical grounds. He did not believe it could be effective unless a new organism unknown to their enemies could be made use of. He stated that as far as he knew no offensive studies on BW had been made. He admitted the possibility that the Kwantung armies had carried out research unknown to the authorities in Tokyo. The Chief Naval Surgeon also denied any knowledge of work on BW. No special protective clothing against a BW attack had been prepared nor had respirators been tested. According to the controller of technical research for the Army, the responsibility for work on BW was in the hands of the Surgeon General. He, himself, had made no provision for BW research in his budgets. He stated that the Japanese believed the U.S. might use BW but that they had not made any defensive preparations as they considered them likely to be of no avail against the overwhelming air superiority of the U.S.

The Surgeon General knew of General Ishii but apparently the latter was not popular in Tokyo and was considered a pushing type of officer.

Origin of Japanese BW Program

Two versions of this were forthcoming. According to Colonel NAITO agitation began in 1932 when Major Ishii returned from a tour of Europe. The Japanese believed that as BW had been prohibited in the Geneva protocols, some authorities at least must have considered it feasible. Ishii continued his agitation until finally the War Ministry in 1937 agreed to provide means for carrying out this work. An institute was started at Pingfan and additions to this had been made every year since that time. Pingfan is about 30 kilometers from Harbin in Manchuria.

According to Colonel Masuda the first application for permission to work on BW came from General Ishii in 1935. Ishii was then the director of the Water Purification Department of the Kwantung armies in Manchuria. At this time a number of Russian spies were captured and bottles of bacterial cultures were found in their possession. Masuda claimed to have actually seen some anthrax cultures himself. Ishii was granted permission to undertake offensive BW studies.

SECRET

233836 - 2

Organisation

The Water Purification Departments (WPD) were an important part of the Medical services of the Japanese armies. There were separate departments at Army group levels and each of these had smaller units down to, and including the divisional Water Purification Unit. There were five permanent stations of the WPD at Harbin, Peking, Nanking, Canton and Singapore.

The normal duties of these units were:-

a) Prevention of infectious diseases
b) Water purification
c) Investigation of epidemics

The WPD for the Kwantung armies had its HQ at Harbin and was under General Ishii. The original laboratories were at the Military Hospital in Harbin. When Ishii started his work on BW an experimental station was constructed at Pingfan. At first only the field trials were carried out here, but in 1940 with the completion of more buildings all the laboratory work was transferred here. The ground plan shows it to have been quite an extensive station with laboratories for the production of vaccines and serum drying etc. The garrison was at one time 3,000 and in 1945 had fallen to 1,500. All the buildings and the records and equipment were destroyed before the Russians occupied the place. This was according to Masuda who only left Manchuria in August 1945.

Both the officers who worked at Pingfan were outspoken in their criticisms of the organisation. There was little collaboration with experts in the different problems they tried to tackle and only poor quality materials were made available to them. There were men working on BW problems in different sections of the institute, but they were not allowed to discuss progress with others. All of them apparently worked only under direct orders from Ishii.

Work at the Pingfan Institute

In the absence of documents and protocols, technical details of the work carried out are very vague and incomplete.

The normal activities of the institute, functioning as headquarters of the WPD, were divided into 4 sections:

1) Immunology (including typhoid and the enteric group, anthrax and virus and rickettsial diseases)
2) Epidemiology
3) Water supplies and purification
4) Vaccine production

The scope of their normal activities can be judged from the statement that over 20 million doses of vaccine were turned out every year. As stated above the workers on BW were scattered in all departments and Masuda stated that only he and General Ishii knew the whole story.

In 1937 Masuda was put in charge of the bomb development section and by 1939 two different types of bomb had been produced. (Sketches of these are included). He stated that since 1939 no new bombs had been developed apart from an abortive attempt to produce a radio controlled cluster projectile. By 1945 no practical BW bomb had been developed or produced.

23076-3

- 3 -

SECRET

They began by considering a number of possible agents which included in the main the enteric group together with glanders and anthrax. Work was done entirely with liquid suspensions of cultures on account of the dangers of using dried suspensions. A few experiments on the survival of crude liquid suspensions of organisms gave such disappointing results that work was soon confined to anthrax with B. prodigiosus as a simulant. Even the spore suspensions of anthrax were said to die out in 3 months.

All growth was carried out on solid media and no experiments were said to have been done on investigating liquid cultures for growth on a large scale. Small duralumin tanks were used for production of bacteria for field trials. About 900 of these were needed to produce the material necessary for a trial. (Since it is said that all work has been done on solid media, it is possible that "trays" are intended instead of "tanks").

Details of the trials are lacking except the statement that in work on anthrax over a period of two years 100 horses and 500 sheep were used. How these animals were exposed is not stated except a reference to the use of infected steel fragments.

No cloud chamber work was done and the only work on cloud estimations in the field is described for dyed broth exploded in bombs. Particles were collected and measured on cards at different distances from the bomb. It is stated that by this method particles down to 50 microns could be detected. There is no mention of methods used for assaying bacterial clouds.

Sprays from aircraft were tried. Using broth thickened with 50% glycerin they found that sprays released from 4,000 metres took an hour to reach the ground. Sprays from lower altitudes had been tried but details were lacking.

A group of about 75 men were available for carrying out field trials. Several accidents occurred. One man died of pulmonary anthrax after mowing the grass on the site of a trial made on the previous day. Two men died of glanders in the early days and work on this agent was suspended. Two men died of plague in 1944. (There is no other reference to any work with this agent.)

The men were issued with rubberised suits (plague suits) and after the trials stripped and washed in 2% cresol or mercuric chloride. Workers and officers at the institute received higher rates of pay.

There is no mention of any work on the mass production of organisms in preparation for a possible offensive.

On the defensive side there was the large scale production of vaccines and sera. This was part of the normal work of the institute and it is impossible to determine what part of this program had any bearing on work going on with BW.

The Japanese policy in China included the careful briefing of medical officers and police officers into the possibilities of BW sabotage. Thus all epidemics were to be looked on as possibly originating from some act of BW sabotage until proved otherwise.

6.2 Arvo T. Thompson 调查

6.2.1 11 Jan. 1946: Stenographic Transcript of Interrogation of Lieutenant General MASAJI KITANO in Tokyo by Colonel S. E. Whitesides and Colonel A. H. Schwichtemberg

资料出处：Fort Detrick, US.

内容点评：1945 年 11 月，美国第二任调查官 A. T. Thompson 中校到达日本前，对日本相关人员的讯问由 S. E. Whitesides 上校和 A. H. Schwichtemberg 上校进行。本资料为 731 部队第二任部队长北野政次（Masaji Kitano）中将的讯问记录。

Stenographic Transcript of Interrogation of

Lt. General MASAJI KITANO in Tokyo

By Colonel S. E. Whitesides and Colonel A. H. Schwichtenberg

On 11 January 1946

INTERROGATIONS. JAPANESE
STENOGRAPHIC TRANSCRIPTS
JAN-FEB 46

013

Stenographic Transcript of Interrogation of

Lt. General MASAJI KITANO in Tokyo

By Colonel S. E. Whitesides and Colonel A. H. Schwichtenberg

On 11 January 1946

COLONEL WHITESIDES : We want to get some information on your Harbin medical installations, chiefly on BW. We realize that on your defensive work you had to work somewhat on offensive to determine your defensive action. What was your position at the Harbin medical installation? Give dates and details.

GENERAL KITANO : Up to 1 August 1942 I was professor of microbiology at the Manchurian Medical College. After that, I replaced General ISHII as Water Purification Chief of the Kwantung Army.

COLONEL WHITESIDES : Were you prepared at any time to use BW as a weapon? If not, why not?

GENERAL KITANO : No. We were not prepared to use it.

COLONEL WHITESIDES : Why were you not prepared?

GENERAL KITANO : In my opinion, it is not good to use BW in warfare and, if used, it is not effective.

COLONEL WHITESIDES : Were you prepared to use it if you had been directed to do so?

GENERAL KITANO : If higher authorities had given the order, I and General KOBAYASHI would have dissented.

COLONEL WHITESIDES : Do you know where General ISHII is?

GENERAL KITANO : I do not know his present whereabouts. I was succeeded by General ISHII which makes him head of the Water Purification Bureau after I left in March 1945.

COLONEL WHITESIDES : What organisms were used in field trials at the Harbin installation or elsewhere?

GENERAL KITANO : Paratyphoid (mostly type A), typhoid, cholera, and pest (plague), and anthrax.

COLONEL WHITESIDES : Any others?

GENERAL KITANO : Dysentery, gas gangrene, and tetanus. My experiments were not conducted in the lines of warfare.

COLONEL WHITESIDES : What prevented you from developing BW as a weapon then?

GENERAL KITANO : It is not good to use BW in warfare and, in my opinion, it is not effective. My work was only along experimental lines.

1127

COLONEL WHITESIDES : Do you think the Harbin installation is still intact?

GENERAL KITANO : The Russians have taken it over and I do not know what has happened to it.

COLONEL WHITESIDES : What amount of time was spent on the research and the other work on protection?

GENERAL KITANO : There was nothing devoted to BW, no time at all.

COLONEL WHITESIDES : How many BW bombs did they drop in tests?

GENERAL KITANO : I do not know the exact figures. I think it is in several tens.

COLONEL WHITESIDES : Do you know what was in the bombs?

GENERAL KITANO : Anthrax.

COLONEL WHITESIDES : Who conducted these tests?

GENERAL KITANO : The second section, under Lt. Colonel IKARI.

COLONEL WHITESIDES : Did these tests have any connection with the Manchurian Medical College.

GENERAL KITANO : No connection.

COLONEL WHITESIDES : Where were these bombs made and, chiefly, where were the bacteria made?

GENERAL KITANO : The section made the bacteria. The bombs were already there when I arrived.

COLONEL WHITESIDES : Did you see the bombs?

GENERAL KITANO : Yes. There were four types.

COLONEL WHITESIDES : Did they have the "mother and daughter" type?

GENERAL KITANO : I do not know.

COLONEL WHITESIDES : Did they have any porcelain bombs?

GENERAL KITANO : Yes.

COLONEL WHITESIDES : Did they have any projectiles for artillery?

GENERAL KITANO : They had been working on that before I went there. Shells were effective only at short range.

COLONEL WHITESIDES : How much did they weigh?

GENERAL KITANO : They were in the form of 50 kilo and 100 kilo bombs. But actually they did not weigh that much.

COLONEL SCHWICHTENBERG: Can you give an estimate of what they did weigh?

Called 50 kilo

GENERAL KITANO : I think the ones that were [illegible] kilo weighed about 20 kilo and the 100 kilo [illegible] kilo.

COLONEL [illegible]: Give an estimate of the [illegible] of the [illegible] ingredients in the bombs.

GENERAL KITANO : I do not know.

COLONEL [illegible] : Do you know Captain Shinjiro [illegible]?

GENERAL KITANO : There was no one by that name under my command. [illegible] is a person by that name who is a [illegible] at Kyoto Imperial University.

COLONEL [illegible] : Could he have been in the Manchurian Medical College?

GENERAL KITANO : I do not know this man. There is a Shinjiro [illegible] at Kyoto Imperial University.

COLONEL [illegible] : Was Shinjiro [illegible] in Manchuria?

GENERAL KITANO : No.

COLONEL [illegible] : Is he a captain?

GENERAL KITANO : No.

COLONEL [illegible] : What is he a professor of?

GENERAL KITANO : Same field as I.

COLONEL [illegible] : What is the status of the Manchurian Medical College [illegible]

GENERAL KITANO : It has been taken over by the Russians. I know nothing about it.

COLONEL [illegible] : Have you heard anything at all since you left?

GENERAL KITANO : I have had no word since I left.

COLONEL [illegible]: Have you heard any rumors?

GENERAL KITANO : Up to the end of the war the college was in [illegible].

COLONEL [illegible] : Have you heard [illegible] two hospitals [illegible] of Harbin?

GENERAL KITANO : I have not heard anything about it.

COLONEL [illegible] : On these tests [illegible] they use them against?

GENERAL KITANO : Monkeys, rats, squirrels, and other [illegible] animals.

COLONEL [illegible] : Did you ever hear of any Chinese prisoners being used in these tests?

GENERAL KITANO : No. We never at all used [illegible].

COLONEL [illegible] : What effectiveness did you find on these tests on [illegible] animals?

GENERAL KITANO : I saw the animals die of the explosion of the bombs.

COLONEL WHITESIDES : What type of bomb was most effective?

GENERAL KITANO : Anthrax.

COLONEL WHITESIDES : What type bomb was most effective; 50 kilo or 100 kilo?

GENERAL KITANO : 100 kilo.

COLONEL WHITESIDES : What job did General ISHII have when you were in charge of water purification of the Kwantung Army?

GENERAL KITANO : He was Commander-General of the 1st Army which was located west of Peiping.

COLONEL WHITESIDES : How long had General ISHII been with the Kwantung Army when you relieved him?

GENERAL KITANO : He had been there since the founding of the unit.

Stenographic Transcript of Interrogation of
Lt. General MASAJI KITANO in Tokyo
By Colonel S.E. Whitesides and Colonel A.H. Schwichtemberg
On 11 January 1946

COLONEL WHITESIDES : We want to get some information on your Harbin medical installations, chiefly on BW. We realize that on your defensive work you had to work somewhat on offensive to determine your defensive action, What was your position at the Harbin medical installation? Give dates and details.

GENERAL KITANO : Up to 1 August 1942 I was professor of microbiology at the Manchurian Medical College. After that, I replaced General ISHII as Water Purification Chief of the Kwantung Army.

COLONEL WHITESIDES : Were you prepared at any time to use BW as a weapon? If not, why not?

GENERAL KITANO : No. We were not prepared to use it.

COLONEL WHITESIDES : Why were you not prepared?

GENERAL KITANO : In my opinion, it is not good to use BW in warfare and, if used, it is not effective.

COLONEL WHITESIDES : Were you prepared to use it if you had been directed to do so?

GENERAL KITANO : If higher authorities had given the order, I and General KOBAYASHI would have dissented.

COLONEL WHITESIDES : Do you know where General ISHII is?

GENERAL KITANO : I do not know his present whereabouts. I was succeeded by General ISHII which makes him head of the Water Purification Bureau after I left in March 1945.

COLONEL WHITESIDES : What organisms were used in field trials at the Harbin installation or elsewhere?

GENERAL KITANO : Paratyphoid (mostly type A), typhoid, cholera, pest (plague), and anthrax.

COLONEL WHITESIDES : Any others?

GENERAL KITANO : Dysentery, gas gangrene, and tetanus. My experiments were not conducted in the lines of warfare.

COLONEL WHITESIDES : What prevented you from developing BW as a weapon then?

GENERAL KITANO : It is not good to use BW in warfare and, in my opinion, it is not effective. My work was only along experimental lines.

COLONEL WHITESIDES : Do you think the Harbin installation is still intact?

GENERAL KITANO : The Russians have taken it over and I do not know what has happened to it.

COLONEL WHITESIDES : What amount of time was spent on the research and the other work on protection?

GENERAL KITANO : There was nothing devoted to BW, no time at all.

COLONEL WHITESIDES : How many BW bombs did they drop in tests?

GENERAL KITANO : I do not know the exact figures. I think it is in several tens.

COLONEL WHITESIDES : Do you know what was in the bombs?

GENERAL KITANO : Anthrax.

COLONEL WHITESIDES : Who conducted these tests?

GENERAL KITANO : The second section, under Lt. Colonel IKARI

COLONEL WHITESIDES : Did those tests have any connection with the Manchurian Medical College?

GENERAL KITANO : No connection.

COLONEL WHITESIDES : Where were those bombs made and, chiefly, where were the bacteria made?

GENERAL KITANO : The section made the bacteria. The bombs were already there when I arrived.

COLONEL WHITESIDES : Did you see the bombs?

GENERAL KITANO : Yes. There were four types.

COLONEL WHITESIDES : Did they have the 'mother and daughter' type?

GENERAL KITANO : I do not know.

COLONEL WHITESIDES : Did they have any porcelain bombs?

GENERAL KITANO : Yes.

COLONEL WHITESIDES : Did they have any projectiles for artillery?

GENERAL KITANO : They had been working on that before I went there. Shells were effective only at short range.

COLONEL WHITESIDES : How much did they weigh?

GENERAL KITANO : They were in the form of 50 kilo and 100 kilo bombs but actually they did not weigh that much.

COLONEL SCHWICHTEMBERG: Can you give an estimate of what they did weigh?

GENERAL KITANO : I think the case that were called 50 kilo weighed about 20 kilo and the 100 kilo weighed about ? kilo.

COLONEL SCHWICHTEMBERG: Give an estimate of the weight of the entire ingredients in the bomb.

GENERAL KITANO : I do not know.

COLONEL WHITESIDES : Do you know Captain Shinjiro xxxxxx?

GENERAL KITANO : There was no one by that name under my command. xx is a person by that name the is a professor at Kyoto Imperial University.

COLONEL WHITESIDES : Could he have been in the Manchurian Medical College?

GENERAL KITANO : I do not know this name. There is a Shinjiro xxxxx at Kyoto Imperial University.

COLONEL WHITESIDES : Was xxxjiro xxxxx in Manchuria?

GENERAL KITANO : No.

COLONEL WHITESIDES : Is he a captain?

GENERAL KITANO : No.

COLONEL WHITESIDES : What is he a professor of?

GENERAL KITANO : Same field as I.

COLONEL WHITESIDES : What is the status of the Manchurian Medical College now?

GENERAL KITANO : It has been taken over by the Russians. I know nothing about it.

COLONEL WHITESIDES : Have you heard anything at all since you left?

GENERAL KITANO : I have had no work since I left.

COLONEL SCHWICHTEMBERG: Have you heard only rumors?

GENERAL KITANO : Up to the end of the war the xxxxx was in Manchuria.

COLONEL WHITESIDES : Have you heard what has happened to the x...x of Harbin?

GENERAL KITANO : I have not heard anything about it.

COLONEL WHITESIDES : On these tests, which BW tests were done x...x.

GENERAL KITANO	: Monkeys, rats, squirrels, and other small animals.
COLONEL WHITESIDES	: Did you ever hear of any Chinese prisoners being used in these tests?
GENERAL KITANO	: No. No humans at all were used in xxxxx China.
COLONEL WHITESIDES	: What effectiveness did you x…x animals?
GENERAL KITANO	: I saw the animals die of the explosion of the bomb.
COLONEL WHITESIDES	: What type of bomb was most effective?
GENERAL KITANO	: Anthrax.
COLONEL WHITESIDES	: What type bomb was most effective? 50 kilo or 100 kilo?
GENERAL KITANO	: 100 kilo.
COLONEL WHITESIDES	: What job did General ISHII have when you were in charge of water purification of the Kwantung Army?
GENERAL KITANO	: He was Surgeon-General of the 1st Army which was located west of Peiping. .
COLONEL WHITESIDES	: How long had General ISHII been with the Kwangtung Army when you relieved him?
GENERAL KITANO	: He had been there since the founding of the unit.

6.2.2 5 Feb. 1946: Stenographic Transcript of Interrogation of Lt. General SHIRO ISHII in Tokyo by Lt. Colonel A. T. Thompson

资料出处： Fort Detrick, US.

内容点评： 本资料为 1946 年 2 月 5 日调查官 A. T. Thompson 在东京对 731 部队首任部队长石井四郎（Shiro Ishii）中将讯问的记录。

Stenographic Transcript of Interrogation.

Of Lt. General ISHII SHIRO in Tokyo

By Lt. Colonel A. T. Thompson

On 5 February 1946

Stenographic Transcript of Interrogation

Of Lt. General SHIRO ISHII in Tokyo

By Lt. Colonel A. T. Thompson

On 5 February 1946

A demonstration of the four water purification apparatus and the one culture apparatus was made. General ISHII also present the completed answers to the questionnaire on field trials. He also presented information in chart form on institutions and personnel concerned with BW research. Also presented was a chart giving the titles of experiments or work conducted at the Hoibo Institute.

Q: You did no BW work except at the Army Medical college and at Hoibo?

A: BW work was done only at Hoibo. Only general preventive medical science was conducted at the Army Medical College.

Q: Was any work done at the Kyoto Imperial University?

A: The professor there did not like that kind of work, so none was undertaken.

Q: The research work was limited to Hoibo institute?

A: Only at Hoibo. A lot of men in my unit and others who do not know anything about it have been spreading rumors to the effect that some secret work has been carried on in BW and they have gone as far as saying an attack with BW was planned by my unit and that a lot of bacteria were being produced, large quantities of bombs manufactured and airplanes being gathered for that purpose. I want you to have a clear understanding that this is false.

Q: In other words, no work was conducted on BW except at the Hoibo institute?

A: That is correct.

Q: Did you expect the enemy to use BW?

A: In my opinion, some countries might.

Q: Which countries did you expect to use it?

A: Soviet Russia and China. They had used it previously and I expected them to use it again.

Q: What did you expect from the United States in the field of BW?

A: I did not think the United States would use BW.

Q: Why?

A: I believed since the United States had money and materials, they would use more scientific methods of warfare.

Q: Do you think BW is practical?

A: You have to have much money and materials to create conditions favorable to BW.

Q: Do you think BW is something that nations will have to contend with in the future?

A: In a winning war, there is no necessity for using BW and in a losing war, there is not the opportunity to use BW effectively. You need a lot of men, money and materials to conduct research into BW. There is little data on the effectiveness of BW as a weapon. I do not know whether BW can be used effectively on a large scale. It might be effective on a small scale.

Q: Do you mean sabotage?

A: It might be effective in such methods of sabotage as dropping bacteria into wells.

Q: It might be effective under those conditions?

A: I believe such methods could be controlled by my methods of water purification. I heard over the radio that Russia had completed its preparations for BW and it frightened me, but I did not know whether it was actual fact or just was printed in "Red Star" or some other newspaper as a "scare." I do not know how far they have advanced in BW and have wondered what they would use if they attacked with BW.

Q: What bacteria do you think the Russians might use?

A: Tularemia, typhus fever, cholera, anthrax, pest.

Q: What makes you believe that the Russians would use these organisms?

A: I heard reports from people returned from Russia that the Russians had been using these organisms in their preparation for BW.

Q: Would it not be difficult to produce typhus organisms on a large scale?

A: If you could produce a lot of lice you might be able to produce a lot of typhus. German and Polish vaccine is prepared from lice. Trouble with lice is that you have to have human infectious blood to infect the lice. Weil's disease is produced in the same manner and it is very hard to get large quantities. If a country was rich enough, it might be able to make that disease a dangerous weapon.

Q: Was any research conducted on BW against food plants?

A: We did not do any experiments on it. Our work was to protect the soldiers.

Q: Did anyone else concern themselves with BW against crop plants?

A: I do not know.

Q: Were you concerned with BW against animals?

A: We did not do any experiments on large animals. We used small animals as test animals. Besides, we had no veterinarians.

Q: Did veterinary laboratories do any research on BW?

A: I do not know. It was such a secret that there was no communication between units Even personnel working on experiments in my unit did not know what they were working on. Only myself, Colonel MASUDA, and one or two other persons knew.

Q: Who were the other persons?

A: There were some who suspected what was going on, but did not know. Colonel MASUDA, Tomosada, and myself knew.

Q: What section of the EM institute did the BW work?

A: When these experiments came up, a number of men from each group were picked out to do the work. They were only together temporarily and were disbanded when the experiment was completed.

Q: Were all the people in such groups informed of the nature of the work?

A: They were not informed of what they were doing. They protested that they could not carry on with their own experiments and that their regular work was being interfered with.

Q: Could not more progress have been made if those working on the experiment had been told what it was all about?

A: If they had known what they were working on they would have shrunk up from fright and asked for more pay. They were not well-trained men and were usually picked from the ranks.

Q: A soldier is a soldier and could you not have ordered them to do the work?

A: They were not soldiers. They were reservists. Those in the branch units were soldiers, but not those in the main unit. I could not order them.

Q: How much research cooperation was given by the Navy on BW?

A: There was no cooperation whatsoever.

Q: Did not some naval medical officers attend your lectures at the Army Medical College?

A: No. Naval officers are too proud. They do not have any brains, but their noses are high.

Q: From captured documents, we are given to understand that certain naval personnel received additional pay for hazardous work which included work with bacteria and certain poison gasses. Evidently, the Navy must have had some part in it. Why did one personnel receive extra pay?

A: I received no reports from the Navy and I heard nothing about it. The number of medical men in the Navy is less than 10 per cent of those in the Army and I doubt if they had any men capable of conduction experiments.

Q: What training in BW was given to the Kempei Tai?

A: There is a Military Police unit in Nakano-ku which was given training by some medical officers from the Army Medical College. It was just a basic information course on how to discover and report BW incidents.

Q: Who conducted these courses?

A: Colonel MASUDA, Tomosada, and Colonel NAITO, Ryoichi.

Q: Would it be possible to obtain copies of their lectures?

A: I will try to find out.

Interpreter : 2nd Lt. F. H. Ellis
Interpreter : T/Sgt. Toshio Kitamura
Stenographer : T/4 K. A. Haack

Stenographic Transcript of Interrogation
Of Lt. General SHIRO ISHII in Tokyo
By Lt. Colonel A.T. Thompson
On 5 February 1946

A demonstration of the four water purification apparatus and the one culture apparatus was made. General ISHII also present the completed answers to the questionnaire on field trials. He also presented information in chart form on institutions and personnel concerned with BW research. Also presented was a chart giving the titles of experiments or work conducted at the Heibo institute.

Q. You did no BW work except at the Army Medical College and at Heibo?

A. BW work was done only at HEIBO. Only general preventive medical science was conducted at the Army Medical College.

Q. Was any work done at the Kyoto Imperial University?

A. The professor there did not like that kind of work, so none was undertaken.

Q. The research work was limited to Heibo institute?

A. Only at Heibo. A lot of men in my unit and others who do not know anything about it have been spreading rumors to the effect that some secret work has been carried on in BW and they have gone as far as saying an attack with BW was planned by my unit and that a lot of bacteria were being produced, large quantities of bombs manufactured and airplanes being gathered for that purpose. I want you to have a clear understanding that this is false.

Q. In other words, no work was conducted on BW except at the Heibo institute?

A. That is correct.

Q. Did you expect the enemy to use BW?

A. In my opinion, some countries might.

Q. Which countries did you expect to use it?

A. Soviet Union and China. They had used it previously and I expected them to use it again.

Q. What did you expect from the United States in the field of BW?

A. I did not think the United States would use BW.

Q. Why?

A. I believed since the United States had money and materials, they would use more scientific methods of warfare.

Q. Do you think BW is practical?

A. You have to have much money and materials to create conditions favorable to BW.

Q. Do you think BW is something that nations will have to contend with in the future?

A. In a winning war, there is no necessity for using BW and in a losing war, there is not the opportunity to use BW effectively. You need a lot of men,, money and materials to conduct research into BW. There is little data on the effectiveness of BW as a weapon. I do not know whether BW can be used effectively on a large scale. It might be effective on a small scale.

Q. Do you mean sabotage?

A. It might be effective in such methods of sabotage as dropping bacteria into wells.

Q. It might be effective under those conditions?

A. I believe such methods could be controlled by my methods of water purification. I heard over the radio that Russia had completed its preparations for BW and it frightened me, but I did not know whether it was actual fact or just was printed in "Red Star" or some other newspaper as a "scare." I do not know how far they have advanced in BW and have wondered what they would use if they attacked with BW.

Q. What bacteria do you think the Russians might use?

A. Tularemia, typhus fever, cholera, anthrax, pest.

Q. What makes you believe that the Russians would use these organisms?

A. I heard reports from people returned from Russia that the Russians had been using these organisms in their preparation for BW.

Q. Would it not be difficult to produce typhus organisms on a large scale?

A. If you could produce a lot of lice you might be able to produce a lot of typhus. German and Polish vaccine is prepared from lice. Trouble with lice is that you have to have human infectious blood to infect the lice. Weil's disease is produced in the same manner and it is very hard to get large quantities. If a country was rich enough, it might be able to make that disease a dangerous weapon.

Q. Was any research conducted on BW against food plants?

A. We did not do any experiments on it. Our work was to protect the soldiers.

Q. Did anyone else concern themselves with BW against crop plants?

A. I do not know.

Q. Were you concerned with BW agents against animals?

A. We did not do any experiments on large animals. We used small animals as test animals. Besides, we had no veterinarians.

Q. Did veterinary laboratories do any research on BW?

A. I do not know. It was such a secret that there was no communication between units. Even personnel working on experiments in my unit did
not know what they were working on. Only myself, Colonel MASUDA, and one or two other persons know.

Q. Who were the other persons?

A. There were some who suspected what was going on, but did not know. Colonel MASUDA, Tomosada, and myself know.

Q. What section of the BW institute did the BW work?

A. When those experiments came up, a number of men from each group were picked out to do the work. They were only together temporarily and were disbanded when the experiment was completed.

Q. Were all the people in such groups informed of the nature of the work?

A. They were not informed of what they were doing. They protested that they could not carry on with their own experiments and that their regular work was being interfered with.

Q. Would not more progress have been made if those working on the experiment had been told what it was all about?

A. If they had known what they were working on they would have shrunk up from fright and asked for more pay. They were not well-trained men and were usually picked from the ranks.

Q. A soldier is a soldier and could you not have ordered them to do the work?

A. They were not soldiers. They were reservists. Those in the branch units were soldiers, but not those in the main unit. I could not order them.

Q. How much research cooperation was given by the Navy on BW?

A. There was no cooperation whatsoever.

Q. Did not some naval medical officers attend your lectures at the Army Medical College?

A. No. Naval officers are too proud. They do not have any brains, but their noses are high.

Q. From captured documents, we are given to understand that certain naval personnel received additional pay for hazardous work which included work with bacteria and certain poison gasses. Evidently, the Navy must have had some part in it. Why did one personnel receive extra pay?

A. I received no reports from the Navy and I heard nothing about it. The number of medical men in the Navy is less than 10 per cent of those in the Army and I doubt if they had any men capable of conduction experiments.

Q. What training is BW was given to the Kempei Tai?

A. There is a Military Police unit in Nakano-ku which was given training by some medical officers from the Army Medical College. It was just a basic information course on how to discover and report BW incidents.

Q. Who conducted those courses?

A. Colonel MASUDA, Tomosada, and Colonel NAITO, Ryoichi.

Q. Would it be possible to obtain copies of their lectures?

A. I will try to find out.

Interpreter : 2nd Lt. F. H. Ellis
Interpreter : T/Sgt. Toshio Kitamura
Stenographer : T/4 K. A. Haack

6.2.3 6 Feb. 1946: Transcript of Interrogation of Lieutenant General Masaji Kitano in Tokyo, Japan by Lieutenant Colonel A. T. Thompson

资料出处： Fort Detrick, US.

内容点评： 本资料为 1946 年 2 月 6 日 Thompson 中校在东京对北野政次（Masaji Kitano）中将讯问的记录。

Copy no. 2

Transcript of Interrogation of
Lieutenant General Masaji Kitano in Tokyo, Japan
By Lieutenant Colonel A. S. Thompson
On 6 February 1946.

Interpreter: 2nd Lt. Francis M. Ellis

Q. Did General Ishii continue direction of the BW research at Heibo during the period that you relieved him as Chief of the Department?

A. He could not give direct orders but he could influence the work carried on.

Q. What personnel at Heibo were informed of the nature of BW research?

A. Only one or two. A few could not help but gained a general idea of what was going on.

Q. Were any protective ointments developed for BW agents?

A. During the time of Ishii a glanders protective ointment was made. I do not know the formula or much about it. An ointment against malaria (insect repellant) was developed. We thought of working on an ointment to prevent contraction of "Forest Tick Fever". In the course of research on the prevention of epidemic hemorrhagic fever we discovered that the oil extracted from white birch was effective in killing the North Manchurian Tick (mite). By refining the oil we discovered the active ingredient. The substance itself was highly volatile and, when applied to the skin, did not persist. I thought of mixing this substance in an ointment in order to stabilize it. This ointment was also conceived as efficacious against Ixodes persulcatus, the carrier of forest tick fever.

Q. What use was to be made of the glanders protective ointment?

A. I do not know.

Q. What BW work was conducted at institutions other than at Heibo?

A. Because of the secret nature of BW, no work was done at other institutions.

Q. It is inconceivable that BW research was limited to a single institution, Heibo, when other research in Japan, equally as classified, was conducted at many institutions.

A. BW is a restricted subject, prohibited by the Geneva Convention, and thus was not an authorized activity.

Q. Who authorized initiation of BW research?

A. Ishii

Q. What support was given BW research by the General Staff?

A. I don't know. It was started before I came to Heibo. Being secret, I don't know. Allotment of the necessary money was made by the Kwantung Army.

Q. Was the Emperor informed of BW research?

A. No. Had the Emperor known, he would have prohibited such work.

Q. What support did the medical profession in Japan lend to BW research?

A. None.

Q. How did the medical profession regard the BW activity?

A. Their opinion was divided, some for, some against it.

Q. What support was given BW by the Surgeon General?

A. None. He was opposed to it.

NOTE: This interview completes the interrogation of General Kitano.

Transcript of Interrogation of
Lieutenant General Masaji Kitano in Tokyo, Japan
By Lieutenant Colonel A.T. Thompson
On 6 February 1946

Q. Did General Ishii continue direction of the BW research at Heibo during the period that you relieved him as Chief of the Department?

A. He could not give direct orders but he could influence the work carried on.

Q. What personnel at Heibo were informed of the nature of BW research?

A. Only one or two. A few could not help but gained a general idea of what was going on.

Q. Were any protective ointments developed for BW agents?

A. During the time of Ishii a glanders protective ointment was made. I do I do
not know the formula or much about it. An ointment against malaria
(insect repellent) was developed. We thought of working on an ointment
to prevent contraction of "Forest Tick Fever". In the course of research
on the prevention of epidemic hemorrhagic fever we discovered that the oil
extracted from white birch was effective in killing the North Manchurian
Tick (mite). By refining the oil we discovered the active ingredient. The
substance itself was highly volatile and, when applied to the skin, did
not persist. I thought of mixing this substance in an ointment in order to
stabilize it. This ointment was also conceived as efficacious against
Ixodes persulcatus, the carrier of forest tick fever.

Q. What use was to be made of the glanders protective ointment?

A. I do not know.

Q. What BW work was conducted at institutions other than at Heibo?

A. Because of the secret nature of BW, no work was done at other institutions.

Q. It is inconceivable that BW research was limited to a single institution, Heibo when other research in Japan, equally as classified, was conducted at many institutions.

A. BW is a restricted subject, prohibited by the Geneva Convention, and thus was not an authorized activity.

Q. Who authorized initiation of BW research?
A. Ishii.

Q. What support was given BW research by the General Staff?

A. I don't know. It was started before I came to Heibo. Being secret, I don't know. Allotment of the necessary money was made by the Kwantung Army.

Q. Was the Emperor informed of BW research?

A. No. Had the Emperor known, he would have prohibited such work.

Q. What support did the medical profession in Japan lend to BW research?

A. None.

Q. How did the medical profession regard the BW activity?

A. Their opinion was divided, some for, some against it.

Q. What support was given BW by the Surgeon General?

A. None. He was opposed to it.

NOTE: This interview completes the interrogation of General Kitano.

6.2.4 6 Feb. 1946: Stenographic Transcript of Interrogation of Lt. General SHIRO ISHII in Tokyo by Lt. Colonel A. T. Thompson

资料出处： Fort Detrick, US.

内容点评： 本资料为 1946 年 2 月 6 日 Thompson 在东京对石井四郎（Shiro Ishii）中将讯问的记录。

Copy #6

SD 3194

[illegible]

Of Lt. General [illegible]

By Lt. Colonel [illegible]

On 8 [illegible]

SECRET

Stenographic Transcript of Interrogation

Of Lt. General ISHII SHIRO in Tokyo

By Lt. Colonel A. T. Thompson

On 8 February 1946

Q: What field experiments were made with the pest organism?

A: Due to the danger of it, there were no field experiments with that organism. There are a great many field mice in Manchuria and it would have been dangerous to conduct field experiments with pest because the mice could very easily carry the organism and start an epidemic. We conducted experiments with pest in the laboratory.

Q: What kind of experiments?

A: We put rats in cages inside the room and sprayed the whole room with pest bacteria. This was to determine how the rats became infected, whether through the eyes, nose, mouth, or through the skin.

Q: What did you find out?

A: The results were not too favorable. We usually got 10 per cent infections.

Q: By which way?

A: That was the total.

Q: What route was the most effective?

A: Through the nose. Also, through an open wound. Animals were shaved and it was found that they could become infected through the microscopic abrasions caused by the shaving. We found that the lymph nodes became inflamed. That is how we know if an animal has been infected.

Q: Was this spray test conducted in a special chamber or in an ordinary room?

A: It was not a special chamber. The windows were double-plated and paper was put all over the walls. The room was made as air tight as possible. Human beings did not enter the room. They conducted the test from an outside corridor.

Q: Was not there any danger in handling the animals after the experiment and also was it not dangerous because of the bacteria still being in the air?

A: After the experiment, we sprayed formalin in the room and did not enter for one day.

Q: How are you protected while handling the animals?

A: We wore protective clothing, masks, and rubber shoes. Before we touched the animals, we put the cages, animals, and all, into a solution of creosol.

Q: How long after the experiment?

A: After one day.

Q: The bacteria could have spread all over the room during that day.

A: Yes, there was a danger of that. We put the cage with the animal into [illegible] container smaller than the culture room to transport it.

Q: Did you have any accidents in the laboratory or near by as a result of the experiments?

A: Yes, a person who handled the animals after the experiment got infected and died.

Q: Did any persons outside of the institute get infected?

A: No. The person who handled the animals went into the room and I believe he caught it from handling the animals. I do not believe the theory that bacteria can be floating in the air after one day.

Q: Was pest ever tested in bombs or shells?

A: We did not try it because it is too weak. It would be destroyed in five minutes in the sunlight.

Q: Do you believe the pest organism has any value as a BW agent?

A: Due to its weakness, I do not believe there is any value in it.

Q: We have heard from Chinese sources that pest was started in Changteh, China, in 1941, by airplanes flying over and dropping pest material and a plague resulted. Do you know about this?

A: No.

Q: The Chinese claimed the Japanese started it.

A: It is impossible from a scientific point of view to drop pest organisms from airplanes.

Q: Rats, rags, and bits of cotton infected with pest were dropped and later picked up by the Chinese and that is how it was to have started.

A: If you drop rats from airplanes, they will die. There is no chance of a human being catching pest as a result of dropping pest organisms from an airplane.

Q: What experiments were conducted with yellow fever virus?

A: None. There is no Aedes aegypti mosquito in Japan and hence there is no necessity for prevention.

Q: Would not yellow fever virus be a good BW agent?

A: There is no virus in Japan.

Q: No culture anywhere?

A: None.

Q: We have evidence that Japan tried to obtain the yellow fever virus from the Rockefeller Institute.

A: I heard that somebody from the Japanese Infectious Disease Institute was sent to try to obtain the yellow fever virus from America, but was refused. This person was a representative of the Imperial Japanese Government.

Q. Why did this representative want to obtain the virus when there was no necessity for making preventive measures against yellow fever? What was the purpose in trying to obtain it?

A. It was probably to be used in preparation of vaccine to inoculate persons who were to travel south through infected areas. I had no concern in this.

Q. Were attempts made to obtain the virus from other countries?

A. There is probably no yellow fever virus in other countries. It must be the United States alone so there were no other attempts.

Q. Have you ever been under the control of the Russian authorities during the last year?

A. No. I am afraid some members in the branch departments have been captured by the Russians. However, these members do not know anything of importance.

Q. Who first authorized the beginning of BW research in Japan?

A. There were no orders giving consent to research in BW. If there were, we would have received all the money, personnel, and materials we wanted to carry on this research. Since there were no orders, we only conducted the BW research on a very small scale (1 to 2 per cent) in the Water Purification Bureau.

Q. Who in the War Ministry gave official approval to permit the work to be carried on?

A. The members of the War Ministry did not seem to have any scientific bent. Most of them were of the old school which depended upon the spirit of the Japanese people and not scientific methods to win the war. They did not listen to any of my requests. I did not ask for help directly from the War Ministry. I had to go through channels which meant through the Kwantung Army.

Q. Did the Kwantung Army get money from the War Ministry for BW research?

A. I would hand in my requisition for funds. There was no appropriation titled, "BW". It all came under Preventive Medicine and Water Purification.

Q. When was official approval first given to start work on BW and by whom?

A. There was no official sanctioning.

Q. That is hard to believe.

A. If I had labeled my request "BW" it would have been cut off by the higherups. It was all under Preventive Medicine and Water Purification. When I received the money, I used it at my own discretion.

Q. Would not have better progress been made if official approval had been obtained?

A. Yes, if the higherups had brains and scientific knowledge, a great deal of progress could have been made. They believed too much in faith.

Q: I want information on who was informed of BW work. Was the Minister of War informed?

A: On the whole, I believe he did not know about it.

Q: So far as you know, was the Minister of War informed?

A: I never reported to the Minister of War personally about BW.

Q: Did the Minister of War have access to BW reports?

A: I personally did not speak to the War Minister and I do not know.

Q: Was the Chief of the Medical Bureau of the War Ministry (Surgeon-General) informed?

A: I think he knew.

Q: How was he informed?

A: Through connections with the Kwantung Army.

Q: Did you have personal contact with the Surgeon-General on BW matters?

A: Not in public, but at private discussions I mentioned it once.

Q: Did he cooperate in BW research?

A: He was opposed to it because there were not enough medical officers and he could not spare any for this type of work.

Q: Was the Kwantung Army commander informed of the progress of the work?

A: I have not met that person to talk to him. Reports concerning BW were considered so highly secret that they were not reported to the Kwantung Army directly. It may have gone by oral methods.

Q: But any army commander would know what work was going on within his command. Was not he informed as the work went along?

A: The work was delegated to the Water Purification Bureau and that was water purification and prevention of disease. There was no sense in giving reports of such a technical nature to a person who would not understand. Most of the work was of a defensive nature. If it was to be used as a weapon, it would come under the Infantry and I would have to report it, but this was confined to medical research.

Q: Who gave the authority to manufacture the BW bombs?

A: There was no official command. All we used were some left-over bomb shells which the Kwantung Army got from some source. The casing was just plated with another iron plate and that became the Uji bomb. We did not require much money.

Q: Was the commander of the Kwantung Army in favor of BW research?

A: I never met that man and I do not know what his opinion was.

Q: I cannot see how this work could be done without anybody's approval.

A: I could not achieve what I had planned due to the fact that I did not receive approval.

Q: I am led to understand that you started this work under your own initiative and carried it out on your own responsibility.

A: Yes.

Q: Would not much more progress have been made if support of a higher command was received?

A: Yes. Since the work was done as part of preventive medicine and water purification, money was drawn from that, and work did not progress as I desired. That is why I believe BW is impossible in Japan.

Q: Was the Emperor informed of BW research?

A: Not at all. The Emperor is a lover of humanity and never would have consented to such a thing.

Q: Who directed the BW work at the Army Medical College?

A: There were no facilities for conducting BW research at the Army Medical College. All the work done there was educating medical officers in basic fundamentals of medicine.

Q: I understand preventive medicine as it applied to BW was taught there.

A: You can take it that way if you want to. They had a water purification course and it probably falls into your category. They experimented on materials for use of the Water Purification Bureau.

Q: Was any instruction given specifically on BW as to its possibilities and to defense against it at the Army Medical College?

A: There was no course of instruction covering possibilities of BW or its use as a weapon. Students were probably taught how to defend against bacteria through all routes of infection.

Q: Who were the chiefs of the Heibo Institute?

A: I was the first. I was succeeded by General KITANO and then I succeeded him.

Q: When were you chief of the Heibo Institute?

A: From 1936 to June 1942 and then again from March 1945 to the end of the war.

Q: Why were you relieved of your command and why was General KITANO put in as chief?

A: In my private opinion, my being sent to the 1st Army was due to the fact that higher-ups did not want me to continue BW research. But, in order to be promoted to Lieutenant General, I had to do some service in the field as a head of a unit. I could not be promoted to that grade if I were in the laboratory. After I had been promoted, I could go back to the laboratory in my new grade.

Q: Which position was the most important?

A: Surgeon-General of the 1st Army was the most important because I was responsible for the health of 5 divisions (100,000 men).

- 5 -

Q: Were any BW bombs manufactured at the Mukden arsenal?

A: I do not know. I just requisitioned them and they were provided.

Q: The UJI type bomb was specially made just for BW. Who made them?

A: The old laboratory in Harbin, which manufactured the water filters, had the facilities for baking the porcelain and the same equipment was used for making the bombs as was used for the manufacture of water filters. Much trouble I had was trying to get technicians for baking porcelain. The technicians occupied a separate room in the factory and they made a small inner-factory for the manufacture of the porcelain bombs.

Q: Why was not the assistance of regular ordnance officers used in making the bombs?

A: In ordnance, they deal with only iron bombs. They would not take the responsibility for making porcelain bombs. It does not take too much trouble to make the bombs. We could manufacture the bombs as we pleased and make any changes or improvements which we felt were necessary. The group that made the porcelain bombs was called the Sakura group (Cherry Blossom group).

Q: I think better bombs would have been made if you had obtained the assistance of ordnance experts. Why was not this done?

A: It is true. But, I did not have direct orders to carry on this work and therefore I had no cooperation from other units. I had to do everything myself.

Q: Why did you not try to get official approval?

A: I did try to get approval but could not.

Q: Who did you try to get approval from?

A: I had to go through channels and the first agency (Kwantung Army) turned my requests down several times. If BW had been a weapon which was very good, it might have been different. But it was more or less some kind of scientific imagination and was still in the theoretical stage. In the Japanese Army, you have to prove over a period of years that a thing is good before it will be accepted.

Q: Why did you not go to your friends in Japan who had friends in high circles?

A: It was difficult. There were not enough men who were scientifically minded to go to for assistance. If it was a proposition that would make them some money, they might help, but not with this.

Q: Had they no patriotic feelings?

A: If there was such a person as Rockefeller who had the cash and the spirit there might have been some chance.

Q: What work was done at Naito Institute with the trans-oceanic balloons?

A: None, I think it was carried out at a scientific laboratory in Japan.

Q: Are you acquainted with the 9th Army Technical Laboratory at Noborito?

A: I heard that the experiments on the balloon were being carried out in Japan, but I do not know there.

Q: Did you have any connection with that unit?

A: No.

Q: What position did Colonel MASUDA, Tomosada, have under you?

A: He is a long standing friend of mine. He occupied many positions. Was head of the Supply Bureau, head of the Water Purification Department which was a small part of the Third Section, he taught at the Army Medical College. He went to Burma for about two years as head of a malaria control unit and came back after having caught malaria.

Q: What part did he play in the BW field trials at [illegible]?

A: Since he was head of the Supply Bureau, he probably had the work of supply for the tests.

Q: Did Colonel MASUDA carry out any BW trials himself? Did he have charge of any trials?

A: I am not sure. He might have been. The organization was always changing.

Q: Would he have any more information on BW experiments than you have given me up to this point?

A: I believe not.

Q: Would anybody else have additional information on BW that we could obtain?

A: I believe not.

Q: Have you been able to obtain copies of the lectures by Colonel MASUDA to the Kempei Tai?

A: I sent a wire to Colonel MASUDA. At present copies have not yet reached my hands.

Interrogator : 2nd Lt. [illegible]
Interpreter : T/Sgt. [illegible]
Stenographer: T/5 [illegible]

-7-

[illegible]

Stenographic Transcript of Interrogation of Lt. General SHIRO ISHII in Tokyo By Lt. Colonel A.T. Thompson On 6 February 1946

Q. What field experiments were made with the pest organism?

A. Due to the danger of it, there were no field experiments with that organism. There are a great many field mice in Manchuria and it would have been dangerous to conduct field experiments with pest because the mice could very easily carry the organism and start an epidemic. We conducted experiments with pest in the laboratory.

Q. What kind of experiments?

A. We put rats in cages inside the room and sprayed the whole room with pest bacteria. This was to determine how the rats became infected, whether through the eyes, nose, mouth, or through the skin.

Q. What did you find out?

A. The results were not too favorable. We usually got 10 per cent infection.

Q. By which way?

A. That was the total.

Q. What route was the most effective?

A. Through the nose. Also, through an open wound. Animals were shaved and it was found that they would become infected through the microscopic abrasions caused by the shaving. We found that the lymph nodes became inflamed. That is how we know if an animal has been infected.

Q. Was this spray test conducted in a special chamber or in an ordinary room?

A. It was not a special chamber. The windows were double-plated and paper was put all over the walls. The room was made as air tight as possible. Human beings did not enter the room. They conducted the test from an outside corridor.

Q. Was not there any danger in handling the animals after the experiment and also was it not dangerous because of the bacteria still being in the air?

A. After the experiment, we sprayed formalin in the room and did not enter for one day.

Q. How are you protected while handling the animals?

A. We wore protective clothing, masks, and rubber shoes. Before we touched the animals, we put the cages, animals, and all, into a solution of cresol.

Q. How long after the experiment?

A. After one day.

Q. The bacteria could have spread all over the room during that day.

A. Yes, there was a danger of that. We put the cage with the animal into another container smaller than the culture medium to transport it.

Q. Did you have any accidents in the laboratory or near by as a result of the experiments?

A. Yes, a person who handled the animals after the experiment got infected and died.

Q. Did any persons outside of the institute get infected?

A. No. The person who handled the animals went into the room and I believe he caught it from handling the animals. I do not believe the theory that bacteria can be floating in the air after one day.

Q. Was pest ever tested in bombs or shells?

A. We did not try it because it is too weak. It would be destroyed in five minutes in the sunlight.

Q. Do you believe the pest organism has any value as a BW agent?

A. Due to its weakness, I do not believe there is any value in it.

Q. We have heard from Chinese sources that pest was started in Changteh, China in 1941, by airplanes flying over and dropping pest material and a plague resulted. Do you know about this?

A. No.

Q. The Chinese claimed the Japanese started it.

A. It is impossible from a scientific point of view to drop pest organisms from airplanes.

Q. Rats, rags, and bits of cotton infected with pest were dropped and later picked up by the Chinese and that is how it was to have started.

A. If you drop rats from airplanes, they will die. There is no chance of a human being catching pest as a result of dropping pest organisms from an airplane.

Q. What experiments were conducted with yellow fever virus?

A. None. There is no aedes egypti mosquito in Japan and hence there is no necessity for prevention.

Q. Would not yellow fever virus be a good BW agent?

A. There is no virus in Japan.

Q. No culture anywhere?

A. None.

Q. We have evidence that Japan tried to obtain the yellow fever virus from the Rockefeller Institute.

A. I heard that somebody from the Japanese Infectious Disease Institute was sent to try to obtain the yellow fever virus from America, but was refused. This person was a representative of the Imperial Japanese Government.

Q. Why did this representative want to obtain the virus when there was no necessity for making preventive measures against yellow fever? What was the purpose in trying to obtain it?

A. It was probably to be used in preparation of vaccine to inoculate persons who were to travel south through infected areas. I had no concern in this.

Q. Were attempts made to obtain the virus from other countries?

A. There is probably no yellow fever virus in other countries. It must be the United States alone so there were no other attempts.

Q. Have you ever been under the control of the Russian authorities during the last year?

A. No. I am afraid some members in the branch department have been captured by the Russians. However, these members do not know anything of importance.

Q. Who first authorized the beginning of BW research in Japan?

A. There were no orders giving consent to research in BW. If there were, we would have received all the money, personnel, and materials we wanted to carry on this research. Since there were no orders, we only conducted the BW research on a very small scale (1 to 2 per cent) in the Water Purification Bureau.

Q. Who in the War Ministry gave official approval to permit the work to be carried on?

A. The members of the War Ministry did not seem to have any scientific bent. Most of them were of the old school which depended upon the spirit of the Japanese people and not scientific methods to win the war. They did not listen to any of my requests. I did not ask for help directly from the War Ministry. I had to go through channels which meant through the Kwangtung Army.

Q. Did the Kwangtung Army get money from the War Ministry for BW research?

A. I would hand in my requisition for funds. There was no appropriation titled, 'BW'. It all came under Preventive Medicine and Water Purification.

Q. When was the official approval first given to start work on BW and by whom?

A. There was no official sanctioning.

Q. That is hard to believe.

A. If I had labeled my request 'BW' it would have been cut off by the higher-ups. It was all under Preventive Medicine and Water Purification. When I received the money, I used it at my own discretion.

Q. Would not have better progress been made if official approval had been obtained?

A. Yes, if the higher-ups had brains and scientific know-how, a great deal of progress could have been made. They believed too much in faith.

Q. I want information on who was informed of BW work. Was the Minister of War informed?

A. On the whole, I believe he did not know about it.

Q. As far as you know, was the Minister of War informed?

A. I never reported to the Minister of War personally about BW.

Q. Did the Minister of War have access to BW reports?

A. I personally did not speak to the War Minister and I do not know.

Q. Was the Chief of the Medical Bureau of the War Ministry (Surgeon-General) informed?

A. I think he knows.

Q. How was he informed?

A. Through connections with the Kwangtung Army.

Q. Did you have personal contact with the Surgeon-General on BW matters?

A. Not in public, but at private discussions I mentioned it once.

Q. Did he cooperate in BW research?

A. He was opposed to it because there were not enough medical officers and he could not spare any for this type of work.

Q. Was the Kwangtung Army commander informed of the progress of the work?

A. I have not met that person to talk to him. Reports concerning BW were considered so highly secret that they were not reported to the Kwangtung Army directly. It may have gone by oral methods.

Q. But any army commander would know what work was going on within his command. Was not he informed as the work went along?

A. The work was delegated to the Water Purification Bureau and that was water purification and prevention of disease. There was no sense in giving reports of such a technical nature to a person who would not understand. Most of the work was of a defensive nature. If it was to be used as a weapon, it would come under the infantry and I would have to report it, but this was confined to medical research.

Q. Who gave the authority to manufacture the BW bombs?

A. There was no official consent. All we used were some left-over bomb shells which the Kwangtung Army got from some source. The casing was just plate with another iron plate and that became the BW bomb. We did not require much money.

Q. Was the commander of the Kwangtung Army in favor of BW research?

A. I never met that man and I do not know what his opinion was.

Q. I cannot see how this work could be done without anybody's approval.

A. I could not achieve what I had planned due to the fact that I did not receive approval.

Q. I am led to understand that you started this work under your own initiative and carried it out on your own responsibility.

A. Yes.

Q. Would not much more progress have been made if support of a higher command was received?

A. Yes. Since the work was done as part of preventive medicine and water purification, money was drawn from that, and work did not progress as I desired. That is why I believe BW is impossible in Japan.

Q. Was the Emperor informed of BW research?

A. Not at all. The Emperor is a lover of humanity and never would have consented to such a thing.

Q. Who directed the BW work at the Army Medical College?

A. There were no facilities for conducting BW research at the Army Medical College. All the work done there was educating medical officers in basic Fundamentals of Medicine.

Q. I understand preventive medicine as it applied to BW was taught there.

A. You can take it that way if you want to. They had a water purification course and it probably falls into your category. They experimented on materials for use of the Water Purification Bureau.

Q. Was any instruction given specifically on BW as to its possibilities and to defense against it at the Army Medical College?

A. There was no course of instruction covering possibilities of BW or its use as a weapon. Students were probably taught how to defend against bacteria through all routes of infection.

Q. Who were the chiefs of the Heibo Institute?

A. I was the first. I was succeeded by General KITANO and then I succeeded him.

Q. When were you chief of the Heibo Institute?

A. From 1936 to June 1942 and then again from March 1945 to the end of the war.

Q. Why were you relieved of your command and why was General KITANO put in as chief?

A. In my private opinion, my being sent to the 1st Army was due to the fact that higher-ups did now want me to continue BW research. But, in order to be promoted to Lieutenant General, I had to do some service in the field as a head of a unit. I could not be promoted to that grade if I were in the laboratory. After I had been promoted, I could go back to the laboratory in my new grade.

Q. Which position was the most important?

A. Surgeon-General of the 1st Army was the most important because I was responsible for the health of 5 divisions (100,000 men).

Q. Were any BW bombs manufactured at the ? arsenal?

A. I do not know. I just requisitioned them and they were provided.

Q. The Uji type bomb was specially made just for it. Who made them?

A. The old laboratory in Harbin, which manufactured the water filters, had the facilities for baking the porcelain and the same equipment was used for making the bombs as was used for the manufacture of water filters. Most trouble I had was trying to get technicians for baking porcelain. The technicians occupied a separate room in the factory and they made a small inner-factory for the manufacture of the porcelain bombs.

Q. Why was not the assistance of regular ordnance officers used in making the bombs?

A. In ordinance, they deal with only iron bombs. They could not take the responsibility for making porcelain bombs. It does not take too much trouble to make the bomb. We could manufacture the bombs as we pleased and make any changes or improvements which we felt were necessary. The group that made the porcelain bombs was called the Sakura group (Cherry Blossom group).

Q. I think better bombs would have been made if you had obtained the assistance of ordinance experts. Why was not this done?

A. It is true. But, I did not have direct orders to carry on this work and therefore I had no cooperation from other units. I had to do everything myself.

Q. Why did you not try to get official approval?

A. I did try to get approval but could not.

Q. Who did you try to get approval from?

A. I had to go through channels and the first agency (Kwangtung Army) turned my requests down several times. If BW had been a weapon which was very good it might have been different. But it was more or less some kind of scientific imagination and was still in the theoretical stage. In the Japanese Army, you have to prove over a period of years that a thing is good before it will be accepted.

Q. Why did you not go to your friends in Japan who had friends in high circles?

A. It was difficult. There were not enough men who were scientifically minded to go to for assistance. If it was a proposition that would make them some money, they might help, but not with this.

Q. Had they no patriotic feelings?

A. if there was such a person as Rockefeller who had the cash and the spirit there might have been some chance.

Q. What work was done at Heibo Institute with the trans-oceanic balloons?

A. None, I think it was carried out at a scientific laboratory in Japan.

Q. Are you acquainted with the 9th Army Technical Laboratory at

A. I heard that the experiments on the balloon were being carried out in Japan, But I do not know where.

Q. Did you have any connection with that work?

A. No.

Q. What position did Colonel MASUDA, Tomosada, have under you?

A. He is a long standing friend of mine. He occupied many positions, was head of the Supply Bureau, head of the Water Purification Department which was a small part of the Third Section, he taught at the Army Medical College. He went to Burma for about two years as head of a malaria control unit and came back after having caught malaria.

Q. What part did he play in the BW field trials at Heibo?

A. Since he was head of the Supply Bureau, he probably had the work of supply for the tests.

Q. Did Colonel MASUDA, carry out any BW trials himself? Did he have charge of any trials?

A. I am not sure. He might have been. The organization was always changing.

Q. Would he know any more information on BW experiments than you have given me up to this point?

A. I believe not.

Q. Would anybody else have additional information on BW that we could obtain?

A. I believe not.

Q. Have you been able to obtain copies of the lectures by Colonel MASUDA to the Kempei Tai?

A. I sent a wire to Colonel MASUDA. At present copies have not yet reached my hands.

Interpreter : 2nd Lt. F. H. Ellis
Interpreter : T/Sgt. Toshio Kitamura
Stenographer : T/4 K. A. Haack

6.2.5 9 Feb. 1946: Transcript of Interrogation of Major Yoshiyasu Masuda in Tokyo, Japan by Lt. Colonel A. T. Thompson

资料出处：Fort Detrick, US.

内容点评：本资料为 1946 年 2 月 9 日 Thompson 在东京对原 731 部队航空班班长、药剂少校增田美保（Yoshiyasu Masuda）讯问的记录。1941 年 11 月 4 日增田美保驾机在常德上空投放了鼠疫跳蚤。

Copy No. 2

Transcript of Interrogation of
Major Yoshiyasu Masuda in Tokyo, Japan
By Lieutenant Colonel A. T. Thompson
On 9 February 1946

Interpreter: 2nd Lt. Francis M. Ellis

NOTE: Information had been received that a Major Sadayoshi Masuda, a former pharmacy officer with pilot training, had participated in the BW airplane field trials at Heibo and that his present address was: c/o Nippon Tokushukogyo Co., Ltd., Minami-shinagawa, Tokyo. Request for his appearance for interrogation was made to Japanese Liaison. A report was received that no one by that name could be located at the address. Later, a Major Yoshitaka Masuda appeared for interrogation.---The source of information may have made an error in the given name. (A.T.T.)

Q. When were you stationed at the Heibo (Pingfan) institute?

A. August 1937 to August 1943.

Q. What has been your training?

A. Sanitary technician, training in nutrition and pharmacy.

Q. What were your duties at the Heibo Institute?

A. Procurement of sanitary equipment and supplies, and supply of such equipment. During the cold months I made trials by plane to see whether the method of packing chemicals and pharmaceuticals used in preventive medicine would withstand air transport.

Q. What was your rank?

A. Major, Pharmacy Officer.

Q. To what section of the Boeki-Kyusui-Bu were you assigned?

A. Second Section.

Q. Did you have flight training?

A. Yes.

Q. What type of planes did you fly in your work?

A. Small transport planes (called "Super"). They were capable of carrying eight stretchers.

Q. Were you acquainted with General Ishii?

A. Yes, he was the head of the unit.

Q. What part did you play in General Ishii's experiments?

A. I was concerned with means of transporting medicines and pharmaceuticals by air; how to pack materials in wood boxes economically; testing bottled fluids as to possible freezing at high altitudes and the effect on such materials of the shock of landing.

Q. We have been informed by your former superior officer, General Ishii, that BW drop and spray trials from aircraft were carried out, and we desire additional information. What part did you have in these trials?

A. I had nothing to do with BW trials.

Q. Who did pilot the planes used in these trials?

A. There were two men. Major Seikin Hirasawa did the dropping and spray trials with Captain Torakasa Gounda as pilot. Major Hirasawa was a medical officer.

Q. Where are Major Hirasawa and Captain Geanda at present?

A. I believe that they are still in Manchuria.

Q. You are giving me false information. You were named by reliable sources as one who took part in the BW trials.

A. I only did the experiments I have mentioned. I had nothing to do with the BW trials.

Q. We will check further into this matter, and you may later have to face our informant and be further questioned as to the truth of your statements.

A. That would be fine.

Q. Did you witness any of the BW trials?

A. I saw the dropping of bombs from the plane but did not see the results.

Q. As a pilot, you evidently had an opportunity to examine the planes used in the BW trials. How was the spray tank mounted on the plane?

A. There were 2 or 3 rather large transports and 1 or 2 bombers. There were three hangars. My plane was kept in the first hangar. The planes used in the trials were kept in the last hangar so I could not see them. I do not know.

Q. We have heard that one person was hurt in one of the trials using airplanes. Who was it?

A. I had heard from Major Hirasawa that some of the tanks had been broken. I do not know of an accident.

Q. How far from the Institute were the experimental grounds for the aircraft trials located?

A. About one and one-half kilometers.

Q. Did you know that BW experiments were being conducted at Heibo?

A. I did not know. I had not heard of them. I knew that they were studying methods of protection against infectious diseases. My unit did what we were ordered. What the other departments were doing was kept secret.

Q. We know that BW research was being conducted at Heibo. We have obtained this information from your superior officers. We will have to take appropriate disciplinary measures if we find that you are not telling us the truth.

A. Hirasawa dropped the bombs. I don't know what the bombs were for but I don't think they were for a good reason. Airplanes flew over the target but they missed the mark. They were bad bombs. I did not see this, I only heard of it.

Q. What bombs were used?

A. I do not know which bombs they were.

Q. Was it the "I", "Ro", "Ha" or "Uji" Bomb?

A. I believe it was the "I" and "Uji" Bomb, I don't really know.

-3-

Q. Do you know Colonel Tomosada Masuda?

A. Yes. The questions you have been asking of me, he would know well.

Q. Why do you say that?

A. Colonel Masuda was there a long time and so I think he would know. He was there the longest, he probably knows I believe. Masuda was next under Ishii.

Q. Who were the persons in charge of the several sections of the Boeki-Kyusui-Bu?

A. I believe they were:

Administrative Section - Colonel Ota
1st Section - Major General Saii Kikuchi
2nd Section - Colonel Iojii Ikari
3rd Section - Colonel Tomasuda Masuda

Q. What instruction on BW was given at the Army Medical College in Tokyo?

A. When I was there, none was given. There are several groups and different courses of instruction.

Q. How did you like to work with General Ishii?

A. We did not think that way. We were working for our country. We did as we were told. I thought General Ishii was a great man, an important man. He was an important person, the head of the unit, therefore, we did not meet him.

Q. Has anyone directed you not to reveal information on BW?

A. No one.

Q. Do you know where General Ishii is at the present time?

A. I do not know.

Q. Is the Boibo Institute intact at present?

A. I had heard that it had been destroyed.

Q. Write your name and present address.

A. (The following name and address was written)

YOSHIYASU MASUDA, NIPPON TOKUSHU, KOGIYO KAISHA
MINAMI SHINAGAWA

EVALUATION: It is apparent that source of information was in error as to given name of Major Masuda. This source will be further interrogated concerning his information that Major Masuda participated in the BW field trials. It is believed that Major Masuda's statements as to his part in the research conducted at Boibo Institute are sincere and that the BW field trials with aircraft were conducted by other persons.

-3-

Transcript of Interrogation of Major Yoshiyasu Masuda in Tokyo, Japan On 9 February 1946

NOTE: Information had been received that a Major Sadayoshi Masuda, a former pharmacy officer with pilot training, had participated in the BW airplane field trials at Heibo and that his present address was: c/o Nippon Tokushukogyo Co., Ltd., Minami-shinagawa, Tokyo. Request for his appearance for interrogation was made to Japanese Liaison. A report was received that no one by that name could be located at the address. Later, a Major Yoshiyasu Masuda appeared for interrogation.----The source of information may have made an error in the given name. (A.T.T.)

Q. When were you stationed at the Heibo (Pingfan) institute?

A. August 1937 to August 1943.

Q. What has been your training?

A. Sanitary technician, training in nutrition and pharmacy.

Q. What were your duties at the Heibo Institute?

A. Procurement of sanitary equipment and supplies, and supply of such equipment. During the cold months I made trials by plane to see whether the method of packing chemicals and pharmaceuticals used in preventive medicine would withstand air transport.

Q. What was your rank?

A. Major, Pharmacy Officer.

Q. To what section of the Boeki-Kyusui-Bu were you assigned?

A. Second Section.

Q. Did you have flight training?

A. Yes.

Q. What type of planes did you fly in your work?

A. Small transport planes (called "Super"). They were capable of carrying eight stretchers.

Q. Were you acquainted with General Ishii?

A. Yes, he was the head of the unit.

Q. What part did you play in General Ishii's experiments?

A. I was concerned with means of transporting medicines and pharmaceuticals by air; how to pack materials in wood boxes economically; testing bottled fluids as to possible freezing at high altitudes and the effect on such materials of the shock of landing.

Q. We have been informed by your former superior officer, General Ishii, that BW drop and spray trials from aircraft were carried out, and we desire additional information What part did you have in these trials?

A. I had nothing to do with BW trials.

Q. Who did pilot the planes used in those trials?

A. There were two men. Major Seikin Hirasawa〔Masayoshi〕 did the dropping and spray trials with Captain Torakasa Gounda as pilot. Major Hirasawa was a medical officer.

Q. Where are Major Hirasawa and Captain Gounda at present?

A. I believe that they are still in Manchuria.

Q. You are giving us false information. You were named by reliable sources as one who took part in the BW trials.

A. I only did the experiments I have mentioned. I had nothing to do with the BW trials.

Q. We will check further into this matter, and you may later have to face our informant and be further questioned as to the truth of your statements.

A. That would be fine.

Q. Did you witness any of the BW trials?

A. I saw the dropping of bombs from the plane but did not see the results.

Q. As a pilot, you evidently had an opportunity to examine the planes used in the BW trials. How was the spray tank mounted on the plane?

A. There were 2 or 3 rather large transports and 1 or 2 bombers. There were three hangars. My plane was kept in the first hangar. The planes used in the trials were kept in the last hangar so I could not see them. I do not know.

Q. We have heard that one person was hurt in one of the trials using airplanes. Who was it?

A. I had heard from Major Hirasawa that some of the tanks had been broken. I do not know of an accident.

Q. How far from the Institute were the experimental grounds for the aircraft trials located?

A. About one and one-half kilometers.

Q. Did you know that BW experiments were being conducted at Heibo?

A. I did not know. I had not heard of them. I know that they were studying methods of protection against infectious diseases. My unit did what we were ordered. What the other departments were doing was kept secret.

Q. We know that BW research was being conducted at Heibo. We have obtained this information from your superior officers. We will have to take appropriate disciplinary measures if we find that you are not telling us the truth.

A. Hirasawa dropped the bombs. I don't know what the bombs were for but I don't think they were for a good reason. Airplanes flew over the target but they missed the mark They were bad bombs. I did not see this, I only heard of it.

Q. What bombs were used?

A. I do not know which bombs they were.

Q. Was it the "I", "Ro", "Ha" or "Uji" bomb?

A. I believe it was the "I" and"Uji" bomb. I don't really know.

Q. Do you know Colonel Tomasada Masuda?

A. Yes. The questions you have been asking of me, he would know well.
Q. Why do you say that?

A. Colonel Masuda was there a long time and so I think he would know. He was there the longest, he probably knows I believe. Masuda was next under Ishii.

Q. Who were the persons in charge of the several sections of the Boeki-Kyusui-Bu?

A. I believe they were:

Administrative Section - Colonel Ota
1st Section - Major General Saii Kikuchi〔Hitoshi Kikuchi〕
2nd Section - Colonel Jojii Ikari〔Tsuneshige Ikari〕
3rd Section - Colonel Tomosada Masuda

Q. What instruction on BW was given at the Army Medical College in Tokyo?

A. When I was there, none was given. There are several groups and different courses of instruction.

Q. How did you like to work with General Ishii?

A. We did not think that way. We were working for our country We did as we were told. I thought General Ishii was a great man, an important man He was an important person, the head of the unit, therefore, we did not meet him.

Q. Has anyone directed you not to reveal information on BW?

A. No one.

Q. Do you know where General Ishii is at the present time?

A. I do not know.

Q. Is the Heibo Institute intact at present?

A. I had heard that it had been destroyed.

Q. Write your name and present address.

A. (The following name and address was written)

YOSHIYASU MASUDA, NIPPON TOKUSHU KOGIYO KAISHA MINAMI SHINAGAWA

EVALUATION: It is apparent that source of information was in error as to given name of Major Masuda This source will be further interrogated concerning his information that Major Masuda participated in the BW field trials. It is believed that Major Masuda's statements as to his part in the research conducted at Heibo Institute are sincere and that the BW field trials with aircraft were conducted by other persons.

6.2.6 20 Feb. 1946: Transcript of Interrogation of Lieutenant Colonel Yoshitaka Sa(s)aki in Kyoto, Japan by Lieutenant Colonel A. T. Thompson

资料出处： Fort Detrick, US.

内容点评： 本资料为 1946 年 2 月 20 日 Thompson 在京都对佐佐木义孝（Yoshitaka Sasaki）中佐讯问的记录。

Transcript of Interrogation of
Lieutenant Colonel Yoshitaka Sasaki in Kyoto, Japan
By Lieutenant Colonel A. T. Thompson
On 20 February 1946

Interpreter: 2nd Lt. Francis M. Ellis

Subject: Interrogation of Lt. Col. Yoshitaka Sasaki

To : WDIT

Interrogator: Lt. Col. Arvo Thompson

Interpreter : 2nd. Lt. F. F. Ellis

Q: What was your position?

A: I was head of the Water Purification Unit at Sango, a branch of the Harbin Water Purification Unit.

Q: What was your rank?

A: I was a Lt. Col. in the medical corps.

Q: What has been your training?

A: I am a surgeon. At present I have a private practice in Kyoto. and am engaged in general surgery.

Q: Will you give me a brief resume of the dates of your tour of duty in Manchuria during the war?

A: I was in Manchuria from December 1940 to January 1943. During this period from December 1940 to April 1941 I was in Harbin. The buildings at Sango had not been completed, and the BKB (Boeki Kyusuibu) work wasn't started until April when half the construction had been finished. I was in Sango from April 1940 to January 1943, although I had been making frequent trips there from Harbin.

Q: When were you at Heibo?

A: In 1937 before the war I was associated with the Harbin BKB as a captain. I was in Heibo in Jan. 1938 to Sept. 1938, and again from Jan. 1940 to Dec. 1940.

Q: What were your duties?

A: The greater part of my duties at Sango were concerned with construction and care of buildings. (Col. Sasaki agreed that this was not a surgeon's job; he was concerned with the supervisory end of the work. Since he had been at Harbin and understood what was required, he was sent to Sango since the administrative details and supervision was much the same.)

Q: What did you do during the two periods you were at Heibo?

A: I was concerned with water purification work.

Q: What do you know of the BW work done at Heibo?

A: I don't know anything of the BW work; I am not a research technician.

Q: Did you know that BW work was going on at Heibo?

A: No, I did not know it. It was a secret.

Q: If you know that it was a secret, you must have known something about it?

A: I was not a technician. When I asked some of the other men what they were doing, they told me the work was secret. The technicians did not discuss their work with one another. We were not permitted in that part of the laboratory in which BW work must have been conducted.

Q: Did you know Gen. Ishii?

A: Yes. I did not see him daily but met him occasionally.

Q: What sort of contact did you have with him?

A: The only contact I had with Gen. Ishii was in the field of preventive medicine and water purification.

Q: Did you ever have any part in BW field trials?

A: No , I never had any part.

Q: Did you see or hear of any?

A: No. There was some Sango Fever (septicemia) in Sango and some technicians were sent there to make tests. We were also warned to see to it that the water was rendered harmless by use of the Ishii Water Filters.

Q: Was Japan in a position to initiate BW?

A: I don't know. I think that Ishii and other laboratory personnel could answer this question.

Q: What persons other than Ishii would know of BW research in Japan?

A: Lt. Col. Masuda, Lt. Col. Fujii, Kitano. The latter would know just a little because he was there for only a short time.

Q: Have you heard whether the Chinese of PW's were used in BW experiments?

A: I do not know.

Q: Did Ishii give any BW training at the EWB institution?

A: No, he did not.

In response to a question about the school at Heibo and instruction therein, Col. Sasaki stated that lectures were given on water purification ; they were not secret, and anyone could attend.

Q: What BW activity was conducted in institutions in Japan proper?

A: I think nothing was done.

Q: Did the Medical Department of the Army authorize BW research?

A: No, I don't know.

Q: Where did Ishii get his backing to work on BW?

A: I think from the Kwantung Army.

Q: How many people at Heibo were engaged in BW research?

A: There were a lot like me in water purification; those on BW, I think, were very few.

Q: Would Japan have used BW if the opportunity had offered itself?

A: If Japan had completed her research, the Emperor would not have allowed it.

Q: Was the Emperor informed on BW research in Japan?

A: I do not know.

Q: What had you heard of German and Russian BW activity?

A: Nothing.

Q: How was Ishii regarded by the medical profession of the Army?

A: A famous man with great executive ability and a good head on his shoulders. Smart.

Q: Did he have many enemies?

A: I think he had a lot of enemies and a lot of friends. He was an important person.

Q: What is your personal opinion of the practicability of BW?

A: My personal opinion is that BW is not practical. It is entirely theoretical.

It is obvious from the answers Lt. Col. Sasaki gave us to all the questions on BW that he knew nothing whatsoever about the investigation being carried out in this field at Heibo. Since such work was top secret and on a relatively small scale compared to the greater part of the work being carried out at Heibo, men in Sasaki's capacity were not likely to be in a position to know about BW.

6.2.7 27 Feb. 1946: SCAP LOCATES AND QUESTIONS GENERAL ISHII by Peter Kalisher, UP Correspondent, Pacific Stars and Stripes

资料出处： Fort Detrick, US.

内容点评： 本资料为 1946 年 2 月 27 日美军报纸 *Pacific Stars and Stripes* 刊登的东京海外特派员 Peter Kalisher 的报道：美军发现石井四郎，加以讯问。

Pacific Stars and Stripes 27/2/46

SCAP LOCATES AND QUESTIONS GENERAL ISHII

by Peter Kalisher
UP Correspondent

Tokyo (UP) - Lt. Gen. Shiro Ishii, head of the Japanese Medical Research Institute, which conducted experiments in certain phases of biological warfare as well as preventive medicine at Ping Fan near Harbin, Manchuria has been located and brought to Tokyo for interrogation after an intensive search by Army intelligence agencies, it was revealed by G-2 SCAP.

The search for Gen. Ishii, who has along been an important intelligence target, was redoubled early last month following a UP dispatch in the Jan. 6 Pacific Stars and Stripes in which the general was charged by Communist sources with having conducted bubonic plaque experiments on American and Chinese POW's.

Shortly thereafter Gen. Ishii was located by the CIC in China Prefecture. An order for him to appear for interrogation was presented to the Japanese and on Jan. 18 he was delivered to SCAP by the Japanese authorities. He is presently living in Tokyo and is not under arrest.

Meanwhile, Lt. Col. A.T. Thompson of the Chemical Warfare Service, flew from Washington to Tokyo on a special order to interrogate Ishii. Under the supervision of Lt. Col. D.S. Tait, technical intelligences, and with the help of Lt. E.M. Ellis of the War Intelligences section and several ATIS interpreters, a 7-week interrogation of Ishii was conducted.

In addition, approximately 25 other Japanese who knew Ishii were queried, including several Japanese medical officers.

Although Ishii denied conducting experiments on prisoners of war or planning any large-scale attempts to develop offensive biological warfare, he did admit inventing a porcelain plaque-bomb, which he said was only used to determine how to combat the effects of a similar bomb should Japan's enemies ever use one.

US Army officers minimized the efficiency of the bomb due to its faulty fuse, Ishii's inventions in the field of preventive medicine they said were more successful. Two water filters for field use were described as "excellent." Samples of the filters have been in Allied hands since September 1944 when they were captured at Sura-Chan on the banks of the Salween River. An anti-dysentery pill was termed only "partially effective."

Ishii maintained that only a small part of the ¥6,000,000 a year appropriation granted him by the Japanese government was ever used to carry on experiments in the field of bacteriology.

He was described as a determined, almost ruthless individual who rose from the rank of colonel in 1941 to Lt. Gen. in 1945. He was appointed Professor of the Manchurian Medical University in 1936, and has been conducting experiments in bacteriology in conjunction with the Japanese Army since then, G-2 revealed.

6.2.8 31 May, 1946: REPORT ON JAPANESE BIOLOGICAL WARFARE (BW) ACTIVITIES BY Arvo T. Thompson, Lt. Col., V.C.

资料出处： National Archives of the United States, R319, B2097.

内容点评： 本资料为美国第二任日本细菌战调查官 Thompson 中校 1946 年 5 月 31 日的《日本细菌战活动报告（1946 年 1 月 11 日至 3 月 11 日）》（《Thompson 报告》）。

ARMY SERVICE FORCES
Camp Detrick
Frederick, Maryland

REPORT

ON

JAPANESE BIOLOGICAL WARFARE (BW) ACTIVITIES

By

Arvo T. Thompson
Lt. Col., V.C.

31 May 1946

Copy 3 of 15 Copies

P R E F A C E

The investigation reported herein was made over the period from 11 January 1946 to 11 March 1946 in accordance with paragraph 1, Movement Orders, Shipment OO-Tokyo-AU, letter AGPO-A-O, 201 Thompson, Arvo T., (21 December 1946), The Adjutant General's Office, Washington 25, D. C., dated 26 December 1945.

TABLE OF CONTENTS

S U M M A R Y

JAPANESE BIOLOGICAL WARFARE (BW) ACTIVITIES

1. Extensive investigations in both the offensive and defensive phases of BW were conducted by the Japanese as a military activity. Japanese Naval interest in BW appears to have been limited to the defensive aspects.

2. BW research and development by the Japanese Army was influenced and directed mainly by Lt. Gen. Shiro Ishii. While Ishii maintained that no official directive existed for the prosecution of this activity and that it was conducted as a phase of military preventive medicine, it is evident from the progress that was made that BW research and development in all its phases was conducted on a large scale, and was officially sanctioned and supported by the highest military authority.

3. Alleged acts of BW sabotage by the Russians and Chinese with the necessity for development of defensive measures against such incidents were the reasons advanced by Ishii for Japanese committment to BW activity. Development of BW as an offensive weapon was never contemplated, he emphasized.

4. The Pingfan installation, located near Harbin, Manchuria, was the principal BW research and development center. Work in this field was also carried on in the Army Medical College in Tokyo. BW being a military activity and highly classified for security reasons, civilian scientists and facilities of civilian research institutes were not utilized for this activity.

5. The causative agents of typhoid and paratyphoid fevers, cholera, dysentery, anthrax, glanders, plague, tetanus and gas gangrene as well as filterable viruses and rickettsiae were considered as possible BW agents. Organisms for field trials were limited to nonpathogenic agents and to two agents pathogenic for both man and animals, B. anthracis (anthrax) and M. malleomyces (glanders).

6. Methods of dissemination of BW agents investigated by the Japanese included bombs, artillery shells, spray from aircraft, and sabotage. By far, the principal effort to develop an effective means of dissemination of infectious agents was devoted to bomb development. Nine aircraft bombs had been developed and tested for this purpose by 1940. They included bombs designed for ground contamination, production of infectious clouds, and fragmentation munitions for production of casualties by wound infection.

SECRET

7. Only a few preliminary experiments were conducted employing modified artillery shells as a BW munition. Dissemination by this means was considered impractical. The same conclusion was reached concerning aircraft sprays after a few preliminary experiments.

8. The Ha bomb and the Type 50 Uji bomb were considered to be the most effective of the munitions developed at Pingfan. While both bombs had several major defects, Ishii believed that, by correction of these defects and further improvement of these bombs by ordnance experts, they could be made into efficient BW munitions.

9. Intensification of measures in preventive medicine and water purification were considered by the Japanese as the most effective defense against BW. Fixed and mobile epidemic prevention and water purification units were responsible for the detection, prevention, and control of outbreaks of infectious diseases in the field. The Military Police (Kempei), in an auxiliary capacity, served as an intelligence organization for the surveillance of possible BW incidents, the collection of evidence, and the apprehension of saboteurs.

10. While definite progress had been made in offensive BW development, at no time was Japan in a position to employ BW as a practical weapon.

CONCLUSIONS

It is the opinion of the investigating officer that:

1. The information regarding Japanese BW activities obtained from presumably independent sources was consistent to the point where it seems that the informants had been instructed as to the amount and nature of information that was to be divulged under interrogation.

2. All information was presumably furnished from memory since all records are said to have been destroyed in accordance with directives of the Japanese Army. Yet, some of the information, especially sketches of the bombs, was in such detail as to question the contention that all documentary evidence had been destroyed.

3. It was evident throughout the interrogations that it was the desire of the Japanese to minimize the extent of their activities in BW, especially the effort devoted to offensive research and development.

4. Failure to fully utilize Japanese scientific capability by restriction of BW research and development to the military with lack of cooperation between the military services precluded progress toward development of BW into a practical weapon.

5. Had a practical BW weapon been achieved, it is unlikely that Japan would have resorted to its use because of fear retaliation by means of chemical warfare. Insofar as could be learned, Japan had no information of American activity in BW.

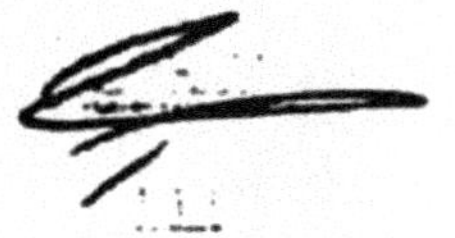

REPORT ON JAPANESE BIOLOGICAL WARFARE ACTIVITIES

1. INTRODUCTION.

The initial investigation of Japanese Biological Warfare (BW) activities was made by Lt. Col. Murray Sanders and Lt. Harry Youngs of the Chemical Warfare Service as a part of the scientific and intelligence survey of Japan conducted by the Scientific and Technical Advisory Section, United States Army Forces, Pacific, during September and October 1945. Report of this investigation is contained in Volume 5, BIOLOGICAL WARFARE, 1 November 1945.

Subsequently, additional personnel associated with this activity became available for interrogation and were interviewed in Japan by personnel from WDIT Section, G-2, GHQ, AFPAC, and from the Chemical Warfare Service. The principal persons interviewed were Lt. Gen. Shiro Ishii and Lt. Gen. Masaji Kitano, former directors of the organization responsible for Japanese biological warfare research and development.

This report pertains mainly to the interrogation of Gen. Ishii and to the information obtained from him. Interrogation of Gen. Kitano and other persons did not add to this information but confirmed, in general, that obtained from Gen. Ishii. Only minor discrepancies were found in the information obtained from persons interviewed individually.

No documentary evidence of Japanese research and development in this field was found during the course of the investigation. All persons interviewed were consistent in their statements that such records had been destroyed, because of their top secret classification, in accordance with existing Army directives. The information obtained was, therefore, presumably from the memory of those interviewed.

Lt. Gen. Shiro Ishii, under whose influence biological warfare research was initiated and prosecuted in Japan, became available for interrogation in Tokyo on 17 January 1946. His whereabouts since the cessation of hostilities had been unknown until CIC sources located him in seclusion at his country home in Chiba prefecture. Upon request from the Counter Intelligence Corps, GHQ, AFPAC, to the Japanese Government, Ishii was returned to his residence in Tokyo. Ishii, suffering from chronic cholecystitis and dysentery, was permitted to remain at his Tokyo residence where all interviews were conducted.

Interrogation of Ishii was conducted at intervals over the period from 22 January to 25 February 1946 by direct interviews through interpreters and by means of questionnaires. On the subject of BW research and development, Ishii's replies to questions were guarded, concise and often evasive. On the subject of preventive medical research, water supply and purification, Ishii spoke freely. It was apparent throughout the interviews that he desired

to emphasize the activities pertaining to preventive medicine, water purification and supply, and to minimize the BW aspects of the organization he directed: The Kwantung Army Boeki Kyusui Bu*.

2. PERSONAL AND MILITARY HISTORY OF LT. GEN. SHIRO ISHII.

In response to a request for his personal history and military experience, Gen. Ishii gave the following information:

Born: 25 June 1892.

December 1920: Graduated from the Medical Department of Kyoto Imperial University.

20 January 1921 - 9 April 1921: Military training as a probational Officer, 3rd Infantry Regiment, Imperial Guard Division.

9 April 1921: Surgeon—1st Lieutenant attached to 3rd Imperial Guard Infantry.

1 August 1922: Attached to Tokyo 1st Army Hospital.

20 August 1924: Surgeon—Captain.

April 1924 - April 1926: Post graduate studies in bacteriology, serology, preventive medicine and pathology at Kyoto Imperial University.

1 April 1926: Attached to Kyoto Army Hospital.

24 April 1928 - April 1930: Went abroad for a tour of inspection and study visiting Singapore, Ceylong, Egypt, Greece, Turkey, Italy, France, Switzerland, Germany, Australia, Hungary, Czechoslovakia, Belgium, Holland, Denmark, Sweden, Norway, Finland, Poland, Soviet Russia, Estonia, Latvia, East Prussia, The United States, Canada and Hawaii.

1 August 1930: Surgeon—Major Instructor at the Army Medical College.

1 August 1935: Surgeon—Lieutenant Colonel.

1 August 1936: Chief of Kwantung Army Boeki Kyusui Bu

1 March 1938: Surgeon—Colonel.

* The literal translation of Boeki Kyusui Bu is, "Anti-epidemic Water Supply and Purification Department."

SECRET

1 August 1940: Chief of Kwantung Army Boeki Kyusui Bu and instructor at the Army Medical College.

1 March 1941: Surgeon—Major General.

1 August 1942: Chief of 1st Army Medical Department.

1 August 1943: Instructor at the Army Medical College.

1 March 1945: Surgeon—Lieutenant General, Chief of Kwantung Army Boeki Kyusui Bu.

1 December 1945: Entered the First Reserves.

3. STIMULUS FOR JAPANESE BW RESEARCH AND DEVELOPMENT.

Throughout the interrogations Ishii maintained that no official directive existed for initiation and conduct of the Japanese BW research and development program. Ishii further declared that he himself was responsible for Japanese interest in BW and that it was largely under his influence that investigation of the offensive phases of BW was conducted in order to prepare an adequate defense against possible enemy BW attack. Since the mission of the Boeki Kyusui Bu was the prevention and control of epidemic diseases and the supply of pure water, he reasoned that development of measures for defense against BW attack was a logical responsibility of his department.

According to Ishii, incidents leading to Japanese investigation of BW potentialities were: numerous instances of poisoning and contamination of wells during the Sino-Japanese conflict; rumors of Russian activity in the field of BW; reports by Manchurian police of the capture of Soviet spies with ampules containing typhus, cholera and anthrax organisms; sabotage of the Japanese Army horse-drawn transport during the building of the Heian-Kokko railway with the loss of 2,000 horses from anthrax; and articles on BW appearing in foreign literature.

Ishii believed that the contamination of wells in the China theater was perpetrated by Chinese guerillas under Russian influence. Personnel from his organization examined over 1,000 wells following an outbreak of cholera resulting in 6,000 deaths among Japanese soldiers in the Shanghai area. Of the wells examined, three were found to be grossly polluted with cholera organisms. Since the investigation was made by competent bacteriologists and the actual bacterial containers were recovered on the scene, Ishii was convinced that this was a deliberate act by saboteurs and not contamination resulting from natural drainage into the wells.

When the Japanese captured the Nanking area, Ishii claimed additional instances were found of contamination of wells with cholera organisms.

Wells marked in Chinese characters "Good Water" were found contaminated whereas wells marked "Bad Water" were found potable.

In reference to foreign literature on BW, Ishii mentioned German articles and the article on "Bacterial Warfare" by Major Leon A. Fox, M.C., U.S. Army. Ishii considered these articles to be fantastic and not based on scientific facts.

Apprehension of Russian activities and intent in the field of BW and the necessity for development of defensive measures against this threat, as well as against the numerous Communist inspired acts of BW sabotage in the Chinese and Manchurian theaters of operation, were the principal reasons advanced by Ishii for Japanese committment to BW activity. He repeatedly emphasized that it was not the Japanese objective to develop BW as an offensive weapon; nor had they ever contemplated initiation of this method of warfare.

4. ORGANIZATION AND ALLOCATION OF THE BOEKI KYUSUI BU.

The initial agency for the prevention and control of infectious diseases in the Japanese Army was, according to Ishii, the Department of Field Prevention of Diseases, established shortly after the Russo-Japanese War. The outbreak of the Sino-Japanese War increased the field of activity of this agency until it embraced an area from the Russo-Manchurian border to the north and Hainan Island to the south. It was concerned with infectious diseases prevalent in the cold northern regions as well as with numerous tropical maladies of the Orient. No uniform method of water purification or supply existed in the Army. Soldiers would not follow instructions regarding the boiling of drinking water; consequently epidemics of water-borne diseases were of frequent occurrence.

The existing field sanitary agency was considered inadequate for the prevention and control of the infectious diseases being encountered in the different operational areas of the Japanese Army. Apprehension of enemy employment of bacteria and poison (as had been encountered in the poisoning and contamination of wells) with the necessity for development of counter measures, further stressed the need for reorganization of the field sanitary agencies.

The Department of Field Prevention of Disease was inactivated and the Boeki Kyusui Bu was organized. According to Ishii, the main objective of this department was the "prevention of diseases coming through water channel."

The Boeki Kyusui Bu was comprised of fixed and mobile units located throughout the overseas theaters of operation as well as in Japan proper.

-4-

SECRET

By July 1938, five Fixed Boeki Kyusui Bu (BKB) installations were established in the overseas theater as follows:

a. Kwantung Army BKB (Harbin)

b. North China Army BKB (Peking)

c. Central China Army BKB (Nanking)

d. Southern China Army BKB (Canton)

e. Southern Army BKB (Singapore)

The fixed BKB installations were assigned to Army groups and were under the direct control of the Army group commander; i.e., Commanding General of the Kwantung Armies.

The mobile BKB consisted of Field BKB and Divisional BKB in the overseas theaters and Divisional BKB and Army District BKB in Japan proper. Like the fixed installations of the Water Supply and Purification Department, the mobile units were assigned to and under direct control of their respective organization commanders. By July, 1938, eighteen (18) Divisional BKB had been organized and were in operation with their respective divisions in the field. Additional mobile units were established as the sphere of activity of the Japanese Army increased. Units of the Water Supply and Purification Department were independent of the Medical Department, the latter department serving only in an advisory capacity to the respective military commanders on medical matters.

5. DUTIES OF THE BOEKI KYUSUI BU.

The following duties and responsibilities were assigned to the units of the Water Supply and Purification Department:

a. Fixed BKB: Research in prevention of epidemic diseases and water supply; production and supply of biological products; production, repair and supply of materials and equipment for epidemic prevention and water supply; execution and guidance on measures for epidemic prevention and water supply; education in epidemic prevention and water supply; physical and chemical examinations; and hospitalization and treatment of patients suffering from infectious diseases.

b. Field BKB: Patrolling for prevention of epidemics and reconnaissance of sources of water; execution and guidance on epidemic prevention measures; examination of water and detection of poison; disinfection and medical examination; purification and supply of water; repair of sanitary water filters; research on epidemic prevention and supply of purified water.

c. Divisional BKB: Divisional units had the same responsibilities as had the field units aside from research and education.

SECRET

Whenever outbreaks of communicable diseases could not be controlled, or when unusual diseases or incidents were encountered by the field and divisional units in areas for which they were responsible, personnel and equipment from the fixed installations were dispatched to deal with the situation.

6. THE KWANTUNG ARMY BOEKI KYUSUI BU.

The Kwantung Army Water Supply and Purification Department, directed by Gen. Ishii from the time of its activation in 1936 until the close of the war, was the agency responsible for prosecution of the Japanese BW research and development program. Except for an interval from August 1942 to March 1945 when Gen Masaji Kitano relieved Ishii as Chief of the Department, the BW activities of this organization were controlled directly by Ishii who was responsible, apparently, only to the Japanese High Command. On matters pertaining solely to preventive medicine and water supply and purification, he was the subordinate to the Kwantung Army commander. On the conduct of BW activities, Ishii evidently had a free hand. Ishii said that the subject of BW was considered so highly secret that formal reports were not submitted.

In response to a question concerning the reasons for his relief as Chief of the Kwantung organization, Ishii stated that it was for the purpose of qualifying him for promotion to Lieutenant General which required field service duty with an Army. He further remarked that, in his opinion, his assignment as Surgeon-General of the 1st Army was made because "higher-ups" did not want him to continue BW research. In any event, the major developments of this research had been completed by the end of 1942, and, due to Ishii's influence, the research continued, to some degree at least, under Gen. Kitano.

Regarding the relationship of the Kwantung Army Boeki Kyusui Bu with the other water supply and purification departments and units, Ishii was emphatic in his statements that he was not the commander of the overall Boeki Kyusui Bu organization of the Japanese Army and, therefore, he had no knowledge of the activity of the departments of the other armies.

Ishii maintained that no official directive had been given by the War Ministry and that no specific appropriations had been granted for BW work. Funds appropriated for research on preventive medicine and water purification were used for BW research. Ishii estimated this diversion of funds for BW research to be about 1 to 2 percent of the appropriation. (Note: From another source it was learned that the yearly budget for preventive medicine research was approximately 6 million Yen). His estimate, however, is not in conformity with a later admission in which Ishii stated that about 20 percent of the research was devoted to BW.

Throughout the interrogation Ishii endeavored to leave the impression that BW research was conducted only on a very small scale and as a part of the research in preventive medicine and water purification. He repeatedly emphasized that offensive aspects of BW were investigated for

-6-

SECRET

the sole purpose of determing BW potentialities in order to learn what defensive measures were necessary from the standpoint of epidemic prevention and water purification.

All persons questioned on the subject were consistent in their replies that the Emperor was uninformed of the Japanese BW activity. Ishii's response to the query was that "BW is inhumane and advocating such a method of warfare would defile the virtue and benevolence of the Emperor." Ishii further stated that had the Emperor been informed of this activity he would have prohibited the work.

Regardless of Ishii's contention that BW research was only a minor phase of the activities of the Kwantung Army Water Supply and Purification Department and that it was conducted without official directive, from scope of the research and the progress that was made, it is evident that BW research and development in all its phases was conducted on a large scale, was officially sanctioned, and was supported by the highest military authority.

a. Organization of the Kwantung Army Boeki Kyusui Bu.

As outlined by Gen. Ishii, the Kwantung Army Water Supply and Purification Department consisted of a headquarters and five branch departments all located in Manchuria. The headquarters was further divided into six sections or departments designated as the General Affairs Department, First Department, Second Department, Third Department, Fourth Department and the Materials Department. With the exception of the Third Department, which was located in Harbin, the headquarters departments were located at Pingfan (Heibo*), the main research installation about 24 kilometers south of Harbin. (See Supplement 1). The branch departments were located at Botanko, Rinko, Songo, Hairaru and Dairen.

At the height of its activities, personnel of the Kwantung Army Water Supply and Purification Department numbered over 2,500 individuals. Personnel included medical officers, pharmacists, hygienic officers, technical officers, engineers, instructors, medical non-commissioned officers and soldiers, fiscal personnel and civilian employees. (See Supplement 2a. for Table of Organization as submitted by Lt. Gen. Kitano).

b. Duties of the Kwantung Army Boeki Kyusui Bu.

An outline of the duties of the several headquarters sections or departments and branch departments of the Kwantung organization as submitted by Gen. Ishii is given in Supplement 2b. In brief, the General Affairs Department of headquarters was responsible for the over-all administration. The First Department was concerned with fundamental research in preventive medicine. The Second Department was concerned with epidemiological

SECRET

-7-

* In Chinese the installation is called "Pingfan," the Japanese name is "Heibo."

SECRET

research and was responsible for execution of measures for prevention of epidemics. The Third Department was responsible for research on matters pertaining to water supply and purification, manufacture and maintenance of water supply equipment and execution of measures for water supply and purification. The Fourth Department was responsible for vaccine and serum production. In addition to the usual supply functions, the Materials Department was responsible for the propagation and supply of all small experimental animals.

The various Branch Departments were responsible for the execution of measures for prevention of epidemics and the supply of purified water in their respective areas. The Dairin Branch was also concerned with research pertaining to improvement of vaccines, serums and diagnostic agents.

7. THE PINGFAN (HEIBO) INSTALLATION.

The Pingfan installation of the Kwantung Boeki Kyusui Bu, located about 24 kilometers south of Harbin, Manchuria, was the principal Japanese BW research center. While Gen. Ishii contended that the primary purpose of the installation was field preventive medicine as it applied to the Kwantung Armies, it is evident, from the extensive investigations and developments that were made in the field of BW, that considerable effort was devoted to this latter activity as a part of the preventive medicine program and for the purpose of development of a BW weapon. Construction of the installation was begun about in 1937, for by that time BW field trials were underway and the first BW munitions had been developed. A small research laboratory in Harbin (See Supplements 3a and 3b for plan) was utilized for the initial investigations prior to completion of the Pingfan Installation. Upon completion of Pingfan, the Harbin laboratory was used mainly for the manufacture and repair of water purification equipment. Gen. Ishii had developed a diatomite tube-type water filter which was adopted by the Japanese Army as standard equipment for field use, and facilities at the Harbin laboratory for baking the diatomite filters were also used for manufacture of the porcelain cases of the Uji-type BW bombs.

An idea of the extent of the facilities at Pingfan for preventive medicine and BW research may be obtained from the sketch of the installation submitted by Ishii (Supplement 3c). (A similar sketch, Supplement 3d, supposedly drawn from memory, was obtained from Gen. Kitano). The installation was self-sufficient to the extent of raising most of its food requirements and experimental animals. Extensive laboratories were provided for research, production of biological products, and for manufacture and repair of equipment. Within the closely guarded walled installation, a separate area was provided for plague research. An attached air base provided air transport for personnel and equipment and aircraft for BW field trials. The installation contained a school for instruction of officers and enlisted personnel in field sanitation regulations, preventive medicine, water purification and supply. Instruction was by lectures, demonstrations and practical exercises.

SECRET

Undoubtedly, a certain amount of indoctrination in BW, at least from the defensive standpoint, must have been given the students. This, however, was denied by Ishii who said that BW development had not reached the stage where instruction of personnel in this field was warranted. A hospital for the examination and treatment of Pingfan personnel and their dependents was also provided. An outline of the research conducted at Pingfan was furnished by Ishii (Supplement 3e).

BW investigation was not conducted by a fixed group of personnel at Pingfan, Ishii said. Personnel from the various departments were temporarily assigned to a particular project or experiment, and once the project, or a particular phase of it, was completed the assigned personnel were disbanded and returned to their respective duties. Aside from a few key individuals, personnel assigned to a project were not fully informed of the nature of the work or purpose of the investigation. This procedure, Ishii admitted, did not promote progress of the work, but was necessary for security reasons.

8. OFFENSIVE BW ACTIVITIES.

a. Organisms Studied: The causative agents of typhoid and paratyphoid fevers, cholera, dysentery, anthrax, glanders, plague, tetanus and gas gangrene, as well as filterable viruses and rickettsiae were investigated from a BW standpoint. Organisms used in field trials with munitions, Ishii said, were limited to the noninfectious agents, B. subtilis and B. prodigiosus, and agents infectious for animals, B. anthracis and M. malleomyces (glanders). Only a single field experiment had been carried out with glanders, Ishii maintained. (The nature of this experiment could not be learned). Because of the danger of infection and a glanders casualty, further experiments were abandoned and work on this agent was limited to efforts toward development of an immunizing agent and a curative ointment. Ishii denied that field experiments had been carried out with P. pestis. Fear of retroactivity and possible spread by rodents were reasons given by Ishii for confining plague investigations to the laboratory

On being requested for his opinion as to the organisms he considered most effective offensively, Ishii said that he could only conjecture and that the effectiveness of a particular agent was dependent on the climate and the sanitary measures in force in the area concerned.

b. Mass Production of Organisms: A culture cabinet invented by Ishii for mass production of organisms for vaccine purposes was the means of production of bacterial agents for BW field trials. The cabinet consisted of a duralumin box with double doors containing a series of trays for surface growth of organisms on solid medium. The trays could be automatically layered with medium to a uniform depth by simply pouring the melted medium through a covered opening in the door. The trays were inoculated by a swab and the growth harvested by scraping with a small metal rake. For mass production, a series of 30 to 40 of the cabinets were employed.

SECRET

With the assistance of technicians from a nearby Japanese military hospital, Ishii gave a demonstration of the use of the culture cabinet. Using seven liters of melted standard agar medium, one cabinet was automatically layered to a depth of 9 millimeters in each tray by laying the cabinet down, pouring the medium through the opening in the door and then raising the cabinet upright. A second cabinet, inoculated with B. coli beforehand, was harvested, yielding about 160 grams of wet surface culture.

Use of this cabinet enabled production greatly exceeding that possible by employment of standard laboratory apparatus. According to Ishii, the cabinet was developed primarily to meet the increasing demands for various vaccines required by the Japanese Armies in the field. At no time were bacterial agents produced and stored in quantity nor available for possible tactical employment.

c. Methods of Dissemination: Methods of dispersion of BW agents investigated at Pingfan included: (1) bombs; (2) artillery shells; (3) dispersion by spray from aircraft. By far the principal effort to develop an effective means of dissemination of infective agents was devoted to BW bombs. A few preliminary experiments were conducted with modified artillery shells and dissemination by spray from aircraft.

(1) Bombs: By 1940, nine (9) aircraft bombs designed for dissemination of bacterial agents had been developed and tested in the field. They included bombs designed for ground contamination, production of infectious clouds, and fragmentation munitions for production of casualties through wound infections caused by contaminated bomb fragments and shrapnel. The earliest munitions were modified chemical warfare bombs. Later bomb developments were of original design and included porcelain and glass case bombs exploded by primacord and a gas expulsion spray bomb.

The bombs, Ishii said, were all developed and manufactured in facilities at the Pingfan installation and the laboratory in Harbin by personnel of his organization without the assistance of regular ordnance personnel. He admitted that more progress in munitions development could have been made had they had the cooperation of bomb specialists. Bombs that were later modified for BW munitions, explosives, and fuzes were obtained by requisition through regular supply channels. One of the main defects of all the bombs developed at Pingfan was the faulty fuzes which, Ishii said, were all modified, obsolete, artillery shell fuzes.

Ishii emphasized that the bombs were experimental models produced in quantities sufficient only to prove their practicability and to determine the measures necessary for defense against like weapons. The following bomb production data furnished by Ishii are surprising in view of his contentions:

Bomb	Approximate Production	Year Made
I	300	1937
Ro	300	1937
Ha	500	1938
Ni	200	1939
Old Type Uji	300	1938
Type 50 Uji	500	1940-1941
Type 100 Uji	300	1940-1942
Ga	50	1940
U	20	1939

Ishii was uncertain as to the number of bombs expended in field trials. He inferred that only a small number of trials were conducted with each bomb and that the remaining bombs were destroyed prior to the Japanese evacuation of Pingfan. From the fact that the first munition was developed and tested in 1937, it is evident that the Japanese activities in the field of BW were well underway prior to this date.

Ishii denied the existence of a "mother and daughter" radio bomb and the Mark 7 bomb mentioned in other reports of Japanese activities. Munitions development did not continue much beyond 1942, for, by 1943, Ishii said, the scarcity of materials began to be felt. By 1944, due to lack of materials and transfer of personnel to the battle fronts, the Pingfan installation had reached a "stifled condition".

The Ha bomb and the Type 50 Uji bomb were considered by Ishii to be the most promising of the munitions developed at Pingfan. By correction of existing defects and further improvement by ordnance experts, he felt that these two bombs could be made into efficient munitions.

When questioned as to where samples of the munitions could be found, Ishii said that all the remaining bombs and the entire Pingfan installation, along with everything of intelligence value, had been destroyed prior to advance of the Russians into the Harbin area. (Note: Entry into the Harbin area for the purpose of verification of Ishii's statements was not possible because of Russian occupation). Since no records, blue prints, photographs or samples of the original bombs could be obtained, Ishii was requested to furnish sketches of the munitions drawn from memory. Reproductions of drawings made from sketches of the bombs submitted by Ishii are attached. (Supplements 4a, 4b, 4c, 4d, 4e, 4f, and 4g).

At several points during the interrogation, when pressed for details, Ishii retorted that, as the director of an organization as extensive as the Kwantung Army Water Supply and Purification Department whose time was occupied largely by administrative matters, he could not be expected to be familiar with minute technical details. The detailed bomb sketches and other technical information obtained from Ishii, however,

indicate an amazing familiarity with detailed technical data. It leads one to question the contention that all records pertaining to BW research and development were destroyed. In all probability, much of the information Ishii presented was compiled with the assistance of his former associates at Pingfan, several of whom were present in Tokyo and vicinity at the time. He had ample opportunity to consult his former associates since the interrogations were intermittent and much of the information was presented by charts and written answers to questionnaires.

(a) I Bomb. The I Bomb, a 20kg modified gas bomb with a capacity of 2 liters, was perhaps the first munition developed for the dissemination of a bacterial liquid payload. Explosion of the bomb head upon impact with the ground blew out the tail with ejection of the liquid fill. The bomb was tested during 1937-1938 by static and drop trials from aircraft. For the trials, the bomb was filled to about 70 per cent capacity with 0.1 per cent fuchsin, 2 to 5 per cent starch solution, or noninfectious agents. A rectangular grid 100 x 500 meters, with either test papers or Petri dishes, depending upon the fill, placed at 20 meter intervals, was used for assessment of dispersion. In winter, a background of snow was used as a means of evaluating the effective area of dispersion of the bomb contents. With a wind velocity of 5 meters per second, an area of dispersion 10-15 x 100-150 meters resulted in case of static explosion. When dropped from aircraft, the bomb buried itself before exploding, resulting in a deep funnel-shaped crater with little effective dispersion of the contents. Depth of the crater depended on the height of release. Dropped from an altitude of 1,000 meters, a crater 0.5-1 meter in depth resulted; from 2,000 meters a crater 1-1.5 meters in depth resulted; a 4,000 meter drop caused a crater 2.5-3 meters in depth. Because of the tendency to bury itself before detonation, its small capacity and large percentage of duds, the I Bomb was considered unsatisfactory and was discarded.

(b) Ro Bomb. The Ro bomb, in size and appearance, was similar to the I bomb. The head was of novel design containing front and rear compartments. Upon contact with the ground, the front compartment exploded throwing the bomb proper 10 to 15 meters into the air. The rear compartment then exploded blowing out the tail and ejecting the contents. The bomb fill for the trials was the same as in case of the I bomb, and it was tested on a similar grid. In static trials an area of dispersion 20-30 x 200-300 meters resulted. Results in drop trials were about the same as with the I bomb. The percentage of duds was greater than in case of the I bomb, largely due to the same defective fuzes. For the same reasons as in case of the I bomb, the Ro bomb was not considered worthy of further improvement and was discarded.

(c) Ha Bomb. The 40kg Ha bomb was a fragmentation bomb designed for destructive effect by projection of bomb fragments and shrapnel contaminated with anthrax spores. The bomb was double walled, having a central burster tube surrounded by an iron fragmentation wall 10 millimeters

-12-

in thickness, and a payload chamber between the wall and the steel bomb case. The payload chamber was of 700 cubic centimeters capacity and contained about 1,500 steel pellets to augment the destructive effects of the bomb fragments. The payload chamber and the steel pellets were coated with a bakelite varnish to prevent corrosion. Armed with nose and tail impact fuzes and containing 3 kilograms of TNT in the nose and tail compartments and central burster tube, the bomb exploded upon impact scattering bomb fragments, shrapnel and anthrax spores at high velocity in a horizontal direction.

Field trials of the Ha bomb were made during 1938 and 1939. Dye solutions and organisms were used as fill for the static tests. Size, distribution and penetrating power of the bomb fragments and shrapnel were determined by using a grid consisting of upright board targets arranged in concentric circles from the point of bomb burst. Test animals were distributed in like pattern. In winter, fragmentation distribution was determined by recovery of particles from the frozen, icy ground. Fragments and shrapnel were projected for distances of 400 to 500 meters with a density of about one fragment or shrapnel per square meter within a radius of 50 meters. Bomb fragments and shrapnel were recovered and examined for viability of attached organisms. Drop trials were made from aircraft for the purpose of determing bomb function and percentage of duds.

Additional fragmentation studies were made by burying the bomb in sand to a depth of 5 meters. The bomb was then exploded electrically and the sand screened to estimate the size of the resulting fragments. Approximately 10 per cent of the recovered fragments weighed from 1 to 3 grams, 20 per cent from 3 to 5 grams, 25 per cent from 5 to 10 grams, 40 per cent from 10 to 15 grams, and 5 per cent were over 15 grams.

The Ha bomb had several defects. It was considered too complex for mass production. The thin bomb case was soldered to the head and tail sections and would not withstand the shock of handling and transportation. Leakage of the bacterial contents often occurred, with danger of infection to the bomb handlers. Suspension of the bomb in aircraft was difficult because the shape of the bomb varied from that of standard aircraft bombs. The heavy explosive charge destroyed from 40 to 65 per cent of the organisms. Regardless of its defects the Ha bomb was considered promising. Ishii believed that, with correction of the defects and further development by bomb experts, the Ha bomb could be made into an efficient munition.

(d) Ni Bomb. The 50kg Ni bomb was of the same general design as the Ha bomb. The bomb body was about 100 millimeters longer, and it had a payload capacity of 1 liter. The explosive charge, however, was only 50 per cent of that used in the Ha bomb. Due to the smaller explosive charge, bacterial survival was greater, but the penetrating force of the bomb fragments and area of dispersion was not as great. Results from tests of the

SECRET

bomb in 1939 were considered to be "rather good," and the bomb was deemed worthy of further development.

(e) U Bomb. The 30kg U bomb was designed to spray liquids by means of compressed air at a predetermined altitude. The bomb had a detachable nose covering a spray head. It was equipped with impact nose fuzes, a delay tail fuze and a self-timing tail mechanism which operated upon release from the airplane. Action of the self-timer allowed the central burster tube to move forward separating the detachable nose from the spray head. The forward motion of the central burster tube also caused release of the compressed air with spraying of the bomb contents through the spray head. Upon reaching the ground, the bomb itself exploded. Only 20 rounds of this bomb were manufactured, Ishii said, and no field experiments were conducted aside from tests to determine bomb function. Because of leakage of the contents, defective fuzes, inaccurate timing mechanism, and because of its complicated structure the U bomb was not considered worth further development and was discarded.

(f) Old Type Uji Bomb. By 1938, the trend in Japanese BW munitions development was towards bombs of simpler design, greater capacity, and requiring a minimum of explosive for fragmentation and dispersion of the viable bacterial contents. This objective was not specifically expressed by Ishii but it is concluded from his criticisms of the earlier munitions and from a consideration of succeeding bomb development. From steel case bombs employing a heavy charge of TNT and black powder, with resultant destructive effect on the payload, later effort was devoted to design and development of ceramic and glass case bombs using primacord or primacord and a minimum of TNT as the explosive charge.

The porcelain case Uji bomb was the result of this trend in bomb development. The original model, designated by Ishii as the "Old Type Uji" bomb, weighed 25 kilograms and had a capacity of approximately 10 liters. The exterior of the porcelain case contained longitudinal grooves to accommodate the explosive of 4 meters of primacord. The bomb was filled through an opening in the nose stoppered by a metal screw cap. A celluloid fin assembly was strapped to the base of the bomb. Equipped with a time fuze in the tail, the bomb was designed to explode in the air at a set altitude with fragmentation of the porcelain case and dispersion of the contents. The porcelain fragments had little penetrating force, but were difficult to detect on the ground. The bomb was tested in 1938 on a field layout much the same as for the I, Ro, and Ha bombs using dye or starch solutions and suspensions of nonpathogenic organisms. In static tests, exploded at a height of 15 meters, an area of dispersion 20-30 by 500-600 meters resulted with a wind velocity of 5 meters per second. In drop tests, areas of dispersion 20-30 by 500-700 meters resulted when the bomb was exploded at altitudes of 200 to 300 meters. Particle size of the disseminated liquid contents ranged from "droplets the size of rain drops, and larger drops due to aggregation, to particles 50 microns in diameter."

SECRET

-14-

Defects of the Old Type Uji bomb were numerous, Ishii said. The porcelain case would not stand rough handling. Leakage of the contents occurred at the union of the metal filling plug and the porcelain case. Weight and dimensions of the bomb were not uniform, contributing to poor trajectory. The bomb was filled to 70 per cent capacity to allow for expansion of contents and the void space caused tumbling of the bomb. The porcelain fins warped during warm weather adding to poor trajectory, became brittle in cold weather, and often became detached in flight. The fuze was faulty and height of burst could not be controlled with any degree of accuracy. Capacity of the bomb was considered satisfactory and the detrimental effect of metal on the bacterial contents was eliminated by use of the porcelain case. The bomb, however, was not considered worthy of further development.

(g) Ga Bomb. The 35 kg Ga bomb was an experimental glass case model of the Old Type Uji bomb. Spiral instead of longitudinal grooves contained the explosive of primacord. Only 20 rounds of this model were manufactured. It had much the same defects as the Old Type Uji bomb and after a few preliminary trials was discarded.

(h) Type 50 Uji Bomb. The 25kg, 10 liters, Type 50 Uji bomb was an improved model of the Uji series of bombs. The nose contained an impact, delay fuze and a bursting tube with 500 grams of TNT. A time fuze in the tail set off the 4 meters of primacord exploding the bomb at a height of 200 to 300 meters. In case the tail fuze and the primacord failed to function, explosion of the bomb with dispersion of the contents was insured upon impact by the explosive train in the nose.

Approximately 500 rounds of this model were manufactured in 1940 and 1941, and extensive field trials were conducted during the period 1940 to 1942. The bomb was tested by static explosion and drop tests from aircraft. For the initial tests the bomb was filled with dye solution and suspensions of nonpathogenic organisms. Later trials were conducted using a suspension of anthrax spores as the payload. The suspension had a concentration of 50 to 100 milligrams of spores per cubic centimeter of liquid. A field layout of test papers or Petri dishes, depending upon the fill, was used for assessment of dispersion. In case of the anthrax trials, large animals including oxen, horses, goats and sheep were used as test animals.

In the drop tests with a wind velocity of 5 meters per second and explosion of the bomb at an altitude of 200 to 300 meters, areas of dispersion 40-60 by 600-800 meters were attained.

Static explosion of the bomb at a height of 15 meters with the same wind velocity gave an area of dispersion approximately 20-30 by 500-600 meters. For the anthrax trials, the bomb was statically

exploded at a height of 15 meters. Animals were then allowed to graze for one or two hours downwind of the explosion over the contaminated ground. Infection, followed by death from anthrax, resulted in almost 70 per cent of the horses and 90 per cent of the sheep allowed to graze over the contaminated ground.

While the Type 50 Uji bomb still had some of the defects of the old model, it was considered more efficient. With correction of these defects and further development in the hands of experts, Ishii felt that the Type 50 Uji bomb could be made into an effective BW munition.

(i) Type 100 Uji Bomb. The 50kg Type 100 Uji bomb was a larger model of the Type 50. This bomb had a payload capacity of approximately 25 liters. As explosive, approximately 12 meters of primacord was used. 300 rounds were manufactured and extensive trials were conducted in much the same manner as with the Type 50 during the period 1940 to 1942. Because of its size and possibility of breakage in handling, this model was not considered as practical as the Type 50.

(2) Artillery Shells. Two types of artillery shells were investigated as a means of dissemination of BW agents. A standard gas shell, designated as the "H" shell, and a shrapnel shell, the "B" shell, were tested in the desert near Hairal. The shells were charged with dye solutions or a suspension of B. prodigiosus in bouillon of a concentration of 200 to 500 milligrams per cubic centimeter. The shells were fired from a distance of 3,000 meters at a target 500 meters square consisting of white test papers or Petri dishes arranged at 20 meter intervals. For tests of the "B" shell, board targets arranged at intervals of 20 meters over an area 500 meters square were used to determine hits. One of the main objectives of the trials was to determine survival of bacteria when dispersed by shell. Since few direct hits on the targets were obtained, Ishii said, no conclusive data resulted and dissemination by this means was considered impractical.

(3) Spray from Aircraft. Ishii stated that about 10 trials had been made in the vicinity of Pingfan for the purpose of evaluating the efficiency of dispersion of agents by spraying from aircraft. The airplane used was equipped with a compressed air tank and a separate tank for the spray liquid. Compressed air released into the spray tank forced the spray liquid out into the air through a duct near the tail of the airplane. Solutions of dyes and suspensions of nonpathogenic organisms were used as test liquids. The dyes employed were 0.1 per cent solutions of fuchsin or anilin red. B. subtilis and B. prodigiosus were used as test organisms. For detection of the colored solutions sprayed from the airplane, a grid of white test papers placed at 50 meter intervals over an area 1,000 meters square was used. Petri dishes with standard agar medium were arranged in like manner for the detection of organisms. Particle size and density were calculated from the test papers by means of a scaled lense or standard test

-16-

SECRET

papers were used for comparison. The concentration of organisms resulting from the spray was estimated by examination of the Petri dishes after incubation in the laboratory.

Release of the spray from altitudes under 500 meters gave detectable results. The diameter of the particles resulting from the spray ranged from 3 millimeters to 50 microns. No organisms were recovered when the spray was released from altitudes over 3,000 meters. Considerable difficulty was experienced with operation of the spray mechanism. On one occasion the compressed air tank burst, injuring the operator. According to Ishii, results from the spray trials were considered unsatisfactory and this method of dissemination was concluded to be inefficient and of no possible operational value.

(4) Sabotage. It is apparent from the frequent references by the Japanese to contamination of wells by the enemy, and from the extensive measures that were instituted for purification of water in the field, that dissemination of infectious agents by saboteurs was seriously considered from both the offensive and defensive standpoint. Ishii inferred that sabotage was perhaps the most effective means of employment of BW. Training of personnel in this activity, as has been mentioned in intelligence reports, was denied.

The only specific information obtained on sabotage activity was learned from Lt. Col. Ryoichi Naito, a former associate of Ishii, who had been concerned with the BW research conducted at the Army Medical College in Tokyo. Ishii maintained that BW investigations at this institution had been limited to defensive investigations in preventive medicine. However, Naito stated that while there was no distinct demarcation between the BW and preventive medical research conducted at the Army Medical College, investigations that had offensive BW implications were carried on. One phase of BW research, Naito stated, was the search for a stable poison that could be used for the sabotage of foodstuffs. Most of this work was concentrated on the thermostabile "fugu toxin" obtained from the livers of "blow-fish". Attempts were made to concentrate this toxin to a lethal dosage of 1 gamma for mice. In a comparable dosage for man, it was calculated that the toxin could be employed practically in sabotage activity. This degree of concentration was not obtained, and further efforts were interrupted by the B-29 raids of November 1944 and ceased altogether with destruction, by fire, of the Army Medical College in April, 1945.

9. DEFENSIVE BW ACTIVITIES.

Augmentation and intensification of measures for preventive medicine and water purification were deemed to be the most effective defense against BW. The widely distributed fixed and mobile units of the Boeki

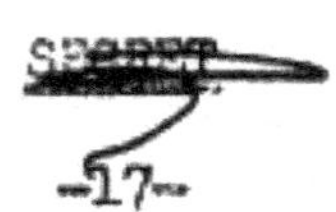

Kyusui Bu were alerted and responsible for the detection, prevention and control of natural outbreaks of infectious diseases as well as diseases of possible enemy introduction. Research in preventive medicine and the production of vaccines, serums and other therapeutic agents at the Pingfan installation and at the Army Medical College were intensified as a means of BW defense. Instruction of medical personnel in preventive medicine pertaining to the defensive aspects of BW was likewise an activity at both institutions.

As a defense against the potentialities of BW munitions revealed by the offensive experimentation at Pingfan, Ishii said that the following measures were developed:

a. Protection by lying down and taking advantage of low ground or objects.

b. Iron helmets and bullet-proof jackets.

c. Reinforced cellophane wrappers and paper wrappers varnished with persimmon juice as a covering for the entire body.

d. Protective clothing of thin, rubberized silk and regular Army gas masks.

e. Protective ointment. Requested for further information on protective ointments, Ishii replied that an ointment effective against the glanders organism had been developed having the following formula:

Mercuric oxycyanate..........	0.1
Starch........................	7.0
Tragacanth powder............	2.0
Medicated soap...	1.0
Glycerine.....................	1.0
Water.........................	100.0

f. Mobile field disinfection cars:

(1) Car "A" for ground disinfection.

(2) Car "B" for disinfection of personnel and clothing.

g. Mobile field laboratory cars for detection and diagnosis.

h. Airplanes for transportation of epidemiological units, equipment and supplies, and for early evacuation of patients.

i. Provision of hospital trains and ships.

j. Increased production of vaccines, serums, and other therapeutic agents including marfanil and penicillin.

k. Early diagnosis and treatment of infectious diseases.

l. Enforcement of preventive innoculation throughout the Army.

As a further defensive measure, liaison was maintained between the Military Police (Kempei) and the Boeki Kyusui Bu. In an auxiliary capacity, the military police served as an intelligence network for the surveillance of possible BW incidents, collection of evidence, and the apprehension of saboteurs. Since the personnel of this organization had no professional training, they were given basic instruction in elementary bacteriology and epidemiology by personnel from the Boeki Kyusui Bu. Instruction included the symptomatology of the more common diseases, manner of their spread, and emergency control measures. They were taught not to place undue emphasis; yet not to overlook seemingly unimportant incidents. Prompt reports were to be submitted to their immediate commanders who in turn would report to the headquarters of the nearest Boeki Kyusui Bu where appropriate action would be taken.

10. NAVAL INTEREST IN BW.

References in captured Japanese documents to a naval Mark 7 bacterial bomb and to special pay for naval personnel engaged in hazardous duty including BW research implied possible naval activity in BW. No evidence supporting this indication was found. The existance of a naval Mark 7 bomb was denied by all Army and Navy personnel who were interviewed.

Adm. Shigetaro Shimada, Minister of the Navy from October 1941 to July 1944, was questioned regarding the document issued by his office listing special pay for BW duty. He denied naval activity in BW and explained the BW reference in the document as having been inserted "by personnel responsible for drafting Navy regulations who possibly imagined BW with an eye to the future." The reference may have originated, Shimada said, in the Office of the Surgeon General of the Navy. Shimada considered BW as impracticable and an ineffective weapon in naval warfare.

It is evident that no cooperation existed between the Army and Navy on BW research. Furthermore, no evidence was found that independent research in this field was conducted by the Navy. Shimada's statements indicate that the Japanese Navy at least had an interest in BW from the defensive standpoint, and that liaison in this phase of BW may have existed between the Surgeons General of the Army and Navy.

-19-

SECRET

11. REASONS FOR LACK OF PROGRESS IN OFFENSIVE BW DEVELOPMENT.

Regardless of the intensive offensive BW investigations conducted at the Pingfan installation, at no time was Japan prepared to employ BW as a practical weapon. Reasons given by Ishii for lack of progress in offensive BW development were, in substance, the following:

a. The primary motive for Japanese BW research was defensive.

b. No official directive existed for BW research, consequently, the necessary funds, personnel and equipment were not available.

c. Lack of competent technical personnel. Only meager compensation was available for casualties from BW research. This field was, therefore, not attractive to qualified investigators.

d. Scientific advisory committees were not available for consultation because of the lack of competent personnel.

e. Lack of essential materials in Japan.

f. Lack of support by the High Command. The importance of science was not recognized. They (personnel in high command) were not capable of impartial judgment and did not respect scientists, therefore, misapprehension and superstition prevailed over scientific facts.

g. Anti-espionage was impossible and Japan feared retaliation.

12. PRACTICABILITY OF BW.

Conclusions as to the practicability of BW expressed by Ishii and others were:

a. The practicability of BW as an offensive weapon remains to be demonstrated.

b. Because of the instability of BW agents and the many essential conditions necessary for the successful initiation of an epidemic, the effective employment of BW on a large scale is doubtful.

c. BW might be effective on a small scale as a means of sabotage.

d. Defense against BW is possible by development of appropriate measures in preventive medicine.

e. Use of BW would not be necessary in a war being won by other weapons and effective use of it could not be made in defeat.

f. BW is not a decisive weapon, at the most, it could be but an auxiliary weapon.

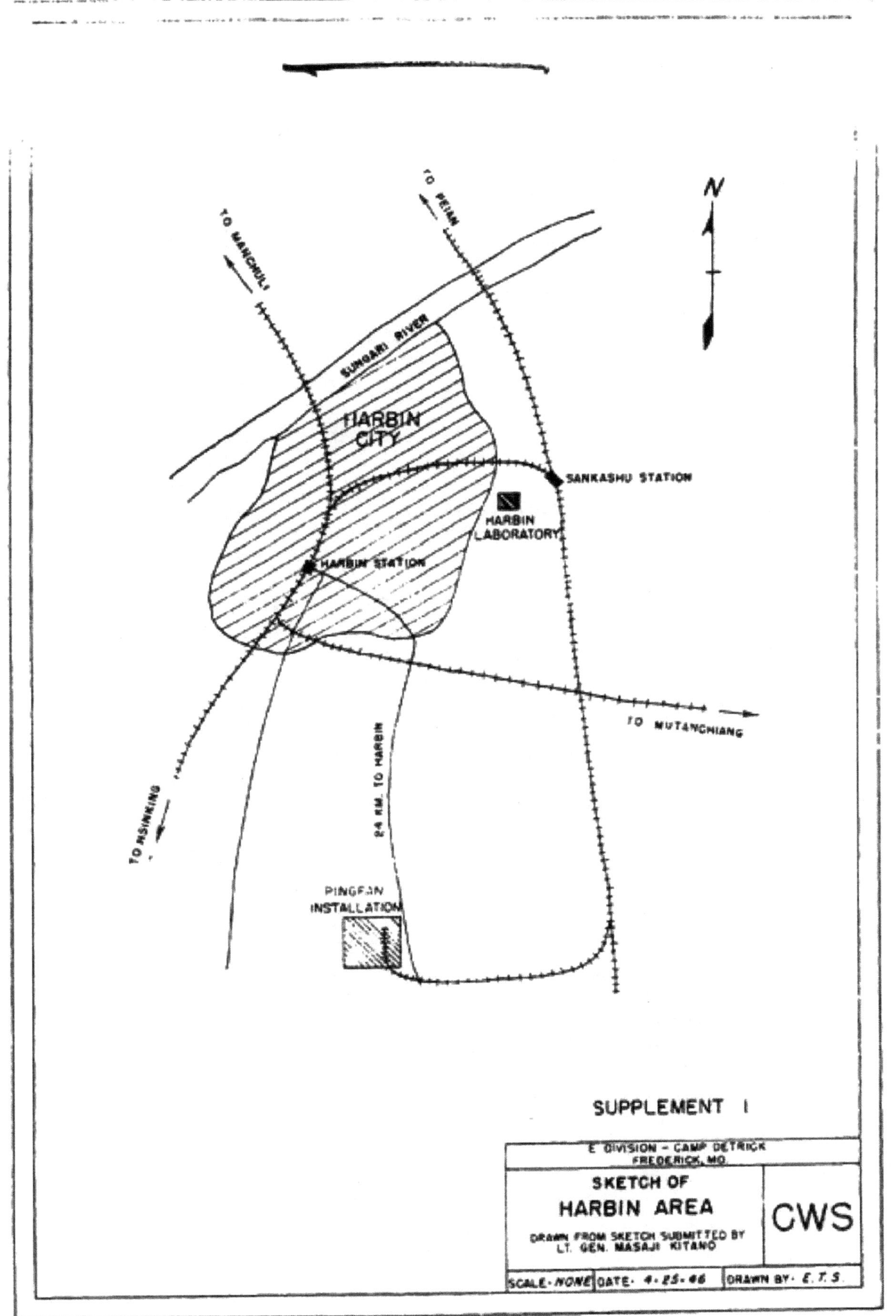
N
TO MANCHULI
TO PEIAN
SUNGARI RIVER
HARBIN
CITY
SANKASHU STATION
HARBIN
LABORATORY
HARBIN STATION
TO MUTANCHIANG
24 KM. TO HARBIN
TO HSINKING
PINGFAN
INSTALLATION
SUPPLEMENT I
E DIVISION - CAMP DETRICK
FREDERICK, MD
SKETCH OF
HARBIN AREA
DRAWN FROM SKETCH SUBMITTED BY
LT. GEN. MASAJI KITANO
CWS
SCALE- NONE
DATE- 4-25-46
DRAWN BY- E.T.S.

SECRET

Supplement 2a

TABLE OF ORGANIZATION OF KWANTUNG ARMY BOEKI KYUSUI BU

Central Office (Headquarters)..........Director - Lt. or Major General (Medical)

General Affairs Section..........Chief - Full or Lt. Colonel (Medical)

1st Section....................Chief - Major General or Colonel (Medical)

2nd Section....................Chief - Full or Lt. Colonel (Medical)

3rd Section....................Chief - Full or Lt. Colonel (Medical)

4th Section....................Chief - Full or Lt. Colonel (Pharmacologist or Medical)

Dairen Detached Office............Chief - Engineer or Surgeon

Branch Offices:

Botanko Branch....................Chief - Major or Lt. Colonel (Medical)

Rinko Branch....................Chief - Major or Lt. Colonel (Medical)

Songo Branch....................Chief - Major or Lt. Colonel (Medical)

Khairalu Branch....................Chief - Major or Lt. Colonel

The personnel of the Headquarters and each branch office is as follows:

Personnel of the Headquarters:

Army Surgeon....................	35
Pharmacologist....................	18
Hygienic officers............about	25
Technical officers...........about	10
Fiscal officers..................	5
Engineers....................about	30
Army Instructors................	3
Interpreters....................	1
N.C.O.......................about	100
Assistant-engineer..............	150
Medical soldiers and other employees	Some

SECRET

Supplement 2a

Personnel of the branch offices:

Army Surgeon......................	1
Pharmacologist....................	1
Hygienic officer..................	1
Fiscal officers...................	1
N.C.O......................about	10
Assistant-engineer.........about	10
Medical soldiers..................	400
Civilian employees................	Some

-2a-

SECRET

Supplement 2b

OUTLINE OF DUTIES OF KWANTUNG ARMY BOEKI KYUSUI BU

I. General Affairs Department.

A. Planning and Control.

B. Business Affairs.

C. Personnel.

D. Intendance.

E. Transportation and Communication.

F. Supervision of Buildings.

G. Medical Affairs.

II. First Department.

A. Investigation and research with regard to the prevention and treating of various infectious diseases.

B. Physical and chemical tests of all kinds.

C. Research relating to the improvement of preventative innoculation liquids, serums for medical treatment, etc.

D. Fundamental research relative to prevention of epidemics.

III. Second Department.

A. Research relative to the execution of measures for the prevention of epidemics.

B. Experiments on materials for the prevention of epidemics.

C. Execution of measures for the prevention of epidemics.

D. Guidance for the prevention of epidemics.

E. Rapid transportation of materials and personnel connected with the prevention of epidemics.

SECRET

Supplement 2b

IV. Third Department.

A. Experiments relating to the improvement of water supply equipment.

B. Execution of measures for water supply.

C. Guidance for the supply of purified water.

D. Manufacture and repair of equipment for water supply.

E. Disinfection.

V. Fourth Department.

A. The manufacture of preventative innoculation liquids, serums for medical treatment, etc.

B. Culture medical experiments.

VI. Materials Department.

A. Custody and supply of materials for the prevention of epidemics, water supply and experiments.

B. Research on preventative medicines.

C. Manufacture of preventative medicines.

D. Propagation and supply of small animals for experimental use.

VII. Branch Departments.

A. Execution and guidance in measures for the prevention of epidemics and water supply in the areas of their responsibility.

B. Investigations relating to the prevention of epidemics and the supply of purified water in the areas of their responsibility.

C. Minor repairs in epidemic prevention and water supply equipment.

VIII. Dairen Branch.

A. Research relating to the improvement of preventive innoculation solutions, serums for diagnosis and treatment, etc.

-2-

Supplement 2b

B. Manufacture and supply of the above mentioned solutions, serums, etc.

C. Research in pathogenic bacteria.

D. Execution of measures for the prevention of epidemics in the areas of their responsibility.

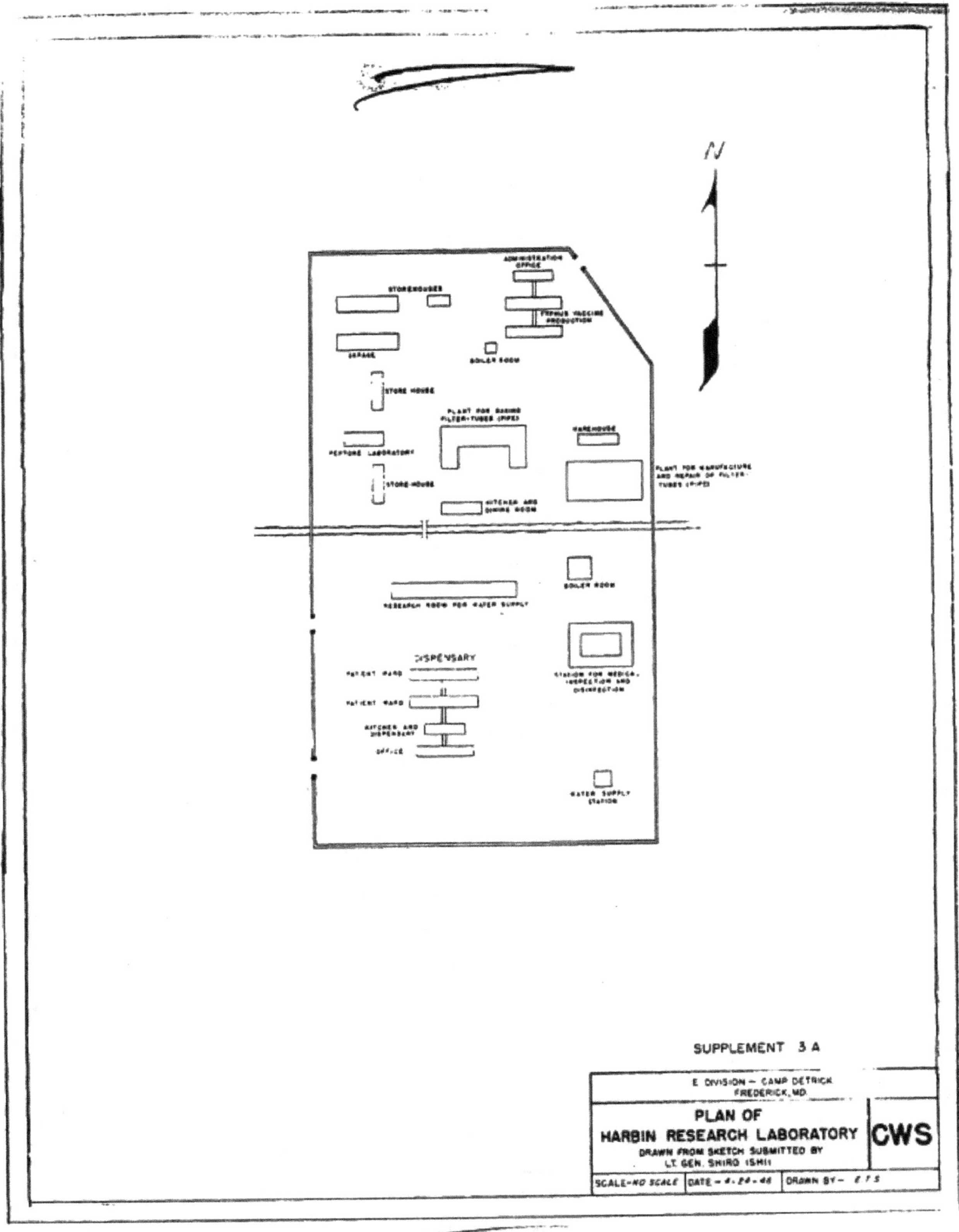
N
ADMINISTRATION OFFICE
STOREHOUSES
BOILER ROOM
STORE HOUSE
WAREHOUSE
STORE-HOUSE
BOILER ROOM
RESEARCH ROOM FOR WATER SUPPLY
DISPENSARY
PATIENT WARD
PATIENT WARD
OFFICE
WATER SUPPLY STATION
SUPPLEMENT 3 A
E DIVISION — CAMP DETRICK
FREDERICK, MD.
PLAN OF
HARBIN RESEARCH LABORATORY
DRAWN FROM SKETCH SUBMITTED BY
LT. GEN. SHIRO ISHII
CWS
SCALE-NO SCALE
DATE —
DRAWN BY —

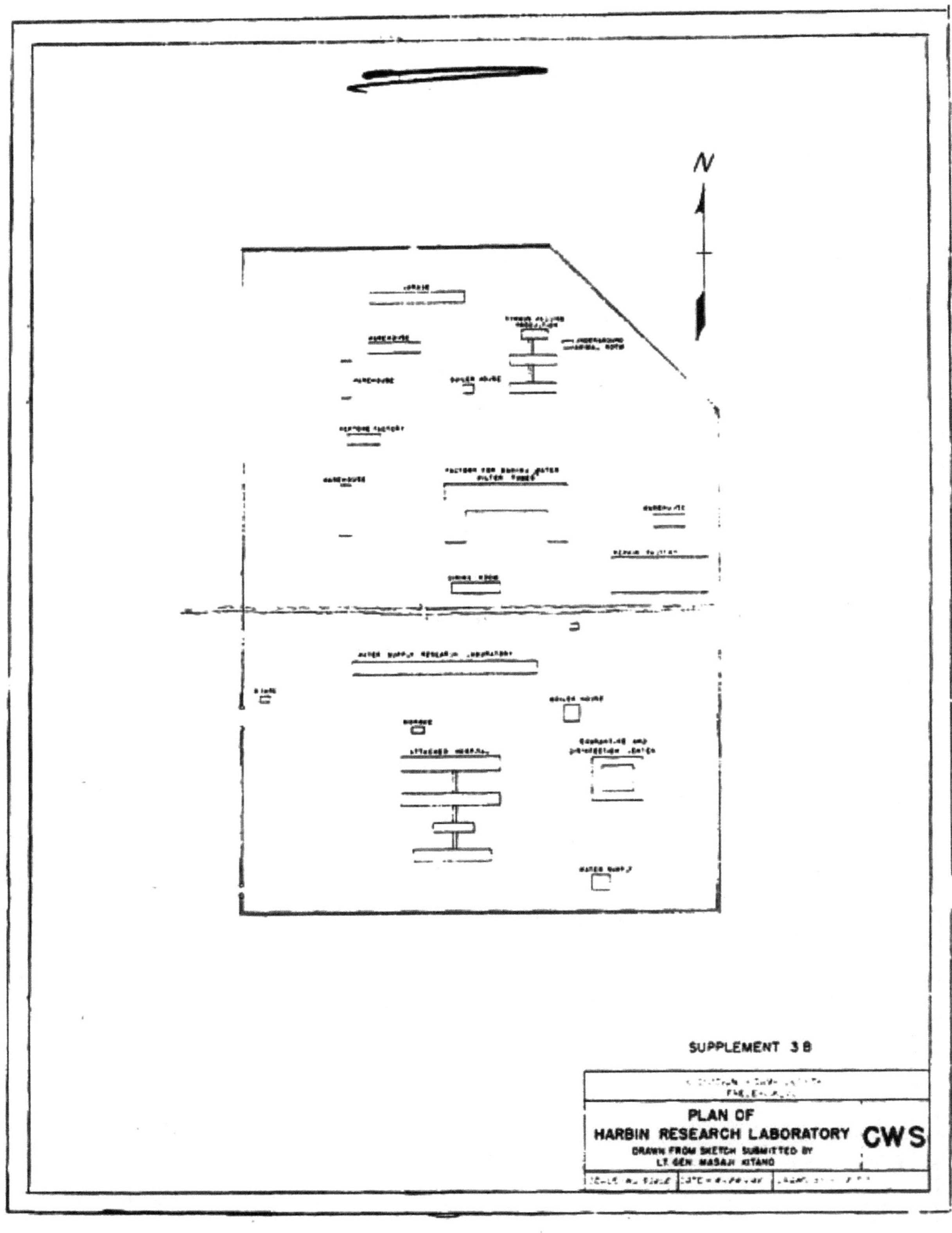
N
SUPPLEMENT 3B
PLAN OF
HARBIN RESEARCH LABORATORY
CWS
DRAWN FROM SKETCH SUBMITTED BY
LT. GEN. MASAJI KITANO

Supplement 3e

OUTLINE OF WORK CONDUCTED BY THE PINGFAN INSTITUTE

I. RESEARCH IN PREVENTIVE MEDICINE:

1. Improvement of Vaccines: Typhoid and paratyphoid, dysentery, cholera, plague, whooping cough, epidemic cerebrospinal meningitis and gonococcus vaccines.

2. Research in Anatoxins: Gas gangrene, tetanus, diptheria and scarlet fever anatoxins.

3. Improvement of Curative Sera: Gas gangrene, tetanus, scarlet fever, erysipelas, diptheria, dysentery, streptococcus, staphlococcus, pneumonia, epidemic cerebrospinal meningitis and plague sera.

4. Measures for Promotion of the Health of Soldiers: Research pertaining to food, rest, sleep and supply of water in Japanese barracks.

5. Prevention of Tuberculosis:

a. Relationship between food, rest, sleep, supply of water and calories needed for military work.

b. Preventive inoculation.

c. Quarantine and disinfection.

6. Research in Rickettsial and Virus Vaccines: Typhus (R.prowazeki), Manchurian fever (R.manchuriae), epidemic hemorrhagic fever, forest tick encephalitis, rabies and small pox vaccines.

7. Vitamin Research.

8. Desiccation Research: Methods for desiccation and storage in the dried state of preventive and curative sera, diagnostic agents and blood plasma.

9. Propagation of Small Animals for Research: Mice, rats, marmots, rabbits and goats.

10. Research in Environmental Hygiene.

11. Research in Self-Supply of Foodstuffs for Members of the Institute.

12. Research in Preventive Methods of Anthrax and Glanders.

SECRET

-1-

Supplement 3e

II. RESEARCH IN DIAGNOSTICS:

1. Research in the Drying and Supply of Diagnostic Agents.

2. Research in Long Period Storage of Diagnostic Sera in the Dried State.

3. Diagnostic Allergic Antigens: Tuberculin, plague, tularemia, Dick and Schick test antigens.

4. Serological Identification.

5. Methods for Diagnosis of Anthrax and Glanders.

III. RESEARCH IN THERAPEUTICS:

1. Surgical Treatment: Early extirpation of the lymphatic glands in pest and anthrax.

2. Internal Treatment: Radical cure of typhoid and paratyphoid carriers.

3. Chemical Treatment: Marfanil, sulforivanol, penicillin.

4. Radical Cure of Patients with Virus Infections: Epidemic hemorrhagic fever, forest tick encephalitis.

5. Serum Therapy: Typhoid, pest, anthrax, dysentery.

6. Research in Effectiveness of Dried Blood Plasma for Field Transfusion: Effectiveness as applied to members of the unit and their families.

7. Physical Treatment: Projection of X-Ray on the spleen for serum sickness.

8. Vaccine Therapy of Typhus.

9. Treatment of Anthrax and Glanders.

IV. RESEARCH IN FIELD DISINFECTION:

1. Methods for field disinfection.

2. Disinfection agents.

Supplement 3a

3. Field disinfection cars for ground disinfection.

4. Field disinfection cars for clothing and personnel.

5. Research in field germ detection cars.

6. Research in prevention and quarantine railway trains and ships.

7. Research in the use of airplanes for disinfection.

V. RESEARCH IN DRUGS AND CHEMICALS:

1. Synthesis of marfanil and sulforivanol.

2. Penicillin production.

3. Extraction of asparagin for Sauton's medium.

4. Extraction of vitamin C from "Yama-hamanasu."

5. Use of birch oil extract for insecticide.

6. Synthesis of vitamin B_1 and B_2.

7. Peptone research.

8. Preparation of meat essence from wild silkworm pupae.

9. Refining of industrial ammonium sulphate for concentration of diptheria toxin.

10. Preparation of pepsin and pancreatin.

11. Fuel for automobiles from birch oil.

12. Substitute fuel from lignite for automobiles.

13. Manufacture of alcohol from resources in Manchuria.

14. Elimination of gum-like matter from cold-proof lubricating oil (a mixture of bean-oil and castor-oil) when alcohol is used as aircraft oil. Preventable by using 80% alcohol and 20% gasoline, or, 80% alcohol and 20% pine root oil.

15. Research in chlorine test paper.

-3-

Supplement 3e

VI. RESEARCH IN SUBSTITUTES FOR CLOTHES AND FOOD:

1. Use of Manchurian wild silkworm for clothing substitute.
2. Food substitutes from Manchurian resources.
3. Cold storage of vegetables.
4. Edible grass as substitutes for vegetables.
5. Edible grass as substitutes for vegetable feeds of small animals.

VII. RESEARCH IN FIELD SUPPLY OF PURIFIED WATER:

1. Cold-proof equipment for sanitary filtering apparatus.
2. Decreasing weight and volume of sanitary filtering apparatus.
3. Substitutes for aluminum and iron in filtering apparatus.
4. Mass production of diatomite filtering apparatus.
5. Methods for determination of disinfection of water in the field.
6. Detection of poison in water.
7. Softening of hard water.
8. Elimination of iron in water filtering tubes.
9. Improvement of methods for washing water filtering equipment.
10. Transporting of small-sized filtering apparatus by dogs.
11. Supply of purified water in bags dropped from aircraft.
12. Methods for increasing capacity of diatomite filtering tubes.

VIII. RESEARCH IN TRANSPORTATION:

1. Air transport of personnel and materials for preventive medicine.
2. Evacuation of patients with infectious diseases by airplane.
3. Research in cold-proof hygiene.

Supplement 3e

IX. RESEARCH IN PREVENTIVE MEDICINE APPLICABLE TO DEFENSE AGAINST BOMBS AND SPRAY FROM AIRCRAFT:

1. Defensive measures against experimental bombs manufactured by the institute.

2. Research in dissemination by spray and measures for defense.

X. MANUFACTURE:

1. **Vaccines:**

a. Dried vaccine.

b. Plague vaccine.

c. Typhoid and paratyphoid vaccine.

d. Gas gangrene vaccine.

e. Tetanus vaccine.

f. Cholera vaccine.

g. Dysentery vaccine.

h. Scarlet fever vaccine.

i. Whooping cough vaccine.

j. Diptheria vaccine.

k. Eruptive typhus vaccine.

(1) Vaccine prepared from eggs.

(2) Vaccine prepared from white rat lungs.

(3) Vaccine prepared from wild squirrel lungs.

2. Curative Sera:

a. Gas gangrene serum.

b. Tetanus serum.

Supplement 3e

c. Diptheria serum.

d. Dysentery serum.

e. Streptococcus serum.

f. Staphlococcus serum.

g. Erysipelas curative serum.

h. Pneumonia curative serum.

i. Epidemic cerebrospinal meningitis curative serum.

j. Plague curative serum.

3. Diagnostic Antigens:

a. Typhoid.

b. Paratyphoid.

c. Eruptive typhus.

d. Tuberculin.

4. Diagnostic Sera:

a. Diagnostic serum for typhoid fever.

b. Diagnostic serum for paratyphoid.

c. Diagnostic serum for all types of dysentery.

d. Diagnostic serum for all types of cholera.

e. Diagnostic serum for epidemic cerebrospinal meningitis.

f. Diagnostic serum for pneumonia.

g. Salmonella factor serum.

5. Materials for Filtering Apparatus:

a. Filtering apparatus (B).

b. Filtering apparatus (C).

Supplement 3e

c. Filtering apparatus (D).

d. Filtering apparatus parts.

e. Water filtering tubes.

6. Drugs:

a. Peptone.

b. Meat essence.

c. Magotin.

d. Marfanil.

e. Penicillin.

f. Birch oil.

7. Repair of Water Filtering Apparatus:

8. Tentative Manufacture of Bombs:

a. I Bomb.

b. Ro Bomb.

c. Ha Bomb.

d. Ni Bomb.

e. U Bomb.

f. Uji Bomb (Old Type).

g. Uji Bomb (Type 50).

h. Uji Bomb (Type 100).

i. Ga Bomb.

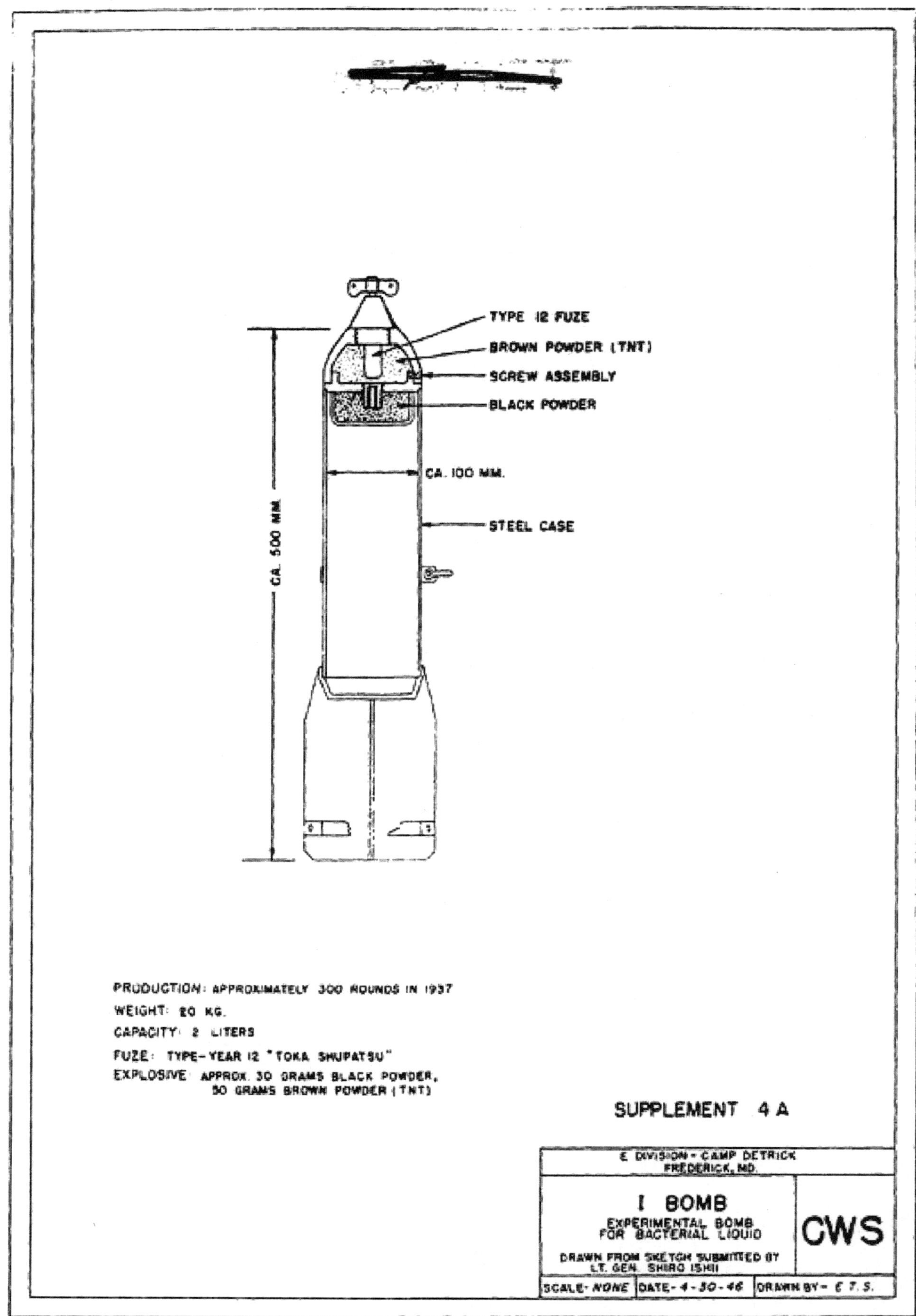
TYPE 12 FUZE
BROWN POWDER (TNT)
SCREW ASSEMBLY
BLACK POWDER
CA. 100 MM.
STEEL CASE
CA. 500 MM.
PRODUCTION: APPROXIMATELY 300 ROUNDS IN 1937
WEIGHT: 20 KG.
CAPACITY: 2 LITERS
FUZE: TYPE-YEAR 12 "TOKA SHUPATSU"
EXPLOSIVE: APPROX. 30 GRAMS BLACK POWDER, 50 GRAMS BROWN POWDER (TNT)
SUPPLEMENT 4 A
E DIVISION - CAMP DETRICK FREDERICK, MD.
I BOMB
EXPERIMENTAL BOMB FOR BACTERIAL LIQUID
DRAWN FROM SKETCH SUBMITTED BY LT. GEN. SHIRO ISHII
CWS
SCALE- NONE
DATE- 4-30-46
DRAWN BY- E.T.S.

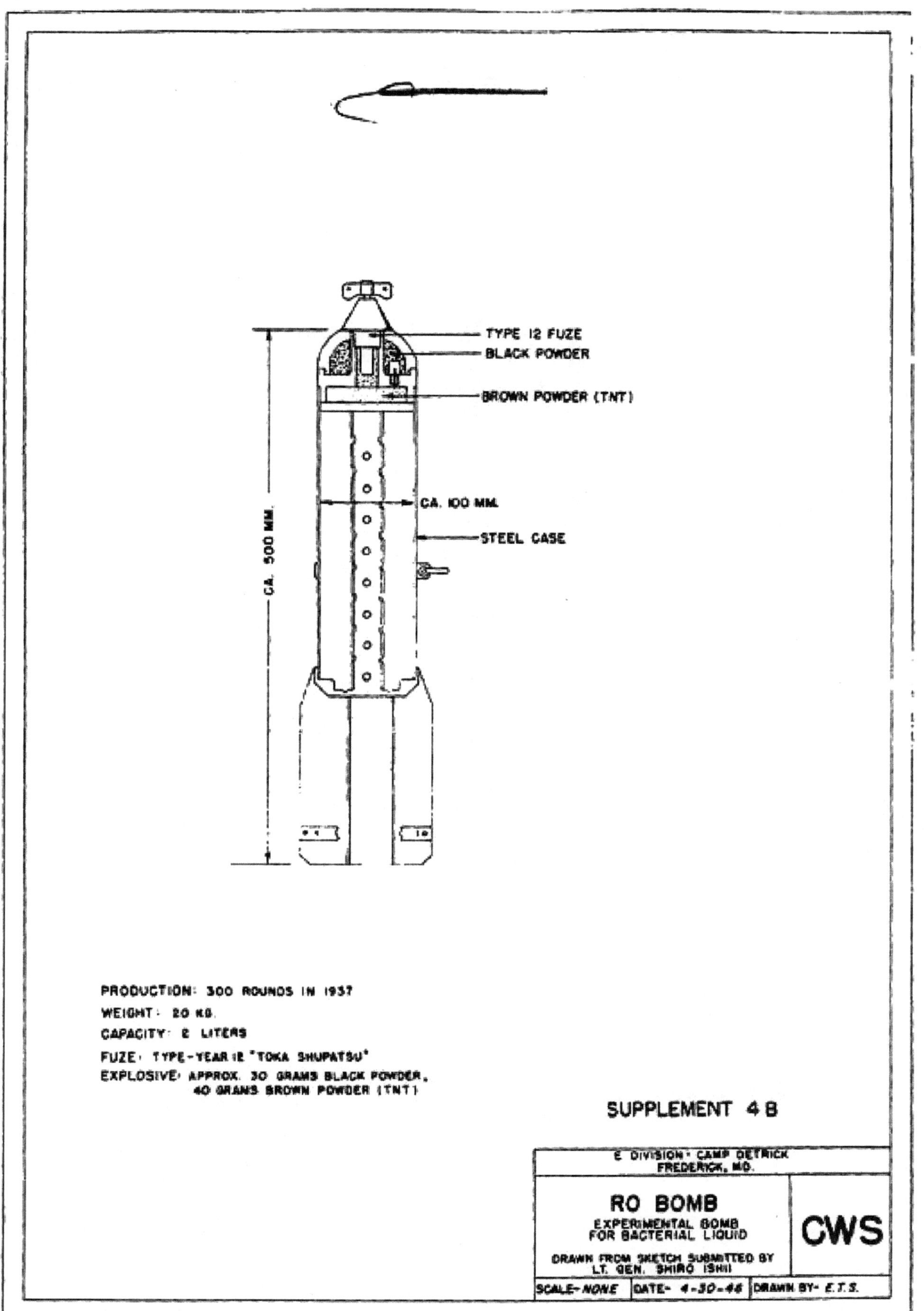
TYPE 12 FUZE
BLACK POWDER
BROWN POWDER (TNT)
CA. 100 MM.
STEEL CASE
CA. 500 MM.
PRODUCTION: 300 ROUNDS IN 1937
WEIGHT: 20 KG.
CAPACITY: 2 LITERS
FUZE: TYPE-YEAR 12 "TOKA SHUPATSU"
EXPLOSIVE: APPROX. 30 GRAMS BLACK POWDER,
40 GRAMS BROWN POWDER (TNT)
SUPPLEMENT 4 B
E DIVISION · CAMP DETRICK
FREDERICK, MD.
RO BOMB
EXPERIMENTAL BOMB
FOR BACTERIAL LIQUID
DRAWN FROM SKETCH SUBMITTED BY
LT. GEN. SHIRO ISHII
CWS
SCALE- NONE
DATE- 4-30-46
DRAWN BY- E.T.S.

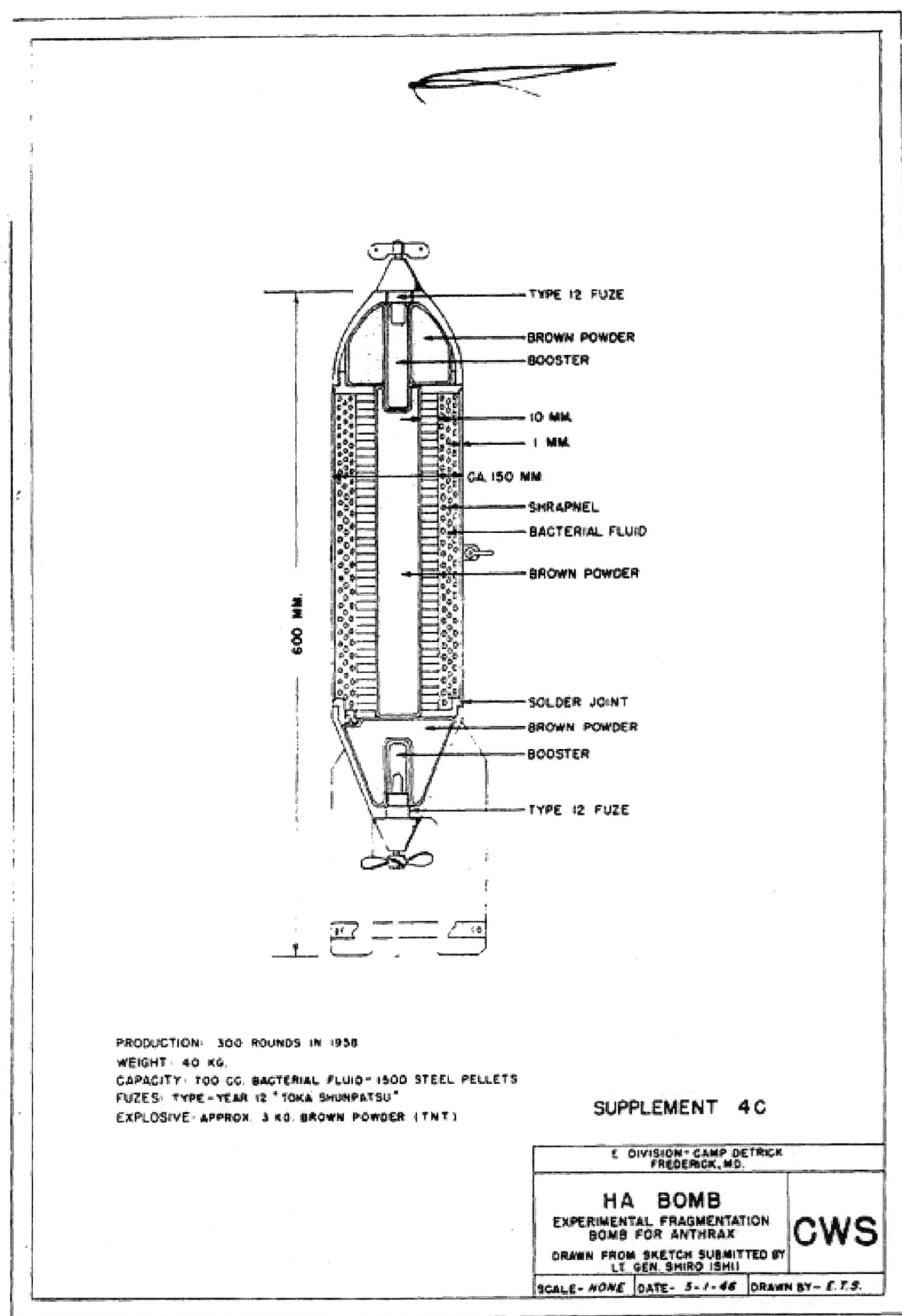
TYPE 12 FUZE
BROWN POWDER
BOOSTER
10 MM
1 MM
CA. 150 MM
SHRAPNEL
BACTERIAL FLUID
BROWN POWDER
600 MM.
SOLDER JOINT
BROWN POWDER
BOOSTER
TYPE 12 FUZE
PRODUCTION: 300 ROUNDS IN 1938
WEIGHT: 40 KG.
CAPACITY: 700 CC. BACTERIAL FLUID - 1500 STEEL PELLETS
FUZES: TYPE - YEAR 12 "TOKA SHUNPATSU"
EXPLOSIVE: APPROX. 3 KG. BROWN POWDER (TNT)
SUPPLEMENT 4C
E. DIVISION - CAMP DETRICK
FREDERICK, MD.
HA BOMB
EXPERIMENTAL FRAGMENTATION
BOMB FOR ANTHRAX
DRAWN FROM SKETCH SUBMITTED BY
LT. GEN. SHIRO ISHII
CWS
SCALE - NONE
DATE - 5-1-46
DRAWN BY - E.T.S.

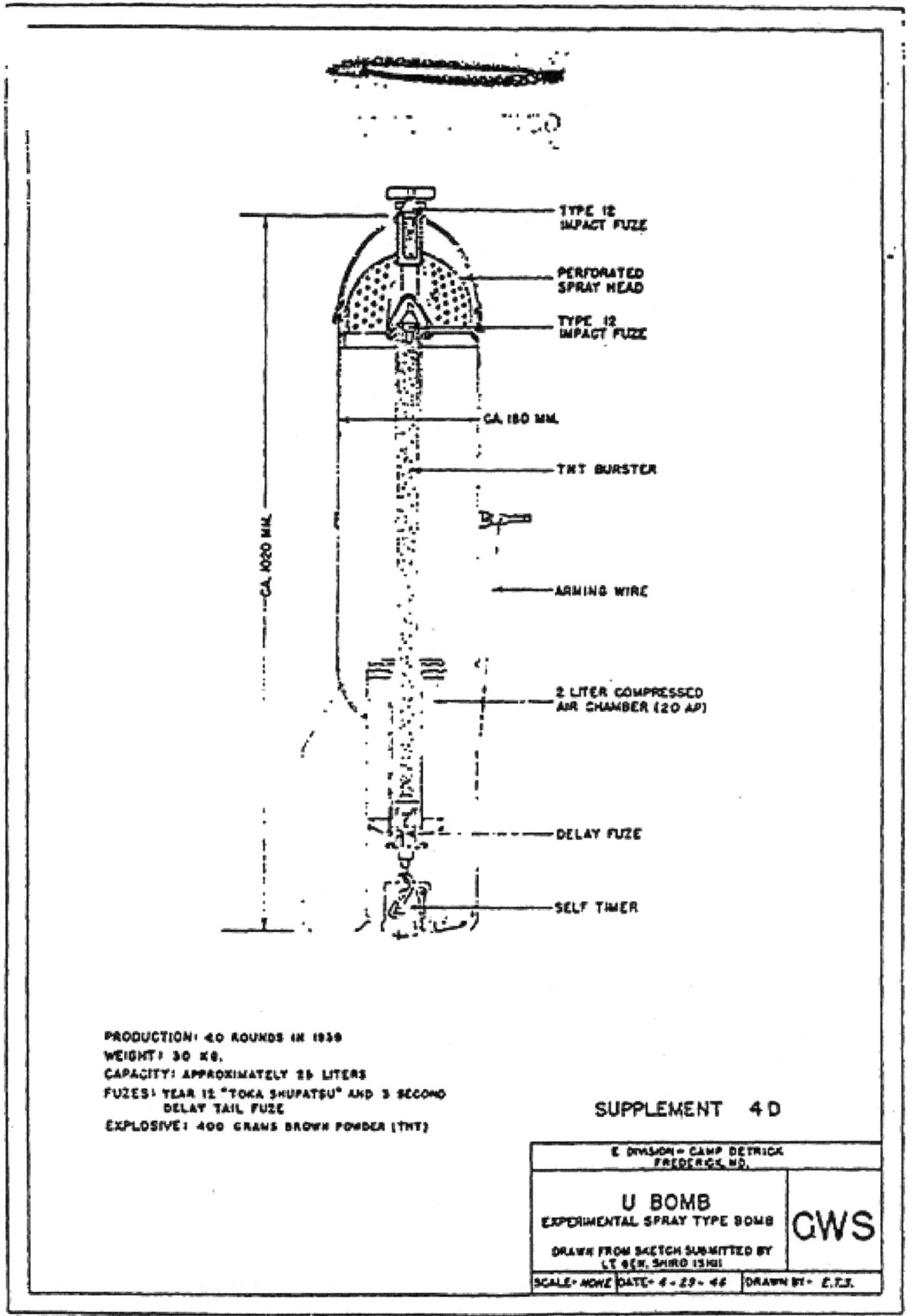
TYPE 12
IMPACT FUZE
PERFORATED
SPRAY HEAD
TYPE 12
IMPACT FUZE
CA. 180 MM.
TNT BURSTER
CA. 1020 MM.
ARMING WIRE
2 LITER COMPRESSED
AIR CHAMBER (20 AP)
DELAY FUZE
SELF TIMER
PRODUCTION: 40 ROUNDS IN 1939
WEIGHT: 30 KG.
CAPACITY: APPROXIMATELY 25 LITERS
FUZES: TEAR 12 "TOKA SHUPATSU" AND 3 SECOND
DELAY TAIL FUZE
EXPLOSIVE: 400 GRAMS BROWN POWDER (TNT)
SUPPLEMENT 4 D
E DIVISION - CAMP DETRICK
FREDERICK, MD.
U BOMB
EXPERIMENTAL SPRAY TYPE BOMB
DRAWN FROM SKETCH SUBMITTED BY
LT GEN. SHIRO ISHII
GWS
SCALE- NONE
DATE- 4-29-46
DRAWN BY- E.T.J.

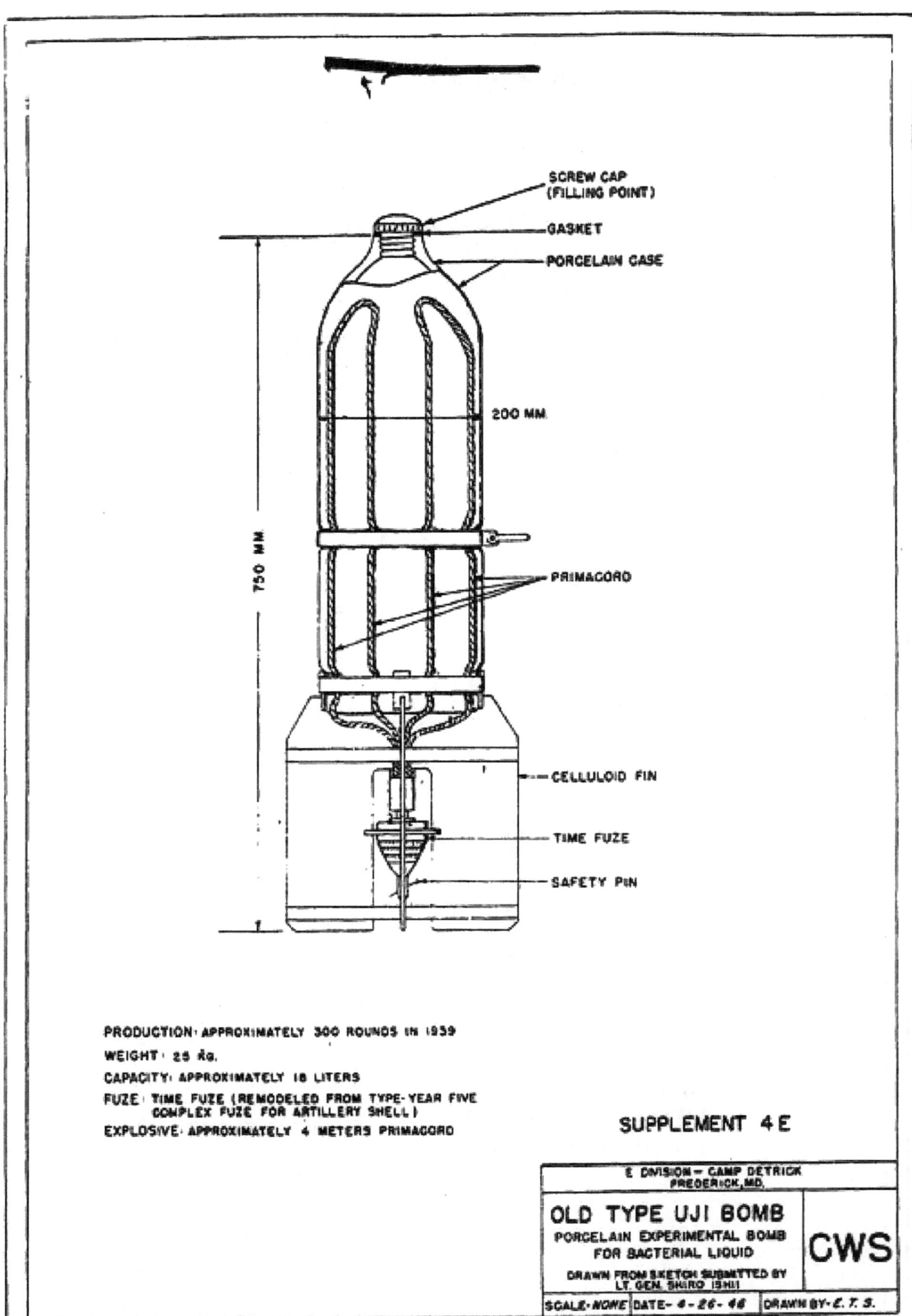
SCREW CAP
(FILLING POINT)
GASKET
PORCELAIN CASE
200 MM
750 MM
PRIMACORD
CELLULOID FIN
TIME FUZE
SAFETY PIN
PRODUCTION: APPROXIMATELY 300 ROUNDS IN 1939
WEIGHT: 25 KG.
CAPACITY: APPROXIMATELY 18 LITERS
FUZE: TIME FUZE (REMODELED FROM TYPE-YEAR FIVE
COMPLEX FUZE FOR ARTILLERY SHELL)
EXPLOSIVE: APPROXIMATELY 4 METERS PRIMACORD
SUPPLEMENT 4 E
E DIVISION – CAMP DETRICK
FREDERICK, MD.
OLD TYPE UJI BOMB
PORCELAIN EXPERIMENTAL BOMB
FOR BACTERIAL LIQUID
DRAWN FROM SKETCH SUBMITTED BY
LT. GEN. SHIRO ISHII
CWS
SCALE-NONE
DATE- 4-26-46
DRAWN BY- E. T. S.

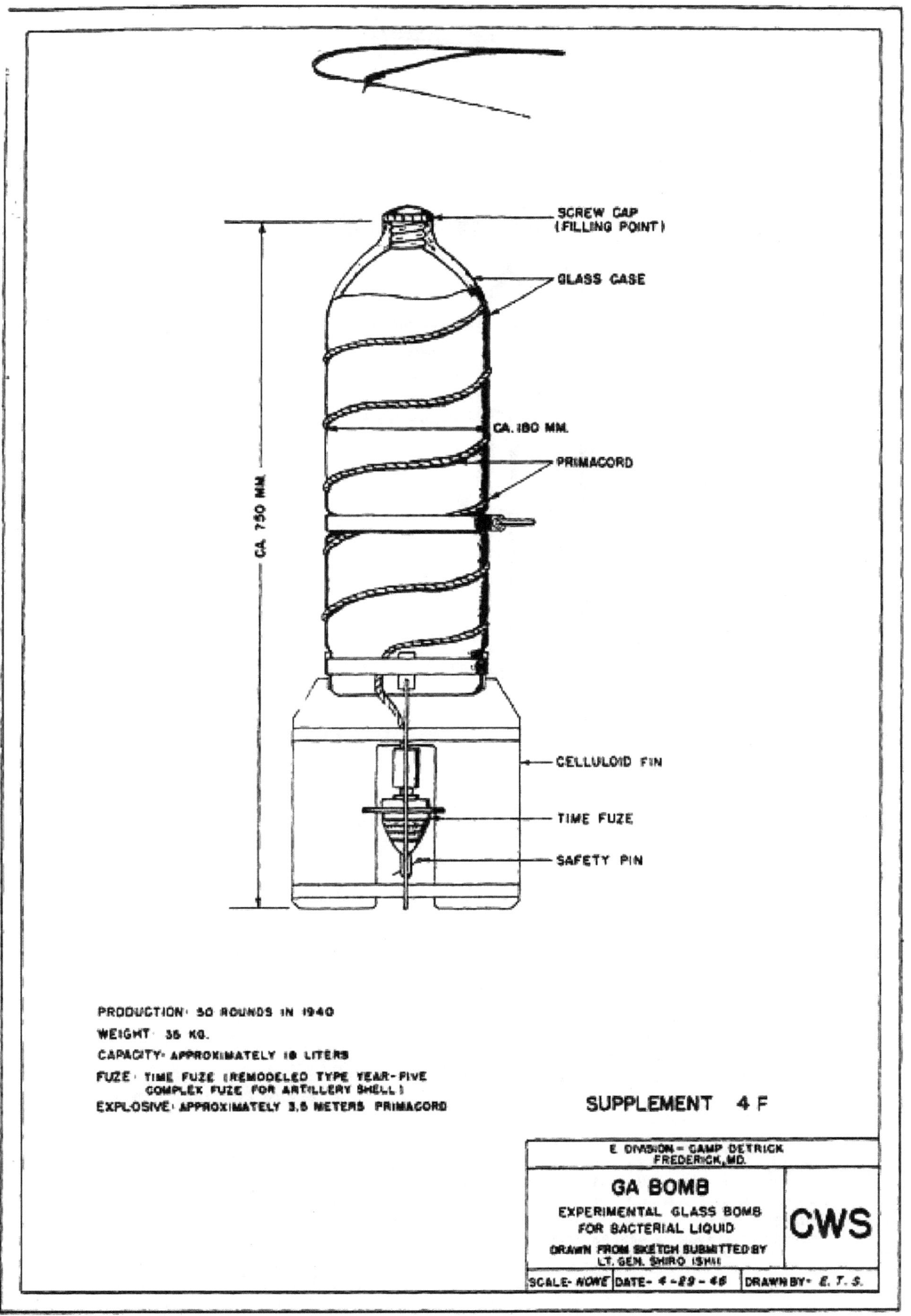
SCREW CAP
(FILLING POINT)
GLASS CASE
CA. 180 MM.
PRIMACORD
CA 750 MM.
CELLULOID FIN
TIME FUZE
SAFETY PIN
PRODUCTION: 50 ROUNDS IN 1940
WEIGHT: 35 KG.
CAPACITY: APPROXIMATELY 10 LITERS
FUZE: TIME FUZE (REMODELED TYPE YEAR-FIVE COMPLEX FUZE FOR ARTILLERY SHELL)
EXPLOSIVE: APPROXIMATELY 3.5 METERS PRIMACORD
SUPPLEMENT 4 F
E DIVISION - CAMP DETRICK
FREDERICK, MD.
GA BOMB
EXPERIMENTAL GLASS BOMB
FOR BACTERIAL LIQUID
DRAWN FROM SKETCH SUBMITTED BY
LT. GEN. SHIRO ISHII
CWS
SCALE- NONE
DATE- 4-29-46
DRAWN BY- E. T. S.

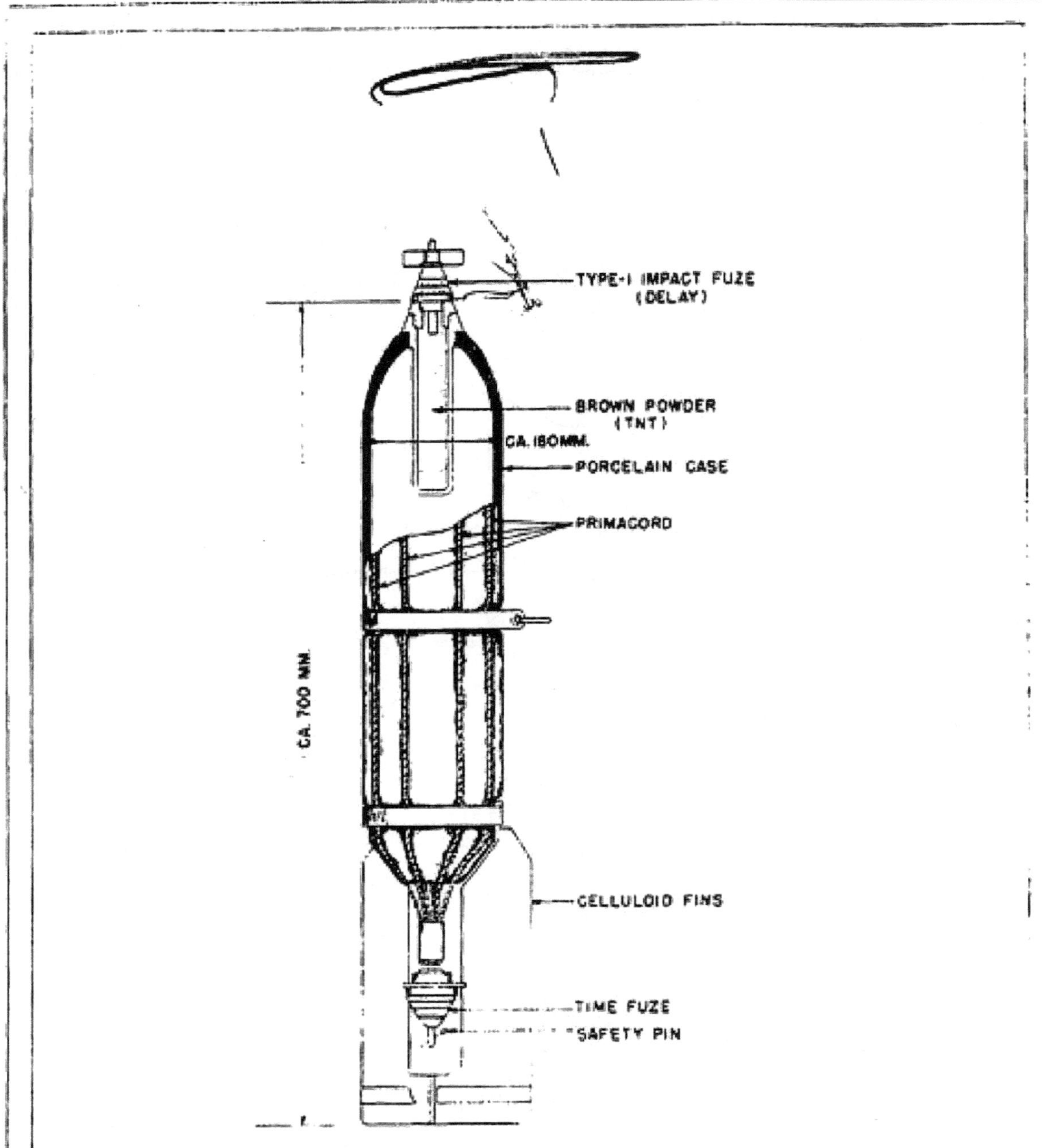

TYPE 50

PRODUCTION: APPROXIMATELY 500 ROUNDS 1940-1942
WEIGHT: 25 KG. CAPACITY: APPROXIMATELY 10 LITERS
FUZE: NOSE FUZE - TYPE I IMPACT (DELAY)
TAIL FUZE - TIME FUZE (REMODELED FROM TYPE YEAR 5 COMPLEX FUZE FOR ARTILLERY SHELL)
EXPLOSIVE: APPROXIMATELY 4 METERS PRIMACORD AND 500 GRAMS TNT.

TYPE 100 (SAME DESIGN)

PRODUCTION: 300 ROUNDS 1940-1942
LENGTH: APPROX. 1600 MM. WIDTH: APPROX. 300 MM.
WEIGHT: 50 KG. CAPACITY: APPROX. 25 LITERS
FUZES: (SAME)
EXPLOSIVE: APPROX. 12 METERS PRIMACORD AND 500 GRAMS TNT.

SUPPLEMENT 4 G

E DIVISION-CAMP DETRICK FREDERICK, MD.	
TYPE 50 UJI BOMB IMPROVED PORCELAIN EXPERIMENTAL BOMB FOR BACTERIAL LIQUID DRAWN FROM SKETCH SUBMITTED BY LT. GEN. SHIRO ISHII	CWS
SCALE- NONE DATE- 4-26-46	DRAWN BY- E.T.S.

6.3 Norbert H. Fell 调查

6.3.1 29 Mar. 1947: Request of Russian Prosecutor for Permission to Interrogate Certain Japanese (Biological Warfare)

资料出处： National Archives of the United States, R319, E468, B428.

内容点评： 本资料为 1947 年 3 月 29 日美军电文情报备忘录，题目：苏联要求讯问有关日本人（细菌战）。提及化学战部队选派 Norbert H. Fell 博士赴日调查，预计 4 月 5 日出发。

Combined Routing - Information - File Form
Plans & Operations Division, WDGS

3-29/612
(FW #5)

Decimal Classification: P&O 000.5 TS (29 March 1947)

x 381
x 091 Russia

Suspense: 1200 31 Mar 47

Subject: Request of Russian Prosecutor for Permission to Interrogate Certain Japanese (Biological Warfare)

Date: 29 Mar 47

Origin: CINCFE

Digest: Rad C 51310 (CM-IN-5288) TOP SECRET

HANDLE BY OFFICER ONLY

Action: Radio to CINCFE advising name of representative, stating that one person considered sufficient and estimating departure on 5 April.
(See M/R on reverse side)

Msg: No. Out 95265 Date Pacific Section

To
- [ ] European
- [x] ~~Pacific~~ Ars
- [ ] Western Hemisphere
- [ ] Control, Rec. & Res.
- [ ] ~~Operations~~
- [ ] Strategic Plans
- [ ] Policy
- [ ] Politico Mil. Survey
- [ ] Base Planning
- [ ] Implementing
- [ ] Plans & Policy
- [ ] Registered Documents
- [ ] Personnel

Comments: For "Biological Warfare", see 381 TS, #67.

Recommendation:
Section Chief G Date 31 Mar
Group Chief Date ~~31 MAR 1947~~ 1 APR 1947

Concurrence:

- [x] Executive, P&O
- [x] Deputy Director, P&O
- [ ] Director, P&O

Original Date Received

Dispatch File

424

Action by Lt. Col. Bagstad

Signed Leo Bagstad Date 31 Mar 47

APR 1 - 1947

26 88827

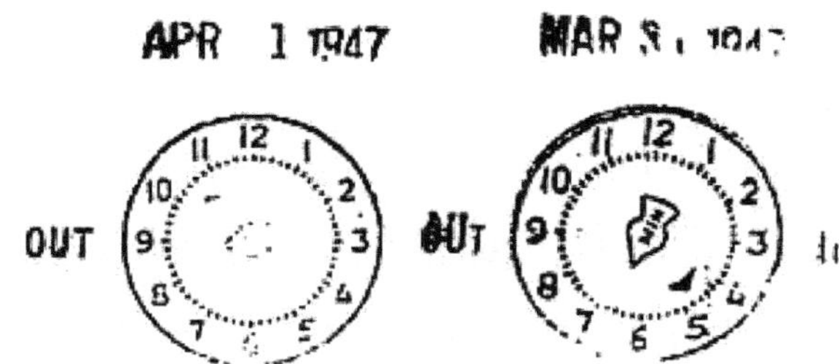

MEMORADNUM FOR RECORD

1. CM-IN 5288 of 29 March concurs in dispatch of interrogators to Japan to interview Japanese BW experts. Radio requests names and ETA of two representatives so that APR can be provided; requests that personnel be placed on TDY for 30 days G2 of FEC; states that USSR may withdraw their offer if reply is based on part 2 of W94446.

2. CM-OUT 94446 grants permission for SCAP controlled Soviet interrogation of BW experts subject to prior interview by U.S. interrogator; also states that interrogation should be granted Soviet on the basis of an amiable gesture toward a friendly government and that future requests will be considered on their individual merits.

3. In CM-IN 1604 of 10 February SCAP requested guidance on Soviet request to interrogate these Japanese and stated that Soviet had offerred to share info gained with U.S. and made certain other offers. In CM-IN 5288 CINCFE states that these offers may be withdrawn by Soviets.

4. Chemical Warfare, Col. Wallington ext 3541 states that his Division considers one interrogator sufficient for this purpose and that Dr. Norbert H. Fell has been selected for the Job. Col. Wallington states that Dr. Fell can be prepared to depart Washington on 5 April.

5. Action: Radio to CINCFE advising name of representative, stating that one person considered sufficient and estimating departure on 5 April.

6. Coordination: P&P - Maj. Liggett ext 2273
CWS - Col. Wallington ext 3541

6.3.2　31 Mar. 1947: TO: CINCFE TOKYO JAPAN, TOPSEC FROM WDGPO REFERENCE CHARLIE FIVE ONE THREE ONE ZERO OF TWO NINE MARCH FOUR SEVEN; 1 Apr. 1947: FROM: WASHINGTON (WDGPO), TO: CINCFE, NR: W 95265

资料出处：National Archives of the United States, R319, E468, B428.

内容点评：本资料为1947年3月31日美国陆军部发送东京美远东司令部的电文：派Norbert H. Fell博士赴日本继续调查，1947年4月5日从华盛顿出发。附1947年4月1日美远东军司令部接收该电文的记录。

TOP SECRET

95265
0119162

TOP SECRET

WAR DEPARTMENT—OFFICIAL BUSINESS

OUTGOING CLASSIFIED MESSAGE

PRECEDENCE	OFFICE OF ORIGIN	EXTENSION
PRIORITY	PLANS AND OPERATIONS PACIFIC SECTION	2495
DATE 31 MARCH 47	P&O 000.5 TS (29 March 1947)	NAME OF OFFICER PREPARING Lt.Col. Bagstad/as

CLASSIFICATION ➡ [ ] RESTRICTED [ ] CONFIDENTIAL [ ] SECRET [XX] TOP SECRET

LIST EACH ADDRESSEE SEPARATELY. USE UPPER CASE AND DOUBLE SPACING BETWEEN EACH ADDRESS AND THROUGHOUT MESSAGE

TO: CINCFE TOKYO JAPAN

COPY FOR P & O MESSAGE-FILE

TOPSEC FROM WDGPO REFERENCE CHARLIE FIVE ONE THREE ONE ZERO OF TWO NINE MARCH FOUR SEVEN

DOCTOR NORBERT HOW FELL HAS BEEN SELECTED BY CWS TO CONDUCT INTERROGATION PD ONE INTERROGATOR CONSIDERED SUFFICIENT UNLESS YOU INDICATE NEED FOR TWO PERSONS PD FIVE APRIL IS ESTIMATED WASHINGTON DEPARTURE DOCTOR FELL

A

COPY FOR P & O MESSAGE FILE

COPY FOR P & O MESSAGE FILE

C 51310 is CM-IN 5288 (29 Mar 47)

DISTRIBUTION	COORDINATION CONTENT AND CLASSIFICATION AUTHENTICATED BY
P&O	TYPED NAME AND GRADE: FRANCIS G. GIDEON Colonel, GSC
ASW	Acting Chief, Pac Sec.
CSA	DIVISION: Operations Group, P&O
AAF	SIGNATURE OF RESPONSIBLE OFFICER
ID	
CWS 42	

W. D., A.G.O. FORM NO. 500, 1 June 1944

This form supersedes W. D., A. G. O. Form No. 500, 2 September 1942, which may be used until existing stocks are exhausted.

COPY FOR P&O MESSAGE FILE

TOP SECRET

FAR EAST COMMAND
GENERAL HEADQUARTERS, ~~U. S. ARMY FORCES, PACIFIC~~ 9?0
ADJUTANT GENERAL'S OFFICE
RADIO AND CABLE CENTER

CONFIDENTIAL

INCOMING MESSAGE

PRIORITY X 201 2nd 2 April 47

FROM : WASHINGTON (WDGPO)

TO : CINCFE

NR : W 95265

000.5 wc (TS-S)

Reference C 51310 of 29 March 47. Doctor Norbert H Fell has been selected by CWS to conduct interrogation. One interrogator considered sufficient unless you indicate need for two persons. 5 April is estimated Washington departure Doctor Fell.

NO SIG

ACTION : G-2

INFORMATION : COMMANDER IN CHIEF, CHIEF OF STAFF, G-1

86235 PRIORITY TOO : 011916 Z
MCN : SA 188/01

"Paraphrase not required. Handle as TOP SECRET correspondence per paras 51 1 and 60 a (4) AR 380-5."

CONFIDENTIAL

A. G. FILE

Handling and transmission of literal plain text of this message as correspondence of the same classification has been authorized by the War Department in accordance with the provisions of paragraphs 16 C, 18 E, 53 A, 53 D (1) (2) (3), and 60-A (1) (2) (3) (4), AR 380-5, 6 March 1946.

COPY No. 14

Incl 10

6.3.3 19 Apr. 1947: MEMORANDUM, TO: Dr. Fell: Roster of Personnel Connected with Shiro ISHII in the Pursuit of Bacterial Warfare, FROM: INVESTIGATION DIVISION, LEGAL SECTION

资料出处：National Archives of the United States, R319, E468, B428.

内容点评：本资料为 1947 年 4 月 19 日盟军总司令部法务局调查科提供 Fell 博士的细菌战调查用石井四郎有关人员名单。

INVESTIGATION DIVISION
LEGAL SECTION

19 April 1947

MEMORANDUM :

TO : Dr. Fell

SUBJECT : Roster of personnel Connected with Shiro ISHII in the pursuit of Bacterial Warfare.

YAM Motoji YAMAGUCHI, Miyagi-ken, Shibata-gun, Murata-machi

HOSA Yasataro HOSAKA, Setagaya-ku, Tomogawa-cho, Okusawa-machi, 3-45.

WAKA Yujiro WAKAMATSU,

YAMA Shiro YAMASHITA, 173, Tsuchirara, Hagi-shi, Yamaguchi-ken.

NISH Takeshi NISHIMURA,

MAC Tokio MACHIDA,

OKI Yukenobu OKI,

MATSUY Hironobu MATSUYAMA,

KANE Korin KANEDA,

SATO U Usaburo SATO,

MARU Shoji MARUYAMA,

SAKAT Shin SAKATA,

MATSUY Shiro MATSUYAMA,

SASAK Bunson SASAKI,

ANDO Keitaro ANDO,

SATO N Noburo SATO,

KUROB Junji KUROBAKI,

MATSUI Toshiro MATSUI,

GO Jiro GOTO,

Civilians (Lt. Col's)

SHIS SHISHIDO (fnu)

ONO Y Yutaka ONO,

IDA IDA (fnu) Kiyoshi

ARIY Shin ARIYAMA,

FUJI FUJITA (fnu)

~~I~~	~~Katsushige IKEDA IDEI~~	Lt. Col.
~~K~~	~~Jun-ichi KANEKO~~	~~Maj.~~
~~T~~	~~YOshifumi TSUYAMA~~	~~Maj.~~
~~H~~	~~Haru HASHIMOTO~~	~~Eng. 5th class.~~
~~I~~	~~Takemoto INOUE~~	Col.
Y	Yukimasa YAGISAWA	Lt. Col.
~~K~~	~~Masaji KITANO~~	~~General -- sucessor to ISHII in 1944.~~
~~M~~	~~MOTOMO (fnu)~~	

HI HIGASHIKUNI (fnu) Prince

CH CHICHIBU (fnu) Prince

KU Mitsuichi KURITSU Wakamatsu-cho, Ushigome-Ku.

AR Torasaburo ARAKI Father-in-law of ISHII and President of Kyoto Imperial University.

NI Eiji NISHIMURA Col.

SA Jun SAKAKURA Lt. Col.

ON Yoshio ONODERA " "

IS Kinzo ISHIYAMA Civilian.

HO Enryo HOJO Col.

SU SUZUKI (fnu) civ.

SAKU Kanichi SAKURAI Civ.

II IIDA (fnu) Civ.

YAK Yukinara YAKIZAWA Civ.

SH Shinichi SHINBO Tech.

TA Yoshiichi TAKAHASHI Tech.

KI Hitoshi KIKUCHI Maj. Gen.

OT Kiyoshi OTA. Col.

IK Hatushige IKARI Col.

MA Tomasada MASUDA COL.

MUR Takashi MURAKAMI Col.

SO Saburo SONADA Col.

IM Kokan IMAZU Col.

KIT Masataka KITAGAWA Col (d)

EG EGUCHI (fnu) Col.

MAS Yashiyasu MASUDA Maj.

TAN TANABE (fnu) Maj.

TAK TAKAHASHI (fnu) Maj.

WA Hotroi WATANABE Eng. 2nd class

FU Hideo FUKATI Eng. 6th class

IS Tachio ISHIKAWA " " "

AN Koji ANDO Eng. 2nd Class

KA Zen KAWAKAMI " " "

SATO SATO (fnu) Col.

NA Ryochi NAITO Lt. Col.

Civilians (Major)

KA KATO (fnu) Fumiya

MUR Yutaka MURAKAMI,

Civ. (Capt.)

MI MITSUDA (fnu) Hayasaki

Civ, (2nd Lt.)

SN SNOJI (fnu)

MA MATSUI (fnu)

IS Shiro ISHII, 77, Wakamatsu-cho, Ushigome-ku, Tokyo.

KO Saburo KOJIMA (densenbyo KENKYUSHO)

HOS Shogo HOSOYA " "

YO Hidetaki YOOHI " "

KU Kozo KUNIMOTO Kyoto Imperial Univ.

KASA Shiro KASAHARA " " "

KAN Hiroshi KANBAYASHI Ministry of war Lt. Gen.

HIR Lt. Col. HIRAGA (fnu) "

ASA " " Asaoka (fnu) "

KAJI " " KAJI (fnu) "

OTU Maj. OTUGURO (fnu)

AKU Col. AKUZUKI (fnu)

SHO Rinnosuke SHOJI Kyoto Imperial Univ.

SASA Kyuco SASAKAWA

INO Ko INOUE

IY IYEMORI (fnu)

MIN Masuzo MINOWADA

HOS Teiji HOSHINO

FUN Shogo FUNSOKA

ARA Senri ARAKI

KINO Ryojun KINOSHITA Osaka Imperial Univesrity.

TANA Eiji TANAGUCHI " " "

TANAB Lt. General TANABE Chief of General Affairs (ISHII Unit)

MIYA MIYAZAKI (fnu) Managing director of S.M.R. Research BURO.

ISHI Kanji ISHIHARA

NIS Katsu NISHI

6.3.4　21 Apr. 1947: CONFERENCE WITH KAMEI, KANICHIRO

资料出处：Technical Library, Fort Dugway Proving Grounds, Utah, US.

内容点评：本资料为 1947 年 4 月 21 日 Fell 博士与亀井贯一郎（Kamei，Kanichiro）的谈话记录。亀井贯一郎为知名外交官。

CONFERENCE WITH KAMEI, KANICHIRO

DATE : 21 April 1947

INTERROGATORS: Dr N. H. Fell, Lt Col R. P. McQuail,
CIC T. Yoshihashi

INTERROGATED : KAMEI, Kanichiro, prominent businessman, and his secretary, ARAMAKI, Hiroto

1. KAMEI identified himself as the director of a Japanese business firm, The Scientific Research and Propagating Institute for Modernizing People's Life and Economy, 3 GOTTOME, GINZA KYOBASHI, TOKYO. His residence is 1112 OMACHI, KAMAKURA. He holds a Ph.D from Columbia University, uses the title of Professor or Doctor, and speaks fairly good English. ARAMAKI is English speaking Japanese, born in HAWAII, educated in US, and employed as KAMEI'S confidential secretary. His address is KAMAKURA SHI, MIDARE BASHI, ZAIMOKUZA 977-6.

2. KAMEI spoke at length on the following:

a. His pre-surrender career as an anti-expansionist politician which culminated in a six month prison term under the TOJO regime.

b. His theories on present day Japanese economy and politics.

c. His belief that his institute and cooperation with the United States would accelerate the recovery of Japan.

d. His fear and distaste of Communism and his cooperation with the CIC to combat its threat.

3. It was explained to KAMEI that information available to the United States indicated that Japanese had not revealed full information on offensive aspects of BW and that due to his previous connection with the investigation, his opinion was solicited. KAMEI stated in substance as follows:

"I was first involved in Lt Col Sander's investigation as an interpreter. In the later stages, I endeavored to persuade the Japanese to reveal everything. I realized that the personnel questioned were evading questions, giving incomplete information, and avoiding responsibility because of fear of being designated "war criminals". Interrogations on BW were carried out too soon after the surrender. Japanese were un-

PA ✓

acf3

easy and would not talk freely. Since then, the occupation has gone well, Japan has settled down, and I believe you can obtain more information if the Japanese concerned are assured that their information will not be used for "war crimes" prosecution. Former General KAWADA, who assists General Eichelberger in the Eighth Army, could help in reassuring the Japanese.

"There were many more offensive experiments and developments in BW than were admitted. It is probable that BW bombs were actually employed in Central China, but I think a group other than General ISHII'S carried out tests and knows the results. I believe that former Colonels NIIZUMI and MASUDA can be helpful. I will confer with them and bring them to see you."

2

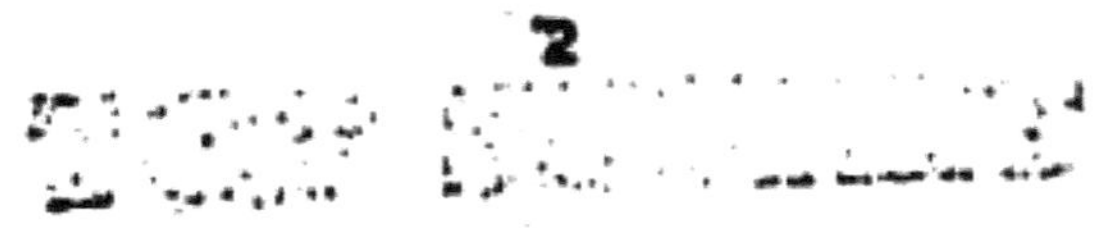

6.3.5　22 Apr. 1947: INTERROGATION OF MASUDA, TOMOSADA

资料出处： Technical Library, Fort Dugway Proving Grounds, Utah, US.

内容点评： 本资料为 1947 年 4 月 22 日 Fell 博士对增田知贞（Masuda, Tomosada）的讯问记录。增田知贞曾任日军驻南京 1644 细菌部队第二任部队长。

INTERROGATION OF MASUDA, TOMOSADA

DATE : 22 April 1947

INTERROGATORS : Dr. N. H. Fell, Lt. Col. R. P. McQuail, Major O. V. Keller, CWO T. Yoshihashi

INTERROGATED : MASUDA, Tomosada, former Colonel, Japanese Medical Corps, and Chief of 2d Section, MANCHU 731
KAMEI, Kanichiro, spokesman for MASUDA

1. MASUDA originally reported 21 Apr 47, but was instructed to see KAMEI and return 22 Apr 47 for interrogation.

2. MASUDA stated that he was a physician at: Chiba Ken, Kimizo Gun, Akimoto Mura, Nishihikasa, 289 Banchi.

3. KAMEI requested permission to relate the conversation between MASUDA and him earlier in the day, and stated in substance as follows:

"MASUDA is eager to cooperate with you. However, information on offensive developments in BW is extremely delicate, and Japanese formerly connected with this field are very loath to speak about it. ISHII was extremely unpopular with his subordinates, and one or more sent anonymous letters shortly after the surrender to SCAP, accusing ISHII of directing human experiments in BW and requesting that he be prosecuted as a war criminal. As a result, Japanese personnel were afraid to reveal information for fear of involving themselves or others. The interrogations conducted by Lt. Col. Sanders and Lt. Col. Thompson were too soon after the surrender. However, if the men who actually know the detailed results of the experiments can be convinced that your investigation is from a purely scientific standpoint, I believe that you can get more information."

"There is no question but that BW trials were made against the Chinese Army in Central China. The bombs were developed originally as a means of developing defensive measures against possible BW on the part of an enemy. However, the strong offensive value of BW bombs, particularly if loaded with anthrax, was soon apparent. Two friends of MASUDA's, NAITO and KANEKO, have definite information on these trials. I suggest a meeting with these men."

"INOUE, of the 1st Demobilization Bureau, should be instructed on the purpose of your investigation. I believe it will reassure any

personnel whom you have reported to be assured from the start that you are not investigating "war crimes"."

4. MASUDA was queried as to his assignments since 1937 and his answer coincided with the information in previous reports. During his tour at the Army Medical College in Tokyo from 1941-43, he was in contact with MANCHU 731. He returned to the unit in 1945 from BURMA, and spent the last month of the war as Chief of 3rd Section supervising the destruction of the installation and records. MASUDA stated that he had the remnants of a note book which he would bring to the next meeting.

5. Out of hearing of MASUDA, and in a whisper to Dr. Fell, KAMEI stated in substance:

"MASUDA admitted to me that experiments were carried out on humans. The victims were MANCHURIAN criminals who had been condemned to death. The personnel involved in carrying out these human experiments took a vow never to disclose information. However, I feel sure that if you handle your investigation from a scientific point of view, you can obtain detailed information."

2

TOP SECRET

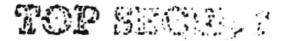

6.3.6　24 Apr. 1947: CONFERENCE WITH KAMEI, KANICHIRO

资料出处： Technical Library, Fort Dugway Proving Grounds, Utah, US.

内容点评： 本资料为 1947 年 4 月 24 日 Fell 博士与亀井贯一郎（Kamei, Kanichiro）的谈话记录。

CONFERENCE WITH KAMEI, KANICHIRO

DATE : 24 April 1947

INTERROGATORS : Dr. N. H. Fell, Lt. Col. R. P. McQuail, Major O. V. Keller, CWO T. Yoshihashi

INTERROGATED : KAMEI, Kanichiro and his Secretary, ARAKAKI, Hinato

1. KAMEI requested a special conference by telephone and upon arrival, stated as follows:

"I contacted INOUE of the 1st Demobilization Bureau about interviews with KANEKO and NAITO. INOUE said he would like to see them first. This indicates a hesitancy to cooperate. You will find that the Japanese are still reluctant to part with information on BW because they are afraid that cooperating and giving information to the United States will be discovered by Communists and passed to Russia. Information about Japanese BW was given fully to Germany, and a large German laboratory was captured intact by the Russians. Thus, the Russians may be well informed on Japanese BW activities. The Japanese have a tendency to feel that continued silence is advisable."

"I will explain briefly the extent of MASUDA's knowledge. Early investigations in BW convinced the Japanese that anthrax was the most effective agent. Several anthrax strains, varying in virulence were discovered. The most promising strain was developed and extensive experiments and tests carried out on animals. Human experiments, using criminals condemned to death by Manchurian courts, were carried out. Infection with anthrax organisms was induced in the following ways:

a. Orally, or by contaminating diet.
b. Inhalation.
c. Infection of open wounds.
d. Injections.

"The tests helped discover an anthrax strain which caused death to humans in about one week after infection, and led the Japanese to consider the use of anthrax as a BW weapon in the following three methods:

a. Against individuals by fifth column, spies, and agents as an effective human poison which left no trace and appeared to be the result of natural causes.

Bombs loaded with anthrax, through which infected bomb fragments would cause injury followed by death from infection.

c. Contamination of water supplies or areas by bacterial showers from airplanes.

Anthrax had the following advantages over other agents: no effective decontamination, long period stability, high virulence, and no effective immunization."

"The Japanese insist that they were forced into BW program by capturing many Russian spies along the MANCHURIAN border, armed with BW agents. The program began as a defensive measure, and as a result, it was learned that anthrax could be employed as an obstacle for denying large areas to the enemy. Study of the defensive aspects led to the discovery of its offensive potential."

"The Japanese are afraid that if they reveal the information that Communists will discover it, write letters to SCAP, tell the Russians, cause publicity, and force the investigation into the open."

"MASUDA, KANEKO and NAITO know the most about BW. If transported to U.S. territory they can reconstruct all records from memory."

"Following the interrogations by Lt. Col. Sanders, the Japanese were relieved that their evasive and incomplete answers were accepted. Lt. Col. Sanders did not know enough about the technical side of the subject. The human experiments were extensive enough to reach scientific conclusions. The methods of infection I mentioned were thoroughly explored and the results and conclusions are in no way based on imagination. KANEKO knows the results of the trials against the Chinese, and these trials included the use of plague. If you are going to interrogate other individuals, I advise that you keep it separate from these three individuals. Due to cliques among former Japanese medical officers, it is difficult to get much cooperation from a large group. ISHII especially should not be involved. There are other individuals who know the detailed data on other agents such as typhoid, but MASUDA knows anthrax, the most effective agent. All of the BW personnel are under the terms of the oath, so you will have to overcome that obstacle.

2

6.3.7 28, 29 and 30 Apr. and I May 1947: CONFERENCES WITH MASUDA, TOMOSADA - KANEKO, JUNICHI, AND NAITO RYO(I)CHI

资料出处：Technical Library, Fort Dugway Proving Grounds, Utah, US.

内容点评：1947年4月28日、29日、30日和5月1日Fell博士与增田知贞（Masuda, Tomosada）、金子顺一（Kaneko, Junichi）、内藤良一（Naito, Ryoichi）的谈话记录。金子顺一是原731部队核心研究人员，内藤良一曾任陆军军医学校防疫研究室主任。

CONFERENCE WITH
[illegible] – [illegible] – [illegible], AND NAITO, RYOICHI

[illegible]

[illegible] : 28, 29 and 30 April and 1 May 1947

[illegible] : Dr E. V. Hill, Lt Col R. P. McQuail, Major O. V. Keller, (29 April only), Mr. S. Yoshihashi

[illegible] : MASUDA, Tomosada, KANEKO, Junichi and NAITO, Ryoichi

1. On 28 April 47, the Japanese arrived at 1600 hours and were instructed to submit an outline of the information they possessed. They agreed to return with completed outline 29 Apr 47. KANEKO gave his address as [illegible], [illegible], and NAITO as OSAKA-[illegible], [illegible].

2. On 29 April 47, the personnel returned with an outline which represented information obtained in previous interrogations, and dealing almost entirely with defensive BW. In answer to questions, the three replied in substance as follows:

"It is hard to report on experiments we have not seen. We have only hearsay to guide us. MASUDA can give you conclusions on the effectiveness of all the agents, but no detail. The basis of BW is discovering the most virulent strain of an effective organism, and MASUDA can give you that. We really do not know exactly who could give you detailed information at this late date."

3. The three Japanese were acquainted with the information KARASAWA and KAWASHIMA revealed to the Russians. The following relevant statements were drawn from:

a. All three:

"KAWASHIMA was not considered important in BW. He was a specialist in production of prophylactic vaccines. KARASAWA was a competent doctor and bacteriologist with engineering ability who worked in mass production of bacteria. YAMAGUCHI was an engineer in charge of bomb experiments. [illegible] is dead. OTA probably knows the general details of all the work at PINGFAN due to his tour as Chief of General Affairs Section. He is not likely to know technical details.

b. MASUDA.

"With regards to your question as to minimum lethal dose of anthrax on humans, 20 mg of moist organisms of most virulent strain were effective on animals, so I presume it would be about that amount for humans. Less virulent strains required up to 100 mg. No effort was made to establish MLD in terms of number of organisms. The Jap-

[illegible] did not employ the LD 50 method of calculation. We heard of a field trial with plague-infected fleas, but it was ineffective.

[illegible] of anthrax is fatal for animals by oral route. I [illegible] about use of smaller quantities. A smaller dose would probably be effective via respiratory tract. There was no field experiments [illegible] of technical difficulties and danger. Laboratory workers were [illegible] despite masks. The aim of BW is to find [illegible] of most virulent strains, and we were satisfied with the [illegible].

[illegible]-infected fleas may remain effective as long as a month depending on temperature, humidity, and other factors of environment. They do not live as long as normal fleas. TANAKA, Hideo of KYOTO was the expert in these matters and could tell you more.

[illegible] were tested against livestock tied to stakes. The animals died from the slightest scratch from an infected bomb fragment. Some animals were 100 m from point of detonation when injured. We heard of human experiments of this type, but never saw them.

[illegible] never heard that total of 1000-2000 humans were used. I cannot estimate the number involved and can only give you effects. I do not know about experiments in which subjects were administered vaccine and then infected. It was not done — we had no vaccine and knew no immunization. ISHII directed the experiments, and those in charge were shifted frequently."

4. The Japanese talked among themselves for a few moments, and Mr Yoshihashi stated that NAITO said, "We might as well tell all as Dr Fell already has a good idea." MASUDA and KANEKO replied that they did not

NAITO then stated:

"We want to cooperate and know we owe it to GHQ, but we have a responsibility to our friends. We took an oath never to divulge information on human experiments. We are afraid some of us will be prosecuted as war criminals. We do not know how much others will be willing to give us. If you can give us documentary immunity, probably we can get everything. The subordinates, not the section chiefs, know the details. If we contact some one who is a Communist, he is liable to tell the Russians."

5. The Japanese were assured that war crimes were not involved, and Dr Fell checked the outline submitted earlier and instructed on those points on which more information was needed.

6. Discussion was again started and the following statements made:

2

[illegible] [illegible] is an authority on epidemic hemorrhagic [illegible] fever, similar to [illegible], with a mortality rate [illegible]

b. [illegible]: "I heard at [illegible] that 10 kilos of infected [illegible] from height of 150 meters from the plane. [illegible] [illegible] infected, and ninety died."

c. [illegible]: "I heard of a trial in which 8 kilos were dropped [illegible] a test of [illegible] spray trial. Both were ineffective."

d. [illegible]: "I may be able to get some detailed information [illegible] I will start contacting personnel in that area."

6. On 30 April, MASUDA, NAITO and KANEKO submitted written statements and MASUDA stated:

"[illegible] I have talked with my friends since our meeting yesterday and [illegible] permission to give you the explanation as to why information on human experiments has not until now been revealed by us. Starting in [illegible], at the inception of the program in human experiments, all personnel who were connected with such experiments took an oath to [illegible] on all details. Dr [illegible] was not told about information [illegible] he was just not told all. Having considered the present world situation, it is my opinion that either the US or the [illegible] will dominate the world. I prefer the United States, and wish to cooperate with [illegible] them. Thus, I feel that the oath is no longer valid. [illegible] agrees with me, and has also influenced me in that belief."

7. The outlines submitted this date gave a fair amount of detailed information and indicated that the required information eventually would be forthcoming. High lights of the papers were:

a. MASUDA: Minimal infectious dose of anthrax and plague on

b. [illegible]: Methods of coating bacteria.

c. KANEKO: Methods of measuring particle size.

8. In a general discussion, the following statements were made:

a. MASUDA: "I know some people in TOKYO who can give me some more detailed information. I will see them.

"Personnel engaged in offensive BW work were carried as medical [illegible] to be in under protection of the League of Nations Covenant. I was

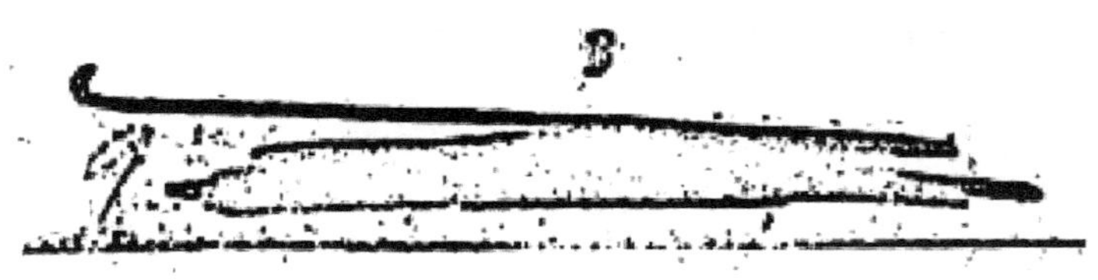

sent to BURMA for [illegible]. I was ordered out of BURMA only because I was badly needed at PINGFAN. We completely destroyed PINGFAN. I had 400 kilos of dried organisms which I destroyed by burning. (Note: This large amount was accepted at this time without question to be checked at a later date. MASUDA later amended his statement to 40 kilos, and said that total production during the life of PINGFAN was about 400 kilos.). All other strains of bacteria were similarly destroyed.

"The four Japanese the Russians will interrogate should know a great deal about offensive BW. Since you want their information and do not want me to contact them, I will write a letter for you to show them. I will tell them to let you know all."

9. NAITO stated that if Dr Fell was interested in BW against plants, YASUBAYASHI, [illegible], of the Penicillium Society in Tokyo, carried out research on the subject.

10. On 1 May, Dr Fell provided the Japanese with a detailed questionnaire of information desired, and MASUDA and KANEKO promised to begin work on a complete report. NAITO promised to contact personnel in the KYOTO-OSAKA area.

-4-

CONFERENCES WITH
MASUDA, TOMOSADA - KANEKO, JUNICHI, AND NAITO, RYOCHI

DATE : 28, 29 and 30 April and 1 May 1947

INTERROGATORS : Dr. H.E. Fell, Lt Col R. P McQuail, Major O. V. Meller, (29 April only), ? G. Yochihashi

INTERROGATED : MASUDA, Tomosada, KANEKO, Junichi and NAITO, Ryochi

1. On 28 April 47, the Japanese arrived at 1600 hours and were instructed to submit an outline of the information they possessed. They agreed to return with completed outline 29 Apr 47. KANEKO gave his address as KAIASEO-CHI, % TOSHIDA, and NAITO as OSAKA-KEW, MYOE-INA BYU, 1 TAPACK MACHI, TAWAHASHI.

2. On 29 April 47, the personnel returned with an outline which represented information obtained in previous interrogations, and dealing almost entirely with defensive BW. In answer to questions, the three replied in substance as follows:

"It is hard to report on experiments we have not seen. We have only hearsay to guide us. MASUDA can give you conclusions on the effectiveness of all the agents, but no detail. The basis of BW is discovering the most virulent strain of an effective organism, and MASUDA can give you that. We really do not know exactly who could give you detailed information at this late date."

3. The three Japanese were acquainted with the information KARASAWA and KAWASHIMA revealed to the Russians. The following reluctant statements were drawn from:

a. All three:

"KAWASHIMA was not considered important in BW. He was a specialist in production of prophylactic vaccines. KARASAWA was a competent doctor and bacteriologist with engineering ability who worked in mass production of bacteria. YAMAGUCHI was a engineer in charge of bomb experiements. KOIKE is dead. OTA probably knows the general details of all the work at PINGFAN due to his tour as Chief of General Affairs Section. He is not likely to know technical details.

b. MASUDA:

"With regards to your question as to minimum lethal dose of anthrax on humans, 20 mg of moist organisms of most virulent strain were effective on animals, so I presume it would be about that amount for humans. Less virulent strains required up to 100 mg. No effort was made to establish MID in terms of number of organisms. The Japese did not employ the XD 50 method of calculation. We heard of one field trial with plague-infected fleas, but it was ineffective.

"Twenty mg dose of anthrax is fatal for animals by oral route. I do not know about use of smaller quantities. A smaller dose would probably be effective via respiratory tract. There was no field experiments because of technical difficulties and danger. Laboratory workers contracted pulmonary anthrax despite masks. The area of BW is to find bacteria of most virulent strains, and we were satisfied with the anthrax.

"Plague-infected fleas may remain effective as long as a month dependent on temperature, humidity, and other factors of environment. They do not live as long as normal fleas. TANAKA, HIDEO of KYOTO was the expert in these matters and could tell you more.

"Bombs were tested against livestock tied to stakes. The animals died from the slightest scratch from an infected bomb fragment. Some animals were 100 meters from point of detonation when injured. We heard of human experiments of this type, but never saw them.

"I never heard that total of 1000-2000 humans were used. I cannot estimate the number involved and can only give you effects. I do not know about experiemnts in which subjects were administered vaccine and then infected. It was not done -- we had no vaccine and knew no immunization. ISHII? directed the experiments, and those in charge were shifted frequently."

b. The Japanese talked among themselves for a few moments, and Mr. Yochihashi stated that NAITO said, "We might as well tell all as Dr Fell already has a good idea." MASUDA and KANEKO replied that they did not know.

NAITO then stated:

"We want to cooperate and know we owe it to GHQ, but we have a responsibility to our friends. We took an oath never to divulge information on human experiments. We are afraid some of us will be prosecuted as war criminals. We do not know how much others will be willing to give us. If you can give us documentary immunity, probably we can get everything. The subordinates, not the section chiefs, know the details. If we contact some one who is a Communist, he is liable to tell the Russians."

4. The Japanese were assured that war crimes were not involved, and Dr Fell checked the outline submitted eariler and instructed on those points on which more information was needed.

5. Discussion was again started and the following statements made:

-2-

a. NAITO. "ISHIKAWA is an authority on epidemic hemorrhagic fever virus disease, native to MANCHURIA, with a mortality rate of ? ?."

b. MASUDA. "I heard at ?, CHINA that 10 kilos of infected fleas were dropped from height of 100 meters from air plane. One hundred people were infected, and ninety died."

c. KANEKO. "I heard of a trial in which 2? kilos were dropped over CHAN__CH, and a test of typhoid spray tried. Both were ineffective."

d. NAITO. "We may be able to get some detailed information in KYOTO. I will start contacting personnel in that area."

6. On 30 April, MASUDA, NAITO and KANEKO submitted written statements, and MASUDA stated:

"I have talked with my friends since our meeting yesterday and request permission to give you the explanation as to why information on human experiments has not until now been revealed by us. Starting in 1938?, at the inception of the program in human experiments, all personnel who were connected with such experiemnts took an oath to remain forever silent on all details. Dr Sanders was not told wrong information -- he was just not told all. Having considered the present world situation, it is my opinion that either the US or the USSR will dominate the world. I prefer the United States, and wish to cooperate with and assist them. Thus, I feel that the oath is no longer valid. MR NAITO agrees with me, and has also influenced us in that belief."

7. The outlines submitted this date gave a fair amount of detailed information and indicated that the required information eventually would be forthcoming. High lights of the papers were:

a. MASUDA. Minimal infectious dose of anthrax and plague on humans.

b. NAITO. Methods of coating? bacteria.

c. KANEKO. Methods of measuring particle size.

8. In a general discussion, the following statements were made:

a. MASUDA. "I know some people in TOKYO who can give us some more detailed information. I will see them.

"Personnel engaged in offensive BW work were carried as medical so as to be under protection of the League of Nations Covenant. I was

-3-

sent to BURMA for objecting. I was ordered out of BURMA only because I was badly needed at PINGFAN. We completely destroyed PINGFAN. I had 400 kilos of dried organisms which I destroyed by burning. (Note: This large amount was accepted at this time without question to be checked at a later date. MASUDA later amended his statement to 40 kilos, and said that total production during the life of PINGFAN was about 400 kilos.) All other strains of bacteria were similarly destroyed.

"The four Japanese the Russians will interrogate should know a great deal about offensive BW. Since you want their information and do not want me to contact them, I will write a letter for you to show them. I will tell them to let you know all."

9. NAITO stated that if Dr Fell was interested in BW against plants, YAGIZAWA, YUKIMASA, at the Penicillium Society in Tokyo, carried out research on the subject.

10. On 1 May, Dr Fell provided the Japanese with detailed questionnaire of information desired, and MASUDA and KANEKO promised to begin work on a complete report. NAITO promised to contact personnel in the KYOTO-OSAKA area.

-4-

6.3.8　1, 2 and 5 May 1947: INTERROGATIONS OF KIKUCHI, HITOSHI

资料出处： Technical Library, Fort Dugway Proving Grounds, Utah, US.

内容点评： 本资料为 1947 年 5 月 1 日、2 日、5 日 Fell 博士对菊池齐（Kikuchi, Hitoshi）的讯问记录。菊池齐曾任 731 部队第一部即研究部部长。

INTERROGATIONS OF KIKUCHI, HITOSHI

DATE : 1, 2, and 5 May 1947

INTERROGATORS : Dr. N. H. Fell, Lt. Col. R. P. McQuail, CWO T. Yoshihashi

INTERROGATED : KIKUCHI, Hitoshi, former Major General, Japanese Medical Corps, Chief of 1st Section, MANCHU 731 Unit.

1. On 1 May, KIKUCHI was told that under the terms of the surrender, he was obliged to reveal full and complete information, and that failure to do so would make him liable to penalties. He stated that this was his first interrogation by United States personnel and gave following biographical data:

OCCUPATION: Unemployed

ADDRESS: Tokyo-To, Kitatama-Gun, Chofu-Machi, Shumofuda, 576 Banchi

DATE OF BIRTH: 1 May 1897 - Shimonoke, Matsui Shi, Iwata Prefecture

EDUCATION: Tokyo High School; Tokyo Imperial University; Medical Course with degrees of MD and PhD, March 1922.

MILITARY ASSIGNMENTS:

1922	First Lieutenant, Medical Corps
1922-25	Medical Officer, Infantry Unit, Hokkaido
1925-27	Imperial University course in bacteriology
1927-30	Medical Officer, First Infantry Regiment, Tokyo
1930-31	Army Medical College, courses in bacteriology
1931-34	3rd Mountain Art. Regt., Medical Officer
1934-36	2d Army Hospital, Tokyo, in charge of medical clinic and contagious diseases ward
1936-41	Army Medical College teacher in bacteriology, production of vaccine for dysentery, paratyphoid and typhoid
1941-42	2d Army Hospital, Tokyo, Commanding Officer of hospital engaged in administrative functions and diagnosis of diseases
1942-46	Kwantung Army Water Purification Unit, Chief of 1st Section (On termination of hostilities, went to Korea and returned by small boat to Japan. He was not in status of a prisoner of war.)

SUPERIORS: During period from Kwantung Unit, General Kitano to March 1945, and General Ishii to the termination of hostilities.

PROMOTIONS: 1922, First Lieutenant; 1926, Captain; 1931, Major; 1936, Lieutenant Colonel; 1940, Colonel; 1945, Major General

2. Questioning was shifted to unit organization and the work of the 1st Section. KIKUCHI volunteered no information. He was confronted with evidence provided by KAWASHIMA and KARASAWA, but pleaded ignorance or denied knowledge in answer to all questions.

3. It was apparent that KIKUCHI was excited and afraid. Mr. YOSHIHASHI talked at length with KIKUCHI on the following:

a. Investigation was to obtain scientific and technical data and was not concerned with "war crimes".

b. Other Japanese concerned were cooperating.

c. He must think situation over and return 1000 hours, 2 May.

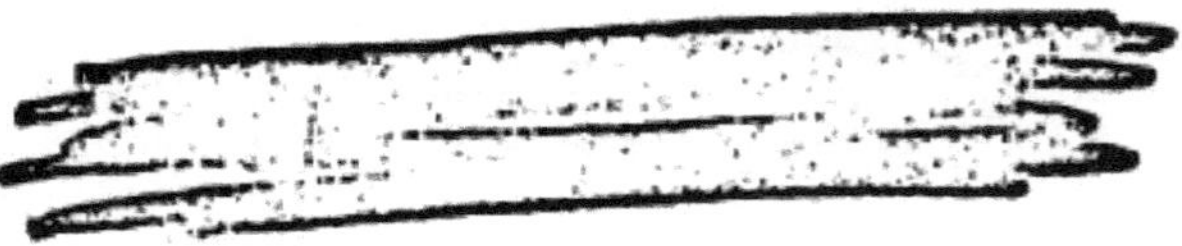

[redacted]

INTERROGATIONS OF KIKUCHI, HITOSHI

oc under YF 420

DATE : 2 and 5 May 1947

INTERROGATORS : Dr N. H. Fell, Lt Col R. P. McQuail, CWO T. Yoshihashi

INTERROGATED : KIKUCHI, Hitoshi, former Major General, Japanese Medical Corps, Chief of 1st Section, MANCHU 731 Unit.

1. On 2 May, Mr Yoshihashi addressed KIKUCHI at length as to the advisability of full cooperation with the United States, and revealing all information for use in medical science. He admitted knowledge of human experiments through rumors, but denied knowledge of details.

2. KIKUCHI read the letter written by MASUDA, stated he realized the need for cooperating with the United States, and he would do his best.

3. Questioning was begun on the testimonies of KAWASHIMA and KARASAWA. KIKUCHI reluctantly replied in substance as follows:

"I did not attend any secret meeting with Ishii in the summer of 1942. I was still CO of 2d Army Hospital in Tokyo. I know nothing about when experiments began. I do not know the minimum lethal dose of anthrax on humans. On livestock, it is 30-40 mg and on sheep 10 mg by oral administration. There were not many experiments of this type. As to injections, it was a smaller dose, perhaps only one mg, but I am not sure because very little was done on this subject. The Japanese had not developed any defense for anthrax. Laboratory workers wore protective clothing and washed in mercuric chloride solution after work. I do not know of fatalities among laboratory workers, but some developed sores as a result — generally around the neck and wrists. These were treated by excising and injecting with anti-serum from horses. The sores were easy to detect, but should be treated promptly.

"Bomb trials were made with bomb in a static position, suspended about two meters from the ground. The "Ha" type bomb, loaded with steel pellets and anthrax, had an effective range of approximately 40 meters with a distribution of one pellet per square meter. With the porcelain "UJI" type, effective range was approximately 200 meters but with favorable winds infected particles were carried to a range of 1,000 meters. With the "Ha" type bomb, wounds from shrapnel were about 100% fatal; wounds from bomb case fragments about 70% to 80% fatal; and wounds from powder container fragments about 90% fatal. There were also fatalities among animals as a result of organisms disseminated through the air at the explosion of the bomb, but I do not know these

[redacted]

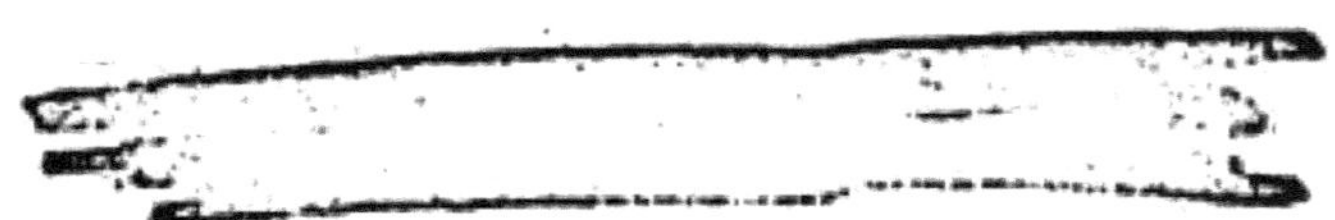

figured. Crude experiments began in 1942, with more advanced and thorough tests in 1943 and 1944. ANDA Station field was opened some time before 1942. I do not think that bombs would be an effective BW weapon because they affect a small area. In summer, areas contaminated with anthrax organisms lose their danger in about three days because the action of wind and rain causes them to fall from the vegetation to the ground. In winter, effectiveness was limited to about seven days. The organisms which fall to the ground probably remain effective for a longer period, but are not so easily picked up by cattle in grazing. To the best of my knowledge, humans were not used in any of these experiments."

4. Mr Yoshihashi explained to KIKUCHI that he was to be interrogated by representatives of the USSR. KIKUCHI requested permission to collect himself and return 3 May. After leaving the office with Mr Yoshihashi, he confided that he was afraid to say anything more at present because he might be accused of lying by the other interrogators. KIKUCHI was instructed to return at 1000 hours, 5 May.

5. On May 5, KIKUCHI was instructed that he was not to reveal information to the Russians on the following subjects:

a. Human experiments.

b. Trials against the Chinese Army.

c. Mass production of fleas.

d. Chain of command of his unit.

e. Instructions by US personnel.

6.3.9 7 May 1947: TELEPHONE CONVERSATION WITH KAMEI, KANICHIRO

资料出处： Technical Library, Fort Dugway Proving Grounds, Utah, US.

内容点评： 本资料为 1947 年 5 月 7 日 Fell 博士与亀井贯一郎（Kamei, Kanichiro）的电话谈话记录，对方提出石井要求书面文件保证免责。

cc under YF 430.

TELEPHONE CONVERSATION WITH KAMEI, KANICHIRO

DATE : 7 May 1947

PERSONNEL : Lt.Col R. P. McQuail, Dr KAMEI, Kanichiro

KAMEI stated in substance as follows:

"I contacted MR MIYAMOTO, a friend and associate of ISHII'S. MIYAMOTO is in the medical supply business, and was awarded many war contracts through ISHII. He gives ISHII financial assistance in gratitude. I convinced him of the necessity of seeing ISHII and advising him to cooperate fully with Dr Fell.

"MIYAMOTO states that ISHII wants documentary guarantee of immunity, but from what you have told me, I will go with MIYAMOTO to see ISHII on 10 May, and emphasize that revealing technical information will help and not damage his position.

"MASUDA returned to his home, but will return on 10 May. He is working on a report with five assistants.

"I received a letter from NAITO and it appears that he is making some progress on contacting personnel in the KYOTO-OSAKA area.

"I shall call at your office on 10 May and tell you more about MASUDA."

6.3.10　7 May 1947: Request Extension of Temporary Duty for Dr. Norbert H. Fell (Request of Russian Prosecutor for Permission to Interrogate Certain Japanese)

资料出处： National Archives of the United States, R331, B1434.

内容点评： 本资料为 1947 年 5 月 8 日美国陆军部对东京远东军司令部 5 月 7 日电文的回复，同意 Fell 博士延长逗留日本一个月。

RESTRICTED
P & O, WDGS

...ed Routing - Information - Fi... Form
Plans & Operations Division, WDGS

027
5-8/143

Decimal Classification: P&O 000.5 TS (F/May 47)	(F/M 3-2)
x 091 Japan x 095 Fell, Dr. Norbert H. x 323.3 Hickam Field	
THIS COPY OF ROUTING FORM TO BE REMOVED ONLY BY P&O RECORD SECTION	SUSPENSE DATE: 1200 - 12 May 47

Subject:	Date	Origin
Request Extension of Temporary Duty for Dr. Norbert H. Fell. (Request of Russian Prosecutor for Permission to Interrogate Certain Japanese.)	7 May 47	CINCFE (Tokyo)

Digest: Rad Nr C-52452, CM-IN 1143.

DECLASSIFIED
Authority NND 770127
BY J.H.T.H. NARS, Date 11/25/85

Action: Radio to CINCFE granting approval of request.

See M/R on reverse side.

MESSAGE NO: 45602 DATE: 9 May 47 Pacific Section

To
- [ ] European
- [x] ~~Pacific~~
- [ ] Western Hemisphere
- [ ] Control, Rec. & Res.
- [ ] Strategic Plans
- [ ] Policy
- [ ] Politico Mil. Survey
- [ ] Base Planning
- [ ] Implementing
- [ ] Registered Documents
- [ ] Personnel
- [ ]
- [ ]
- [ ]

- [x] ~~Operations~~
- [ ] Plans & Policy

Comments:

Recommendation:
Section Chief ______ Date 9 MAY 1947
Group Chief ______ Date 9 MAY 1947

1630

Concurrence:

- [x] Executive, P&O
- [ ] Deputy Director, P&O
- [ ] Director, P&O

Original Date Received 8 May 47

- [ ] Dispatch
- [ ] File

224

Action by Lt Col Bagstad

Signed Lew Bagstad Date 8 May 1947

MAY 9 - 1947

RESTRICTED
P & O, WDGS

25 88827

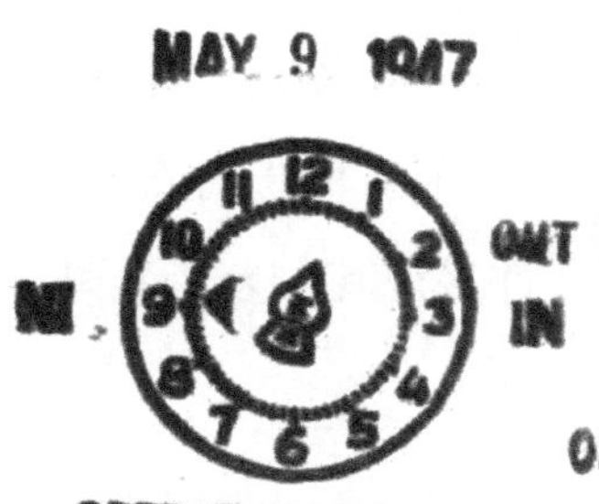

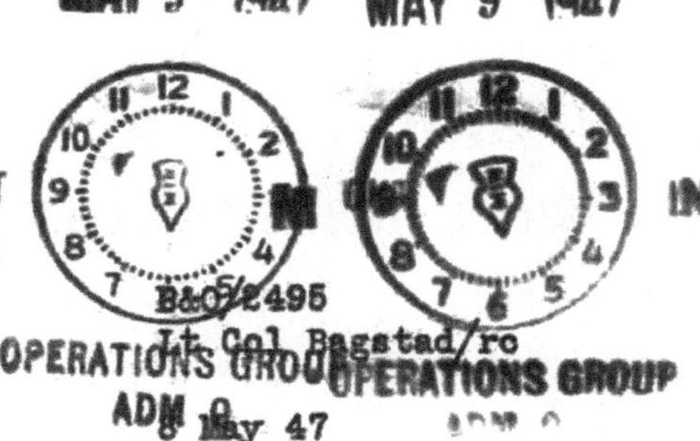

B&O/2495
Lt Col Bagstad/ro
8 May 47

MEMO FOR RECORD:

1. CM-IN-1143 of 7 May 47 from CINCFE requests 30 day extension of TD for Dr. Fell. Also 35 pounds extra baggage allowance, 3 day delay enroute at Hickam and travel by military or commercial air in U.S.

2. Dr. Fell is presently in Tokyo concerning interrogation of Japanese BW experts. Chief of CWS, Col Wallington (3541) recommends that this request be approved. Dr. Fell is an employee of the Chemical Corps. B

3. Action: Rad to CINCFE granting approval of request.

4. Coordination: Cml Corps, Col Wallington, 3541.

5. Cml.C., Maj Williams, X 71431 will take necessary action to amend Dr. Fell's orders. B

6.3.11 8 and 9 May 1947: INTERROGATIONS OF ISHII, SHIRO

资料出处： Technical Library, Fort Dugway Proving Grounds, Utah, US.

内容点评： 本资料为 1947 年 5 月 8 日、9 日 Fell 博士对石井四郎的讯问记录。石井四郎答应不向苏联人透露情报，并提出：如果以书面文件保证其本人、上司与部下免于追究责任，可以向美方提供所有的资料。

INTERROGATIONS OF ISHII, SHIRO

a.c. under YP 430

DATE 8 and 9 May 1947

PRESENT Dr. E. H. Fell, Lt. Col. R. P. McQuail, CWO T. Yoshihashi, Capt. Fenton (Medical Officer, 361st Station Hospital), Unknown Japanese Physician

1. Interrogation was held at ISHII's home: Tokyo-To, Shinjuku-Ku, Wakamatsu-Cho 77, Wakamatsu So.

2. ISHII was bedridden and appeared to be in ill health.

3. Following facts were explained to ISHII:

a. Investigation was for technical and scientific information and not war crimes.

b. Interrogators were familiar with previous statements made by him.

c. The information he had concealed was of interest now.

d. His statement on human experiments and trials of BW against Chinese Army was wanted.

e. Kawashima and Karasawa had told the Russians all they knew.

4. ISHII replied at length in substance as follows:

"I will not reveal information to the Russians. I told Lt. Col. Sanders in 1945 that I wouldn't. I recently received a warning not to talk to Russians. (This was a warning sent to ISHII by a G-2 agent on instruction of AC of S, G-2, FEC.) Anyway, I cannot give detailed technical data. All the records were destroyed. I never did know many details, and I have forgotten what I knew. I can give you general results."

"Japan was forced into study of defensive BW as a result of use by Chinese and Russian agents. I never heard of ANDA until I returned to Pingfan in 1945. I did not visit the location."

"I am responsible for all that went on at Pingfan. I am willing to shoulder all responsibility. Neither my superiors or subordinates had anything to do with issuing instructions for experiments. If you ask me specific questions, I can tell you general

nm

results. Major Hinofuji was in charge of experimental work in anthrax. I read about the Nimpo incident in the Chinese paper 'Shinko'. I was in Manchuria and do not know anything about the matter."

"I am wholly responsible for Pingfan. I do not want to see any of my subordinates and superiors get in trouble for what occurred. If you will give documentary immunity for myself, superiors, and subordinates, I can get all the information for you. Masuda, Kaneko, and Naito, whom you say you know, can give you a lot. I would like to be hired by the U.S. as a BW expert. In the preparation for the war with Russia, I can give you the advantages of my 20 years research and experience. I have given a great deal of thought to tactical problems in the use and defense against BW. I have made studies on the best agents to be employed in various regions and in cold climates. I can write volumes about BW, including the little thought of strategic and tactical employment."

5. Mr. Yoshihashi explained to ISHII that he would soon be interrogated by the Russians and was not to reveal information on:

a. Human experiments.
b. Mass production of fleas.
c. Trials against Chinese forces.
d. Instructions by United States personnel.

6. The interrogators were of the opinion that ISHII's sickness might be used as an excuse to refuse interrogation by the Russians and resolved to explore the possibility.

7. On 8 May, the purpose of visiting ISHII was to establish his physical condition and discover if it were possible to use "poor health" as a reason to refuse the Soviets an opportunity to interrogate him. Capt. Fenton, Medical Officer from 361st Station Hospital, conferred with General ISHII's personal physician. Capt. Fenton announced that ISHII was in good health, and there was no reason not to interrogate him either singly or in conjunction with USSR.

8. After examination, ISHII appeared to be in such a cooperative mood that what was intended to be a short visit lasted for two hours. ISHII was notified that no decision had been reached on immunity for himself or his subordinates, but was shown a copy of the letter from Masuda. ISHII stated in substance as follows: "I will tell everything needed, but it is such a broad field that I would like to know what aspects Dr. Fell is interested in. I know very little about the experiments which went on at Anda after I left. I suggested that Kitano be contacted and

2

questioned about humans getting pulmonary anthrax as a result of bomb bursts. I do not think the Germans got much information from the Japanese. The Germans were eager to get the data, but were always stalled off. The free balloons were a secret project, and I did not know of their existence until I read about them in the newspaper. I do not know if their use as a BW agent was contemplated on high level information. It is such a problem that I can write a book on the subject. I used to think up a problem, assign experts to follow down on the defensive, and offensive aspects, and submit a report. For this reason, I do not know the details of experiments."

"With regard to anthrax, I considered it the best agent because it could be produced in quantity, was resistant, retained its virulence, and was eighty to ninety per cent fatal. The best epidemic disease I considered to be plague. The best vector borne disease I consider to be epidemic encephalitis."

"As to responsibility for destruction of Pingfan, I do not know of formal instructions. I was in Harbien until 9 August when I found out officially that the Japanese were at war with USSR. When I returned on that date, Pingfan was already burning. I was unable to get even my personal documents from my office. Masuda must have been in error or mistaken when he stated that he had 400 kilos of dried anthrax organisms. That is too much."

9. ISHII was again instructed as to answers he should give in the forthcoming interrogations with the Soviets. It was evident at this time that more instructions must be given at a later date.

10. On 9 May ISHII was presented with an outline questionnaire prepared by Dr. Fell on data desired. Mr. Yoshihashi and Dr. Fell read the outline completely and explained all terms to ISHII. ISHII interrupted the explanation on a few occasions to ask questions and to inject ideas. There was doubt in ISHII's mind as to the advisability of fully cooperating without documentary immunity. However, it appeared that he would do some work on the outline in the interim. ISHII then stated in substance the following: "I prefer to be interrogated at my home instead of the NYK Building because of my health, and I am afraid to leave my house."

11. The minimum infectious dose of cholera was reduced by constantly increasing the virulence of the best strain. The final MID attained was 10^{-4} of an original liquid culture, and this was equivalent to about 3,000 organisms. In plague, the MID was approximately 10^{-7}. "Artificially induced plague starts as the typical bubonic type, but three days before death the subjects develop pneumonic plague which was then infectious by person to person transmission, i.e., by droplet infection. No one from

3

the Kwangtung Army Stables was allowed to visit Pingfan, nor was anyone from Pingfan allowed to visit the Stables. I was in no way connected with the Stables and know nothing of their activities."

12. ISHII did not specifically state that his technical discussion pertained to humans, but it was obvious.

6.3.12　10 May, 1947: INTERROGATION OF MURAKAMI, TAKASHI

资料出处： Technical Library, Fort Dugway Proving Grounds, Utah, US.

内容点评： 本资料为 1947 年 5 月 10 日 Fell 博士对村上隆（Murakami, Takashi）的讯问记录。村上隆曾任 731 部队总务部部长、第二部（实战研究和野外实验部）部长。

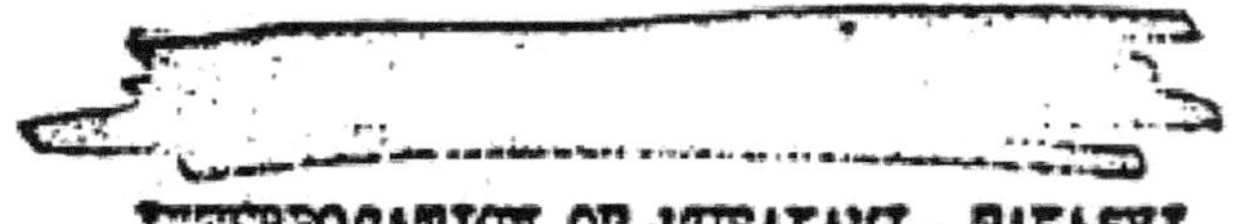

cc under YF 430

INTERROGATION OF MURAKAMI, TAKASHI

DATE : 10 May 1947

INTERROGATORS : Dr. N. H. Fell, Lt Col R. P. McQuail, CWO T. Yoshihashi

INTERROGATED : MURAKAMI, Takashi, former Colonel, Japanese Medical Corps, Chief of 2d Section, MANCHU 731 Unit

1. MURAKAMI stated that he intended to become a practicing physician in June at Fukuoka Ken, Yawata Shi, Yachiyo Machi, Nishi Ichome. He related that he was repatriated from RABAUL, NEW BRITAIN, 16 Nov 46, and this was his first interrogation by United States authorities.

2. MURAKAMI was told that under terms of the surrender, he was obliged to reveal full and completed information, and failure to do so would make him liable to penalties. In answers to questions, MURAKAMI stated in substance as follows:

"I was assigned to Kwantung Army Water Purification Unit from Mar to July 43, and was CO of the 2d Section for period July 41-July 43. My assignment to the Unit was a surprise. I was not suited for it as I am a medical officer and a hematologist — I am not a bacteriologist. Perhaps one reason for my assignment was because I was a member of the Military Attache Staff in Moscow 1933-35, and could serve as a consultant on Russian matters, but this never proved necessary. I destroyed all documents in my possession and must depend on my memory. I did a great deal of experimental work with the bacteria bomb, but little success was obtained due to inaccuracy and faulty design of the bombs. My work was that of establishing particle size of BW charge and the danger space from the bombs. I heard of cases of individuals who contracted pulmonary anthrax without being struck by a bomb fragment, but do not know first hand."

3. MURAKAMI was acquainted with the following facts:

a. KAWASHIMA and KARASAWA, prisoners of USSR, had told of human experiments.

b. He was involved as Chief of 2d Section and CO of a BW expedition against the Chinese.

c. He would be interrogated by USSR authorities in a few days.

d. Investigation by Dr Fell was to obtain valuable information for the US, and that he must not reveal to USSR information on the following:

(1) Human experiments;

(2) BW trials against the Chinese;

(3) Mass production of fleas;

(4) Chain of command of the unit;

(5) Instructions by United States authorities.

4. KURAKAMI stated in substance as follows:

"I will cooperate as you direct. It will not be hard for me to deny information because I was engaged chiefly in administrative duties. In addition, I did not understand a great deal of what was going on since I was a doctor and not interested. I actually do not know about ANDA Station because it was established after I left, and the dates of the experiments you mention are all wrong. I will not have any trouble in the interrogations."

5. MURAKAMI confirmed the following biographical data:

BIRTH: 23 October 1900, FUKUOKA Prefecture.

EDUCATION: 24 Mar 24, graduated KUMAMOTO Medical College.

MILITARY ASSIGNMENTS:
1924-26, Medical Officer, 47th Inf Regt;
1926 , NAGOYA Arsenal;
1927-29, KUMAMOTO Medical University, special student and Research Course;
1929-33, KUMAMOTO Garrison Hospital;
1933-35, Military Attache Staff, MOSCOW;
1935-39, 1st TOKYO Garrison Hospital -
1936, Member, Medical Affairs Bureau, War Ministry 1936, Minister's Secretariat of War Ministry 1936, Army General Staff Headquarters.
1939-43, KWANTUNG Army Water Purification Unit;
1943-45, Medical Dept, 8th Area Army, RABAUL, NEW BRITAIN;
1946 , Repatriated

PROMOTIONS:
1924 - 2d Lieutenant; 1927 - 1st Lieutenant; 1930 - Captain;
1937 - Major; 1940 - Lieutenant Colonel; 1943 - Colonel.

DECORATIONS: Five

6.3.13　10 May, 1947: INTERROGATION OF OTA, KIYOSHI

资料出处：Technical Library, Fort Dugway Proving Grounds, Utah, US.

内容点评：本资料为 1947 年 5 月 10 日 Fell 博士对大田澄（Ota，Kiyoshi）的讯问记录。大田澄曾任 731 部队第二部、第四部、总务部部长，南京 1644 部队部队长。

cc under YF438

INTERROGATION OF OTA, KIYOSHI

DATE : 10 May 1947

INTERROGATORS : Dr. N. H. Fell, Lt. Col. R. P. McQuail, CWO T. Yoshihashi

INTERROGATED : OTA, Kiyoshi, former Colonel, Japanese Medical Corps, and Chief of 4th Section, Manchu 731 Unit

1. OTA identified himself as OTA, KIYOSHI, identical to the Ota, Akira, listed in the Japanese Army register. "Akira" is sometimes mistakenly read as "Sumi", thus leading to the confusion as to his identity. He gave his present occupation as a physician at Yamaguchi Ken, Hagi Shi, Chinto, Funatsu 2502.

2. OTA was confronted with the following facts:

a. Kawashima and Karasawa revealed to the Russians information on human experiments and field trials against the Chinese Army.

b. Dr. Fell's investigation was for the purpose of learning the technical and scientific data of the experiments and was not concerned with war crimes.

c. Masuda was cooperating with Dr. Fell and wrote a letter to OTA and others. (Letter was shown to OTA.)

3. OTA stated in substance as follows:

"I was assigned to Kwantung Army Water Purification Unit during periods 1936-1941 and 1943-1945. As Chief of the 4th Section, I was principally engaged in executive and administrative duties. General Ishii frequently directed members of my section without going through me, and thus I do not know exactly what went on. I can try to contact my former subordinates who were directly in charge of the experiments. I recall four field trials at Anda about 1941, but the bombs were ineffective due to faulty design and missed the target area. I would like to think over and refresh my memory about trials against Chinese Army before I make any statements."

4. Mr. Yoshihashi explained to OTA the fact that he was to be interrogated by the Russians in a few days and he must not reveal information on:

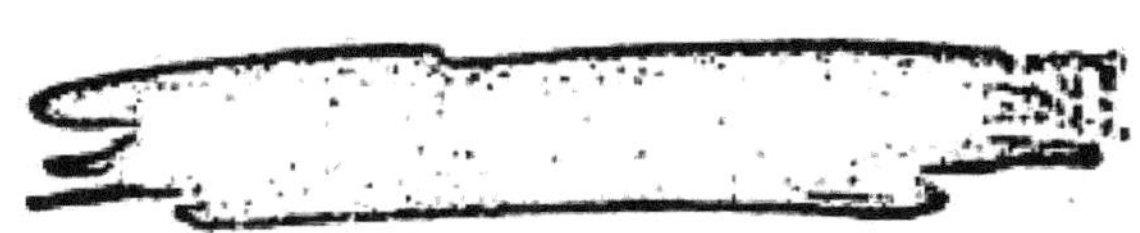

a. Human experiments.
b. Field trials on Chinese Army.
c. Mass production of fleas.
d. Chain of command of the Unit.
e. Instructions by United States personnel.

5. OTA replied:

"I appreciate your help. I do not believe that Kawashima and Karasawa were in a position to know much about the experiments. Most of what they know is probably hearsay and perhaps witnessing a few experiments at Anda. I have not thought of Pingfan since I returned to Japan and need a few days to prepare myself mentally for interrogation. I will think and confer with Masuda and return for another talk with you."

6. OTA appeared to be an intelligent, cooperative professional man. He answered questions directly and appeared sincere in his statements.

7. OTA received final instruction 14 May as to his conduct during interrogation by the USSR.

6.3.14 10 May 1947: INTERRAGETION OF IKARI, TSUNESHIGE

资料出处： Technical Library, Fort Dugway Proving Grounds, Utah, US.

内容点评： 本资料为 1947 年 5 月 10 日 Fell 博士对碇常重（Ikari, Tsuneshige）的讯问记录。碇常重曾任 731 部队第二部部长。

INTERROGATION OF IKARI, TSUNESHIGE

DATE : 10 May 1947

INTERROGATORS : Dr N. H. Fell, Lt Col R. P. McQuail, CWO T. Yoshihashi

INTERROGATED IKARI, Tsuneshige, former Colonel, Japanese Medical Corps, Chief of 2d Section, MANCHU 731 Unit

1. IKARI stated that he was a practicing physician at Kumamoto Ken, Shimomashiki Gun, Toyoda Mura, Oaza Tsukawara 186.

2. IKARI was acquainted with following facts:

a. Under terms of surrender, he was obliged to reveal full and complete information, and failure to do so would make him liable to penalties.

b. KAWASHIMA and KARASAWA, prisoners of USSR, had told of human experiments.

c. Investigation was for purpose of obtaining scientific and technical data, and was not connected with "war crimes".

d. A number of his colleagues were cooperating with Dr Fell and submitting detailed information on human experiments.

3. IKARI stated in substance as follows:

"I will cooperate and reveal all I remember. This is my first interview by United States authorities. I specialized in bacteriology early in my career. In April 1939, I was assigned to Manchu 731 Unit. I left PINGFAN 12 Aug 45 for Korea, and was repatriated 27 Nov 45. To the best of my knowledge, no one in the unit at that time was taken prisoner by the Russians. I was a member of the General Affairs Section Apr 39 to Aug 43, and Chief of 2d Section Aug 43 to Aug 45. During period 1941-43, I handled general affairs of 2d Section. I did not go on an expedition to China in 1941. I was in SINGKING on anti-epidemic work. I have not thought of the unit for a long time. I am not mentally prepared for detailed questioning as I have just had a long trip. I must think and refresh my memory."

4. IKARI was instructed to telephone Dr Fell later in the day to arrange for a meeting with MASUDA.

6.3.15 15 May 1947: FROM: WAR (CHEMICAL CORPS), TO: CINCFE (G-2) (CHIEF CHEMICAL OFFICER FOR FELL) NR: W 98097

资料出处：National Archives of the United States, R331, B1434.

内容点评：本资料为 1947 年 5 月 15 日美国陆军部化学战部队发送美远东军司令部（G-2）化学战部队长官 Fell 的电文：Norman 博士为 Fell 博士准备的讯问用问题。

FAR EAST COMMAND
GENERAL HEADQUARTERS, ~~U. S. ARMY FORCES, PACIFIC~~
ADJUTANT GENERAL'S OFFICE
RADIO AND CABLE CENTER

~~CONFIDENTIAL~~

INCOMING MESSAGE

PRIORITY 15 May 47

FROM : WAR (CHEMICAL CORPS)

TO : CINCFE (G-2) (CHIEF CHEMICAL OFFICER FOR FELL)

NR : W 98097

Rered C 52423 and telcon 6 May this radio in 17 parts.

Part 1: The questions following were prepared by Dr Norman for use by Dr Fell during interrogation.

Part 2: What were the main crops considered by the Japanese group concerned with crop destruction?

Part 3: What plant diseases, organisms, or insects were studied?

Part 4: Was the intent to attack by sabotage or by direct application of the agent to the crop by airplane?

Part 5: Where was the laboratory work carried out? What sort of facilities did the laboratories have?

Part 6: Who were the chief technical people involved, and what positions had they held previously?

Part 7: Were field trials carried out? On a small plot basis or on a large scale? Were any of these in isolated areas or on islands?

Part 8: How was it proposed to distribute the agents for crops? By dropping test tube cultures, or use of bombs or sprays from airplanes? If either of the latter, what kind of equipment was developed?

Part 9: Was attention given to defensive measures, such as spraying of crops that had previously been treated?

Part 10: Were any experiments carried out on effects on crops of chemicals such as oil, war gases, or poisons or

04192 PRIORITY

"Paraphrase not required. Handle as TOP SECRET correspondence per para 51 1 and 60 a (4) AR 380-5."

~~CONFIDENTIAL~~

Handling and transmission of literal plain text of this message as correspondence of the same classification has been authorized by the War Department in accordance with the provisions of paragraphs 16-C, 18-E, 53-A, 53-D (1) (2) (3), and 60-A (1) (2) (3) (4), AR 380-5, 6 March 1946.

COPY NO.

FAR EAST COMMAND
GENERAL HEADQUARTERS, ~~U. S. ARMY FORCES, PACIFIC~~
ADJUTANT GENERAL'S OFFICE
RADIO AND CABLE CENTER

INCOMING MESSAGE

~~CONFIDENTIAL~~ PRIORITY

WASHINGTON MSG NBR W 98097 DTD 15 MAY 47 CONTINUED:

weed killers?

Part 11: Were experiments carried out on burning of crops or vegetation by incendiaries and/or spraying or treating?

Part 12: Were there any gardens or field plots at or near the BW installation? How big were they? Were they isolated from other farms? What crops were growing?

Part 13: Did you see men working in the plots, spraying or dusting the plants? Did any of the crops die or change color? Did airplanes fly over them at low altitude?

Part 14: Do you know if grain or vegetables from these plots were fed to animals or men?

Part 15: Were there any agronomists, plant pathologists, botanists, crop breeders, or entomologists on the technical staff of the BW installation? What sort of work were they doing?

Part 16: Were chemical weed killers in use in Japan before the war? If so, what substances were used? Were they available during the war?

Part 17: What crop diseases do you know of or can recognize? Do any of these cause serious losses in the vicinity of the BW installation?

NO SIG

ACTION: G-2

ADDED DIST: COMMANDER IN CHIEF, CHIEF OF STAFF (20 May 47) 23 may 47 Copy no 5 Destroyed md

~~CONFIDENTIAL~~

04192 PRIORITY TOO: 142038 Z
MCN: YB 47/15

-2-

"Paraphrase not required. Handle as TOP SECRET correspondence per para 51 1 and 60 a (4) AR 380-5."

Handling and transmission of literal plain text of this message as correspondence of the same classification has been authorized by the War Department in accordance with the provisions of paragraphs 16-C, 18-E, 53-A, 53-D (1) (2) (3), and 60-A (1) (2) (3) (4), AR 380-5, 6 March 1946.

COPY NO. 12

20

6.3.16 29 May 1947: INTERROGATION OF WAKAMATSU, YUJIRO

资料出处： Technical Library, Fort Dugway Proving Grounds, Utah, US.

内容点评： 本资料为1947年5月29日Fell博士对若松有次郎（Wakamatsu，Yujiro）的讯问记录。若松有次郎曾任100部队（又称关东军军马防疫厂）部队长。

INTERROGATION OF WAKAMATSU, YUJIRO

DATE : 29 May 1947

INTERROGATORS : Dr. N. H. Fell, Lt. Col. R. P. McQuail, CWO T. Yoshihashi

INTERROGATED : WAKAMATSU, Yujiro, former Major General Veterinary Corps, Japanese Army, and Commanding General KWANTUNG Army Stables, MANCHU 100.

1. WAKAMATSU identified himself and stated he was unemployed and lived at Yamaguchi Prefecture, Hagi-Shi, Hijihara 172.

2. WAKAMATSU gave the following biographical data:

BORN: 1897

EDUCATION: 1919 - Graduated, undergraduate college;
1922 - Tokyo University, Dept. of Agriculture, Degree as Doctor Veterinary Medicine.

ARMY CAREER: 1922 - Appointed 1st Lt Veterinary Corps, assigned to 13th Cav Regt, Chiba Ken

1924 - Military Government, Karafuto

1925 - 1st Sig Regt

1926 - Appointed Capt, assigned 12th Cav, Fukuoka Ken

1927 - Student, Infectious Diseases Institute, in veterinary bacteriology.

1929 - Army Military Academy, veterinary instructor

1930 - Studied six months in preparation for European Tour and left for Germany late in the year. Spent total of thirty months in Europe studying general bacteriology, principally at Koch Institute of Bacteriology.

6.3.17 20 Jun. 1947: 005: Brief Summary of New Information About Japanese B.W. Activities, TO: Chief, Chemical Corps, THROUGH: Technical Director, Camp Detrick, Commanding Officer, Camp Detrick, FROM: Chief, PP-E Division, Camp Detrick

资料出处：National Archives of the United States, R331, B1434.

内容点评：本资料为美军 Camp Detrick PP-E 部门主任 Fell 提交化学战部队司令的《日本细菌战活动新情报简要总结》(《Fell 报告》)。

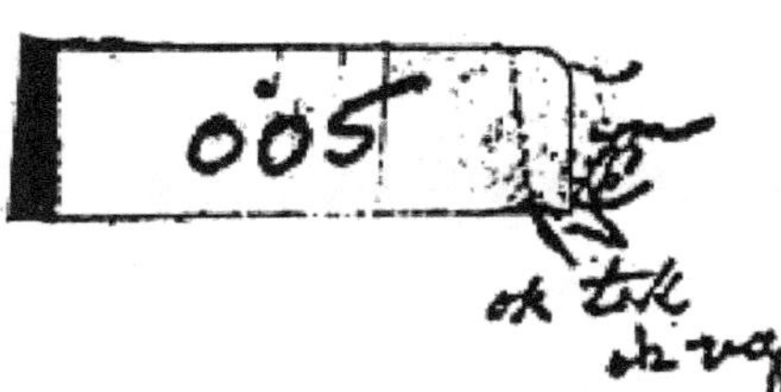

HHP/arc/3
20 June 1947.

SUBJECT: Brief Summary of New Information About Japanese B.W. Activities

TO : Chief, Chemical Corps

THROUGH: Technical Director, Camp Detrick
Commanding Officer, Camp Detrick

FROM : Chief, PP-E Division, Camp Detrick

1. During February 1947 information was received from G-2, Far East Command, that new data might be available concerning Japanese B.W. activities. This information was based largely on numerous anonymous letters sent to the C-in-C, F.E.C., from various former members of the Japanese B.W. organization (Boeki Kyusui Bu), describing various experiments carried out on human beings at the main B.W. installation, Pingfan in Manchuria. G-2 considered this information reliable enough to justify a request that a representative from Camp Detrick be sent to the theatre in order to evaluate the information that had been collected.

2. The undersigned proceeded to Tokyo, Japan, under orders dated 4 April 1947 for temporary duty with G.H.Q., G-2, F.E.C. Upon arrival on 15 April he reviewed the file that had been collected and agreed with representatives of G-2 that the information seemed reliable enough to justify further interrogations of leading members of the former Japanese B.W. organization. Through a fortunate series of circumstances and with the help of an influential Japanese politician, (who seems sincerely desirous of cooperating completely with the U.S.), it was finally possible to get the key Japanese medical men who had been connected with B.W. to agree to reveal the entire story. The results obtained are as follows:

a. 19 of the key figures in the B.W. program (several men who had important positions have died) assembled and spent almost a month preparing a 60-page report in English on B.W. activities directed against man. This report was prepared largely from memory, but there were some documents still available that were of assistance to the group. A summary of the many details in this report will be given below.

b. It was found that extensive experimentation had been carried out in the field of crop destruction. The group engaged in this work was small, consisting of one botanist and one plant physiologist with a small group of assistants; however, research had been carried on

SUBJECT: Brief Summary of New Information About Japanese B.W. Activities

actively for nine years. The botanist agreed to cooperate fully and eventually submitted a 16-page report in English covering research on crop diseases. No studies were made on growth regulating hormones, but plant pathogens were investigated extensively. Most of those studied at Camp Detrick had been investigated by the Japanese and in addition many others received attention. Fungi, bacteria, and nematodes were studied, particularly for their effects on practically all grains and vegetables, especially those grown in Manchuria and Siberia.

As an example of the type of work performed, the effects of various pathogens on more than 500 varieties of wheat were studied in the laboratory, in greenhouses and in field plots. Not much work was done on dissemination of plant pathogens but a great deal of study was devoted to geographical and climatic factors. Research was carried out on the various factors relating to infection, the production of agents on a large scale, collection of smut spores after field cultivations, estimated losses that might be expected from the use of pathogens, and defensive measures.

This report has not been analyzed at Camp Detrick as yet; however, after a preliminary inspection, Dr. Norman believes that it contains much interesting and worthwhile information.

c. An interesting report was received on the theoretical and mathematical considerations involved in particle-size determinations, and on droplet distribution of B.W. materials dispersed by bombs or aircraft sprays.

d. Twelve field trials were conducted against Chinese civilians and soldiers. A summary of the results and a map of the villages and towns involved were submitted. A brief description of this summary and the tactics employed will be given below.

e. A short report was received from one individual who had been connected with the free balloon project. In this report it was admitted that considerable attention had been given to using the balloons for dissemination of B.W. agents, but it was concluded that they were unsatisfactory for this purpose. However, full details about the balloons may be obtained, if desired, from other individuals connected with the project throughout its existence.

f. An original printed document representing a series of lectures given to spies and saboteurs by one of the leading B.W. officials is available. A translated summary of this document is on hand at Camp Detrick.

SUBJECT: Brief Summary of New Information About Japanese B.W. Activities

g. It was found that an organization completely separate from Pingfan had carried on a considerable amount of research in the veterinary B.W. field. At the present time 10 members of this group are engaged in preparing a report that will be available sometime in August.

h. General Ishii, the dominant figure in the B.W. program, is writing a treatise on the whole subject. This work will include his ideas about the strategical and tactical use of B.W. weapons, how these weapons should be used in various geographical areas, (particularly in cold climates), and a full description of his "AKIDO" theory about biological warfare. This treatise will represent a broad outline of General Ishii's 20-years' experience in the B.W. field and will be available about 15 July.

i. It was disclosed that there were available approximately 8,000 slides representing pathological sections derived from more than 200 human cases of disease caused by various B.W. agents. These had been concealed in temples and buried in the mountains of southern Japan. The pathologist who performed or directed all of this work is engaged at the present time in recovering this material, photomicrographing the slides, and preparing a complete report in English, with descriptions of the slides, laboratory protocols, and case histories. This report will be available about the end of August. SOURCE OF SLIDES

j. A collection of printed articles totaling about 600 pages covering the entire field of natural and artificial plague has been received; there is also on hand a printed bulletin of approximately 100 pages dealing with some phase of B.W. or C.W. warfare. These documents are both in Japanese and have not been translated.

5. The human subjects used at the laboratory and field experiments were said to be Manchurian coolies who had been condemned to death for various crimes. It was stated positively that no American or Russian prisoners of war had been used at any time (except that the blood of some American POW's had been checked for antibody content), and there is no evidence to indicate that this statement is untrue. The human subjects were used in exactly the same manner as other experimental animals, i.e., the minimum infectious and lethal doses of various organisms was determined on them, they were immunized with various vaccines and then challenged with living organisms, and they were used as subjects during field trials of bacteria disseminated by bombs and sprays. These subjects also were used almost exclusively in the extensive work that was carried out with plague. The results obtained with human beings were somewhat

SUBJECT: Brief Summary of New Information About Japanese B.W. Activities

fragmentary because a sufficiently large number of subjects to permit statistically valid conclusions was not used in any of the experiments; however, in the case of the diseases which had the most emphasis, such as anthrax, it is probable that several hundred subjects were employed during a period of several years.

4. A brief summary of the many details given in the 60-page report on B.W. activities directed against man is as follows:*

ANTHRAX

a. Infectious or lethal dose

The MID_{50} (minimum infectious dose for 50% of the animals employed) was determined to be 10 milligrams subcutaneously for both man and horse, and orally it was 50 milligrams for man (the Japanese workers seldom did plate counts, but expressed all concentrations in terms of milligrams of moist organisms derived from saline suspensions obtained from cultures grown on solid medium; however, they did give a conversion factor for anthrax, i.e. 1 mg = 10^9 organisms). The MID_{50} for other usual laboratory animals was about the same as that we have found. It seems probable, however, that the strain used by the Japanese was considerably more virulent orally than was our strain, although we did little work on the oral route. The mortality rate in infected humans was 60% when infection occurred subcutaneously, 50% orally, and 100% through open wounds and by inhalation. An interesting finding was that horses immunized with an attenuated spore vaccine were highly resistant to subcutaneous infection, but only slightly resistant to infection by the oral route.

b. Direct infection

Data are given for the preparation of suspensions used, the incubation period and the clinical course of the disease. The post-mortem findings are also covered in considerable detail.

c. Immunization experiments

The methods of preparation of vaccines employed are given in detail. It was found that a heat-killed vaccine gave no protection, while an attenuated spore vaccine gave complete protection

* Unless otherwise mentioned all of the data given herein refer to experiments on humans.

SUBJECT: Brief Summary of New Information About Japanese B.W. Activities

against 4 mld orally; however, the living spore vaccine in humans was followed by such violent reactions that it was concluded it could not be employed except in emergencies.

d. Bomb trials

Full details and diagrams of the field trials are given. In most cases the human subjects were tied to stakes and protected with helmets and body armor. The bombs of various types were exploded either statically, or with time fuses after being dropped from aircraft. No determinations were made of cloud concentration, nor of particle size, and the meteorological data are rather crude. The Japanese were not satisfied with the field trials with anthrax. However, in one trial with 15 subjects, 6 were killed as a result of wounds from the bombs, and 4 were infected by bomb fragments (3 of these 4 subjects died). In another trial with a more efficient bomb ("UJI") 6 of 10 subjects developed a definite bacteremia, and 4 of these were considered to have been infected by the respiratory route; all four of these latter subjects died. However, these four subjects were only 25 meters from the nearest of the 9 bombs that were exploded in a volley.

e. Pollution of pastures

The usual experiment was to explode five bombs statically five meters from the ground in a straight line across a field, and then have various animals graze along lines at different distances from the bomb burst. It was found that all types of animals grazing within 25 meters of the explosion sites and within an hour after the explosion, contracted the disease, and 60 - 100% of those grazing 50 meters away became infected. The contaminated grass was infective for at least 4 days, and after one month about 35 per cent of the spores was still found on the grass. During the observation of animals after trials of this type, it was found that usually 25 per cent of normal animals kept in the same barns with the infected animals developed secondary infections.

f. Spraying experiments

In a typical experiment four human subjects were placed in a glass room 10 m^3 in size, and 300 cc. of a 1 mgm/cc suspension were introduced using an ordinary disinfectant sprayer. No particle size determinations were made, but two of the four subjects developed skin lesions which eventually resulted in generalized anthrax.

g. Stability

- 6 -

SUBJECT: Brief Summary of New Information About Japanese B.W. Activities

Extensive data are given on the stability of anthrax spores. The Japanese found, as we did, that adding 0.5 per cent phenol was one of the best methods of insuring stability. Their data show that spore suspensions are stable for more than 10 years in 0.5 per cent phenol, dried egg white, soil, chocolate, bread, and face powder, and for at least 5 years in tooth powder, butter, cheese, milk and cream.

b. Accidental and laboratory infections

After one field trial for pollution of pasture land, three laborers entered the area without wearing protective clothing. All three developed skin lesions but were cured with serum. However, two other laborers living with these three also contracted the disease and one of these died. Several laboratory workers contracted the disease presumably by the respiratory route even though they were protected with masks.

PLAGUE

a. Infectious or lethal dose

The MID50 was found to be 10^{-6} mgm subcutaneously and 0.1 mgm orally. Respiration for 10 seconds of air containing 5 mgm/m^3 was infectious to 80 per cent.

b. Direct infection

The incubation period was normally 3 - 5 days and death occurred within 3 - 7 days after onset of fever. In most cases of artificially induced plague which terminated fatally the usual bubonic form became pneumonic three days before death and was then highly infectious.

c. Immunization experiments

Three avirulent strains were used for vaccines and gave about 80 per cent protection against a challenge subcutaneously with 1000 MID. An acetone extract of a virulent strain gave considerably less protection.

d. Bomb trials

A summary of 3 or 4 of the best trials is given below (in these trials the concentration of bacilli on the ground around the subjects was measured with plates).

SUBJECT: Brief Summary of New Information About Japanese B.W. Activities

Concentration on the ground mm/m2	Infected (exposure)	Type of Infection
over 20	6/6	– Eye-plague, tonsil-plague
over 5	7/10	
over 1	3/10	– Generalized plague
under 1	1/20	

The conclusions from all the bomb trials was that plague bacilli were not a satisfactory B.W. weapon due to their instability but that it was much more practical to spread plague by means of fleas.

e. Spraying experiments

The results indicated that this method was highly effective, both with subjects held within a room and also exposed to bacilli spread from aircraft at low altitudes. 30 – 100 per cent of the subjects used in various trials became infected and the mortality was at least 60 per cent.

f. Stability

No success was attained in stabilizing plague bacilli either in suspensions or by drying.

g. Infected fleas

A great deal of work was done on methods of breeding fleas and infecting them through rats. Methods were developed for producing many kilograms of normal fleas (one gram = 3,000 fleas), and for infecting them on a production basis. This flea work is described in great detail and represents an excellent study.

It was found that infected fleas survived for about 30 days under the best conditions and were infective for that length of time. It was also found that one flea bite per person usually caused infection. It was also found that if subjects moved freely around a room containing a concentration of 20 fleas per square meter 6 of 10 subjects became infected and of these 4 died.

Bomb trials were carried out using the "UJI" porcelain bomb with primacord explosive. The fleas were mixed with sand before being filled into the bomb. About 80 per cent of the fleas survived the explosion which was carried out in a 10 meter square chamber with 10 subjects. 8 of the 10 subjects received flea bites and became infected and 6 of the 8 died.

TYPHOID, PARATYPHOID A AND B, AND DYSENTERY (Bacillary)

Very little work was done on these diseases in humans except to determine the MID and to test various types of vaccines.

a. Typhoid

The MID_{50} orally was 4 mgm and this produced only mild and typical cases with no deaths. The best vaccine protected only 8 of 13 subjects challenged with 160 mgm of freshly isolated organisms (in the control group 12 of 13 became infected).

The stability of typhoid bacilli in soil was tested and it was found that these organisms survived 27 days without a significant decrease and then gradually diminished in number. A laborer collecting soil samples 17 days after the start of this experiment contracted typhoid fever.

Typhoid organisms were coated successfully with gelatin and would then withstand several times the amount of chlorine that would kill the normal bacilli.

b. Paratyphoid A and B

The MID_{50} orally for man was 1 mgm with both of these organisms. No immunization experiments were performed with human subjects.

c. Dysentery

The MID_{50} orally for the Shiga organism was 10 mgm, and for 2 Flexner strains it varied from 10 to more than 200 mgm. Results with heat killed vaccines of all these strains were almost completely negative; any effectiveness attributed to the vaccines was probably more the result of the natural acquired immunity of the subjects tested.

CHOLERA

a. Infectious dose

The MID_{50} orally was 10^{-6} mgm of most organisms and 10^{-5}

SUBJECT: Brief Summary of New Information About Japanese B.W. Activities

cc. of a mixture of freshly isolated organisms and feces. About half of the cases so induced terminated fatally within 5 days.

b. Immunization experiments

The results with heat-killed and formaldehyde-killed vaccines were negative, but a vaccine produced by the ultra-sonic method using 6300 kc for 30 minutes gave complete protection in a small group of 5 subjects; the challenge dose was approximately 10,000 MID.

c. Spray trials

In one trial in which the organisms were sprayed at low altitude from aircraft, 8 of 24 subjects became infected but there were no deaths.

d. Stability

Suspensions of the organism were very unstable and the Japanese had no success in drying them, even with the lyophil process.

GLANDERS

The Japanese did not do very much work with this organism because they definitely were afraid of it. They had 7 cases of laboratory infections, of which 2 died, 2 were cured by amputation and 3 received effective serum therapy.

a. Infectious dose

The MID_{50} subcutaneously for man was 0.2 mgm and this produced a mortality of 20%. Fairly good details are given about the clinical course of the disease and postmortem findings.

b. Immunization experiments

Heat killed vaccines had no protective effects with guinea pigs and no experiments were done on man.

c. Bomb trials

Only one trial was conducted using 10 human subjects and 10 horses. Three of the horses and one of the men became infected, but there are no data on cloud concentration or density of the organisms on the ground.

SUBJECT: Brief Summary of New Information About Japanese B.W. Activities

d. Spraying experiments

These experiments carried out in chambers were highly effective. In one trial one gram of dried bacilli were placed in a small glass box and stirred with a fan; a rubber tube attached to the box was inserted into the noses of 3 human subjects and all 3 became infected after inspiration of an estimated 0.1 mgm.

EPIDEMIC HEMORRHAGIC FEVER ("Songo")

This is a so-called "new" disease which appeared in Manchuria in 1938-1939. (It probably was endemic for certain sections of Manchuria at that time). The B.W. group conducted extensive research on this disease and isolated a virus that proved to be mite-borne. Full details are given about the epidemiology of the disease, the clinical course, pathology and causative agents.

CONCLUSIONS (Given at end of the 60-page report)

Various diseases, other than those described above, were investigated in the earlier stages of the B.W. program. These included tuberculosis, tetanus, gas gangrene, tularemia, influenza and undulant fever. It was found that the intravenous infection of tuberculosis bacilli caused rapid development of general miliary infections but that it was not easy to infect man by the respiratory route. In general it was concluded that the only two effective B.W. agents they had studied were anthrax (and this agent was considered mainly useful against live-stock) and the plague-infected flea. The Japanese were not even satisfied with these agents because they thought it would be fairly easy to immunize against them.

8. In the field trials with B.W. the usual tactic was to direct one or more battalions against the Chinese at two points about a mile apart on a railroad. When the Chinese were driven back the Japs would then tear up the mile of track, and spray or spread in some other manner the desired B.W. agent, and then stage a "strategic retreat". The Chinese would come rushing back into the area within 24 hours, and then within a few days plague or cholera would develop among the Chinese troops. In all these cases the Japanese tried to leave spies behind in the contaminated area to report on the results, but they admitted that this frequently was not successful and results were not clear. However, of the 12 trials that were reported all but three were said to have given positive results. In two trials with plague-infested fleas scattered from aircraft at about 200 meters altitude, definite localized epidemics resulted. In one of these 96 cases were known to have been produced of which 90 per cent died.

SUBJECT: Brief Summary of New Information About Japanese B.W. Activities

In three other trials with plague-infected fleas scattered by hand along railroads, small epidemics were produced in every case, but no figures are available. In two trials with cholera and two with typhoid in which the organisms were hand-sprayed on the ground and into water supplies around the railroad area, positive results were obtained in all cases.

6. The undersigned believes that the Japanese have given us a true story with all the details they could remember. However, it is probable that after analyzing the various reports we may be able to ask specific questions that can be answered. It is evident that we were well ahead of the Japanese in production on a large scale, in meteorological research, and in practical munitions. (General Ishii insisted on using solid media for large-scale production because he did not believe virulence could be maintained in liquid media. The lack of good meteorological data and the poor progress in the field of munitions may be attributed to the constant dissension that existed among the various services in the Army, the Army and the scientists, and among the scientists themselves; the Pingfan unit had practically no help from the Air Force or Ordnance). However, the data on human experiments, when we have correlated it with the data we and our Allies have on animals, may prove invaluable; and the pathological studies and other information about human diseases may help materially in our attempts at developing really effective vaccines for anthrax, plague, and glanders. It also seems possible that now that we have had a complete admission from the Japanese about their B.W. research, we may be able to get useful information about their actual work in the field of C.W., death rays, and Naval research.

ROBERT H. FELL
Chief, PP-E Division

HHF/ars/3
20 June 1947

SUBJECT: Brief Summary of New Information About Japanese B.W. Activities

TO : Chief, Chemical Corps

THROUGH: Technical Director, Camp Detrick
Commanding Officer, Camp Detrick

FROM : Chief, PP-E Division, Camp Detrick

1. During February 1947 information was received from G-2, Far East Command, that new data might be available concerning Japanese B.W. activities. This information was based largely on numerous anonymous letters sent to the C-in-C, F.E.C., from various former members of the Japanese B.W. organization (Beoki Kyusui Bu), describing various experiments carried out on human beings at the main B.W. installation, Pingfan in Manchuria. G-2 considered this information reliable enough to justify a request that a representative from Camp Detrick be sent to the theatre in order to evaluate the information that had been collected.

2. The undersigned proceeded to Tokyo, Japan, under orders dated 4 April 1947 for temporary duty with G.H.Q., G-2, F.E.C. Upon arrival on 15 April he reviewed the file that had been collected and agreed with representatives of G-2 that the information deemed reliable enough to justify further interrogations of leading members of the former Japanese B.W. organization. Through a fortunate series of circumstances and with the help of an influential Japanese politician, (who seems extremely desirous of cooperating completely with the U.S), it was finally possible to get the key Japanese medical man who had been connected with B.W. to agree to reveal the entire story. The results obtained are as follows:

a. 19 of the key figures in the B.W. program (several men who had important positions have died) assembled and spent almost a month preparing a 60 report in English on B.W. activities directed against man. The report was prepared largely from memory, but there were some documents still available that were of assistance to the group. A summary of the many details in this report will be given below.

b. It was found that extensive organization had been carried out in the field of crop destruction. The group engaged in this work was small, consisting of one botanist and one plant physiologist with a small group of assistants; however, research had been carried out

SUBJECT: Brief Summary of New Information About Japanese B.W. Activities

actively for nine years. The botanist agreed to cooperate fully and eventually submitted a 10-page report in English covering research on crop diseases. No studies were made on growth regulating hormones, but plant pathogens were investigated extensively. Most of those studied at Camp Detrick had been investigated by the Japanese and in addition many others received attention. Fungi, bacteria, and nematodes were studied, particularly for their effects on practically all grains and vegetables, especially those grown in Manchuria and Siberia.

As an example of the type of work performed, the effects of various pathogens on more than 200 varieties of wheat were studied in the laboratory, in greenhouses and in field plots. Not much work was done in dissemination of plant pathogens but a great deal of study was devoted to geographical and climatic factors. Research was carried out on the various factors relating to infection, the production of agents on a large scale, collection of smut spores after field cultivation, estimated losses that might be expected from the use of pathogens, and defensive measures.

This report has not been analyzed at Camp Detrick as yet, however, after a preliminary inspection, Dr. Herman believes that it contains much interesting and worthwhile information.

c. An interesting report was received on the theoretical and mathematical considerations involved in particle-size determination, and as droplet distribution of B.W. materials dispersed by bombs or aircraft sprays.

d. Twelve field trials were conducted against Chinese civilians and soldiers. A summary of the results and a map of the villages and towns involved were submitted. A brief description of this summary and the tactics employed will be given below.

e. A short report was received from one individual who had been associated with the free balloon project. In this report it was admitted that considerable attention and been given to using the balloons for dissemination of B.W. agents, but it was explained that they were unsatisfactory for this purpose. However, full details about the balloons may be obtained, if desired, from other individuals connected with the project throughout its existence.

f. An original printed document representing a series of lectures given to spies and saboteurs by one of the leading B.W. officials is available. A translated summary of this document is on hand at Camp Detrick.

-2-

SUBJECT: Brief Summary of New Information About Japanese B.W. Activities

g. It was found that an organization completely separate from Pingfan had carried on a considerable amount of research in the veterinary B.W. field. At the present time 10 members of this group are engaged in preparing a report that will be available sometime in August.

h. General Ishii, the dominant figure in the B.W. program, is writing a treatise on the whole subject. This work will include his ideas about the strategical and tactical use of B.W. weapons, how these weapons should be used in various geographical areas, (particularly in cold climates), and a full description of his "AERBO" theory about biological warfare. This treatise will represent a broad outline of General Ishii's 20-years' experience in the B.W. field and will be available about 15 July.

i. It was disclosed that there were available approximately 8,000 slides representing pathological sections derived from more than 200 human cases of disease caused by various B.W. agents. These had been concealed in temples and buried in the mountains of southern Japan. The pathologist who performed or directed all of this work is engaged at the present time in recovering this material, photomicrographing the slides, and preparing a complete report in English, with descriptions of the slides, laboratory protocols, and case histories. This report will be available about the end of August.

j. A collection of printed articles totaling about 600-pages covering the entire field of natural and artificial plague has been received; there is also on hand a printed bulletin of approximately 100 pages dealing with some phase of B.W. or C.W. warfare. These documents are both in Japanese and have not been translated.

3. The human subjects used at the laboratory and field experiments were said to be Manchurian coolies who had been condemned to death for various crimes. It was stated positively that no American or Russian prisoners of war had been used at any time (except that the blood of some American POW's had been obtained for antibody content), and there is no evidence to indicate that this statement is untrue. The human subjects were used in exactly the same manner as other experimental animals, i.e., the minimum infectious and lethal dosage of various organisms was determined on them, they were immunized with various vaccines and then challenged with living organisms, and they were used as subjects during field trials of bacteria disseminated by bombs and sprays. These subjects also were used almost exclusively in the extensive work that was carried out with plague. The results obtained with human beings were somewhat

SUBJECT: Brief Summary of New Information About Japanese B.W. Activities

fragmentary because a sufficiently large number of subjects to permit statistically valid conclusions was not used in any of the experiments; however, in the case of the diseases which had the most emphasis, such as anthrax, it is probable that several hundred subjects were employed during a period of several years.

4. A brief summary of the many details given in the 60-page report on B.W. activities directed against man is as follows:*

ANTHRAX

a. Infectious or lethal dose

The MID sub 50 (minimum infectious dose for 50% of the animals employed) was determined to be 10 milligrams subcutaneously for both man and horse, and orally it was 50 milligrams for man (the Japanese workers seldom did plate counts, but expressed all concentrations in terms of milligrams of moist organisms derived from saline suspensions obtained from cultures grown on solid medium, however, they did give a conversion factor for anthrax, i.e., 1 mgm = 10 [8] organisms). The MID50 for other usual laboratory animals was about the same as that we have found. It seems possible, however, that the strain used by the Japanese was considerably more virulent orally than our strain, although we did little work on the oral route. The mortality rate in infected humans was 66% when infection occurred subcutaneously, 90% orally, and 100% through open wounds and by inhalation. An interesting finding was that horses immunized with an attenuated spore vaccine were highly resistant to subcutaneous infection, but only slightly resistant to infection by the oral route.

b. Direct infections

Data are given for the preparation of suspensions used, the incubation period and the clinical course of the disease. The post-mortem findings are also covered in considerable detail.

c. Immunization experiments

The method of preparation of vaccines employed are given in detail. It was found that a heat-killed vaccine gave no protection, while an attenuated spore vaccine gave complete protection

* Unless otherwise expressed all of the data given herein refer to experiments on humans.

SUBJECT: Brief Summary of New Information About Japanese B.W. Activities

against 4 mld orally; however, the living spore vaccine in humans was followed by such violent reactions that it was concluded it could not be employed except in emergencies.

d. Bomb trials

Full details and diagrams of the field trials are given. In most cases the human subjects were tied to stakes and protected with helmets and body armor. The bombs of various types were exploded either statically, or with time fuses after being dropped from aircraft. No determinations were made of cloud concentration, nor of particle size, and the meteorological data are rather crude. The Japanese were not satisfied with the field trials with anthrax. However, in one trial with 15 subjects, 8 were killed as a result of wounds from the bombs, and 4 were infected by bomb fragments (3 of these 4 subjects died). In another trial with a more efficient bomb ("UJI"), 6 of 10 subjects developed a definite bacteremia, and 4 of these were considered to have been infected by the respiratory route; all four of these latter subjects died. However, these four subjects were only 25 meters from the nearest of the 9 bombs that were exploded in a volley.

e. Pollution of pastures

The usual experiment was to explode five bombs statically five meters from the ground in a straight line across a field, and then have various animals graze along lines at different distances from the bomb burst. It was found that all types of animals grazing within 25 meters of the explosion sites and within an hour after the explosion, contracted the disease, and 60 - 100% of those grazing 80 meters away became infected. The contaminated grass was infective for a least 4 days, and after one month about 33 per cent of the spores was still found on the grass. During the observation of animals after trials of this type, it was found that usually 25 per cent of normal animals kept in the same barns with the infected animals developed secondary infections.

f. Spraying experiments

In a typical experiment four human subjects were placed in a glass room 10 m [3] in size, and 300 cc. of a 1 mgm/cc suspension were introduced using an ordinary disinfectant sprayer. No particle size determinations were made, but two of the four subjects developed skin lesions which eventually resulted in generalized anthrax.

g. Stability

-5-

SUBJECT: Brief Summary of New Information About Japanese B.W. Activities

Extensive data are given on the stability of anthrax spores. The Japanese found, as we did, that adding 0.5 per cent phenol was one of the best methods of insuring stability. Their data show that spore suspensions are stable for more than 10 years in 0.5 per cent phenol, dried egg white, soil, chocolate, bread, and face powder, and for at least 5 years in tooth powder, butter, cheese, milk and cream.

h. Accidental and laboratory infections

After one field trial for pollution of pasture land, three laborers entered the area without wearing protective clothing. All three developed skin lesions but were cured with serum. However, two other laborers living with these three also contracted the disease and one of these died. Several laboratory workers contracted the disease presumably by the respiratory route even though they were protected with masks.

PLAGUE

a. Infections or lethal dose

The MID50 was found to be 10 [-6] mgm subcutaneously and 0.1 mgm orally. Respiration for 10 seconds of air containing 5 mgm/m [3] was infectious to 80 per cent.

b. Direct infection

The incubation period was normally 3 - 5 days and death occurred within 3 - 7 days after onset of fever. In most cases of artificially induced plague which terminated fatally the usual bubonic form became pneumonic three days before death and was then highly infectious.

c. Immunization experiments

Three avirulent strains were used for vaccines, and gave about 50 per cent protection against a challenge subcutaneously with 1000 MID. An acetone extract of a virulent strain gave considerably less protection.

d. Bomb trials

A summary of 3 or 4 of the best trials is given below (in these trials the concentration of bacilli on the ground around the subjects was measured with plates).

-6-

SUBJECT: Brief Summary of New Information About Japanese B.W. Activities

Concentration on the ground mgm/m [2]	Infected (approx.)	Type of Infection
over 20	5/6?	-- Eye-plague, tonsil-plague
over 8	7/10	
over 1	3/20	-- Generalized plague
under 1	1/30	

The conclusions from all the bomb trials was that plague bacilli were not a satisfactory B.W. weapon due to their instability but that it was much more practical to spread plague by means of fleas.

e. Spraying experiments

The results indicated that this method was highly effective, both with subjects held within a room and also exposed to bacilli spread from aircraft at low altitudes. 50 - 100 per cent of the subjects used in various trials became infected and the mortality was at least 60 per cent.

f. Stability

No success was attained in stabilizing plague bacilli either in suspensions or by drying.

g. Infected fleas

A great deal of work was done on methods of breeding fleas and infecting them through rats. Methods were developed for producing many kilograms of normal fleas (one gram = 3,000 fleas), and for infecting them on a production basis. This flea work is described in great detail and represents an excellent study.

It was found that infected fleas survived for about 30 days under the best conditions and were infective for that length of time. It was also found that one flea bite per person usually caused infection. It was also found that if subjects moved freely around a room containing a concentration of 20 fleas per square meter 6 of 10 subjects became infected and of these 4 died.

Bomb trials were carried out using the "UJI" porcelain bomb with

SUBJECT: Brief Summary of New Information About Japanese B.W. Activities

primacord explosive. The fleas were mixed with sand before being filled into the bomb. About 50 per cent of the fleas survived the explosion which was carried out in a 10 meter square chamber with 10 subjects. 8 of the 10 subjects received flea bites and became infected and 6 of the 8 died.

TYPHOID, PARATYPHOID A AND B, AND DYSENTERY (Bacillary)

Very little work was done on these diseases in humans except to determine the MID and to test various types of vaccines.

a. Typhoid

The MID20 orally was 4 mgm and this produced only mild and typical cases with no deaths. The best vaccine protected only 8 of 13 subjects challenged with 100 mgm of freshly isolated organisms (in the control group 12 of 13 became infected).

The stability of typhoid bacilli in soil was tested and it was found that these organisms survived 27 days without a significant decrease and then gradually diminished in number. A laborer collecting soil samples 17 days after the start of this experiment contracted typhoid fever.

Typhoid organisms were coated successfully with gelatin and would then withstand several times the amount of chlorine that would kill the normal bacilli.

b. Paratyphoid A and B

The MID80 orally for man was 1 mgm with both of these organisms. No immunization experiments were performed with human subjects.

c. Dysentery

The MID50 orally for the Shiga organism was 10 mgm, and for 2 Flexner strains it varied from 10 to more than 200 mgm. Results with heat killed vaccines of all these strains were almost completely negative; any effectiveness attributed to the vaccines was probably more the result of the natural acquired immunity of the subjects tested.

CHOLERA

a. Infectious dose

The MID50 orally was 10 [-4] mgm of most organisms and 10 [-8]

SUBJECT: Brief Summary of New Information About Japanese B.W. Activities

cc. of a mixture of freshly isolated organisms and feces. About half of the cases so induced terminated fatally within 5 days.

b. Immunization experiments

The results with heat-killed and formaldehyde-killed vaccines were negative, but a vaccine produced by the ultra-sonic method, using 6300 kc for 50 minutes gave complete protection in a small group of 8 subjects, the challenge dose was approximately 10,000 MID.

c. Spray trials

In one trial in which the organisms were sprayed at low altitude from aircraft, 8 of 24 subjects became infected but there were no deaths.

d. Stability

Suspensions of the organism were very unstable and the Japanese had no success in drying them, even with the lyophil process.

GLANDERS

The Japanese did not do very much work with this organism because they definitely were afraid of it. They had 7 cases of laboratory infections, of which 2 died, 2 were cured by amputation and 3 received effective serum therapy.

a. Infectious dose

The MID50 subcutaneously for man was 0.2 mgm and this produced a mortality of 20%. Fairly good details are given about the clinical course of the disease and postmortem findings.

b. Immunization experiments

Heat killed vaccines had no protective effects with guinea pigs and no experiments were done on man.

c. Bomb trials

Only one trial was conducted using 10 human subjects and 10 horses. Three of the horses and one of the men became infected, but there are no data on cloud concentration or density of the organisms on the ground.

SUBJECT: Brief Summary of New Information About Japanese B.W. Activities

d. Spraying experiments

Those experiments carried out in chambers were highly effective. In one trial one gram of dried bacilli were placed in a small glass box and stirred with a fan, a rubber tube attached to the box was inserted into the noses of 3 human subjects and all 3 became infected after inspiration of an estimated 0.1 mgm.

EPIDEMIC HEMORRHAGIC FEVER ("Songo")

This is a so-called "new" disease which appeared in Manchuria in 1938-1939. (It probably was endemic for certain sections of Manchuria at that time.) The B.W. group conducted extensive research on this disease and isolated a virus that proved to be mite-borne. Full details are given about the epidemiology of the disease, the clinical course, pathology and causative agents.

CONCLUSIONS (given at end of the 60-page report)

Various diseases, other than those described above, were investigated in the earlier stages of the B.W. program. These included tuberculosis, tetanus, gas gangrene, tularemia, influenza and undulant fever. It was found that the intravenous infection of tuberculosis bacilli caused rapid development of general miliary infections but that it was not easy to infect man by the respiratory route. In general it was concluded that the only two effective B.W. agents they had studied were anthrax (and this agent was considered mainly useful against livestock) and the plague-infected flea. The Japanese were not even satisfied with these agents because they thought it would be fairly easy to immunize against them.

5. In the field trials with B.W. the usual tactic was to direct one or more battalions against the Chinese at two points about a mile apart on a railroad. When the Chinese were driven back the Japs would then tear up the mile of track, and spray or spread in some other manner the desired B.W. agent, and then stage a "strategic retreat". The Chinese would come rushing back into the area within 24 hours, and then within a few days plague or cholera would develop among the Chinese troops. In all these cases the Japanese tried to leave spies behind in the contaminated area to report on the results, but they admitted that this frequently was not successful and results were not clear. However, of the 12 trials that were reported all but three were said to have given positive results. In two trials with plague-infected fleas scattered from aircraft at about 200 meters altitude, definite localized epidemics resulted. In one of these 86 cases were known to have been produced of which 90 per cent died.

SUBJECT: Brief Summary of New Information About Japanese B.W. Activities

In three other trials with plague-infected fleas scattered by hand along railroads, small epidemics were produced in every case, but no figures are available. In two trials with cholera and two with typhoid in which the organisms were hand-sprayed on the ground and into water supplies around the railroad area, positive results were obtained in all cases.

6. The undersigned believes that the Japanese have given us a true story with all the details they could remember. However, it is probable that after analyzing the various reports we may be able to ask specific questions that can be answered. It is evident that we were well ahead of the Japanese in production on a large scale, in meteorological research, and in practical munitions. (General Ishii insisted on using solid media for large-scale production because he did not believe virulence could be maintained in liquid media. The lack of good meteorological data and the poor progress in the field of munitions may be attributed to the constant dissension that existed among the various services in the Army, the Army and the scientists,and among the scientists themselves; the Pingfan unit had practically no help from the Air Force or Ordnance). However, the data on human experiments, when we have correlated it with data we and our Allies have on animals, may prove invaluable, and the pathological studies and other information about human diseases may help materially in our attempts at developing really effective vaccines for anthrax, plague and glanders. It also seems possible that now that we have had a complete admission from the Japanese about their B.W. research, we may be able to get useful information about their actual work in the field of C.W., death rays, and Naval research.

Herbert H. Fell
Chief, PP-E Division

6.3.18 24 Jun. 1947: 006: Letter from NORBERT E. FELL, Chief PP-E Division to Assistant Chief of Staff, G-2, HHQ, Far East Command, through: Technical Director, Camp Detrick, Commanding Officer, Camp Detrick

资料出处：Technical Library, Fort Dugway Proving Grounds, Utah, US.

内容点评：本资料为 1947 年 6 月 24 日 PP-E 部门主任 Fell 予美远东军司令部 G-2 副参谋长的联络函，称此调查所获资料由情报系统掌握，不用于“战争犯罪”程序。

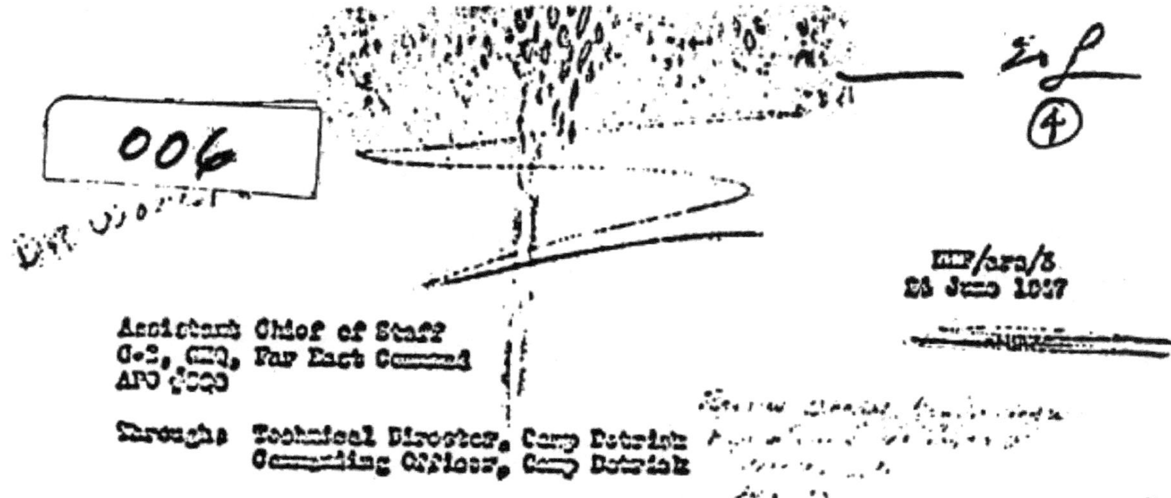

EHP/ara/3
23 June 1947

Assistant Chief of Staff
G-2, GHQ, Far East Command
APO 500

Through: Technical Director, Camp Detrick
Commanding Officer, Camp Detrick

JAPANESE INTE
24 JUNE 47

1. Enclosed is a report that has been submitted to the Chief, Chemical Corps and which represents a general summary of the information received to date. It is felt here that a formal, technical report need not be prepared until additional information now being gathered in Japan can be made available at Camp Detrick.

2. It has not been decided whether the undersigned or some other member of the staff here will return to Japan in August or September to collect the additional material, but it is presumed that someone will be sent over there. It is requested, therefore, that all additional information turned in to G-2 be held there until further notice.

3. The material which Colonel McQuail shipped here (slides, photomicrographs, and printed documents) has been received in good condition. However, the transcriptions of the Japanese stenographic records of the joint interrogations have not arrived and it would be appreciated if you will notify us whether these were sent to Camp Detrick or to G-2, General Staff. It is also hoped that if Colonel McQuail has prepared a more or less formal report covering all the G-2 angles in this investigation, a copy may eventually be forwarded to Camp Detrick to complete the file here.

4. It is requested that H. HAMADA, the plant physiologist who worked with Yagisawa in the field of research on crop destruction, be asked to prepare an independent report on all the work done by his group. It is hoped that by getting such a report we may be able to amplify some of the important information which Yagisawa has already given us.

5. The information that has been received so far is proving of great interest here and it certainly will have a great deal of value in the future development of our program.

-1-

6. Enclosed are the 2 specimen booklets of photomicrographs that were given us for inspection. These should be returned to the Japanese who are preparing the additional photomicrographs at the CIC office in Kanazawa.

7. At a conference yesterday at which the Chief of the Chemical Corps and representatives of the War, State, and Justice Departments were present, it was informally agreed that the recommendations of the G-2, FEC, and the Chief, Chemical Corps would be accepted; i.e. that all information obtained in this investigation would be held in intelligence channels and not used for "War Crimes" purposes. It is believed that a meeting of the SWNCC subcommittee will be held 23 June and that a radio along the lines you desire will be dispatched shortly.

8. The undersigned wishes to express again his appreciation of the complete cooperation of G-2, FEC in this investigation, and of the many courtesies and helpful advice extended by the AC of S, G-2, the CG, and the C-in-C, FEC.

NORBERT H. FELL
Chief, PP-B Division

Incls

1. Copy of report on B.W. investigation.

2. Two booklets of photomicrographs.

24 June 1947

Assistant Chief of Staff
G-2, HHQ, Far East Command
APO# 00

Through; Technical Director, Camp Detrick
Commanding Officer, Camp Detrick

1. Enclosed is a report that been submitted to the Chief, Chemical Corps and which represented a general summary of the information received to date. It is felt here that a formal, technical report need not be prepared until additional information now being gathered in Japan can be made available at Camp Detrick.

2. It has not been decided whether the undersigned or some other member of the staff here will return to Japan in August or September to collect the additional material, but it is presumed that someone will be sent over there. It is requested, therefore, that all addition information turned in to G-2 be held there until futher notice.

3. The material which Colonel McQuail shipped here (slides, photomicrographs, and printed documents) has been received in good condition. However, the transcriptions of the Japanese stenographic records of the joint interrogrations have not arrived and it would be appreciated if you will notify us whether these were sent to Camp Detrick or to G-2, General Staff. It is also hoped that if Colonel McQuail has prepared a memo or long formal report covering all the G-2 angles in this investigation, a copy may eventually be forwarded to Camp Detrick to complete the file here.

4. It is requested that H. HAMADA, the plant physiologist who worked with Yagasama in the field of research on crop destruction, be asked to prepare an independent report on all the work done by his group. It is hoped that by getting such a report we may be able to amplify some of the important information which Yagasama has already

given us.

5. The information that has been received so far is proving of great interest here and it certainly will have a great deal of value in the future development of our program.

#

6. Enclosed are the 2 (illegible) booklets of photomicrographs that were given us for inspection. These should be returned to the Japanese who are preparing the additional photomicrographs at the CIC office in (illegible).

7. At a conference yesterday at which the Chief of the Chemical Corps and representatives of the War, State and Justice Departments were present, it was informally agreed that the recommendations of the C.in.C, FEC, and the Chief, Chemical Corps would be accepted, i.e. that all information obtained in this investigation would be held in intelligence channels and not used for "War Crimes" programs. It is believed that a meeting of the SWNCC sub-committee will be held 23 June and that a radio along the lines you desire will be dispatched shortly.

8. The undersigned wishes to express again his appreciation of the complete cooperation of CoS, FEC in this investigation, and of the many courtesies and helpful advice extended by the AC of S, G-2, the G-3, and the C.in.C, FEC.

NORBERT E. FELL
Chief, PP-E Division
(PP-E: Pilot Plant-Engineering)

Encl:
1. Copy of report on B.W. Investigations.
2. Two booklets of photomicrographs.

6.3.19　30 Jun. 1947: From: CINCFE Tokyo Japan, To: WDGID, Nr: C-53704

资料出处：National Archives of the United States, R331, B1434.

内容点评：本资料为1947年6月30日美远东军司令部于东京发送美国陆军部的电文：就战争犯罪征求Fell博士意见。

WAR DEPARTMENT
CLASSIFIED MESSAGE CENTER
CONFIDENTIAL
INCOMING CLASSIFIED MESSAGE

30 JUN 47

PARAPHRASE NOT REQUIRED. HANDLE AS TOP SECRET CORRESPONDENCE PER PARAs 51i and 60a (4) AR 380-5

From: CINCFE Tokyo Japan

To: WDGID

Nr: C 53704 30 June 1947

Urad WAR 80671 and pertinent previous radios, particularly ourad C 51169*should be brought to attention of Doctor Norbert H. Fell, Chemical Corps. War Crimes should consult Doctor Fell for clarification as he is expert investigator with latest local information. Provisions of SWNCC 351/1, 5th March 1947, should be considered by War Crimes. Aggressive prosecution will adversely affect US interests under paragraphs 3E and 5, urad WX 95147, 24th July 1946.

End

* As received

Directorate for Freedom of Information
And Security Review
Office of the Assistant Secretary of Defense
(Public Affairs)
Room 2C-757, Pentagon, Washington, D.C.

Note: C 51169 is CM IN 4565 (25 Mar) ID (Believed to be in error)

See CM IN 1088 (7 Jun) Deceived

DOWNGRADED TO CONFIDENTIAL on 8 JUL 1977
DECLASSIFY on
Classified by

ACTION: Gen Noce

INFO: Gen Chamberlin, Gen Norstad, Gen Waitt

CM IN 4778 (30 Jun 47) DTG 300415Z mk

DECLASSIFIED BY ORDER OF THE SEC ARMY BY TAG PER 770475

CONFIDENTIAL

COPY NO. 12

...NG OF AN EXACT COPY OF THIS MESSAGE IS FORBIDDEN

6.4 Edwin V. Hill 与 Joseph Victor 调查

6.4.1 12 Dec. 1947: SUMMARY REPORT ON B.W. INVESTIGATIONS, TO: GENERAL ALDEN C. WAITT, Chief Chemical Corps, FROM: EDWIN V. HILL, M. D. Chief, Basic Sciences, Camp Detrick, Md.

资料出处：Technical Library, Fort Dugway Proving Grounds, Utah, US.

内容点评：继 Fell 博士后，美国又派遣了两名研究人员 Edwin V. Hill 与 Joseph Victor 赴日继续调查日军细菌战。本资料为1947年12月12日马里兰州美军Camp Detrick基础科学部门主任Edwin V. Hill医学博士提交美国化学战部队长官Alden C. Waitt上将的《细菌战调查总结报告》(《Hill报告》)。

5

Confidential? Officially ... Chief, 14 July 1954 ... F Albrecht ... 7 54

CmlC
Control No. 6909C

APO 500
12 December 1947

SUBJECT: SUMMARY REPORT ON B. W. INVESTIGATIONS

TO : GENERAL ALDEN C. WAITT,
Chief Chemical Corps
Pentagon, 25, Washington, D. C.

1. Introduction: Pursuant to Letter Orders AGAO-C 200.4 (15 Oct 47). (Tab A). Dr. Edwin V. Hill and Dr. Joseph Victor arrived in Tokyo, Japan, October 28, 1947. Investigations were conducted as outlined below. Through the wholehearted cooperation of Brigadier General Charles A. Willoughby, Assistant Chief of Staff, G-2, General Headquarters, Far East Command, who placed all facilities of G-2 at our disposal, the mission was greatly expedited. It is noteworthy that information supplied by interviewed persons was submitted voluntarily. No question of immunity guarantee from war crimes prosecution was ever raised during these interviews.

2. Object:

A. To obtain additional information necessary to clarify reports submitted by Japanese personnel on the subject of B. W.

B. To examine human pathological material which had been transferred to Japan from B. W. installations.

C. To obtain protocols necessary for understanding the significance of the pathological material.

3. Method:

A. The following personnel were interviewed regarding B. W. subjects with which they had worked either at Harbin or in Japan:

Subject	Doctors who were interviewed	
Aerosols	Masahiko Takahashi, Junichi Kaneko	Tab B.
Anthrax	Kiyoshi Ota	Tab C.
Botulism	Shiro Ishii	Tab D.
Brucellosis	" " , Yujiro Yamanouchi, Kozo Okamoto, Kiyoshi Hayakawa	Tab E, F, G, R.
Cholera	Tachio Ishikawa, Kozo Okamoto	Tab R.
Decontamination	Yoshifumi Tsuyama	Tab H.
Dysentery	Masaaki Ueda, Tomosada Masuda, ~~Saburo Kojima,~~ Shogo Hosoya, ~~Kaname Takahashi~~	Tab I, J, K, L, M

TOP SECRET

Camp Detrick
Control No. [illegible]

egraded Confidential
By authority of Chief Chemical Officer.
By [signature]
Grade and Org. Lt Col CmlC
Date 4 Aug 57

TOP SECRET

Subject Doctors who were interviewed

Fugu Toxin	Tomosada Masuda	Interim Report
Gas Gangrene	Shiro Ishii	Tab L, M.
Glanders	" " , Tachio Ishikawa	Tab A, J.
Influenza	" "	Tab N.
Meningococcus	" " , Tachio Ishikawa	Tab O.
Mucin	Masaaki Ueda, Senji Uchino	Tab P.
Plague	Shiro Ishii, Tachio Ishikawa, Masahiko Takahashi, Kozo Okamoto	Tab B, R.
Plant Diseases	Yukimasa Yagizawa	Tab S.
Salmonella	Kiyoshi Hayakawa, Kanau Tabei, Saburo Kojima	Tab Q, K, F.
Songo	Shiro Kasahara, Masaji Kitano, Tachio Ishikawa	Tab T, U.
Small Pox	Shiro Ishii, Tachio Ishikawa	Tab V.
Tetanus	Shiro Ishii, Shogo Hosoya, Kaoru Ishimitsu	Tab M, W, X.
Tick encephalitis	Shiro Kasahara, Masaji Kitano	Tab Y.
Tsutsugamushi	Shiro Kasahara	Tab Z.
Tuberculosis	Hideo Futagi, Shiro Ishii	Tab AA
Tularemia	Shiro Ishii	Tab AB
Typhoid	Kanau Tabei, Kozo Okamoto	Tab K, AC
Typhus	Shiro Kasahara, Masayoshi Arita, Toyohiro Hamada, Masaji Kitano, Tachio Ishikawa	Tab AD, AE, AF, AG, AH, AI.
Index to Slides		Tab AJ

B. The pathological material submitted to us in Kanazawa was in a completely disorganized condition. It was necessary to arrange this material according to case number, tabulate the number of specimens and inventory the specimens.

C. Information furnished by people who were interviewed was given from memory except in the case of Dr. Shiro Kasahara, who had a record of temperature charts and pertinent clinical data in 3 subjects with experimental Songo Fever. (Tab T, U.)

2

MC-670

TOP SECRET

A. Not only was additional information obtained about subjects previously submitted in the Japanese B. W. report, but much information was gathered about many human diseases which were intensively investigated by the Japanese, but not previously reported.

The subtended lists indicate diseases mentioned in previous reports and those which were studied but not previously reported:

Previously Reported	Not Reported
Anthrax	Botulism
Aerosols	Brucellosis
Cholera	Decontamination
Glanders	Fugu Toxin
Plague	Gas Gangrene
Plant Diseases	Influenza
Salmonella	Meningococcus
Songo	Mucin
Tetanus	Small Pox
Typhoid	Tick Encephalitis
Typhus	Tuberculosis
	Tularemia
	Tsutsugamushi

B. The pathological material in Kanazawa was brought from Harbin by Dr. Tachio Ishikawa in 1943. It consists of specimens from approximately 500 human cases, only 400 of which have adequate material for study. The total number of human cases which had autopsies at Harbin was less than 1,000 in 1945, according to Dr. Kozo Okamoto (Tab R). This number was about 200 more than were present in Harbin at the time Dr. Ishikawa returned to Japan. As a result of inventory of specimens which were first submitted, it was evident that much material was being withheld. However, it required only slight encouragement to obtain an additional collection of specimens which was considerably greater than that first submitted.

Below are tabulated lists of the number of cases for the various diseases as well as the number of cases which have adequate material for study. There were 850 recorded cases, with adequate material for 401 cases and no material for 317 cases. This was explained by Dr. Okamoto who suspected that not more than 500 cases were taken from Harbin by Dr. Ishikawa.

Disease	Human Cases Adequate Material	Total
Anthrax	31	36
Botulism	0	2
Brucellosis	1	3
Carbon Monoxide	0	1
Cholera	50	135

HC-670

TOP SECRET

Disease	Human Cases Adequate Material	Total
Dysentery	12	21
Glanders	20	22
Meningococcus	1	5
Mustard Gas	16	16
Plague	42	180
Plague Epidemic	64	66
Poisoning	0	2
Salmonella	11	14
Songo	52	101
Small Pox	2	4
Streptococcus	1	3
Suicide	11	30
Tetanus	14	32
Tick Encephalitis	1	2
Tsutsugamushi	0	2
Tuberculosis	41	82
Typhoid	22	63
Typhus	9	26
Vaccination	2	2

C. Specific protocols were obtained from individual investigators. Their descriptions of experiments are detailed in separate reports. These protocols readily account for the tabulated pathological material and indicate the extent of experimentation with infectious diseases in human and plant species.

5. Evidence gathered in this investigation has greatly supplemented and amplified previous aspects of this field. It represents data which have been obtained by Japanese scientists at the expenditure of many millions of dollars and years of work. Information has accrued with respect to human susceptibility to these diseases as indicated by specific infectious doses of bacteria. Such information could not be obtained in our own laboratories because of scruples attached to human experimentation. These data were secured with a total outlay of ¥250,000 to date, a mere pittance by comparison with the actual cost of the studies.

Furthermore, the pathological material which has been collected constitutes the only material evidence of the nature of these experiments. It is hoped that individuals who voluntarily contributed this information will be spared embarrassment because of it and that every effort will be taken to prevent this information from falling into other hands.

EDWIN V. HILL, M. D.
Chief, Basic Sciences
Camp Detrick, Md.

Incls: Tab A-AJ
Tab A w/d

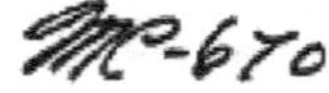

6.4.2 Interview of Doctors

01 29 Oct. 1947: REPORT ON DYSENTERY, INFORMATION BY: Tomosada MASUDA in Tokyo

资料出处： Technical Library, Fort Dugway Proving Grounds, Utah, US.

内容点评： 本资料为 1947 年 10 月 29 日于东京，增田知贞（Tomosada Masuda）向调查官 Edwin V. Hill 与 Joseph Victor 提供的情报，题目：痢疾。

Regraded ~~Confidential~~ CONFIDENTIAL 6909.C
By authority of Chief Chemical I
Officer.
By
Grade and Org. Lt Col, Cml
Date 4 Aug 54 REPORT ON DYSENTERY

032 INFORMATION BY: October 29, 1947

Tomosada MASUDA

in

Tokyo

Types:

Shiga, Flexner and Y (German). Organisms isolated from stools of cases in Manchuria.

Media:

Agar;
Extract fish 10 parts. Proportions tested varied from 2-10-25 optimum - 24 parts was optimum;
Peptone parts. Proportions tested varied from 10-25. The later was optimum.
NaCl 2;
H_2O 1000
pH 7.4 to 7.6 adjusted with NaCl and Na_2CO_3

Substitutes for:

Extracts, fish

Extract (Liebig, Arrow — Susuki Co.) This was better than fish extract.

Extract of silk worm cocoon.

Substitutes for:

Peptone - Witte (teru-uchi)

Casein, cod fish, sardines. The latter were studied by Dr Arai. Methionine 0.1% was better than peptone.

Fish extract of Bonita, tuna, or sardine, had head and tail discarded, carcass was filletted, steamed over boiling water and the juice concentrated in the water beneath the carcass. Later, the extract was concentrated by heating to a sticky mass. This extract was furnished by medical supply of the Army. The extract is a by-product of the fish industry which prepares these fish for sale.

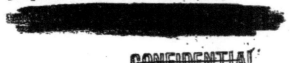

CONFIDENTIAL

Effective Vitamins:

Addition of Orizanin, Sankyo Co., containing B1 and added in the proportion of 1 cc per 100 cc of medium, increased growth of organisms. Growth was measured by nephthelometry. Virulence was determined by infectivity of various weights of organisms.

Traces of beta-naphthol increase bacterial yield.

Glucose added to medium did not increase growth, but increased infectivity when employed as 10% solution mixed with the organisms. Comparison was made with 0.85% NaCl. Glucose with bacteria was injected intraperitonially.

Vegetable products were extracted by boiling and the filtrate could be substituted for fish or beef extract. Carrots, raddishes, green peas and other plants were tested. Milk and gelatine were also used, but no tests were made with regard to growth rate and virulence.

No completely synthetic media were studied.

Maintenance of Organisms:

Bacilli did not retain virulence on culture media. They were inoculated in deep agar cultures containing 0.8% agar in air tight sealed test tubes for two months, and then passed through mice to enhance virulence. Moisture was 5/6ths total weight.

Doses:

MID Mouse was 10 milligrams (?)

Ten (10) mice were tested with each dose. Rabbit was also employed but little information was remembered. MID human was reported. Two - three people were tested with each dose.

Chinese were more resistant than Japanese or Caucasians. Disease lasts 3 - 5 weeks. In man, infection was oral with 10% glucose added to milk. It was thought that since ~~Ip.~~ glucose mixed with bacteria increased infectivity of bacteria in mice, it might have the same effect in oral administration. However, ~~xxxxxxxx~~ in mouse experiments of ten (10) mice infected, two (2) received 10% glucose as control in 1 cc volume. Occasional control mice died from the glucose injections. It was decided that 5% glucose was better than 10%. Glucose experiments were recent and no detailed studies were made with respect to the effects of intraperitonial glucose.

Effects of "mucoid" were Examined:

"Mucin" was purchased from American sources, or prepared from ox or pig stomach. Work was carried out by Major Ueda in 1942, and Prof. Uchino, Senji at Kyoto who worked on the chemistry of this material. It was

Regraded ~~Confidential~~ CON...
By authority of Chief Chemical Officer.
By ___
Grade and Org. Lt Col. CmlC
Date ~~found that "Mucoid"~~ in medium or in infectious fluid increased infectivity. However, effects of "Mucoids" were unpredictable since many preparations were inactive. Details were supplied later by Dr Ueda in Kanazawa.

Toxins:

Only Shiga was used. Old broth cultures, exact age not known, were passed through Chamberlain filters and concentrated at low temperature vacuum distillation. Concentrated broth was dialyzed through cellophane. No studies were performed on effects of toxins. These were thought to have been attempts to produce anti-serum as described below.

Immunisation Procedures:

Toxin was injected subcutaneously into horses, (see Hosaya and Kogima) to produce anti-serum.

A.
Killed organisms, by heat 60°C for 30 minutes.

In Man, 1 milligram per cc of saline injected at weekly intervals in doses of 0.5, 1.0, 1.0 cc subcutaneously for three weeks. The three strains, Shiga, Flexner and Y, were mixed in equal parts. Severe reactions sometimes with necrosis usually follow. This vaccine was ineffective.

Formalised organisms of similar mixtures, dosage and administration, resulted in the same reactions and effects.

B.
Tablets containing 5 mgm Shiga, 2.5 mgm Flexner and 2.5 mgm Y which had been formolized and dried, were coated by "Keratin" or "Sarol". The bacilli had been grown in broth for 48 hours, 10% Formalin added and stored at 5° centigrade for two weeks. They were then centifuged, lyophilised, and ground in a ball mill. Tablets were fed 1 a day for 7 days.

This treatment was ineffective since cases of dysentery occurred in treated troops. However, the French literature had recommended 10-day treatment, but the Japanese could not follow this course due to its expense. Development of this procedure was conducted in rabbits which were given moist material orally in equivalent doses for 10 days. Agglutinins appeared in dilutions of 1:500 and were highest 2 – 3 weeks after the last treatment. However, none of the rabbits was challenged.

C. Formalin Treatment: Scrapings of 24-hour agar cultures were placed in 10% formalin for 2 weeks in a concentration of 20 mgm per cc. They were dialyzed for 24-hours until traces of formalin were no longer

3

present. Preservation was 0.5% "Masonin" or "Carbol". The final preparation contained 20 mgm of bacteria per cc and was injected in quantities of (1.0 – 0.5?) — 1.0 — 1.0 at first, second and third weekly intervals, and a question was raised whether this had been reported to Dr M. Sanders. Dr Masuda did not know whether there were reactions. However, there was no significant protection.

D. Supersonic Treatment of Bacteria: Experiments were conducted by Watanabe, Hotori, but were discontinued after his death. Dr Masuda assumes that lack of activity along these lines resulted from the negative effects of these preparations.

There were no studies with x radiation, ultra violet rays, aeration of agitation of cultures.

Treatment

Sulphadiazine, Sulphaguanidine were helpful.

Symptomatic colonic application of $AgNO_3$ and oral $MgSO_4$ were tried.

02　3 Nov. 1947: REPORT ON MUCIN, INTERVIEW WITH Dr. Katsumasa UEDA

资料出处： Technical Library, Fort Dugway Proving Grounds, Utah, US.

内容点评： 本资料为1947年11月3日Edwin V. Hill、Joseph Victor与京都大学教授上田正明（Katsumasa UEDA）的谈话记录，题目：粘蛋白。

Regraded Confidential
By authority of Chief Chemical Officer.
By [signature]
Grade and Org. Lt Col CmlC
Date 4 August 1954

6409-Cp

CONFIDENTIAL

REPORT ON MUCIN

INTERVIEW WITH: November 3, 1947

Dr Katsumasa UEDA

Dr Katsumasa Ueda was interrogated on the subject of mucin on 3 November 1947, with Warrant Officer Taro Yoshihashi acting as interpreter. Dr Ueda stated that a series of reports on "Mucous Substances Pertaining to Bacterial Biological Research" were published in Volume 2 of the Reports of the Army Medical School, Epidemic Research Unit and, that a copy of this book was given to Lt Col Sanders. The individual papers contained in this report are as follows:

1. Soluble acetic acid fraction of alkaline extract of hog stomach mucous membrane and its effect on increasing the infectivity of bacteria. - Report No. 621.

2. Acetic acid insoluble fraction of hog stomach mucous membrane and its effect on increasing the infectivity of bacteria. - Report No. ________.

3. Acetic acid soluble fraction of hog stomach mucous membrane and its effect on increasing the infectivity of bacteria. - Report No. 884.

4. Hog stomach mucin and mucoid obtained by a different method and their infectivity promoting effect. - Report No. 417.

5. Toxicity of mucin and mucoid for mice. - Report No. 918.

6. Increasing the infectivity of bacteria by mucous substances obtained from plant and animal proteins and polysaccarides. - Report No. 942.

7. Mechanism of increasing the infectivity of bacteria by mucous substances. - Report No. 873.

The existence of these reports, which contain much information of current value, was unknown to the writer and to those (actively) working in the field at Detrick. The location of these reports should be ascertained and if they cannot be found, then arrangements will be made to have a copy of this report which is in our possession translated.

CONFIDENTIAL

03 4 Nov. 1947: MUCIN, INTERVIEW WITH: Dr. Katsumasa UEDA

资料出处：Technical Library, Fort Dugway Proving Grounds, Utah, US.

内容点评：本资料为 1947 年 11 月 4 日 Edwin V. Hill、Joseph Victor 与上田正明（Katsumasa UEDA）的谈话记录，题目：粘蛋白。

Regraded Confidential
By authority of Chief Chemical Officer.
By [signature]
Grade and Org. [illegible]
Date 4 August 1954

~~CONFIDENTIAL~~

R 6909.R
P

MUCIN

INTERVIEW WITH: November 4, 1947

Dr Katsumasa UEDA

a. Hog stomach is extracted with three volumes of solution of 0.5% sodium carbonate at pH 10 and to the extract is added 30% acetic acid to bring the pH to 4.6. Material is then filtered. The filtrate, which is termed mucoid, is stated to be the most active constitutent biologically and is concentrated in vacua, acetone washed and dried. The percipitate which is termed mucin is further purified by treating as described above with 0.5% sodium carbonate followed by precipitation with acetic acid. The mucin is dried by washing with acetone.

b. In bacteriological investigations 0.1 cc of a bacterial suspension is mixed with 0.4 cc of 5% mucin or mucoid and injected into mice intra-peritoneally. It was stated that in their experience, different lots of mucin or mucoid prepared at ten different times gave approximately the same results. The following table shows the effectiveness of preparations of mucin and mucoid in increasing the infectivity of a variety of organisms for mice.

EFFECT OF MUCIN AND MUCOID ON INCREASING THE INFECTIVITY OF VARIOUS ORGANISMS FOR MICE

Organism	Mucin	Mucoid	Control
Typhoid	2×10^{-5} mg	2×10^{-8} mg*	2×10^{-2} mg
Dysentery	4×10^{-2} mg	4×10^{-3} mg	0.4 mg
Cholera	1×10^{-4} mg	$1 \times 10^{-3.4}$ mg	1.4 mg
Gartner	10^{-3} to 10^{-5} mg	10^{-3} to 10^{-5} mg	

* 2×10^{-8} is equivalent to approximately 20 organisms and was administered in a volume of 0.1 cc.

c. The mucin and mucoid as produced was found to be toxic for

CONFIDENTIAL

mice. Approximately 0.5 mgm injected intra-peritoneally was sufficient to kill a mouse in 24 hours. A dose of 2.5 mgm killed mice in 5 hours. Animals dying from the effects of injected mucin showed hematuria and, at an autopsy congestion of the intermediate zone of the kidney and lesions in the liver, intestine and spleen. Peritonitis was present. Photographs of these lesions will be obtained. It was found that when solutions of mucin or mucoid were heated to 100° centigrade for 30 minutes, the toxic factor was destroyed. Heating mucin did not produce a coagulum, nor render the material more difficult to inject. Mucin or mucoid heated to remove the toxic factor was used for animal experiments with the organisms mentioned in the table above. Dr Ueda also mentioned that the toxicity of mucin for animals could be destroyed by treatment with formalin and carbonic acid. The toxic factor in mucin and mucoid can also be removed by adsorption on activated carbon at PH 4.2. None of the above mentioned treatments destroyed the infection promoting effect of the mucin or mucoid. A number of other substances were tried, but were found to be ineffective in reducing the toxicity of the material. These were KI, Trypsin, Diastase, $NaNO_2$, $KMnO_4$, H_2O_2 and S_nCl_2.

c. Human gastric mucin was prepared by the method described earlier in this report, but was found to be only 0.0001 as active as hog mucin in increasing the infectivity of bacteria. Mucins were also prepared from whales, sharks, snakes, eels and fish, and were found to be approximately as effective as human gastric mucin. Virulence promoting proteins were extracted from soy beans, Japanese sweet potatoes and Yamaimo. Seaweed extract called "Funori" was found to be the best of all substitutes, but was still only 0.1 to 0.01 as active as mucoid.

Milk casein was also tested and found to be somewhat more effective than Funori. The various preparations which were intensively investigated and listed in the order of decreasing activity - mucoid, milk casein, Funori and mucin. Dr Ueda stated that when mucin was injected into mice intra-peritoneally and organisms subcutaneously, the virulence promoting effect was present; however, if the organisms are administered intra-peritoneally, and the mucin subcutaneously, this effect was not observed.

d. The effect of mucin on stimulating the growth of bacillus typhosus in vivo is given below:

Mucoid + Bouillon - Increased Growth

Mucoid + Serum - Excellent Growth

Mucoid + Agar - Very little Growth

Chemical studies on active mucin and mucoid preparations were conducted by Prof Serji Uchiro of the Dept of Biochemistry of Kyoto University.

CONFIDENTIAL

04　7 Nov. 1947: SONGO, EPIDEMIC HEMORRHAGIC FEVER, INTERVIEW WITH: Dr. Tachio ISHIKAWA

资料出处： Technical Library, Fort Dugway Proving Grounds, Utah, US.

内容点评： 本资料为 1947 年 11 月 7 日 Edwin V. Hill、Joseph Victor 与石川太刀雄丸（Tachio ISHIKAWA）的谈话记录，题目：关于孙吴　流行性出血热。石川太刀雄丸曾任 731 部队第一部石川班（病理研究）班长。

Regraded ~~Confidential~~
By authority of Chief Chemical
Officer.
By ______
Grade and Org. ______
Date ______

CONFIDENTIAL ~~CONFIDENTIAL~~ 6909-e

SONGO
EPIDEMIC HEMORRHAGIC FEVER

INTERVIEW WITH: November 7, 1947

Dr Tachio ISHIKAWA

at

Kanazawa

Introduction:

Dr Ishikawa in 1939 or 1940 received specimens of kidney and spleen from autopsies performed in N. E. Manchuria near the town of Songo. The clinical features of this disease are described in the report. Because of the symptoms as well as extensive hemorrhage in the renal medula in the interstices between collecting tubules and the absence of organisms in Giemsa stained sections, he assumed the disease was caused by a virus. A commission directed by Dr Shiro Kasahara was organized for the study of this disease.

Symptoms:

By direct inoculation into M, it has been determined that the incubation period is 10 - 13 days. At this time, there appear fever to 39° - 40° C, headache, flushing, delerium. The first bout of fever may subside for 4 - 6 days and then return, about 16 - 17 days after inoculation. During fever, there is hemoconcentration, RBC rise to 8,000,000, ecchymosis in the gums and on the inner parts of thighs and arms and generalized petechiae, leucocytosis of 30,000-100,000 with increase mainly in polymorphonuclear leucocytes, shock with blood pressure as low as $\frac{70}{50}$, pulse 120 per minute, severe albuminuria, even hematuria or oligurid. Injection sites bleed, blood thrombin may be low, Wasserman reaction is usually 1 plus. Mortality is 30%. Liver function is believed to diminish because of decreased urinary excretion of Sodium Santorin.

Infectivity of blood and tissues of M is present only at the time of fever. Liver and kidney contain the agent. In rats, mice and rabbits, the agent, passed through Chamberlain filters, produces corneal and testicular lesions. In monkeys, it produces renal lesions when sufficiently virulent or dosage is large enough. M cases were sacrificed with CH_3Cl at intervals during the course of the disease to study virus content of organs and pathogenesis. Of 101 cases in the files, approximately 50 were experimental.

Pathology - Generalized hemorrhages occur in all organs and tissues. A

~~CONFIDENTIAL~~

Regraded ____
By authority of Chief Chemical Officer.
By ____
Grade and Org. ____
Date ____

CONFIDENTIAL

unique distribution of hemorrhage in the kidneys is noted in that the bleeding is confined to the medulla. Nephrosis is a prominent feature. Spleen is not enlarged. Liver has focal necroses, hemorrhage and often intense myalopoeisis. Endothelial hypertrophy in splenic and liver sinusoids is conspicuous. Pitutary hemorrhages with oceassional necroses are the rule, according to Ishikawa. Subendocardial hemorrhages in the left auricle are frequent. Interstitial pneumonia and pulmonary edema are frequent. Decreased spermatogenesis is common as well as hemorrhage in the zona reticularis of the adrenal. Hemorrhages also are found in the brain, especially the medulla, as well as in the pancreas. Dr Ishikawa feels that the thymus undergoes hyperplasia in this disease. No cases of residued neurological disturbances are seen clinically.

2

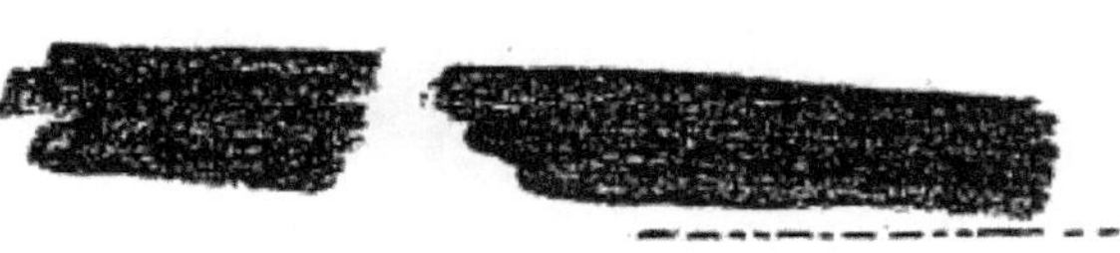

05　13 Nov. 1947: SONGO, EPIDEMIC HEMORRHAGIC FEVER, INTERVIEW WITH: Shiro KASAHARA and Masaji KITANO

资料出处： Technical Library, Fort Dugway Proving Grounds, Utah, US.

内容点评： 本资料为 1947 年 11 月 13 日 Edwin V. Hill、Joseph Victor 与笠原四郎（Shiro Kasahara）、北野政次（Masaji Kitano）的谈话记录，题目：孙吴　流行性出血热。笠原四郎曾任 731 部队第一部笠原班（病毒研究）班长。

Regraded Unclassified
By authority of Chief Chemical Officer.
By ____________
Grade and Org. Lt Col CmlC
Date 4 August 195_

6908-C

CONFIDENTIAL

SONGO
EPIDEMIC HEMORRHAGIC FEVER

INTERVIEW WITH: November 13, 1947

Shiro KASAHARA and

Masaji KITANO

Both men were extremely cooperative and gave information freely. Slight hesitancy appeared before admitting details of human experiments. However, assurance that we know the results and the number of such experiments overcame reluctance to talk about it. These men did not take part in the preparation of the combined report of Masuda.

Introduction:

Original experiments were undertaken during an epidemic in Songo, Manchuria in 1939. Blood from a soldier with fever was injected into 2 monkeys in 5 cc doses, s.c. One monkey had fever on the 5th day. The second had no response. During the period of fever, 5 cc of blood from the first monkey was injected into a 3rd monkey with negative results.

2 rabbits injected i.t. with 1 cc of blood from the above patient. One developed inflammation with edema and redness of the scrotum as well as orchitis showing inter-stitial edema and slight histiocytic infiltration. This animal was sacrificed on the 7th day — the other 2 had no reaction.

Another epidemic appeared in 1941 and the third in 1942. In November of 1942, human experiments were started. All tissues were sent to Dr Ishikawa.

203 mites picked from field mice in that area were emulsified in 2 cc saline and injected s.c. in one man with positive results. Another emulsion containing 60 mites produced no effect in another subject. In this way, the subsequent human material was derived from the first case which had been injected with 203 mites. In general, the incubation period was between 2 and 3 weeks. Some cases have a spike of fever for one day at two weeks after injection and a subsequent elevation of temperature 2 days to a week. Blood from the first experimental case was drawn during fever 20 days after injection of the mites. Ten cc were injected s.c. into the second case; 13 days after this injection, the second case developed fever. On the 13th day, 5 cc drawn from this second case were injected into a 3rd man as well as into white mice and monkeys. Subsequent cases were produced either by blood or blood free

CONFIDENTIAL

extracts of liver, spleen or kidney derived from individuals sacrificed at various times during the course of the disease. Morphine was employed for this purpose.

Results may be summarized as follows;

1. Only during fever does blood contain virus — 5 experiments.

2. During fever a mixture of kidney, spleen and liver contain virus — 5 experiments — eventhough these organs reveal no histological changes in this time.

3. In 5 of 7 experiments with each of the following: blood, serum, plasma, w.b.c., r.b.c., platelets and filtrates of the above through Chamberlain L2, L3, L5, L9 and Seitz E.K. were positive results seen.

4. On the other hand, after natural death, which usually coincides with a rapid fall in temperature, extracts of concentrated liver and spleen were not infectious although these organs show severe histological changes — 10 experiments.

5. Mites fed on sick people did not transmit the disease — 2 cases.

6. Virus grew on mouse and chick embryo which were on agar slants in horse serum, one positive result in 3 experiments tested in man. However, no growth of virus was observed in chorioallantoic membrane and yolk sack — 3 experiments.

7. Blood from febrile man was injected s.c. into horses. After incubation period of 30 - 50 days, fever appeared lasting 5 to 7 days in 6 of 15 experiments. Blood of febrile horses was injected into other horses with positive results in one of two cases. Conversely, blood of febrile horses injected into man was positive in 2 of 8 experiments. These last experiments were undertaken because coincident with human epidemic an unidentified disease appeared in horses. The disease produced experimentally resembled that found naturally during the epidemic.

Mortality of the natural disease in Japanese soldiers was 30% when the disease was first discovered. By symptomatic treatment, i.e. forcing fluids, i.v., Ringer's solution and 10% glucose, insulin, etc., mortality was reduced to 15%. However, mortality in experimental cases was 100% due to the procedure of sacrificing experimental subjects.

Mites transmitting the disease live on field mice. Although they bite man, they cannot live on him. These mites are found only at the time of the epidemics which are seasonal and described in Kasuda's report. At this time, mites are full of larvae and contain no ova.

Regraded Confidential
By authority of Chief Chemical Officer.
By [signature]
Grade and Org. Lt Col CmlC
Date 4 August 1954

CONFIDENTIAL

Disease Produced by this Agent in other Animals:

Monkey -

Incubation period 5 - 11 days, develops fever but no lessions and does not die. About 30% are susceptible.

Rabbit -

Develop orchitis and scrotal inflamation following i.t. injection of 1 cc of blood.

Mice -

Act as carriers, but do not show symptoms. This was proven with subject #4 who was injected s.c. with 5.0 cc emulsion of mouse kidney, liver and spleen. This mouse had received an i.p. injection of 1 cc of blood from subject #2 at the time of fever. The mouse was sacrificed one month after the i.p. injection.

Guinea Pig -

Resistant.

Rat -

Partly resistant. The degree of resistence had not been accurately determined.

Horse -

Incubation period 1 month to 50 days. Fever and albuminuria, but no hemorrhage.

No attempts were made to transmit the disease with urine or feces.

3 CONFIDENTIAL

Regraded ~~Confidential~~ CONFIDENTIAL
By authority of Chief Chemical
Officer.
By ____________
Grade and Org. Lt Col Cml C
Date 5 August 1954

FEVER CHARTS

Subject 1

1942 injected
Nov 6 ~~max~~/ 2030 mites in 2.0 cc saline

Date	
7	36.6
8	36.7
9	36.8
10	37.1
11	37.5
12	36.7
13	36.6
14	36.7
15	36.7
16	36.4
18	36.6
19	38.6 A
	36.7 P
20	36.7
	36.3
21	36.7
	36.8
22	36.7
	37.0
23	36.8
	37
24	36.9
25	36.7
	37.3
26	38.7
	39.4 - 10 cc blood injected s.c. into Subject 2
27	38.4
	39.0
28	39.0
	37.1
Nov 29	35.6
	37.2
30	36.5
	39.1
Dec 1	36.4
	36.8
2	36.7
	36.7

(Temperatures in °C)

Value next to date is morning temperature. Other value is evening temperature C

CONFIDENTIAL

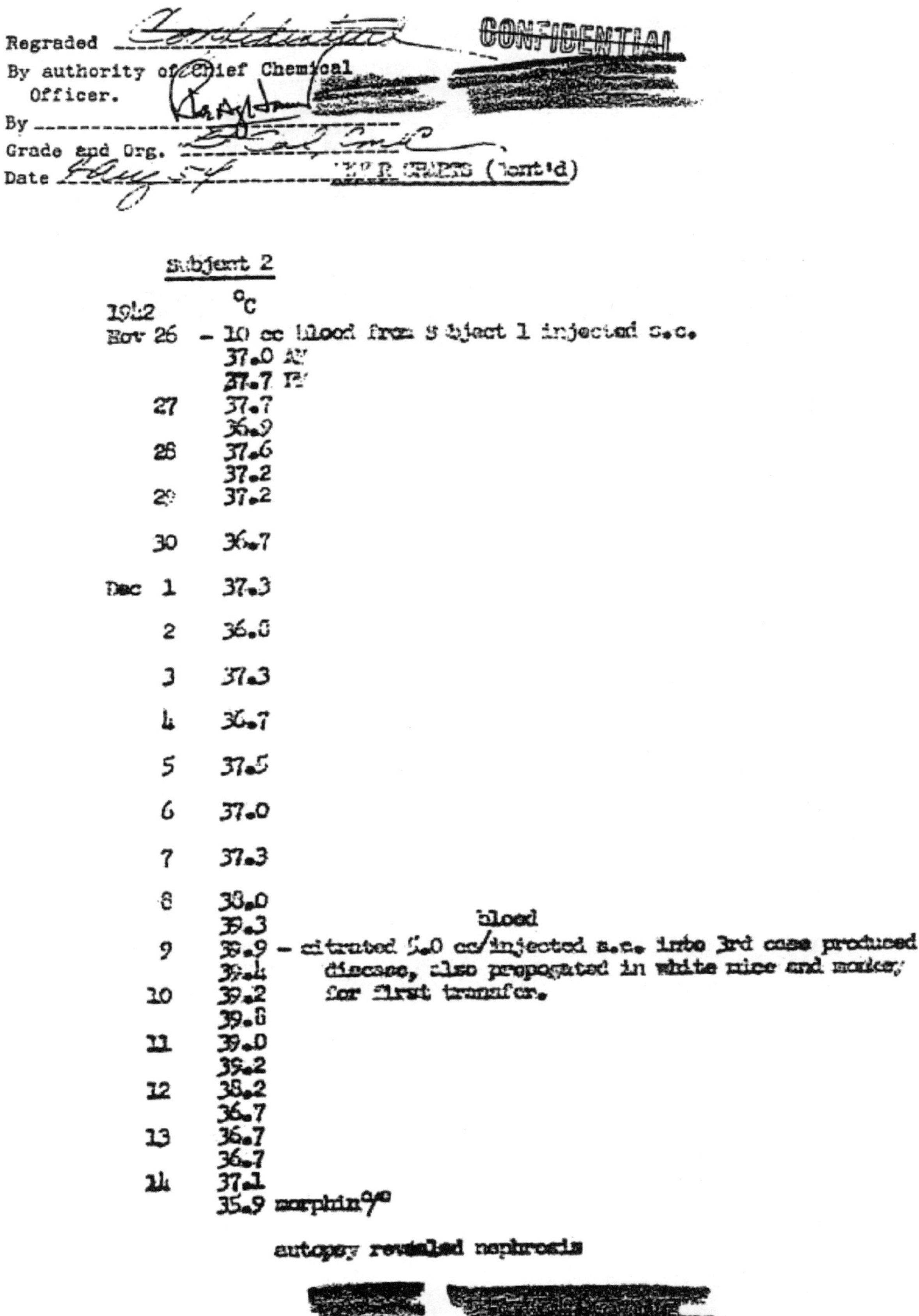

Regraded Unclassified
By authority of Chief Chemical Officer.
By
Grade and Org.
Date

CONFIDENTIAL

FEVER CHARTS (Cont'd)

Subject 2

1942	°C	
Nov 26		- 10 cc blood from Subject 1 injected s.c.
	37.0 AM	
	37.7 PM	
27	37.7	
	36.9	
28	37.6	
	37.2	
29	37.2	
30	36.7	
Dec 1	37.3	
2	36.8	
3	37.3	
4	36.7	
5	37.5	
6	37.0	
7	37.3	
8	38.0	
	39.3	
9	39.9	- citrated 5.0 cc blood injected s.c. into 3rd case produced disease, also propogated in white mice and monkey for first transfer.
	39.4	
10	39.2	
	39.8	
11	39.0	
	39.2	
12	38.2	
	36.7	
13	36.7	
	36.7	
14	37.1	
	35.9	morphine

autopsy revealed nephrosis

2

CONFIDENTIAL

Regraded ____________
By authority of Chief Chemical Officer.
By ____________
Grade and Org. ____________
Date ____________

CONFIDENTIAL

FEVER CHART (Cont'd)

Subject 4.

S.c. injection of 5.0 cc emulsion of 10% mouse liver, spleen and kidney in saline. Mouse had received i.p. injection of 1.0 cc of blood from Subject 2 on 12/9 and was 9° 1 month later.

Day	°C
1	37.3
2	37.3
3	37.5
4	37.1
5	37.0
6	36.7
7	36.8
8	36.1
9	37.0
10	37.0
11	36.4
12	37.0
13	37.3
14	37.7
15	37.0
16	37.3
17	37.7 40.0
18	[illegible] 40.5
19	39.8 39.3
20	38.5 39.4
21	38.5 39.1
22	36.6 9° morphin

3

CONFIDENTIAL

06 13 Nov. 1947: TYPHUS, INFORMATION FROM: Masaji KITANO

资料出处： Technical Library, Fort Dugway Proving Grounds, Utah, US.

内容点评： 本资料为 1947 年 11 月 13 日北野政次（Masaji Kitano）提供的情报，题目：斑疹伤寒。

CONFIDENTIAL

CONFIDENTIAL

6909 C AF

Officer.
By
Grade and Org.
Date August 1954

TYPHUS

INFORMATION FROM: November 13, 1947

Masaji KITANO

Dr Kitano has no knowledge of systematic studies on man. He believed some experiments were performed in which comparisons were made between the resistance of vaccine treated and controlled individuals infected with various doses of Typhus rickettsia. His main problem was the mass production of vaccine.

Methods for vaccine production are described below:

1. Emulsified Mouse Lung -

Rickettsia were instilled i.n. into mice. Pneumonic lungs resulting therefrom on the 5th day, were ground up and emulsified in saline. This emulsion injected s.c. afforded protection in guinea pigs.

2. Chick Embryo and Yolk Sack -

Innoculation according to Cox Method.

3. Exudate of Squirrel Peritonitis -

A 10% emulsion of infected squirrel brain suspended in saline was injected i.p. into squirrels. 5 days later, the peritoneal exudate was harvested. This exudate protected man and guinea pig. Optimum production of this vaccine occurred when squirrels were kept at 15° centigrade.

A diagnostic test for typhus was developed as a by-product of this study. The emulsified lung of vaccine was centrifuged. The supernatal fluid was mixed with the patient's serum at room temperature. Flocculation occurred within 30 - 60 seconds when the patient had typhus. In human cases infected experimentally with 2.0 cc of blood, the above test is positive within the first 5 days of fever. Fever in these cases appear after an incubation period of 10 - 12 days.

In the Japanese army, only few soldiers had been immunized against typhus. Mass production of vaccine began in 1944. Therefore the material was used sparingly.

CONFIDENTIAL

CONFIDENTIAL ~~CONFIDENTIAL~~

6909-C AG

By [signature]
Grade and Org. Lt Col. [illegible]
Date 9 August 1954

~~The following reports were~~ written by Dr Kitano at our request:

On a New Diagnostic Method of Typhus Fever in Early Stage of the Disease

by Masaji Kitano

1. Preparation method of antigen

a. White mice are nasaly infected with strain of R. moaseri. Lungs which are grown with abundant rickettsial bodies are ground with glass pieces, and emulsified with ten times volume of physiological saline. The emulsion is centrifugalized for 10 minutes at 3,000 r.p.m. Precipitates are again ground, emulsified. This is repeated three times. Lastly, supernatant fluid is centrifugalised at 10,000 r.p.m. for 30 minutes. To this precipitate is added physiological saline solution to a consenteration of lungs from 15 mice in 15 cc volume, and phenol is added to 0.5%. This is stored for about one month at 4° C. This is used as antigen.

Rickettsial bodies are neither demonstrable microscopically, nor in the inoculation test of experimental animals. This emulsion of lung tissue is brownish in color.

b. We also succeeded in preparing the antigen from R. prowazeki, using Manchurian ground squirrel (citelus).

2. Diagnostic method

Certain amount of physiological saline is taken in 9 series of hole objective glass. Same volume of test serum is added to the first glass. Half volume of the dilution is then transferred to the second one. Thus, successive twice fold dilutions of serum are prepared in 8 series of the glass, except the last one which contains only saline (control).

One platin loopful antigen is added to each of the dilutions, moved for 30 seconds. After 5 minutes, it is tested whether the precipitation occurrs or not (examine with naked eye).

3. This test will show positive result after 5 days, from the onset of the disease.

This method of diagnosis is simple, and accurate more than the Weil-Felix Reaction.

6909.C AH

On a New Preparation Method of Typhus Vaccine

By Masaji Kitano

Manchurian ground squirrel (Citellus mongolicus umbratus, Thomas), one of hibernate mamals, is inoculated with typhus strain. It is kept under a temperature between 10° C and 18° C with restricted amount of foods. At its highths of infection, peritoneal cavity is opened under anesthethics of chloroform or ether. The peritoneum is carefully scratched and washed with 0.2% formalised physiological saline. This wash is used as vaccine.

For the maintenance of strain, either an emulsion made from 1/4 to 1/3 quantity of brain of infected animal, or 1cc peritoneal wash of 0.2% citrated sterilized physiological saline, is inoculated into a susceptible animal. This method of preparation is especially practicable in Manchuria, where there are abundant wild ground squirrels for the purpose of obtaining a large quantity of typhus vaccine economically. However, further improvement of this vaccine in order to obtain a more homogeneous suspension is necessitated.

On the other hand, a release method of rickettsial bodies from cells for the purpose of purification is contrived, however, this is rather tedious and there is also a great deal of loss of rickettsial bodies.

07 TICK ENCEPHALITIS, INFORMATION FURNISHED BY: Drs Yukio KASAHARA and Masaji KITANO

资料出处： Technical Library, Fort Dugway Proving Grounds, Utah, US.

内容点评： 本资料为笠原幸雄（Yukio KASAHARA）、北野政次（Masaji KITANO）提供的情报，题目：壁虱脑炎。具体日期不详。

6909-C

TICK ENCEPHALITIS

INFORMATION FURNISHED BY:

Drs Yukio KASAHARA and

Masaji KITANO

In May 1943, lumberjacks in the Batanko area, Manchuria, became ill with fever and a paralyzing disease. During May and June, the disease is most prevalent. Mortality was 50%. In this area, material was gathered from 408 ticks and a fresh human case.

Transmission experiments:

One cc of 10% suspension of human brain was injected i.C. into each of 2 monkeys. After an incubation period of about 7 days, fever appeared with temperature up to 40° C. One monkey recovered, the other developed paralysis when the fever was subsiding about the 12th day. It was sacrificed and found to have a non-purulent meningoencephalomyelitis. Blood drawn at the height of fever produced the disease in successive i.C. transfers in monkeys. However, its infectivity decreased and by the 4th transfer had disappeared.

1st passage from human case into monkeys
+ ↓ +
1st passage from monkey blood
+ ↓ −
2nd " " " "
+ ↓ −
3rd " " " "
+ ↓ −
4th " " " "
− −

Emulsion of 408 ticks instilled i.n. into 5 mice after an incubation period of 5 - 7 days produced fever, ruffled fur and weakness in 2. One mouse was sacrificed on the 2nd day of fever. Brain emulsion of this mouse was injected i.C. into 7 mice. Thereafter it was transferred indefinitely by i.C. inoculation and produced symptoms similar to those of St Louis encephalomyelitis.

Mouse brain suspension from the 2nd mouse transfer was injected i.C. in dose of 1.0 cc in man and produced symptoms after an incubation

period of 7 days. Highest temperature was 39.8° C. This subject was sacrificed when fever was subsiding, about the 12th day.

A second man received similar mouse brain emulsion i.n. in a dose of 1.0 cc. After an incubation period of 10 days the same symptoms appeared.

Symptoms:

Fever is the first change. When the fever begins to subside, motor paralysis appears in the upper extremities, neck, face, eyelids and respiratory muscles. There are no significant sensory changes. No paralysis is observed in the tongue, muscles of deglutition or lower extremities. After recovery, paralysis may be permanent. Both Kasahara and Kitano observed it longer than 6 months.

Pathological changes occur mainly in the cervical cord and medulla. Lesions were also observed in thoracic cord to 7th vertebra and in pons, thalamus, cerebrum and cerebellum. Anterior horn cells show degeneration. There is also perivascular round cell infiltration and gliosis. Myelin studies have not been done.

Filtration experiments were performed with Chamberlain filters L_2 and L_3 and Seitz EK which were all positive in mice.

The virus grows in chorioallantoic membranes and chick embryo inoculated i.C. In the latter, it was transferred through 5 embryoes; on the 6th day after transfer it was inoculated i.C. After the 5th embryo passage, it was successfully transferred to mice.

There is no vaccine.

6909-C 2

TSUTSUGAMUSHI FEVER

The 2 cases of Tsutsugamushi Fever in Dr Ishikawa's collection were explained by Drs Kasahara and Kitano. They came from the Niigata Neurological Hospital. A weak strain of the virus obtained from Formosa is used as fever therapy for the treatment of general paresis. This fever is as effective as any in the treatment of neurological syphilis. No work was done in Harbin. The strain is maintained by successive passage through rabbit testicle.

08　15 Nov. 1947: PLANT AGENTS, INTERVIEW WITH Dr. Yukimasa YAGISAWA

资料出处： Technical Library, Fort Dugway Proving Grounds, Utah, US.

内容点评： 本资料为 1947 年 11 月 15 日 Edwin V. Hill、Joseph Victor 与八木泽行正（Yukimasa YAGISAWA）的谈话记录，题目：植物病菌。八木泽行正曾任 731 部队第二部八木泽班（植物菌）班长。

Regraded ~~Confidential~~ ~~CONFIDENTIAL~~
By authority of Chief Chemical Officer.
By [signature]
Grade and Org. Lt Col, CmlC
Date 4 August 1954

6989-C S

PLANT AGENTS

INTERVIEW WITH: November 15, 1947

Dr Yukimasa YAGASAWA

Dr Yukimasa Yagasawa was interviewed on Nov 15, 1947 for the purpose of securing the answers to a number of questions which have been submitted by Dr Norman of Camp Detrick:

1. The staff of the Japanese on B.W. research group on Plant Agents consisted of only two professionals; Dr Yagasawa served as Chief of the branch for a period of ten years, Dr Hamada served in a professional capacity for two years. Sub-professional staff of the unit consisted of only ten men.

2. The geographic area of the world considered as a target for the dissemination of plant diseases consisted of Siberia and the Pacific N.W.

3. Only those agents were selected for intensive development which past history indicated were capable of producing great damage to growing crops. The geographical area for which these agents would be suitable was selected as a secondary consideration.

4. Stinking Smut of Wheat was selected for intensive development because it produced great damage in the growing wheat on Manchuria and Siberia. Approximately one-third of all the wheat grown in Manchuria is infected with this disease. It was believed that western Oregon and Nebraska because of their climate would be suitable targets for this disease. For test purposes, a large number of varieties of American wheat were planted and experimentally infected with the agent. The variety Marquis was found to be almost completely resistant, whereas Kota was extremely susceptible. The other varieties of wheat occupy a position intermediate in susceptibility. The agent for offensive use was to have been collected as a by-product from flour milling operations in Manchuria and the occupied areas of China. According to Dr Yagasawa, the collection of smut also has the beneficial effect of controlling the disease in these areas in addition to furnishing a large amount of material for experimental uses.

Nematosis of wheat and rye was selected for the same reasons as Stinking Smut in wheat — this disease is prevalent in Manchuria and approximately 80% of wheat fields are heavily infected. The disease

CONFIDENTIAL

Regraded ______ CONFIDENTIAL
By authority of Chief Chemical Officer.
By ______
Crade and Org. ______
Date ______

was originally introduced into Japan from Canada in contaminated poultry feed about 15 years ago, but its spread was effectively controlled. Due to the wide spread distribution of the disease in Manchuria, almost unlimited quantities of agent could be collected as a by-product of milling operations. Dr Yagasawa was so impressed with this disease that he felt that it would even be worth while to deliberately infect fields of wheat with Nematosis in order to collect the agent. Approximately 500 tons of this material could be produced in the field with a loss of 2,500 tons of grain. The recommended innoculum for B.W. purposes is 5 kilograms per acre and would result in a 100% destruction of the crop in the case of susceptible varieties of wheat. Most Japanese and Australian varieties of wheat are 80% susceptible. Russian varieties 25%, and American varieties intermediate between Japanese and Russian. The Florence variety of wheat was stated to be only 10% susceptible.

Both Stinking Smut and Nematosis of wheat and rye were considered to be superior to the other plant agents investigated because of the serious damage which they are capable of producing, and the availability of unlimited quantities of agent.

In addition to the two diseases mentioned above, the following diseases are considered to be most effective as crop destroying agents:

a. Downy Mildew of Potato (Phytopthera Infestans);

b. Claviceps Purpurea for rye;

c. Gibberella Saubinetti for cereals;

d. Rice Blast for rice.

Chinese and Indian varieties are extremely susceptible to this disease. For American and Japanese varieties of rice, Piricularias Oryzae would have been selected. As a matter of fact, the Japanese were very much afraid that this particular disease might have been used against them.

The following qualities were considered to be essential for an effective plant pathogen:

a. Infectivity - spread from plant to plant;

b. Ease of production;

c. Stability;

d. Persistence;

e. Ease or difficulties of control measures.

2

CONFIDENTIAL

A survey of the literature was conducted on stem rusts, and it was decided that because of the difficulty in producing the agent experimentally that it was not worth while to conduct extensive experimentation.

Ophiobolus or Take-all of wheat was selected for investigation because Yagasawa believed it would be a formidable disease in the United States and Russia. Field experiments demonstrated that wheat could be only infected at the time of planting and not later. For this reason, further work was not conducted on this agent. Field investigations were conducted for only one season. Had unlimited time and facilities been available, Dr Yagasawa would have continued experimentation on this agent.

Blade Blight of Barley (Helminthosporium Graminaum) was investigated only from the academic point of view. This disease is prevelant in Manchuria and certain areas of China and occassionally destroys 100% of the grain crop.

No plant pathogens were developed to the stage where they could have been used offensively although facilities could have been made available in Harbin for the production of large quantities of agent. Lack of confidence on the part of the staff officers prevented its application. According to Dr Yagasawa, approximately 1,000 tons of bran was in stock at all times in Harbin and could have been used for the production of plant pathogens had the order been given. Physical facilities were available for autoclaving and handling 100 tons of bran per day. Some agents were produced on a semi-large scale in quantities of 100 to 500 kilograms at a time. Gibberella Saubinetti and Phytophthera were the agents prepared in these quantities. If larger quantities of material had been required, Dr Yagasawa felt that the facilities of the fermentation industry could have been pressed into use for this purpose. By fermentation industry, he was referring to the manufacturing process used in the preparation of soy bean sauce.

Artificial media was not used to produce plant pathogens on a large scale. The only experiment using artificial media which was conducted was one in which Czapeks solution, plus 1% sucrose was used for the production of Gibberella Saubinetti. The agent grew very slowly in this media. This synthetic media was not used on a large scale because sugar was critically short and bran was available in unlimited quantities at very low cost.

No plans had been prepared for future large scale preparation of innoculum. A 1% innoculum was used. The production of innoculum was carried from the test tube to an Erlenmeyer flask containing solid medium and thence to 20 to 40 liter aluminum flasks or trays.

Dr Yagasawa mentioned a disease attacking wheat and oats which was discovered in Japan approximately ten years ago which may not have been

reported in the American literature. This disease is produced by Cephalosporium Gramineum and attacks all varieties of wheat and oats. Thus far, no varietal resistance to the disease has been discovered. The agent can be grown experimentally in Czapeks media and produces abundant spores. This disease was investigated by Dr Ikaka of the Okayama Agriculture Station and by Dr Nishikato of Ohara Agriculture Research Laboratory of Okaya. An attempt will be made to obtain a copy of a mon graph written in Japanese and a brief description of the disease which appears in English for the files at Camp Detrick. Dr Yagasawa believes that this agent has possibilities in B.W.

4

CONFIDENTIAL

09 15 Nov. 1947: TUBERCULOSIS, INTERVIEW WITH Dr. Hideo FUTAGI

资料出处：Technical Library, Fort Dugway Proving Grounds, Utah, US.

内容点评：本资料为 1947 年 11 月 15 日 Edwin V. Hill、Joseph Victor 与二木秀雄（Hideo FUTAGI）的谈话记录，题目：肺结核。二木秀雄曾任 731 部队第一部二木班（结核菌）班长。

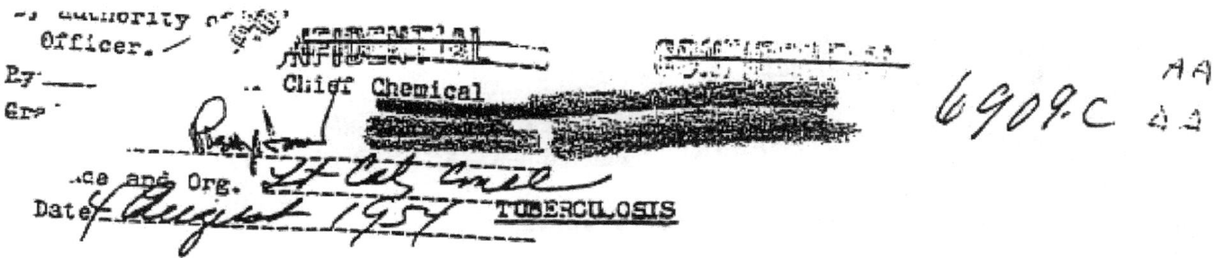

Officer.
By
.. Chief Chemical
Gr
Date
TUBERCULOSIS
6909.C

INTERVIEW WITH: November 15, 1947

Dr Hideo FUTAGI

Experiments carried out on M are described below.

Respiratory Infection:

The effect of inhalation of Cl Tuberculosis hominis was compared in 5 tuberculin positive and 5 tuberculin negative individuals. An emulsion containing 1.0 mgm bacilli (wet weight) in 1.0 cc of saline was discharged in 30 seconds threw a rubber bulb atomizer into a nasal and oral mask worn by the subject. The subjects were studied daily for sputum and blood cultures, temperature, erythrocyte sedimentation rate (E.S.R.) and x-rays of chest. Sputum specimens were obtained thrice daily. Culture medium was Oka-Katakura, a modification of Petroff's medium.

Results -

1. Tuberculin negative cases. One day following exposure there was a slight rise in temperature to 38° C lasting 1 day. Two weeks later, an abrupt rise in temperature to 38.50 C appeared. This subsided slowly during the following month. With fever, sputum cultures were positive at some time in all subjects, E.S.R. increased but x-ray revealed no changes. Tonsils were not examined. No fatalities occurred. Tuberculin reaction became positive just before onset of fever.

2. Tuberculin positive cases. In contrast to the previous group, the temperature rise following inhalation was greater and lasted longer going to [illegible]° C for 2 - 3 days. It returned to normal and remained that way for the next 3 months. However, as in the first group sputum became positive in the second and 3rd week in 2 of 5 cases. X-ray revealed no changes and there were no fatalities. E.S.R. increased during fever.

Conclusions -

1. Comparison of reaction of tuberculin positive and negative individuals to inhalation of 1 mgm Cl. Tuberculosis hominis revealed significant differences in the clinical course without x-ray changes.

2. Tuberculin positive individuals were more resistant to infection by inhalation of these bacteria.

3. Tuberculin negative cases developed positive tuberculin reaction

just before bacteria appeared in sputum.

4. Blood cultures were negative in both series.

Intravenous Infection:

A.

Various doses of Calmette BCG. (Cl tuberculosis bovis) were compared with similar doses of Cl tuberculosis hominis in tuberculin positive individuals. Doses were 10.0, 1.0, 0.1/0.01 0.001 mgm (wet weight) for each individual, the series involving 10 cases. Clinical and laboratory data were obtained as described above.

Results -

1. Calmette BCG. Beginning the day after injection, there was a rapid elevation of temperature which reached maximum of 40° C in 2 - 3 weeks and remained elevated for about 2 months. Blood culture was positive for the 1st 3 - 4 days and sputum became positive in 2 - 3 weeks. X-ray at this time showed signs of miliary tuberculosis of the lungs. E.S.R. increased throughout the febrile period. The patients recovered after 2 months of fever. The above description applies to those receiving 1.0 - 10.0 mgm of bacteria. The symptoms and signs were less severe and there were no x-ray changes in cases receiving less than these doses so that the one receiving 0.001 mgm had a positive sputum after 2 weeks, but only relatively slight fever. All subjects recovered in this series.

2. Cl Tuberculosis Hominis. The clinical course and changes were similar to those described for the other group. In contrast to the other group, all doses produced miliary tuberculosis which was fatal within 1 month in those injected with 10.0 and 1.0 mgm. The others were severely ill, lived longer but probably died later. The experiment was discontinued after 3 months and these patients were not followed thereafter.

Conclusion -

1. In tuberculin positive subjects, Cl. tuberculosis hominis was much more virulent than BCG (bovine) when injected i.v.

2. BCG produced miliary tuberculosis when injected i.v.

B.

Effects of i.v. injection of Cl. tuberculosis hominis in individuals with positive or negative tuberculin reactions. The following doses (mgm wet weight) were injected: 10.0, 1.0, 0.1, 0.01, 0.001 and 0.0001.

By authority of Chief Chemical Officer.
By [signature]
Grade and Org. [signature]
Date: 4 August 195[illegible]

Resultx -

1. Reaction in tuberculin positive cases was similar to that described in the previous series A2. Death at 1 month occurred following a stormy course with fever immediately post-injection in those receiving 1.0 and 10 mgm. Blood and sputum cultures as well as x-ray changes were as described. However, one receiving 0.1 mgm survived although the illness was severe. With 0.01 mgm sputum become positive for 2 days during the 3rd week and fever was slight. The one receiving 0.001 mgm had only slight post injection fever but no positive sputum. Smaller dose than this produced no changes.

2. Tuberculin negative individuals showed less fever immediately after injection. However, with 10.0 and 1.0 mgm doses the course was fatal in 1 month, with 0.1 mgm dose it was fatal in 3 months. These cases revealed miliary tuberculosis at autopsy. The dose of 0.01 mgm produced a reaction similar to that observed with inhalation of 1.0 mgm (see above). One receiving 0.001 mgm had a positive sputum in the 3rd week. Lesser dose produced no changes. Tuberculin reaction became positive in all cases in the third week.

Conclusion -

1. Intravenous Cl. tuberculosis hominis was less severe clinically, but had a greater mortality in tuberculin negative than in tuberculin positive individuals.

2. It produced miliary tuberculosis.

3. The tuberculin reaction became positive in tuberculin negative cases.

<u>Intracutaneous Injection:</u>

Comparison of Calmette B.C.G. with Cl. tuberculosis hominis in tuberculin positive individuals. Doses of 0.1, 0.01, 0.001, 0.001 and 0.00001 mgm in 0.1 cc of each species were injected into the skin over the back beginning at the level of the scapula. B.C.G. was injected in the right side and Cl. tuberculosis hominis in the left. Three subjects were used.

Results -

Doses of 0.001 mgm or more produced abscesses with axillary and cervical lymphadenitis in both series. No pulmonary changes occurred. The B.C.G. infections subsided after 3 months while those with Cl. tuberculosis hominis progressed throughtout the 6 months they were studied. Termination of the observations occurred with the war's end.

Conclusion -

1. Cl. tuberculosis hominis produced a chronic, progressive inflammation lasting more than 6 months when injected i.c. in tuberculin posi-

Regraded ~~CONFIDENTIAL~~
By authority of ~~Chief Chemical~~
Officer.
By [signature]
Grade and Org. Lt Col [illegible]
Date 4 Aug 1954

~~CONFIDENTIAL~~

tive individuals.

2. B.C.G. results in a similar but less severe infection of shorter duration.

Subcutaneous Injection:

The experiment was similar to that with intracutaneous injection. However, the effects were more severe. Infectious dose was between 0.001 and 0.0001 mgm. With Cl. tuberculosis hominis abscesses developed draining sinuses after 1 month which did not heal but progressed during 6 months of observation. B.C.G. lesions were less severe and healed in 3 months.

Oral Administration:

Feeding 100 mgm of dry Cl. tuberculosis hominis in milk to 3 individuals who were tuberculin positive produced no disease.

Immunization:

B.C.G. in doses of 0.001 mgm were injected into the axillae of Manchurian children. After 2 - 3 weeks, the previously negative tuberculin reaction became positive.

Source of Bacteria:

The original stock was derived from a natural case. Virulence was maintained by passage through guinea pigs.

CONFIDENTIAL

10　17 Nov. 1947: BRUCELLOSIS, INTERVIEW WITH Dr. Kiyoshi HAYAKAWA

资料出处： Technical Library, Fort Dugway Proving Grounds, Utah, US.

内容点评： 本资料为 1947 年 11 月 17 日 Edwin V. Hill、Joseph Victor 与早川清（Kiyoshi HAYAKAWA）的谈话记录，题目：波状热。

Regraded Confidential
By authority of Chief Chemical Officer.
By [signature]
Grade and Org. Lt Col, Cml C
Date 4 Aug 54

CONFIDENTIAL

6409-C F

BRUCELLOSIS

INTERVIEW WITH: November 17, 1947

Dr Kiyoshi HAYAKAWA

Interview with Dr Hayakawa who was in charge of media preparation at Harbin from 1937 - 1940. The work on Brucellosis was begun there in 1939 and Dr Hayakawa's association with this phase terminated after 6 months at which time he left Japan to work in Dr Thomas Francis' department at the University of Michigan.

Strain - B. Melitensis was derived from a sheep in Manchuria where the disease is endemic in cattle and other live stock, as well as in people. B. abortus is also found there. B. melitensis was propogated by guinea pig passage and cultured on Francis' medium.

Experiments:

M.

A subject was injected s.c. with 0.01 mgm of B. melitensis. After an incubation period of between 2 - 3 weeks, undulant fever appeared. With the fever, blood cultures became positive. The subject was followed for 6 months and had fever episodes throughout that period. The outcome and subsequent course of this case was unknown to Dr Hayakawa because he left the unit at that time. Continuation of the study was the responsibility of Dr Yujiro Yamanouchi and possibly Dr Kozo Okamoto.

Rabbit -

Agglutinins appeared in blood after s.c. injection of B. melitensis vaccine containing 0.5% phenol.

From 1942 to the end of the war, Dr Hayakawa served in Singapore where he was concerned with classification of salmonella organisms, particularly paratyphoid, and certain studies differentiating scrub typhus from tsutsugamushi fever. The results of these studies are in press, to be printed in English. He also furnished an English translation of the Japanese Army manual for preparation of vaccines.

CONFIDENTIAL

11 18 Nov. 1947: SALMONELLA, DYSENTERY, TYPHOID, INTERVIEW WITH: Dr. Saburo KOJIMA, Assistant Director of National Institute of Health

资料出处： Technical Library, Fort Dugway Proving Grounds, Utah, US.

内容点评： 本资料为 1947 年 11 月 18 日 Edwin V. Hill、Joseph Victor 与日本国立卫生研究所副所长小岛三郎（Saburo KOJIMA）的谈话记录，题目：沙门氏菌、痢疾、伤寒。

Regraded ~~Confidential~~ ~~CONFIDENTIAL~~ 6909-C
By authority of Chief Chemical
Officer.
By ________
Grade and Org. ________
Date 4 Aug 54 SALMONELLA, DYSENTERY, TYPHOID

INTERVIEW WITH: November 18, 1947

Dr Saburo KOJIMA,
Assistant Director of
National Institute of Health

Dr Kojima had almost no experience with B.W. aspects of these diseases. From a few studies at Harbin, he was familiar with the fact that plate cultures of Shiga organisms were quite avirulent, the contents of 2 plates producing only slight diarrhia. Virulence was not enhanced by passage through man. He suggested that Shiga organisms be obtained from a fresh natural case. Such organisms can be maintained virulent by i.p. passage in mice. In M these organisms are infectious only by oral administration. He has heard that these live organisms injected into man produce reaction only at the site of injection.

Animal Experiments:

Typhoid can be transmitted to mice, guinea pigs by s.c. and i.v. injection. Shiga dysentery following i.p. injection in massive doses in mice, guinea pigs, or rabbits may be fatal. In a few cases, simultaneously feeding dysentery bacilli with large quantities of alkali to neutralize gastric acidity may cause intestinal infection. Although feeding S. typhi/murium S. enteritidis and S. cholerae suis, etc. kill mice within a week, S. typhi and S. para-typhi do not harm mice except by i.p. injection. The infectious dose of these agents administered i.p. is 0.01 loopful or less. For Shiga dysentery i.p. injection of laboratory culture of 1 loopful is fatal. However, freshly isolated strains require only 0.1 to 0.01 loopful.

Vaccines:

There is a field experiment in which inhabitants of a large village are divided into two groups. One was treated with vaccine for typhoid, para-typhoid and dysentery. The other served as control. Natural cases were more frequent in the control group with respect to typhoid and para-typhoid, but dysentery was just as common in each group.

Human Experiments:

Although Dr Kojima took no part in any of these, he is certain that they were performed. He believes they were planned so that the effects of various vaccines could be studied.

CONFIDENTIAL

Regraded ~~Confidential~~ CONFIDENTIAL
By authority of Chief Chemical Officer.
By ______
Grade and Org. Lt Col CmlC
Date 4 August 54

VACCINES

1. Heated for 30 minutes to 50 - 60° centigrade;

2. Formolized;

3. Autolyzed;

4. Toxoid;

5. Live dysentery.

Important feature of the vaccine is the strain of bacteria. With the proper strain, vaccine seems to be effective. Effective strains are the S. form of number 58 (Boxhill) and a new strain. On the other hand, former strains and Rawling strain were not effective.

All of these vaccines were administered s.c. The oral vaccine formerly used has been discontinued because it is not effective.

2 CONFIDENTIAL

12　18 Nov. 1947: TOXINS: Gas Gangrene, Tetanus and Shiga Dysentery, INTERVIEW WITH Dr. Shogo HOSOYA

资料出处： Technical Library, Fort Dugway Proving Grounds, Utah, US.

内容点评： 本资料为1947年11月18日 Edwin V. Hill、Joseph Victor与细谷省吾（Shogo HOSOYA）的谈话记录，题目：毒物：气性坏疽、破伤风、志贺痢疾。细谷省吾曾为陆军军医学校防疫研究所成员、东京大学传染病研究所所长。

Regraded ~~Confidential~~ ~~CONFIDENTIAL~~
By authority of Chief Chemical
Officer.
By ________
Grade and Org. Lt Col, CmlC
Date 4 Aug 54 TOXINS: Gas Gangrene, Tetanus and Shiga Dysentery

6909-CM

INTERVIEW WITH: November 18, 1947

Dr Shogo HOSOYA

Preparation of Gas Cangrene toxoids

Cl. Welchi, V. Septique, V. novei and Cl. histolyticus - cultured in liver - liver broth.

Toxin + 50% $Zn\ Cl_2$

Precipitate washed with H_2O

10% $Na_2\ HPO_4$

eluate $Zn_3\ (PO_4)_2$

HCHO

Toxoid + Alum → mixed alum toxoids for immunization.

Effective in guinea pigs and horses.

Tetanus toxin prepared the same way except culture medium was peptone medium (horse meat). Phosphate PH 7.2 Fatal dose for mouse 1 Y.

Preparation of Shiga Toxin and Toxoids -

Shiga dysentery bacillus grown on agar medium containing 2.5% agar in broth, for 24 hours of 37°C.

~~CONFIDENTIAL~~

Suspended in
Saline solution - 60°C for 30 minutes

Supersonic treatment - 20 minutes

Centrifuged

Supernatant — Precipitate

C CL_3COO H (pH 4.0 - 4.2)

— Filtrate (Endotoxin)

Precipitate
H_2O neutralized

$(NH_4)_2SO_4$ 1/3 Saturated

Precipitate — Filtered

\+ $(NH_4)_2SO_4$ 2/3 Saturated

Precipitate (Exotoxin)

Wash in H_2O neutralized

Electrodialysis (in center chamber)
pH (5 - 4.5) 100 V.

Precipitate + H_2O neutralized → Toxin-MLD for

20 min at 100° C — Mice 0.1 Y

Toxoid

Never tested in controlled human experiments. Antitoxin is strongly bacterestatic and is produced by the toxoid. It protects mice and rabbits against exotoxin and bacteria. Exotoxin produces nervous symptoms in rabbits. Endotoxin causes diarrhea and colonic and Cecal ulcers in rabbits.

Antibody contains only small agglutinin and precipitation titre for exotoxin.

There are about 15 strains of dysentery producing exotoxin.

2

13　20 Nov. 1947: AEROSOLS, INTERVIEW WITH: Dr. Takahashi

资料出处： Technical Library, Fort Dugway Proving Grounds, Utah, US.

内容点评： 本资料为 1947 年 11 月 20 日 Edwin V. Hill、Joseph Victor 与高桥（Takahashi）的谈话记录，题目：喷雾。

Regraded Confidential
By authority of Chief Chemical Officer.
By
Grade and Org. Lt Col CmlC
Date 4 Aug 54

Control No. 6909C

AEROSOLS

INTERVIEW WITH: November 20, 1947

Dr Takahashi

Dr Takahashi was interviewed on the subject of aerosols on November 20 for the purpose of supplementing the information available in the Masuda report.

The octagonal shaped chamber used for human experimentation had a capacity of 20 cubic meters. For the generation of the aerosol, an insect type sprayer similar to the flit gun was used. In some cases, the atomizer is located within the chamber, but operated manually from the outside, whereas in other cases it is located outside of the chamber and the aerosol produced is conducted to the chamber through a rubber hose. The rate of atomization was approximately 1 cc of bacterial suspension per second. For human experiments two concentrations of bacterial suspensions were used - 1 mgm per cc and 100 mgm per cc. The chamber was vented to the outside so that the pressure within the chamber was constant during the experiment. Individuals were placed inside the chamber and then the bacterial aerosol was introduced in the manner as stated above. No attempt was made to permit the concentration of bacteria in the air in the chamber to reach equilibrium before animals were exposed. The exposure period was always within the time interval required for the concentration of organisms in the chamber to go from zero concentration to equilibrium concentration. The time of exposure varied and was usually from 10 seconds and up.

The concentration of aerosol was determined by exposing agar plates on the floor of the chamber about the subject during the period of the test. The plates were incubated and colony counts were made. According to Dr Takahashi, these accounted for only one-half to one-third of the calculated number of organisms. It was realized that only the large particles which settled out of the air were picked up by these plates and that the smaller particles which still remained ambient escaped detection.

The only particle size determination on aerosols which were made consisted of exposing a cardboard card 1-1/2 meters in front of the aerosol generator. Dyes were used as tracers and the stained particles on the card were then measured. Size of the particles ranged from 2 millimeter to 10 mu. Some attempts were made to plot percent of distribution curves. Dr Takahashi stated that in his opinion, particles of 10 mu or less would penetrate the lung.

The most recent sampling method which had been developed just before the end of the war consisted of taking a vacuum bottle 500 cc in

~~capacity containing 20~~ cc of bouillon and breaking the vacuum so that a 500 cc ~~sample of aerosol~~ was drawn into the bottle. It was then agitated, progressive dilutions were made and plate counts were conducted. The accuracy of this method of sampling aerosols was not determined.

It was realized that methods of stabilizing bacterial aerosols needed to be developed. Agar, gelatine, saline, bouillon, and egg white were tested for their stabilizing effect. It was realized that some of these materials increased the viscosity of the suspension and the particle size of the resultant aerosol — but, this was relatively of little importance. No effective adjuvant for increasing the stability of organisms in the aerosol form was developed.

The infective dose for various organisms mentioned in the Masuda report assumed no loss of viability incident to spraying or settling and 100% retention of the inhaled material. The following experiments were conducted in the exposure chamber:

Plague - 4 experiments with 4 - 5 subjects each;

Anthrax -10 " " 4 - 5 " " , only 2 subjects developed the disease;

Typhus - 1 experiment with 2 persons;

Small Pox - 1 experiment with 1 - 2 persons;

Glanders - 5 - 6 experiments;

Tuberculosis- 1 - 2 experiments;

Dysentery - 2 - 3 experiments;

Brucellosis - 2 -3 experiments with 1 - 2 subjects each;

Gas gangrene- 2 - 3 " " 1 - 2 " " ;

Cholera - 2 - 3 " " 1 - 2 persons " ;

Songo - 2 - 3 " " 1 - 2 " " .

14 20 Nov. 1947: TYPHUS, INTERVIEW WITH Dr. ARITA

资料出处： Technical Library, Fort Dugway Proving Grounds, Utah, US.

内容点评： 本资料为 1947 年 11 月 20 日 Edwin V. Hill、Joseph Victor 与有田（Arita）的谈话记录，题目：伤寒。有田（正义）曾任 731 部队第四部有田班（斑疹伤寒）班长。

CONFIDENTIAL CONFIDENTIAL 6909-C AD

Regraded ____________
By authority of Chief Chemical Officer.
By ____________
Grade and Org. Lt Col Cml C TYPHUS
Date 4 Aug 1954

INTERVIEW WITH: November 20, 1947

Dr ARITA

Dr Arita worked in Harbin from April 1942 under Dr Kitano. His task was mass production of typhus vaccine. The information was essentially like that supplied by Dr Kitano.

Methods:

1. Castaneda - employing white mice;
2. Chick Embryo inoculation;
3. Squirrel inoculation.

Mouse vaccine was prepared as follows: i.n. instilation of R. mooseri. Pneumonic lung was removed 5 days later, frozen to minus 20° C, thawed at room temperature and ground. It was then emulsified in one part saline to one part lung. Emulsion was centrifuged at 3,000RPM for 10 minutes and the supernatant was recentrifuged at 10,000 RPM for 30 minutes. The sediment was suspended in the same amount of saline that had been added to the original lung. It was stored with 0.2% phenol and injected s.c. in doses of 0.5 and 1.0 cc at an interval of 7 days. This suspension contained $4 - 5 \times 10^9$ rickettsia per cc. Efficacy of this material was tested in guinea pigs. However, Dr Arita knew that human tests with this material were performed in another branch under the supervision of Dr Hamada.

Diagnostic Test:

This procedure again is essentially that outlined by Dr Kitano starting with pneumonic mouse lung which was emulsified in equal parts of saline; the emulsion was centrifuged at 3,000 RPM for 10 minutes, to the sediment was added the same amount of saline used in the original emulsification. This was centrifuged at 10,000 RPM for 30 minutes. The supernatant was filtered through Seitz E.K. and filtrate preserved with 0.5% phenol. The filtrate served as diagnostic fluid which was mixed at room temperature with serum of animals with typhus. The flocculation which occurs within 30 - 60 seconds is specific for typhus and occurs with no other disease.

CONFIDENTIAL

15 22 Nov. 1947: BOTULINUM, BRUCELLOSIS, GAS GANGRENE, INFLUENZA, MENINGOCOCCUS, SMALL POX, TETANUS, TULANEMIA, INTERVIEW WITH Dr. Shiro ISHII

资料出处： Technical Library, Fort Dugway Proving Grounds, Utah, US.

内容点评： 本资料为 1947 年 11 月 22 日 Edwin V. Hill、Joseph Victor 与石井四郎（Shiro ISHII）的谈话记录，题目：肉毒杆菌、波状热、气性坏疽、流感、脑膜炎、天花、破伤风、兔热病。

Regraded ~~Confidential~~
By authority of Chief Chemical Officer.
By ______
Grade and Org. Lt Col, CmlC
Date 4 Aug 54

W/6909.C
D

CONFIDENTIAL

BOTULISM

INTERVIEW WITH:

November 22, 1947

Dr Shiro ISHII

Experiments in M were conducted with 5 subjects who were fed a 2-day old culture. Two of the subjects died.

CONFIDENTIAL

Regraded ~~Confidential~~
By authority of Chief Chemical
Officer.
By Rhelly ...
Grade and Org. Lt Col, CmlC
Date 4 Aug 54

CONFIDENTIAL 709.C

BRUCELLOSIS

INTERVIEW WITH:

November 22, 1947

Dr Shiro ISHII

Experiments in M were carried out by the subcutaneous injection of more than 20 subjects. Does not remember the result of such experiments except that undulant fever followed injection and persisted for many months.

CONFIDENTIAL

6904-c L

Regraded Confidential
By authority of Chief Chemical Officer.
By [illegible]
Grade and Org. Lt Col CmlC
Date 4 Aug 54

GAS GANGRENE

INTERVIEW WITH: November 22, 1947

Dr Shiro ISHII

Although Welchi, Septique, Nobei and Histolytica were investigated, most studies were conducted with Cl. Welchi.

Subcutaneous Injection

Studies with M employed about 10 - 20 subjects. Cl. Welchi was cultured for 2 days in liver - liver broth. It had been derived from natural cases and from soil samples isolated in Manchuria near the border. Virulence was maintained by passage through guinea pigs. Cultures are kept alkaline because virulence disappears at below pH 6.

Human feces contain both virulent and avirulent Cl. Welchi which may be differentiated by guinea pig injection.

Dose:

Subcutaneous injection of 1.0 - 5.0 cc of a 2-day culture produced widespread subcutaneous emphysema in 1 day. When emphysema involved 0.5 body surface the subject died, usually on day 2 - 3.

In the Nomohan incident at Manchurian-Siberian border, 1939, more than half of Japanese wounded developed gas gangrene.

Bomb Burst Experiments with "Ha" bomb were performed twice each with 5 - 6 cases, all of whom became infected.

Immunization tests with gas gangrene toxoid, described by Dr Hosoya were carried out with about 10 subjects, half of whom had been immunized.

Autopsies were performed on all experimental subjects who died.

Regraded Confidential
By authority of Chief Chemical Officer.
By [signature]
Grade and Org. Lt Col, CmlC
Date 4 August 54

CONFIDENTIAL

6909-C

N

INFLUENZA

INTERVIEW WITH: November 22, 1947

Dr Shiro ISHII

Influenza virus derived from American source, strain not known, was maintained by mouse and ferret passage.

Transmission experiments in M. Six experiments each with 2 subjects were treated as follows with infectious material derived from ferret lung:

1. Injected s.c.;
2. Injected i.p.;
3. Inhalation;
4. Nasal Instillation;
5. Injected intrapulmonary;
6. Painted pharynx.

Results: Three subjects had short period of fever which rose up to 38° C for about 2 - 3 days.

CONFIDENTIAL

Regraded Confidential CONFIDENTIAL
By authority of Chief Chemical Officer.
By
Grade and Org.
Date 4 August 54

6909c

MENINGOCOCCUS

INTERVIEW WITH: November 22, 1947

Dr Shiro ISHII

Meningococcus type 3, mucus producing strain, was derived from a natural case.

Transmission experiments in H were performed with 5 subjects for each experiment carried out as follows:

1. Subcutaneous injection;
2. Intraperitoneal " ;
3. Intraspinal (lumbar);
4. Painting larynx,
5. Inhalation;
6. Nasal installation;
7. Lung injection.

Results: All 5 cases of intraspinal injection were positive and died. No other cases became infected.

CONFIDENTIAL

Regraded
By authority of Chief Chemical Officer.
By
Grade and Org.
Date 4 August 1954

CONFIDENTIAL

6909.CV

SMALL POX

INTERVIEW WITH: November 22, 1947

Dr Shiro ISHII

Experiments in M:

Small pox virus was obtained from a natural case in Manchuria. The contents of vesicles were dried and inhaled from paper bags by 10 subjects. All became ill, developing large geographically shaped erythematous, swollen and hemorrhagic areas on the body measuring up to 20 - 30 cm in greatest dimension. None developed vesicles. About 4 died.

CONFIDENTIAL

Regraded ~~Confidential~~
By authority of Chief Chemical
Officer. Ishikawa
By
Grade and Org. Lt Col, CmlC
Date 4 August 1954

~~CONFIDENTIAL~~

6908-C

TETANUS

INTERVIEW WITH: November 22, 1947

Dr Shiro ISHII

Experiments with M were conducted about 10 x with each of 2 subjects receiving lethal doses of 0.1 to 2.0 cc of cultures of B. tetanus s.c. Comparisons were made between immunized and non-immunized subjects. Immunization was carried out with Dr Hosoya's tetanus toxoid and was effective in all cases.

Serum therapy has effectively cured 100% of 50 cases, 20 of them experimental. None were sacrificed. Antiserum contained 2000-10,000 International Units per cc. Serum was administered intrathecally and i.m.

There were no inhalation or oral administration experiments.

CONFIDENTIAL

~~CONFIDENTIAL~~ ~~CONFIDENTIAL~~ 6909-C A B B

Regraded ~~CONFIDENTIAL~~
By authority of Chief Chemical Officer
By [signature]
Grade and Org. Lt Col, CmlC
Date 4 August 1954 TULAREMIA

INTERVIEW WITH: November 22, 1947

Dr Shiro ISHII

Experiments in M were conducted with 10 subjects who were injected s.c. All developed fever lasting as long as 6 months. None died or were sacrificed.

~~CONFIDENTIAL~~

16　22 Nov. 1947: INTERVIEW WITH Dr. Kozo OKAMOTO

资料出处： Technical Library, Fort Dugway Proving Grounds, Utah, US.

内容点评： 本资料为 1947 年 11 月 22 日 Edwin V. Hill、Joseph Victor 与冈本耕造（Kozo OKAMOTO）的谈话记录。冈本耕造曾任 731 部队第一部冈本班（病理）班长。

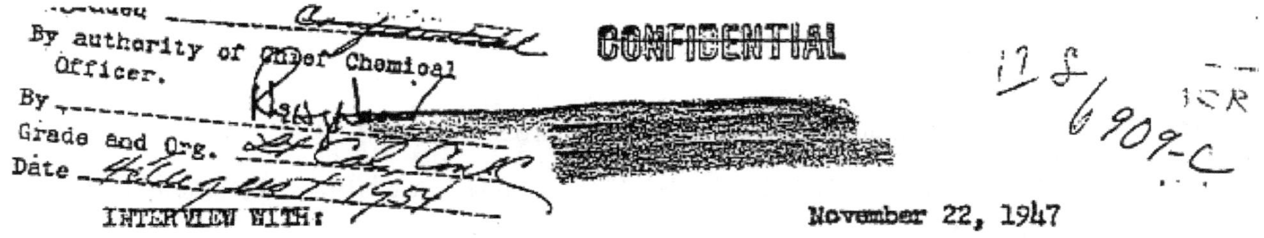
By authority of Chief Chemical Officer.
By
Grade and Org.
Date

CONFIDENTIAL

INTERVIEW WITH: November 22, 1947

Dr Kozo OKAMOTO

Dr Okamoto was pathologist at Harbin from 1938 to 1945. He performed no experiments, only worked up autopsies without being informed of specific protocols.

The following is a list of experimental diseases and the approximate number of each disease disclosed by his autopsies:

Disease	No. of Cases	Mode of Infection
Plague	50	Respiratory and injection
Typhoid	> 8	5 oral, 3 injected and sacrificed
Dysentery	> 20	Oral, Shiga & Komagome
Cholera	50	Oral
Anthrax	30	Respiratory, injection and oral
Glanders	> 5	Injection ?
Typhus	5	Injection ?
Others not Infectious	20	
Malta Fever	1	Pathological diagnosis was tuberculosis

Between 1938 - 1945 there were about 500 autopsies of subjects used in experiments. About 5 pathologists were employed, Dr Ishikawa being one of them. All the autopsies of experimental M subjects at Harbin number less than 1000. If Dr Ishikawa has slides of these cases, he took them without the knowledge of others and doubts that he has more than 500 cases since all those obtained after he left Harbin in 1943 remained at Harbin and numbered about 200.

CONFIDENTIAL

17　24 Nov. 1947: ANTHRAX, INTERVIEW WITH: Dr. Kiyoshi OTA

资料出处： Technical Library, Fort Dugway Proving Grounds, Utah, US.

内容点评： 本资料为 1947 年 11 月 24 日 Edwin V. Hill、Joseph Victor 与大田澄（Kiyoshi OTA）的谈话记录，题目：炭疽。大田澄为 731 部队第一部大田班（炭疽）班长，曾任 731 部队第二部、第四部部长等职。

Regraded ~~Confidential~~
By authority of Chief Chemical Officer.
By [signature]
Grade and Org. Lt Col, CmlC
Date 4 Aug 54

ANTHRAX

h/6909.C C

CONFIDENTIAL

INTERVIEW WITH: November 24, 1947

Dr Kiyoshi OTA

Experiments were conducted in Mukden, beginning in the laboratory of the Manchurian Railway more than 10 years ago. Strains were selected from cattle and soil contaminated areas. Most virulent strains were isolated and virulence was increased by passage in guinea pigs, mice and rats. Rough colonies were most virulent.

Culture Medium
- Peptone 0.5%
- Agar 2.0 - 3.0%
- NaCl 1.0%
- Crimson B 10%
- Amino Acids
- Soy bean extracts 1.0% or
- Meat extract (Liebig) 1.0% or
- Silk worm cocoon extract 1.0%

Experiments in M:

Dose Mgm	Injection Site	No. Infected	No. Deaths
1	Ear	0/3	
1	Ear	0/3	
1	Skin painting	0/5	
0.1	" S.C.	3/3	
0.2	" "	3/3	
0.5	" "	3/3	
1.0	" "	3/3	
5.0	" "	3/3	1/3
50.0	Oral	1/10	1/10
100.0	"	2/10	2/10
> 200.0	"	> 30/30	> 30/30 Intestinal
1.0 - 25.0	Inhalation	0/4	0/4 Phlegmon
50	"	1/1	1/1 Intestinal Phlegmon

Laboratory Accidental Infections - 10 cases, all died.

Bomb Tests - 10 M and other subjects - 1 [illegible]

CONFIDENTIAL

18 24 Nov. 1947: SHIGA DYSENTERY, PARATYPHOID, TYPHOID, INTERVIEW WITH: Dr. TABEI

资料出处： Technical Library, Fort Dugway Proving Grounds, Utah, US.

内容点评： 本资料为 1947 年 11 月 24 日 Edwin V. Hill、Joseph Victor 与田部（TABEI）的谈话记录，题目：志贺痢疾、副伤寒、伤寒。田部（井和）曾任 731 部队第一部田部班（伤寒）班长。

Regraded ~~Confidential~~ CONFIDENTIAL
By authority of Chief Chemical
Officer.
By [illegible]
Grade and Org. Lt Col. CmlC
Date 4 August [illegible]

6909-C

J

SHIGA DYSENTERY

INTERVIEW WITH: November 24, 1947

Dr Tabei

One subject was injected i.v. with 10 mgm Shiga Dysentery. He developed diarrhea and tenesmus on the 3rd day and hanged himself on the 4th day. Blood and stools revealed no dysentery bacilli. He had acute enteritis with mucosal petechiae, desquamation of epithelium and submucosal edema and infiltration by eosinophiles and polymorphonuclear leucocytes. There was no colitis.

CONFIDENTIAL

Regraded Unclassified
By authority of Chief Chemical Officer.
By
Grade and Org. Lt Col CmlC
Date 8 August 1954

CONFIDENTIAL

6909 C

PARATYPHOID

INTERVIEW WITH: November 24, 1947

Dr Tabei

Strain Kurokawa was derived from a patient who contracted the disease in Central China. The organism was extremely motile.

Experiments in M:

30 mgm wet weight were fed in 100 cc 8% sucrose. After an incubation period of 3 – 6 days, fever and diarrhea appeared lasting five days. Blood and stools are positive during fever and stools remain positive for 7 days after fever subsided. The symptoms may recur over many months. A patient may be reinfected by oral feeding on 3 successive occasions but then becomes resistant.

The disease was highly contagious. When a patient was placed in a room with 3 normal people, the others invariably contracted the disease.

There were no passage studies for changes in virulence. The bacilli were cultured in bile agar from blood of a patient with fever.

M.I.D. Paratyphoid A

Dose	Number Infected	
Mgm		
0.1	2/2	
0.01	2/2	M.I.D.
0.001	0/2	

6909C AC

TYPHOID

INTERVIEW WITH: November 24, 1947

Dr TABEI

Dr Tabei was in Harbin from 1938 - 1943.

Strains:

V, VW, and W Strains according to classification of Margaret Pitt, and Felix in England. V was 100 x as virulent as W in mice, tested by i.p. inoculation. VW was intermediate. V was taken from a natural case in Manchuria.

Infectivity in M:

Method -

Different doses of different strains mixed with 100 cc 8% sucrose or 100 cc of milk and fed to Manchurians. Individuals with no typhoid antibody titre were selected. Subjects numbered 36.

Results -

Dose Mgm	Number Infected with V	VW	W Strain
0.1	0/2	1/2	0/2
1.0	0/2	0/2	0/2
10.0	1/2	1/2	0/2

Symptoms -

Diarrhea occured the day following ingestion and lasted only 1 day. After 5 - 6 days, fever rose above 38° C and lasted about 1 month. For the first 2 days of fever, there was bacteremia. Later the agglutinin titre increased. Urine and stools showed bacteria 10 days after the onset of fever. It is the impression of Dr Tabei that those with initial diarrhea did not develop other symptoms, although antibody titer of all subjects increased.

Because of these results, it seemed to Dr Tabei that VW was the most infectious strain and was used in subsequent studies in man.

Immunity Studies with M:

~~Vaccine was prepared~~ in Dairen, "D" Denkon at the Kitasato Labor-

atory in Tokyo and a third vaccine (A) at the Army medical school. Immunized subjects were challenged with 100 mgm (wet weight) WW. Three experiments were repeated. The following represents 1 experiment. Sixty persons were employed:

Challenge Dose WW	Vaccine V	Vaccine D	Vaccine A	Control
100 mgm	2/5	3/5	3/5	4/5 Infected

Deaths occurred in 2 cases and 3 committed suicide.

Conclusion:

None of the vaccines immunized against a dose of 100 mgm WW.

Nasopharyngeal Infection:

1 mgm of WW was suspended in 1.0 cc of saline and instilled by drops into the nasopharynx. 7/14 became infected.

Respiratory Infection:

Five subjects were placed in a chamber and exposed to 2 gm dry bacilli per cubic meter for 10 minutes. No subject was infected. One experimenter became infected. The bacteria were lyophilized and ground in a ball-mill. Individual particles contained 50-100 bacteria determined from slide counts. No evidence as to the viability of these organisms was obtained. However, subjects developed severe cough, copious sputum, nausea and headache. O titer increased, but there was no change in H titer. Stools became positive for bacteria.

Virulence:

Virulence of strain was increased by passage through M, 3 being employed for each passage. Dose initially employed was 100 mgm, but in successive passages was reduced to 0.1 which was M.I.D. About 36 subjects were employed.

Trauma:

One subject was exposed to a bomb burst containing buckshot mixed with 10 mgm bacilli and 10 gm of clay. The buckshot had grooves which were impregnated with the bacteria-clay mixture. Bomb burst 1 meter from the rear of the subject. He developed symptoms of typhoid fever with positive laboratory signs.

Laboratory Infections occurred in 2 Japanese investigators who seemed to be much sicker than Manchurians although none died. It was the

impression of Dr Tabei that Manchurians had much more natural resistance than Japanese.

Number of bacilli per mgm wet weight, Typhoid 1.3 x 10^9, paratyphoid 1.3 x 10^9, Shiga dysentery 1.7 x 10^9, staphylococus 3.0 x 10^9. Typhoid has little contagious value since no instance of infection from contact with patients was seen.

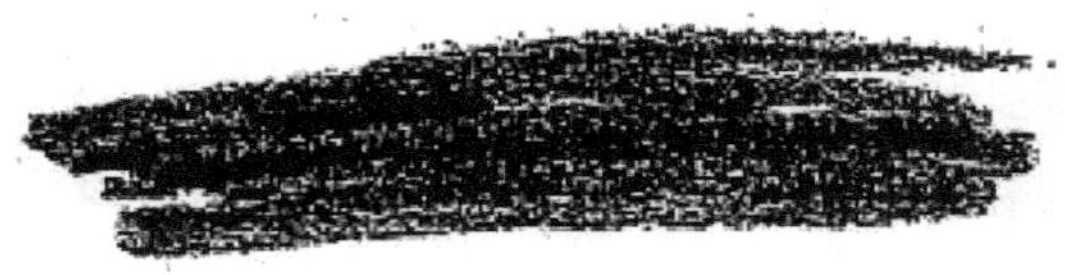

19　25 Nov. 1947: BRUCELLOSIS, INTERVIEW WITH: Dr. Yujiro YAMANOUCHI

资料出处：Technical Library, Fort Dugway Proving Grounds, Utah, US.

内容点评：本资料为 1947 年 11 月 25 日 Edwin V. Hill、Joseph Victor 与山野内裕次郎（Yujiro YAMANOUCHI）的谈话记录，题目：波状热。

Regraded ~~Confidential~~
By authority of Chief Chemical Officer.
By
Grade and Org. LtCol Cml C
Date 4 Aug 54

CONFIDENTIAL

6409.C E

BRUCELLOSIS

INTERVIEW WITH: November 25, 1947

Dr Yujiro YAMANOUCHI

Dr Yamanouchi was at Harbin for only 1-1/2 years, 1939 - 1940, where he worked on brucellosis.

Strain:

In most experiments, B. melitensis was employed. It was derived from sheep and natural cases in Manchuria. B. melitensis was preferred to B. abortus obtained from cows because it was easier to cultivate.

Medium:		
	liver or meat extract	1.0%
	peptone	1.0%
	orizanin B	1.0%
	NaCl	0.3%
	glucose	1.0%
	cystein	0.1%

1 mgm B. melitensis is equivalent to 1.5×10^9 bacilli.

Experiments in M: Injected s.c. in saline.

Dose mgm	Number infected	Number died
5.0	2/2	0
1.0	2/2	1/2 died after 1
0.5	2/2	0
0.1	1/2	0
0.05	1/2	0

Symptoms:

Patients have undulant fever for 1 - 4 weeks. Blood cultures positive during fever. All patients had low agglutin titres before infection. Titres rose to about 1/10,000 during infection even in some without symptoms.

CONFIDENTIAL

Regraded Confidential
By authority of Chief Chemical Officer.
By [signature]
Grade and Org. Lt Col Cml C
Date 4 Aug 54

CONFIDENTIAL

Virulence:

There were no systematic studies.

Vaccines:

1. Heated B. melitensis to 65° C for 1 hour

Experiments in mice - 0.1 - 0.15 mgm in saline were injected i.p. with a 5 day interval between 2 injections. Two weeks after the last injection, the mice were challenged with i.p. injection of 2.5 mgm, 0.5 mgm being fatal. 7-8/10 of immunized mice survived while 0/10 control mice survived.

2. Supersonic treatment of B. melitensis for 15 minutes. Experiments in mice conducted as described above.

8-9/10 of immunized mice survived while 0/10 control mice survived. Stability studies with B. melitensis: Showed that at - 10° C survival in broth occurs in 60 - 70% at the end of 1 month. At room temperature, there is no stability.

Studies with S. paratyphoid A indicated that phosphate buffer pH 7.2 in broth at -5° C, aids stability so that 70-80% survive and retain virulence at 1.5 months.

2 CONFIDENTIAL

20 25 Nov. 1947: TETANUS, INTERVIEW WITH: Dr. Kaoru ISHIMITSU

资料出处：Technical Library, Fort Dugway Proving Grounds, Utah, US.

内容点评：本资料为 1947 年 11 月 25 日 Edwin V. Hill、Joseph Victor 与石光熏（Kaoru ISHIMITSU）的谈话记录，题目：破伤风。

Regraded ~~CONFIDENTIAL~~
By authority of Chief Chemical Officer.
By [signature]
Grade and Org. Lt Col Cml C
Date 4 August 54

~~CONFIDENTIAL~~

6909-C X
X

TETANUS

INTERVIEW WITH: November 25, 1947

Dr Kaoru ISHIMITSU

Dr Ishimitsu was at Harbin from 1938 - 1945. Except for a few studies with Tetanus toxoid, he spent most of his time as chief of the library and translations.

Experiment in M:

Comparison was made between 2 subjects injected with tetanus bacilli, 1.0 cc of a 48 hour culture, and 2 subjects previously receiving tetanus alum toxoid prepared according to the method of Hosoya.

Treatment	Time	Subjects 1	2	3 Tetanus Toxoid	4
1st		0	0	0.5 mgm	0.5 mgm
2	1 week	0	0	1.0 mgm	1.0 mgm
3	2 weeks	0	0	1.0 mgm	1.0 mgm
	4 weeks	Tetanus bacilli and Fullers Earth - 1.0 cc s.c.			
	5 weeks	Trismus 30 hrs Death	Trismus 38 hrs Death	Normal	Normal

The above demonstrates the immunizing effect of tetanus alum toxoid against tetanus bacilli.

CONFIDENTIAL

21 26 Nov. 1947: TYPHUS, INTERVIEW WITH Dr. Genji SAKUYAMA

资料出处： Technical Library, Fort Dugway Proving Grounds, Utah, US.

内容点评： 本资料为 1947 年 11 月 26 日 Edwin V. Hill、Joseph Victor 与作山元治（Genji SAKUYAMA）的谈话记录，题目：斑疹伤寒。

CONFIDENTIAL

6909 C AI

By

Gra... ... Lt Col CmlC

Date 4 August 1954

TYPHUS

INTERVIEW WITH:

November 26, 1947

Genji SAKUYAMA

Dr Sakuyama worked in Harbin 1939 – 1945 where he assisted in studies on tick-encephalitis, Songo and typhus.

EXPERIMENTS IN M:

Compared effects of vaccines prepared from lung exudate of rats and peritoneal exudate of field squirrels with control subjects. Virulent agent derived from guinea pig brain and injected as 1.0 cc of a 0.1% infected brain emulsion.

Results:

Vaccine	No.of Subjects	Vaccine Interval 7 days	Deaths After Challenge 4 weeks later
Rat Lung	5	1.0 cc .0 cc	1-2/10
Squirrel	5	1.0 cc .0 cc	
Control	5		3/5

Controls developed temperature to 40° C lasting more than 2 weeks after incubation period of 9 – 10 days. Vaccinated subjects had an incubation period varying from 12 to 18 days with fever to 37.5 – 38.5° C lasting 1 – 6 days. Concluding that vaccine offered limited degree of protection and both types of vaccine were equally effective.

In guinea pigs, it was found that extracts of spleen, liver, kidney and brain from infected rats or squirrels were without any immunizing action.

Stability of lyophilized R. mooseri and R. tsutsugamushi were compared at refrigerator temperature. Substrate was spleen emulsion R. mooseri lost no activity after 2 years while R. tsutsugamushi lost activity in 1 week.

Tick-encephalitis was first described by Smorodintseff in Virus Forschung, 1940.

Regraded CONFIDENTIAL
By authority Chemical
Officer.
By [illegible]
Grade and Org. Lt Col Cml C
Date August 1954

6909.C

INDEX FOR SLIDES

*Insufficient or no slides.

Anthrax

17, 18, 26, 53, 91, 225, 318, 320, 325, 328, *383, 385, 389, 390, 396, 397, 399, 400, 401, 403, 404, 405, 406, 407, *408, 393, *394, [illegible], 409, 410, 412, 413, 414, 416, 417, *743.

Botulinus:

*454, *455.

Brucellosis

311, *312, *742.

Cholera:

*20, 24, 57, 67, 88, *81, *82, 86, *87, *89, 92, *93, *97, 100, 102, 105, *106, *107, 111, *115, *116, *120, 122, *125, 126, *128, 130, *131, *132, 133, *134, *135, *136, *137, 138, *139, *140, *141, *142, *143, *144, 145, *147, *148, *149, 150, *151, *153, *154, 155, *160, *161, *165, [illegible], *168, *169, 173, *174, *177, 178, *181, *182, *183, *184, *192, *214, 226, *227, 230, *249, 250, *255, 257, *260, *261, 265, *269, 271, 272, 280, 284, 289, *291, 292, *293, 295, 297, *306, 321, 322, 323, 340, 341, *343, *344, 352, 356, 357, 376, 377, 379, *459, *461, *462, *463, *476, *603, *604, *605, 380, *606, *607, *608, *609, *610, 611, *613, *612, *618, *619, *620, *625, 624, *626, *627, *632, *629, 630, *633, *634, *635, *621, 655, *676, *900.

Co-intoxication:

*286

Dengue:

*902

Dysentery:

49, *103, 104, 117, 112, 119, *135, 187, 206, 258, 270, *280, *278, 301, 302, *313, *316, 317, *566, *730, *903.

Implosion:

*645, *646, *651, *652, *653

Fleck-typhus:

*2, *22, 27, 77, *479, *484, *489, *491, *515, *533, *534, *571, 577, 580, 582, *593, *595, 599, 600, *648, *669, *749, *850, *083, 732, 598.

Glanders:

16, 50, 85, 146, 152, 167, 176, 178, 180, 190, 193, 205, 207, 221, 222, 224, 229, 254, 256, 727, *731, *778.

Frost-bite:

*581, 672.

Intoxication (unknown genesis):

*353, *420.

Iperyt-gas:

360, 361, 362, 363, 364, 365, 366, 367, 368, 369, 370, 371, 372, 373, 374, 375.

Malaria:

*405

Meningococcus Meningitis:

*223, *240, *296, 339, *839.

Paratyphoid C:

315, *502.

Small Pox:

37, *38, *39, 40.

2

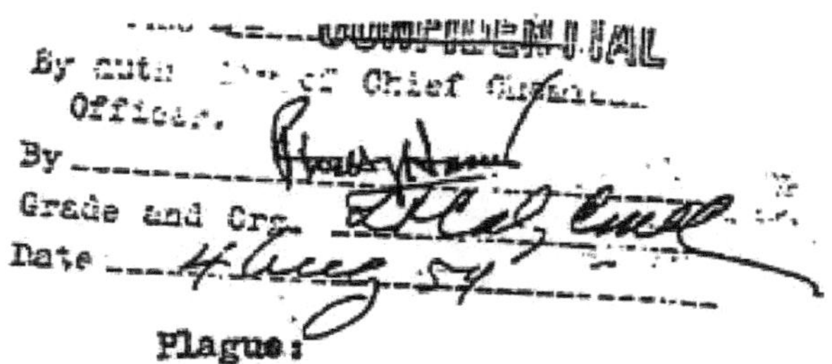

Plague:

*25, 62, 63, *65, 68, 69, 71, *84, 88, *121, *129, *156, *158, *159, *162, *163, *164, 170, *171, *172, *188, *189, 191, *196, 197, *198, *199, 200, *201, 202, *206, *210, *211, 212, 213, 215, *217, 228, *233, *234, *235, 236, *244, *247, *248, *307, *308, 309, 349, 350, 351, 355, 358, 380, 381, *441, *448, *492, *493, *496, *498, *499, *500, *501, *503, *505, *507, *508, *510, *511, *512, *514, *516, *517, *518, *519, *520, *521, *522, *523, *524, *525, *526, *527, *528, *529, *530, *531, *532, *536, *537, *535 *539, 540, *541, *542, *543, *544, *545, *546, *547, *554, *556, *557, *555 *558, *559, *560, *561, *562, *563, *564, *572, *573, *579, *614, *615, *616, 617, *621, *622, *623, *628, *631, *636, *639, *634, *644, *656, *662, *663, *664, *665, 678, 701, 703, 704, 705, 706, 707, 709, *711, 712, *713, 717, 719, *779, *782, *784, 785, 788, *790, *793, 798, 799, *812, *814, *815, 819, *822, *826, *830, *832, *833, *864, *865, *866, *867, *870, *871, *888, *890, *894, *895, *897, *899, 708, *910, *912, *896.

Recurrence fever:

319

Salmonella:

1, 3, 4, 5, *6, 7, 8, 9, 10, 11, 12, *13, *14, 15.

Sepsis, due to streptococcus:

*242, *488, 490.

Songo epidemic hemorrhagic fever:

551, 585, *602, 667, 673, *722, *739, 751, 754, 758, 760, 762, 766, 768, 771, 772, 773, *774, 775, *776, *777, 780, 781, 783, 786, 787, 789, 791, *794, 795, 798, 800, 801, *802, *803, *804, *805, *806, 792, 797, *807, 808, *809, *810, *811, *813, 816, *817, *818, *820, *821, *823, *824, *825, *827, *828, *831, *834, 835, 836, *837, *838, *840, 842, *843, *844, 845, *846, 847, 848, *849, *851, *852, *856, *857, *858, *859, *860, *861, *868, *872, *873, *874, *875, *878, *879, *881, *882, *886, *887, 891, 892, *893, *898, *901, *904, *905, *908, *910, *911, 902 *912, *913, [illegible]

Suicide:

32, 33, *34, *35, 41, 42, *43, 44, 45, 46, 52, 90, *245, *246, *427, *428, *429, *430, *431, *457, *755, *767, 360, 375, *91, *744, *745, *746, *747, *748.

Tetanus:

*231, 232, *647, 649, *657, *658, *666, 668, 670, 671, 673, 680, *681, *682, *683, 684, *685, *686, *687, 688, 689, *690, *691, 692, *693, *694, 695, *696, 697, *724, *725, 726.

Tsutsugamuchi disease:

*504, *829.

Tick-Encephalitis:

*885, 986.

Tuberculosis:

*36, *51, 55, 56, *64, *66, 70, *78, *216, 83, 218, 219, 238, 266, 276, 285, *294, 299, 301, 305, 312, 314, 338, *348, *382, *391, 392, 395, *418, *419, 424, *425, *426, 432, *433, *435, 436, *437, *447, *449, *450, *451, 452, 453, *458, *464, *465, 466, 468, *469, 470, 471, 472, 473, 477, 478, *497, *506, *513, 538, *549, *550, *553, *565, *566, *569, *574, *576, 584, *589, 596, 597, 601, *675, 698, 710, 716, 718, *723, 728, 734, *756.

Typhoid:

29, 58, *72, 75, 194, 195, *203, *209, 241, *252, 262, *263, 264, 267, *268, *273, 274, 275, 279, 310, 315, 324, *326, *329, *332, *334, *335, *333, *336, 337, *345, *346, *347, 354, *359, *364, *402, *442, *443, *444, *445, *446, *460, *486, *495, *590, *594, *637, *638, *642, *659, *660, *662, 674, 699, 700, 702, *714, *715, *720, *721, *729, *740.

Vaccination:

*331, *591.

Other diseases:

Cancer of liver - *48, *251, *385, 757.

Sarkom - *440.

Liver-cirrhosis - *467

Acute nephritis - 47, 220.

Icterus - *438, *763.

4

22　28 Nov. 1947: TYPHUS, INTERVIEW WITH Dr. Toyohiro, HAMADA

资料出处： Technical Library, Fort Dugway Proving Grounds, Utah, US.

内容点评： 本资料为 1947 年 11 月 28 日 Edwin V. Hill、Joseph Victor 与滨田丰博（Toyohiro HAMADA）的谈话记录，题目：斑疹伤寒。

CONFIDENTIAL
Regraded
By authority of Chief Chemical
Officer.
By
Grade and Org.
Date 4 Aug 54

6909-c AE

CONFIDENTIAL

INTERVIEW WITH: November 28, 1947

Dr Toyohiro HAMADA

Dr Hamada worked in Harbin from 1943 - 1945.

Strain Typhus prowazeki was obtained from a Japanese patient "Ito" in Manchuria. It is still available at the Institute for Epidemic Diseases in Tokyo.

Experiments in H:

a. Transmission:
Guinea pig blood from infected animal was injected s.c. in doses of 1 cc into each of 3 subjects. One contracted the disease from which he recovered.

b. Diagnostic Studies:
Same dose of infected guinea pig blood was injected into 4 subjects. Following an incubation period of 10 - 12 days, 3 of the 4 subjects had fever. Hamada-Kitano reaction (similar to that described by Kitano, but claimed to have been worked out by Hamada) was positive on 5 - 6 day of fever while the Weil-Felix reaction was positive at 9 - 12 day of fever.

Antibody Experiments:

Rabbits -

R. murine or R. prowazeki was injected into mice. Exudate of rickettsia and leucocytes was mixed with 10-15 cc saline. Mixture was injected i.v. into rabbits at 5 day intervals at 5 - 7 successive times. Antibodies produced in rabbits were absorbed as follows:

R. prowazeki = A B X

R. murine = B C X

X19 = D X X

The resulting antiserum was used to standardize suspension of rickettsia.

CONFIDENTIAL

Regraded CONFIDENTIAL
By authority of Chief Chemical Officer.
By ________
Grade and Org. ________
Date 4 Aug 54

CONFIDENTIAL

A common antiserum was thereby obtained which contained different antibodies and could be used for quantitating the concentration of antigen. Reaction occurred at room temperature.

Attempts to change R. murine to R. prowazeki: R. murine from guinea pig was injected i.p. into field squirrels maintained at 15 – 18° C without food. After 5 days the peritoneal exudate was suspended in saline and injected into other squirrels. Five successive transfers produced a change in the rickettsia so that they had antigenic properties of R. prowazeki as well as similar biological characteristics producing i.v. infection without scrotal reactions in guinea pigs. Formerly the reverse of these effects were the rule with this strain of R. murine. This strain originated in a Manchurian coolie in Dairen, and is no longer available. Attempts to repeat these observations with Japanese strains of R. murine have been unsuccessful.

Serum Treatment:

R. prowazeki transferred through squirrel peritoneum was suspended in saline and in doses of 20 – 100 cc injected i.v. into horses at 5 day intervals for 15 x. Two weeks after the last injection, the serum titre was 10,000 whereas original titre had been 10 – 20. Treatment with 10 cc of this serum on the fifth day of disease in M decreased severity and shortened the period of illness.

CONFIDENTIAL

23　29 Nov. 1947: DECOMTAMINATION, INTERVIEW WITH Dr. Yoshifumi, TSUYAMA

资料出处：Technical Library, Fort Dugway Proving Grounds, Utah, US.

内容点评：本资料为 1947 年 11 月 29 日 Edwin V. Hill、Joseph Victor 与津山义文（Yoshifumi TSUYAMA）的谈话记录（两份），题目：除污 / 解毒（decomtamination）。

Regraded Confidential
By authority of Chief Chemical
Officer.
By
Grade and Org. Lt Col Cml
Date 4 Aug 57

CONFIDENTIAL

6909-C H

DECONTAMINATION

INTERVIEW WITH: November 29, 1947

Dr Yoshifumi, TSUYAMA

Dr Tsuyama worked at the Army Medical School from 1943 - 1945 and was concerned with methods of decontamination of equipment and personnel.

1. Spray Disinfection:

Gasoline engine power sprayer on truck. Antiseptics were phenol 2.0%, lysol 1.0%, mykesol 1.0%, ogsol 1.0 - 2.0%. These were used on clothing, material, barracks. Particle size of 80-120 micra most efficient at a concentration of 200 - 300 cc / M^3. Such sprays were effective against the following organisms: Typhoid, dysentery, cholera, plague, glanders, tuberculosis, diptheria, meningococcus. These sprays were ineffective against anthrax. Lethal effects were obtained in 30 minutes. Soap or alcohol aided penetrating action of sprayed substance.

Particle size was obtained by a method employing principles of Stokes law. The rate of fall of particles of an aerosol was measured in a 3 meter cylinder. Substrate was dyed and the appearance of stain on a filter paper pad at the bottom of the cylinder was used to calculate particle size. The variables in this method were temperature, height of fall, size of particle and density of air. The constant is gravity. Particle size was controlled by constants of the nozzle and pressure within the system. Under operating conditions, particle size was a function of pressure.

Effects of aerosols were measured by spraying upon filter paper or materials impregnated with bacteria.

2. Fire Disinfection: Gasoline spray of 50 - 70 gm per M^2.

3. Formaldehyde Disinfection:

Variable factors are:

a. Concentration - 15-30 gm M^3 is optimum

b. Temperature - 20° C " "

c. Humidity - 80% " "

d. Specific Bacteria:
Typhoid, cholera, dysentery, plague, glanders, menin-

CONFIDENTIAL

Regraded [illegible]
By authority of Chief Chemical Officer.
By [illegible]
Grade and Org. Lt Col, CmlC
Date 4 Aug 54

~~CONFIDENTIAL~~

gonococcus destroyed in 2 hours.

Tuberculosis, Welchii and tetanus destroyed in 7 hours.

Anthrax spores destroyed in 24 hours.

c. Environment or media of bacteria:
Clothes, shoes, metal, etc.

This type of spray is useful for articles that should not be soaked such as leather goods or woolens.

4. __Vapor Disinfection:__ Steam at 100° C for 30 minutes.

5. Chloropicrate gas for extermination of mice, rats, fleas, bed bugs. Concentration of 5 gm per M^3 for 2 hours was effective.

Dr Tsuyama is to write a more detailed report on this subject.

2

~~CONFIDENTIAL~~

Regraded ~~Confidential~~
By authority of Chief Chemical Officer.
By [signature]
Grade and Org. Lt Col CmlC
Date 4 August 54

CONFIDENTIAL 17

NAME : Dr Yoshifumi Tsuyama

ADDRESS : Uneva, Uchinadamura, Kahokugun, Ishikawa Ken

PAST POSITION: In Japanese Army - Army Medical College in Tokyo

PERIOD OF MEDICAL RESEARCH: 1943 - 1945

The theme of my research (work) was "disinfection" of the field army, especially infected tuberculose anthrax and digestive infectious diseases such as typhoid fever, dysentery and cholera, etc.

The chief experiments of my work are four.

1. Spray Disinfection

Is the germicidal affect of "spray disinfection" quite enough? If it is not, then which method is given and how?

This question was removed by me, and its key points are next:

a. Size of Particles must be measured. Too large, or too small is not favorable, and the most favorable size of particles is about 80 - 120 M (mean value of its diameter).

The size of particles is measured by careful experiment and mathematical calculation. This formula is so called "Stokes Law", and of course its diameter is comparatively calculated to Ag. dest. (pure water). Experimental method is shown in next figure. This is my original apparatus:

Time of beginning spray noted, and then particles are turned down on the prepared filter paper.

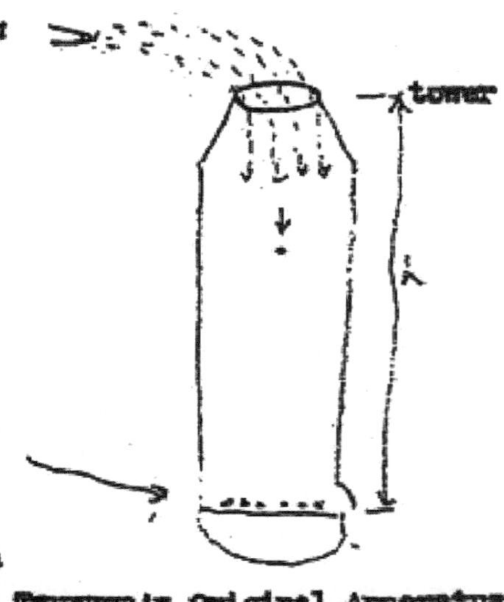

Tsuyama's Original Apparatus

CONFIDENTIAL

Regraded ~~Confidential~~
By authority of Chief Chemical
Officer.
By [signature]
Grade and Org. Lt Col, CmlC
Date 4 Jan 54

The kind of particles is dependent upon the pressure, the diameter of the spray-mouth (spray lock) and the viscosity of its solution, especially important components are former two. When the diameter of the spray-mouth is 1 mm, the favorable pressure is about 20～30 Pond (1.5～1.8 atmosphere).

b. <u>Necessary quantity of the disinfection solution must be determined;</u>

This is determined by physical and bacteriological method. According to my experimental determination, <u>it is about 100～350 cc per 1 M² of the infectious surface, but for the soldiers' clothes, it is about 200～300 cc per 1M².</u>

c. <u>The kind of germs must be considered.</u>

Typhoid, dysentery, cholera, diptheria, Tbc, and anthrax spores are experimented with cholera bacteria being easiest, but anthrax spore the most difficult.

d. <u>Necessary time to kill these germs must be considered.</u>

Commonly, it takes 30 minutes, but for Tbc 2 – 3 hrs is necessary and anthrax spore is not killed at 7 hrs or more.

e. <u>The Kind of Drug:</u>

Phenol – 2%

Lysol – 3%

Kresol – 0.5% – 1%

Neosyndilon – 0.2 – 0.5%

Ogsol – 1 – 2% Dichlor Kresol

Chlorcalkachlor – ?

Dichlorcalkachlor – ?

Methiolate – 0.05 – 0.1%

Formalin – 3%

Formalin alcohol mixture – (Fl 5% Al 95%)

Sublimat ($HgCl_2$) – 0.1%

etc. 

2

CONFIDENTIAL

Unfavorable Points

1. It is not a perfect disinfectant;

2. Germicidal effect is superficial;

3. The clothes are dampened so they cannot be worn immediately.

4. Because large quantities of chemicals are necessary to disinfect large units, from the standpoint of supply considerable difficulties will be experienced in employment of it in the battlefield, for example:

   For a total disinfection of a fully equipped soldier, the minimum quantity of disinfectant is 2 – 3 liters. If computed on the basis of amount of phenol necessary, it is 40 – 60 gms therefore for 1,000 people 40 – 60 kgms. For one horse, approximately 60 – 100 gms are needed, and for one automobile approximately 100 gms.

8. Conclusion:

It is most advantageous to use spray disinfection for men, automobiles, material, airplanes, and leather goods and steam disinfection for disinfecting clothing which can withstand the heat.

2. Formaldehyde Disinfection:

The germicidal effect of formaldehyde gas is dependent upon the following components:

Quantity (= gas pressure : P)

Temperature (T)

Humidity (H)

Kind of Germs (K)

Time (T)

Quality of the infectious object (Q) and, therefo. next formula is given:

$$E = f\ (P.T.H.K.T.Q)$$

Regraded Confidential
By authority of Chief Chemical Officer.
By
Grade and Org. Lt Col. Crill
Date 4 Aug 54

CONFIDENTIAL

	Formalin g. in 1 M³	T.	H.	T.
Typhoid	15 - 20 g	15-20°c	90-100%	3 h
Dys.	20	"	"	3
Cholera	15	"	"	3
Pest.	15	"	"	3
Diph.	15	"	"	4-5
Tbc.	30	"	"	7
Anth. Spore	60-70	"	"	24

Conclusion:

This method can be employed in disinfecting hospital wards and barracks, but in order to obtain effective results, a considerable amount of technical skill is required.

Formaldehyde vacuum disinfection (60° c, 30') is effective, but unsuitable for mass disinfection. Even by using a boiler with the dimensions of 2 - 3 meters in length and 1.3 meters in diameter, it is possible to disinfect only about 5 or 6 men's clothing.

3. Vapor Disinfection:

Hitherto, it was thought that clothing, wool blankets, etc. would not withstand vapordisinfection, but I experimented with the samples of clothing and wool blankets by the following methods;

95 - 100° c non-pressurized steam disinfection,

disinfection by boiling,

formaldehyde vacuum disinfection,

and the extent of the damage caused was calculated on the basis of qualitative changes in contrast to the degree of disinfection accomplished, and the following conclusion was drawn:

the damage caused by vapor disinfection was almost negligible and only slightly inferior in germicidal quality in comparison to formaldehyde

4

CONFIDENTIAL

CONFIDENTIAL

vacuum disinfection.

In other words in:	Damage	Degree of Disinfection
Non-disinfected	0%	100%
Vapor disinfection	5-10%	90- 95%
Boiling	20-30%	70 -80%
Formaldehyde vacuum disinfection	3- 5%	95 -97%

a. Therefore, for mass disinfection of clothing, wool blankets, etc., 90° - 100° c vapor disinfection is favorable.

b. Not much time is required for drying.

c. Only water, fuel, and simple apparatus being necessary, it can be easily employed in the battle zone.

d. The degree of disinfection is high

90° - 100° c 25'

e. Heavy equipment is necessary to conduct a formaldehyde vacuum disinfection, but this disadvantage is eliminated by using vapor disinfection.

4. Chloropicrin Gas Disinfection;

It is suitable for disinfecting houses, warehouses and ships in which the plague bacteria was detected. It is possible to exterminate rats, lice, bed-bugs, and eliminate plague bacteria simultaneously.

Quantity 1 - 2 liters, per 1 M^2, 1 - 5'

General Conclusions;

a. For disinfecting large units in the battlefield, the fundamental method which could be easily employed anywhere would be the method whereby water and heat are used.

b. Using of chemicals would be limited to the minimum.

c. Steam generator - Non-pressurized steam disinfection, chemical spraying disinfection, chemical disinfection of men by shower;

Drying of clothing;

Equipped with water supply.

5

CONFIDENTIAL

Decontamination cars (A&B) equipped to give the above disinfecting methods are to be allotted to units per 1,000 men.

d. Accordingly, combined total disinfection could be accomplished systematically with the rate of 100 men per hour.

e. In special cases, fire disinfection (to use extreme heat generated by atomic energy most suitable) gas disinfection, etc., will be combined to conduct the disinfection.